ECONOMIC CONCEPTS
A PROGRAMMED APPROACH

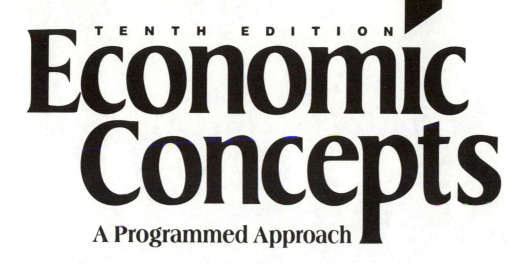

TENTH EDITION

Economic Concepts

A Programmed Approach

ROBERT C. BINGHAM
Late Professor of Economics
Kent State University

Revised by
WILLIAM HENRY POPE
Formerly of Ryerson Polytechnical Institute

McGraw-Hill, Inc.
New York St. Louis San Francisco Auckland Bogotá
Caracas Lisbon London Madrid Mexico City Milan
Montreal New Delhi San Juan Singapore
Sydney Tokyo Toronto

ECONOMIC CONCEPTS: A Programmed Approach

4 5 6 7 8 9 0 MAL MAL 9 0 9 8 7 6 5

ISBN 0-07-045591-0

This book was set in Caledonia by Waldman Graphics, Inc.
The editors were Scott D. Stratford, Michael R. Elia, and Edwin Hanson;
the production supervisor was Annette Mayeski.
The cover was designed by Joseph A. Piliero.
Malloy Lithographing, Inc., was printer and binder.

This book is printed on recycled paper.

Library of Congress Cataloging-in-Publication Data

Bingham, Robert C.
Economic concepts: a programmed approach / Robert C. Bingham.—
10th ed. / revised by William Henry Pope.
p. cm.
ISBN 0-07-045591-0
1. Economics—Programmed instruction. I. Pope, W. H. (William
Henry), (date). II. Title.
HB171.5.B52 1993
330'.07'7—dc20 92-27518

CONTENTS

PREFACE

Though this tenth edition has been revised specifically for use with McConnell-Brue's *Economics*, twelfth edition, it can be used along with any current mainstream principles of economics textbook.

And, indeed, it *should* be used by all those who have heard that economics is a tough subject and are worried about getting through the course.

What you have to do is take it one step at a time. This programmed book does precisely that. In so doing, it leads you easily through all the cause-and-effect relationships that you will meet in any principles of economics textbook.

This edition has been extensively revised to take account of the recent switch from national income accounting based on the gross national product (GNP) to that based on the gross domestic product (GDP). The major revisions have occurred in Sections 4, 5, and 6.

Section 12 has been revised to stress the least-cost rule and the profit-maximizing rule in combining resources. The added emphasis has been achieved through the deletion of thirteen frames and the addition of six.

In Section 13, five frames have been added to show more clearly terms-of-trade advantageous to both countries when production and trade occur on the basis of comparative advantage. Also in Section 13, the last ten pages have again been updated to match the similar updating to the 1990 United States balance of payments figures of McConnell-Brue's twelfth edition. With the nation's net international indebtedness continuing to set new records and with the resulting trade deficit continuing in the close to $100 billion annual range, it is important that the cause and effect relationship be examined carefully using the actual real world figures.

William Henry Pope

HOW TO USE A PROGRAMMED BOOK TO LEARN BASIC ECONOMICS

A programmed book is neither textbook nor workbook. Instead, it is a new way to learn. This new way of learning is based on the question-and-answer method Socrates used 2,400 years ago to teach his students.

What a programmed book is: A programmed book is made up of *frames*. There are several frames on each page of the book. Altogether there are 1,998 in this programmed book. If you thumb through the book you will see these frames. Here is an example of a frame.

1-1

The *lower* the price flour millers have to pay for wheat the *more* wheat they buy from farmers. On the other hand, when the price of wheat *rises* millers (increase/decrease) the amount of wheat they purchase from farmers.

decrease

This frame and every other frame has a small amount of new information in it. Each frame also contains one or more questions. The frame has enough information in it to enable you to respond to the questions correctly by applying things you already know or have learned in previous frames.

People also seem to learn things best when they learn them a little bit at a time—when they learn them in small steps. Each frame is a small step. Even though each step is small, by taking a number of small steps people can learn things which are both complex and difficult.

People also seem to learn best when they take an active part in learning—when they answer questions at every step of the way. The questions in a programmed book are not all alike. Some ask you—as in the question in the frame above—to make a choice; some require you to fill in one or two words or numbers; and a few frames call for you to write in a phrase or even a complete sentence.

Each frame or step includes the response to the question asked. As soon as you have responded to the question, you can find out whether your response was correct or not. Each step is small and is written in such a way that you will almost always come up with the correct response. The frames are arranged in such a way that you learn new things by building on what you have already learned: you progress from simple and familiar to difficult and unfamiliar ideas and ways of doing things.

Using a programmed book is a lot like having your own personal tutor! It teaches by telling and by asking and by correcting you when you are wrong and letting you know when you are right. A tutor seldom lectures you. He or she talks to you, giving you one small piece of information or one simple idea at a time. Your tutor makes you take part in the learning process by questioning you and frames the questions so you *know* the correct response. Your tutor doesn't give the response away by the way the questions are asked. He or she makes you think for yourself, and doesn't ask you to be a parrot. With a tutor you can learn at your own speed. When you have trouble with an idea or bit of information, you can slow down. And when the subject matter is easy you can speed up. Most people learn more from a tutor than they can learn from a lecture or from reading a book.

How to use a programmed book: Anyone can learn something from a programmed book, but to learn the most you have to use the programmed book in the right way. Here is how to use this book to get the most out of it.

1. In addition to the programmed book, you need two things:
   a. A pen or pencil. A pencil is better.
   b. A small card or sheet of paper (about 2 × 8 inches) to cover the correct response while you are deciding on your answer to the question.

2. There are several different kinds of questions. The three most common kinds are:
   a. *Choice questions* in which the possible responses are underlined in parenthesis and have a slash (/) between them. For example:
      Most human beings have (two/four/twelve) legs.
   b. *Fill-in questions* in which there are one or more blanks. *One* word or number is to be written in each blank. For example:
      A typical human being has __________ head and walks on his or her own ________________ .
   c. *Completion questions* in which there is a blank which begins with an asterisk (*) and is from one-half to several lines along. These questions are to be answered in your own words. The number of words you use is up to you. The blank is long enough for you to write your response on it. For example:
      Define a normal human being.* ____________________

      ____

There are several other kinds of questions which you find every so often. What you have to do to answer these questions will be fairly obvious or will be indicated in the frame.

3. The correct responses for a frame are on the left side of the page. Keep them covered until you have answered all of the questions in each frame. Answer each question by actually writing out the response or circling your response to the question. Don't just think your answer. Commit yourself in writing!

4. Only after you have responded to the question in writing should you look to see what the correct response is. Don't look ahead. You won't

learn very much when you peek because you are substituting memorizing for thinking.

5. There are often equally good ways of giving a correct answer. The printed response for any frame is usually just one way to express the correct response. You will have to judge for yourself whether your response and the printed response mean the same thing.

6. Start with the first frame in each section of the book and work through to the last frame. Do not skip frames!

7. When you make a mistake:
   a. First, look back at the question. Perhaps you just misread the question or made a "silly" mistake and you can see why you are wrong.
   b. If you didn't misread the question or make a silly mistake, go back several frames and review them. This review will usually tell you why you made the mistake and show you how to get the correct response.

8. Do not use the programmed book for too long a period at any one time. An hour is probably the longest you should use the program without a break. If you find yourself making one mistake after another, quit for a while. When you start again, begin with the first frame following the last *Review Frame* you did. When you stop, try to stop at a *Review Frame*.

9. Work at your own speed. Don't try to go too fast. If you are making a lot of mistakes, you are either going too fast or have been studying for too long a time. Either go more slowly or stop for a while.

10. At the end of the book there are *Review Tests* for each section. At the end of each section, you will be directed to take a review test. Depending upon how well you do on the review test, you may want to repeat some or all of the frames in that section.

If you have used a programmed book before, you already know how easily, how much, and how rapidly you can learn from it. If you have never used the programmed approach before, you will be pleasantly surprised by how little time and effort it requires and how much and how well you can learn.

There is a lot more in your first course in economics than is included in this programmed book. *Economic Concepts: A Programmed Approach* covers only those parts of economics which are the most important and the most difficult for beginning students to learn. If you are also using a regular economics textbook, this programmed book will enable you to master the fundamentals and will get you over the really tough spots in your textbook. You can learn the easier material in your textbook without a program. You can learn the more difficult and advanced material by yourself after you have mastered the basic economics in this programmed book.

ECONOMIC CONCEPTS
A PROGRAMMED APPROACH

Graphs and Their Meaning

section 1

As was said in the Preface, this programmed book "*should* be used by all those who have heard that economics is a tough subject and are worried about getting through the course.

"What you have to do is take it one step at a time. This programmed book does precisely that. In so doing, it leads you easily through all the cause-and-effect relationships that you will meet in any principles of economics textbook."

Since these relationships are always shown in diagrams—in graphs—that's where we start.

When you wish to go somewhere new, you will probably need directions. If it's not much more than around the corner, then something along these lines would probably get you there: "Go straight along this street until you get to the third traffic light, then go left two blocks, and that's where the arena is, just across the street from the bank." However, if it's in the next state, you would probably like to be given a map. And that's all a graph is: a map that reveals economic relationships more clearly than can be done in words or in a table. So, let's start.

1-1

Look at the space below.

What do you see in this space? A ____________________.

point (dot, speck)

1-2

Can you explain precisely where this point is located? Yes/No

No—not unless you have some other point in the space with which you can compare it

1-3

Suppose we add another point in the space and label it 0 (zero) and label the first point *A*. The space now looks like this.

You can see that point *A* is to the (right/left) of point 0. Point *A* is also (above/below) point 0.

right
above

1-4

Look at point B in the space below.

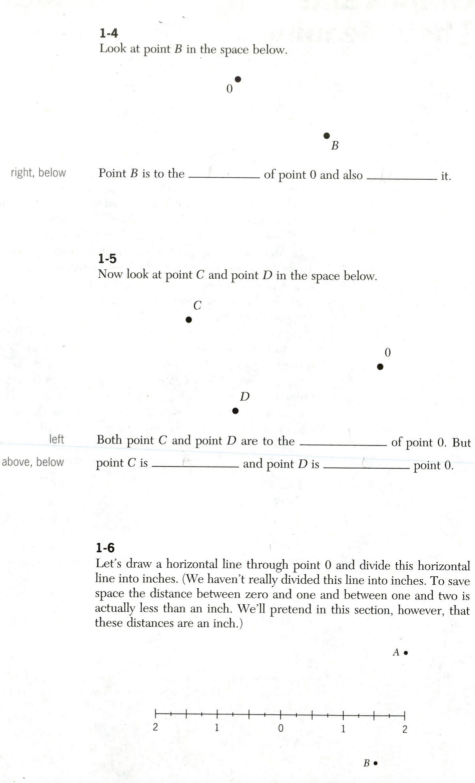

right, below Point B is to the ________ of point 0 and also ________ it.

1-5

Now look at point C and point D in the space below.

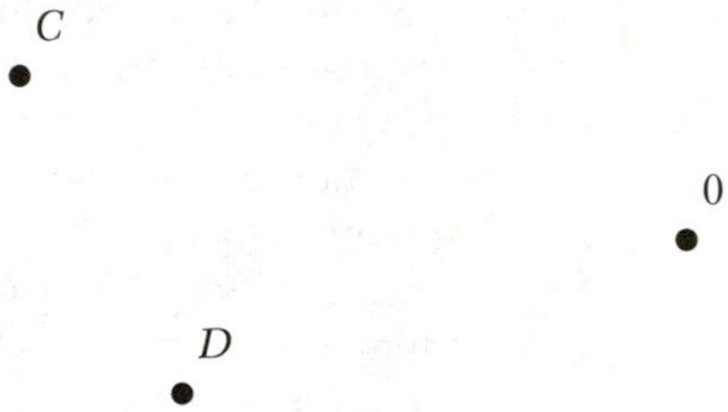

left Both point C and point D are to the ________ of point 0. But

above, below point C is ________ and point D is ________ point 0.

1-6

Let's draw a horizontal line through point 0 and divide this horizontal line into inches. (We haven't really divided this line into inches. To save space the distance between zero and one and between one and two is actually less than an inch. We'll pretend in this section, however, that these distances are an inch.)

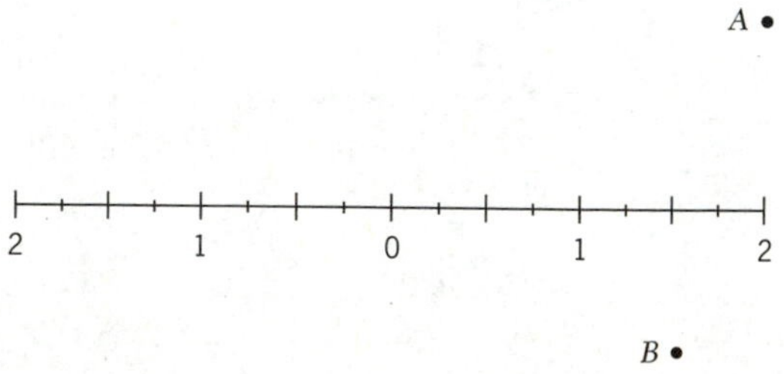

2 Point A is located ________ inches to the right of point 0.

1½ Point B is ________ inches to the right of 0.

1-7

In the space below,

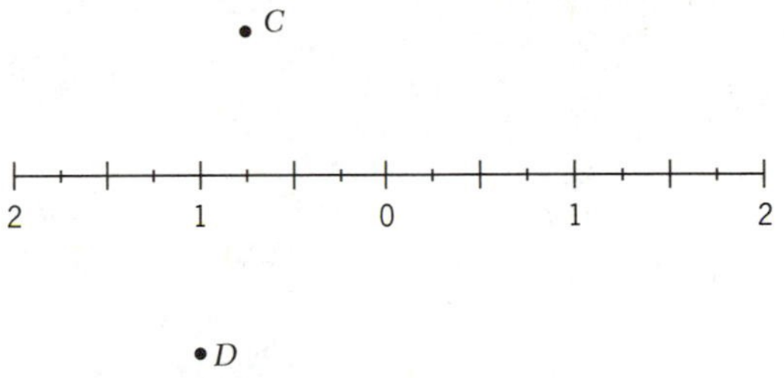

¾ point *C* is __________ of an inch to the left of 0; and point *D* is
1 __________ inch to the left of 0.

1-8

Let's draw a vertical line through point 0 and divide this vertical line into inches. (Again we are pretending that the line is divided into inches.)

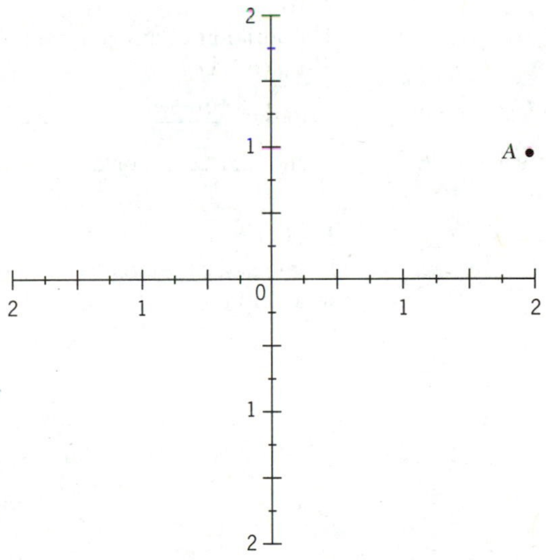

Not only is point *A* 2 inches to the right of point 0, but it is also
1 __________ inch above 0.

1-9

And in the space that follows:

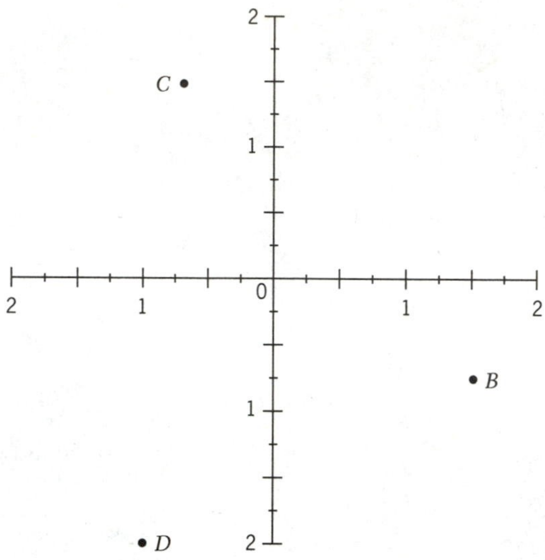

¾ Point *B* is __________ of an inch below 0.

1½ Point *C* is __________ inches above 0.

2 Point *D* is __________ inches below 0.

1-10

The location of any point, in short, can be described by measuring the distance it lies

right, left (either order) to the __________ or __________ of point 0

above, below (either order) and __________ or __________ point 0.

1-11

In geometry the point where the horizontal and vertical lines cross, instead of being called point 0, is called the ***origin***. Point *E* in the space below

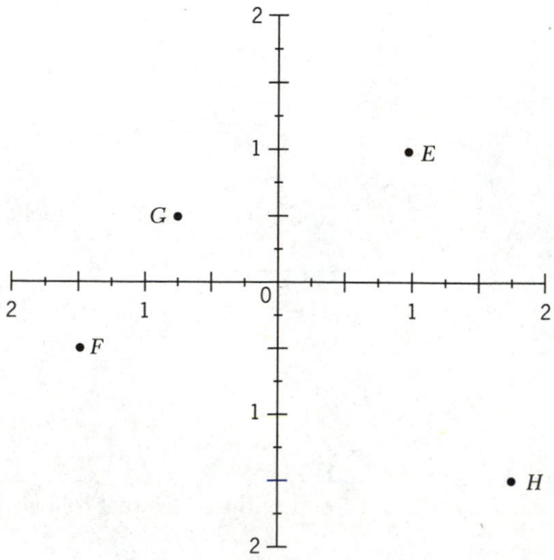

1, right, 1, is located ______ inch to the ______ ; and ______

above inch ______ the origin.

1-12

Looking back at the diagram in frame **1-11**, we can see that point F is

origin located 1½ inches to the left of the ______ and ½ of an inch below

origin the ______.

1-13

How would you describe the location in frame **1-11** of the following points?

¾ of an inch to the left and ½ inch above the origin

Point G: ° ______________________________

______________________________.

1¾ inches to the right and 1½ inches below the origin

Point H: ° ______________________________

______________________________.

1-14

Just as we call point 0 the origin, we call the horizontal line in our diagrams the horizontal ***axis***. The vertical line, similarly, is called the vertical

axis ______ .

1-15

And instead of talking about the distance to the right or left of the origin, we can call distances to the *right* of the origin *plus* (+) or positive distances; and distances to the *left* of the origin *minus* (−) or negative distances. Thus in the diagram below,

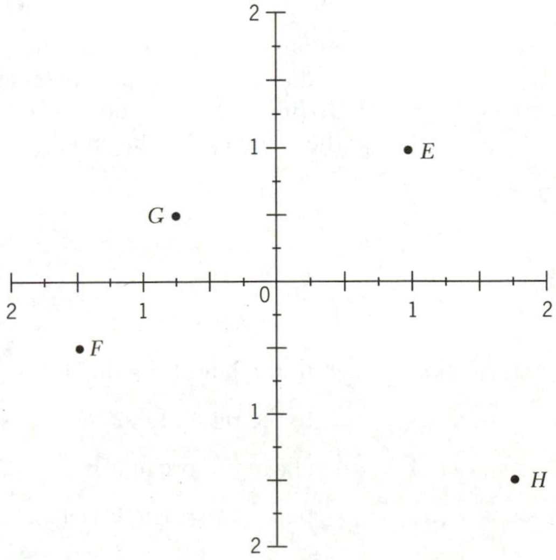

plus
minus

point E is a (plus/minus) 1 inch along the horizontal axis from the origin; and point F is a (plus/minus) 1½ inches along the horizontal axis from the origin.

1-16

minus
horizontal, plus

And in the diagram in frame **1-15**, point G is a ________ ¾ of an inch along the ________ axis; and point H is a ________ 1¾ inches along the same axis from the origin.

1-17

Similarly, we call the distance *above* the origin a *plus* (+) or positive distance; and the distance *below* the origin a *minus* or negative (−) distance. Looking only at the distances along the vertical axis from the origin in the diagram in frame **1-15**:

+	Point E is a (+/−) 1 inch from the origin.
−	Point F is a (+/−) ½ inch from the origin.
+	Point G is a (+/−) ½ inch from the origin.
−	Point H is a (+/−) 1½ inches from the origin.

1-18

two

Every point in a diagram, therefore, has (one/two/three) dimensions.

1-19

horizontal
vertical

The first dimension of any point is its plus or minus distance from the origin along the ________ axis. The second dimension is its plus or minus distance from the origin along the ________ axis. (Mathematicians call the horizontal axis the ***abscissa*** and the vertical axis the ***ordinate***; but you don't need to remember this. We'll continue to call them the horizontal and vertical axes.)

1-20

If a point lies

− (minus or negative)	to the left of the origin it is a ________ distance from the origin.
+ (plus or positive)	to the right of the origin it is a ________ distance from the origin.
+ (plus or positive)	above the origin it is a ________ distance from the origin.
− (minus or negative)	below the origin it is a ________ distance from the origin.

1-21

It is customary in describing the location of a point to write first its horizontal distance from the origin and to write second its vertical distance from the origin. A point that is located at $+2$, -1 is, thus, 2 inches (to the right/to the left/above/below) the origin; and 1 inch (to the right/to the left/above/below) the origin.

to the right
below

1-22

A point located at $-1\frac{1}{2}$, $+1$ is $1\frac{1}{2}$ inches __________ and 1 inch __________ the origin.

to the left of
above

1-23

In the diagram below,

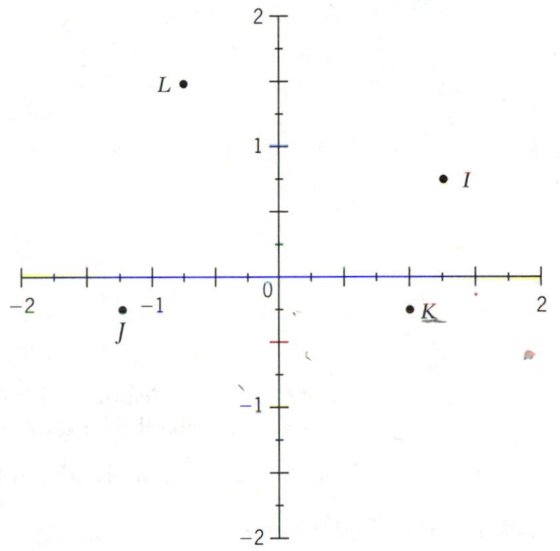

we can describe the location of point I as $(+/-)$ __________ inches and $(+/-)$ __________ of an inch.

$+$, $1\frac{1}{4}$
$+$, $\frac{3}{4}$

1-24

Using the diagram in frame **1-23**,

Point J is located at __________ , __________ .

Point K is located at __________ , __________ .

Point L is located at __________ , __________ .

$-1\frac{1}{4}$, $-\frac{1}{4}$
$+1$, $-\frac{1}{4}$
$-\frac{3}{4}$, $+1\frac{1}{2}$

1-25

If you can read the location of a point on a graph you can also mark the location of a point on a graph. For example, if a point were located at -2, $+1$ you would place it __________ inches to the __________ of the origin and __________ inch __________ the origin.

2, left
1, above

1-26
Just to be sure you can plot any point you might encounter, plot the following points on the graph below; and label each of the points.

M: +2, −1½
N: −1¼, −1¼
P: +1½, + 1½
Q: −1, +1

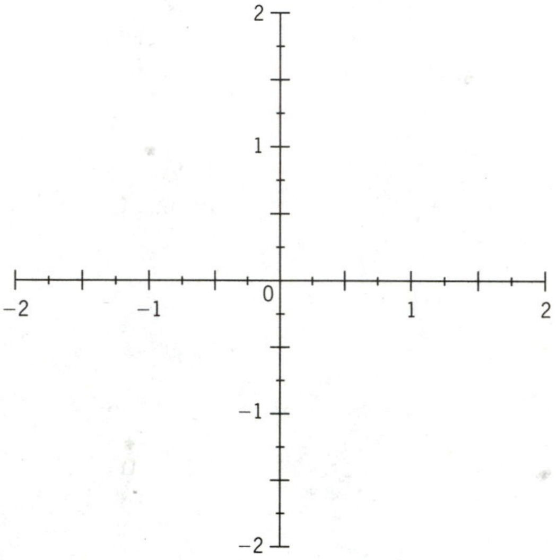

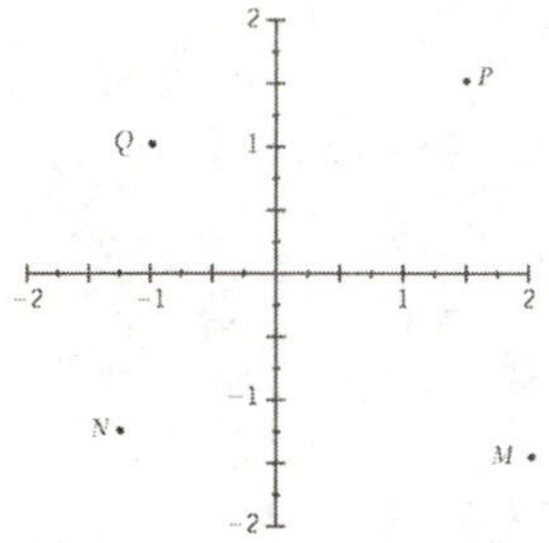

1-27 Review Frame
We can describe the location of any point by stating how far it is along the ________ axis and how far it is along the ________ axis from the ________ .

horizontal, vertical
origin

1-28 Review Frame
A point which is
to the right of the origin is preceded by a ________ sign. (+)
to the left of the origin is preceded by a ________ sign. (−)
above the origin is preceded by a ________ sign. (+)
below the origin is preceded by a ________ sign. (−)

1-29 Review Frame
A point which is
2 inches below and 1½ inches to the right of the origin is located at ________, ________.

+1½, −2

2 inches to the left and 1½ inches above the origin is located at ________, ________.

−2, + 1½

1-30 Review Frame

A point with a dimension of

1, left — −1, −2 is located ______ inch to the ______ and

2, below — ______ inches ______ the origin.

3, right — +3, +4 is located ______ inches to the ______ and

4, above — ______ inches ______ the origin.

1-31

Suppose we know a family that has an annual income of $40,000 which saves $4,000 each year. If we let distances along the horizontal axis represent annual income we can let distances along the vertical axis represent annual ______ .

saving

1-32

Let's agree to let 1 inch represent $20,000. A point indicating a $40,000 a year income would lie ______ inches to the ______ of the origin. And a point indicating $4,000 a year saving would lie ______ tenths of an inch ______ the origin.

2, right
2
above

1-33

So a single point can be used to present the economic fact that a family with an income of $40,000 a year saves $4,000 a year.

Still letting 1 inch represent $20,000 and measuring income horizontally and saving vertically, a point 3 inches to the right and 4/10 of an inch above the origin would mean that a family with an income of $ ______ saves $ ______ a year.

$60,000, $8,000

1-34

Some families with small annual incomes don't save anything during a year. For example, a family with an income of only $20,000 a year might save nothing during a year. To show that when income is $20,000 saving is $0 we would plot a point at (+/−) 1 inch and neither above nor below the ______ axis.

+
horizontal

1-35

Other families with still smaller incomes save negative amounts. They spend more than their income by borrowing or dipping into past savings. To indicate that when income is $10,000 saving is −$2,000 we would plot a point at +½ of an inch and at a ______ 1/10 of an inch.

− (minus or negative)

1-36

Below is a blank graph on which 1 inch represents $20,000. Each inch has been divided into tenths which represent $2,000. Continue to measure income horizontally and saving vertically and plot the following four points.

Income	*Saving*
$10,000	– $2,000
20,000	0
40,000	4,000
60,000	8,000

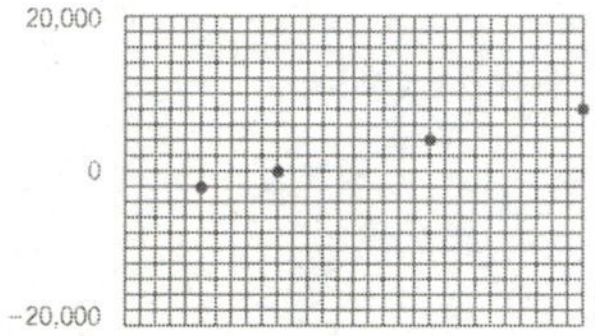

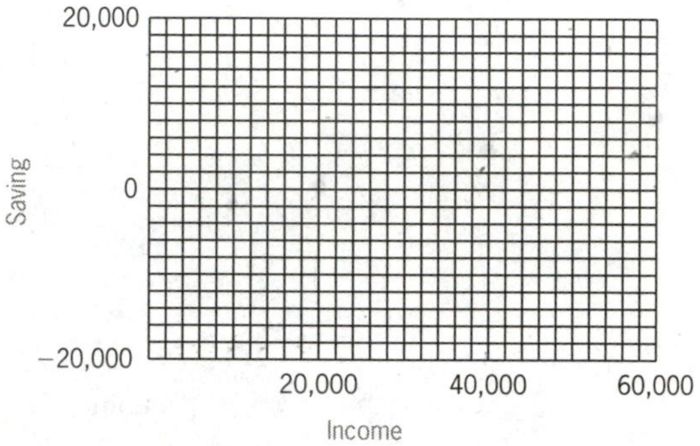

1-37

The four points you plotted in the last frame give you a diagram that looks like the one below. Take a ruler or a straight edge and draw a line through the four points.

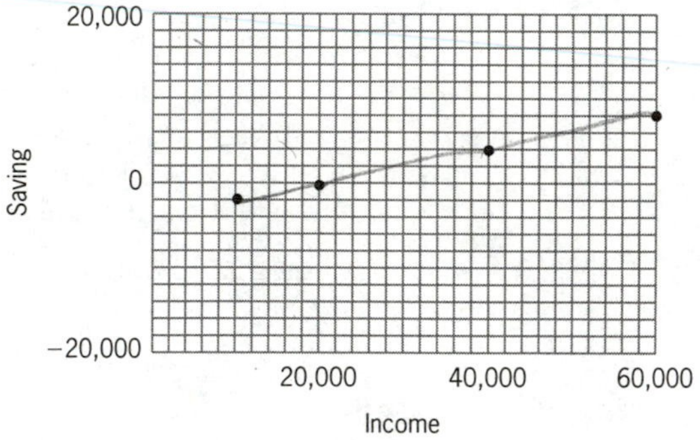

1-38

If you will look back at the line you drew through the four points in frame **1-37** you will be able to discover how much saving is done by families with incomes other than those represented by the points you

$800 plotted. For example, when income is $24,000 saving is $ ________. You can also see that families save $1,600 when their income is $28,000

$32,000 and save $2,400 when their income is $ ________ .

1-39

The line which you drew through the four points in frame **1-37** is also called a ***curve***. But regardless of whether you call it a line or a curve, once you have drawn it you are able to determine the amount of

saving, income ________ families do at almost any level of ________ .

1-40

more
less

Reading the curve in frame **1-37** you can see that the more income families have the (more/less) saving they will do; and the less income they have the (more/less) saving they will do.

1-41

increases
decreases

Put another way, when income increases, saving (increases/decreases); and when income decreases, saving (increases/decreases).

1-42

increases
decreases

The relation between income and saving is called a ***direct*** (or ***positive***) relation because saving increases when income __________ ; and decreases when income __________ .

1-43

up

Imagine that we start at the vertical axis and walk from left to right along the curve we drew in frame **1-37**. As we walk along the curve it will also be like walking (up/down) a hill.

1-44

upward

Since we always talk about moving along a curve *from left to right*, we can say that the curve in frame **1-37** slopes (upward/downward).

1-45

increases
decreases

And a curve such as the one in frame **1-37** that slopes upward tells us that when whatever we are measuring on the horizontal axis

increases whatever we are measuring vertically __________ .

decreases whatever we are measuring vertically __________ .

1-46

a direct, positive
upward

Instead of talking about "whatever we are measuring on the horizontal axis" and "whatever we are measuring vertically," let's call the things measured on the two axes ***variables***. Then we can say that when two variables increase and decrease together the relation between the two variables is (a direct/an inverse) one; or a (positive/negative) relationship; and that the curve showing this relationship slopes __________ .

1-47

saving and income increase and decrease together
slopes upward (from left to right)

In summary, the direct or positive relation between saving and income means that * ____________________ and that the curve relating saving and income * ____________________ .

1-48

The relation between two variables is not always a direct one. Suppose the relation between the *rate of interest* people have to pay to borrow money and the *amount of money* they will borrow is shown by the diagram below.

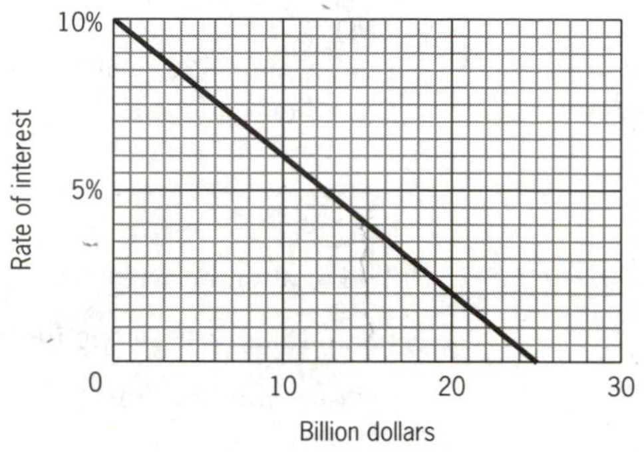

10 In this diagram we have let 1 inch represent $ ________ billion on
horizontal, 5 the ________ axis; and 1 inch represent ________ percent on
vertical the ________ axis.

1-49

If we look closely at this graph we can see that when the rate of interest
10 is 6 percent people will borrow $ ________ billion; and that they
2 would borrow $20 billion if the rate of interest were ________ percent.

1-50

rate Each point on the curve in frame **1-48** shows a ________ of
interest, money ________ and the amount of ________ people will
borrow ________.

1-51

By reading the graph you can complete the table below.

	When the rate of interest is	*People will borrow*
10	________ %	$ 0 billion
$5	8%	________ billion
	6%	10 billion
4	________ %	15 billion
	2%	20 billion
$25	0%	________ billion

1-52

Looking back at the table you completed in the last frame you can see that when the rate of interest decreases the amount of money people

increases — will borrow __________ ; and that were the rate of interest to increase

decrease — the amount of money borrowed would __________ .

1-53

The relation, in short, between the rate of interest and the amount of

an inverse — money borrowed is (a direct/an inverse) one.

1-54

The relation between the rate of interest and the amount of money borrowed can't be a direct one since the two variables don't increase and decrease together. The relation between them is ***inverse*** (or ***negative***)

decreases — because when one variable increases the other __________ ; and when

increases — one variable decreases the other __________ .

1-55

We have redrawn the graph from frame **1-48** below.

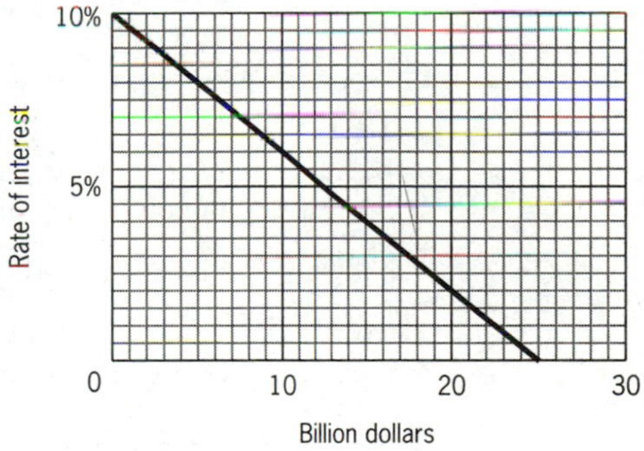

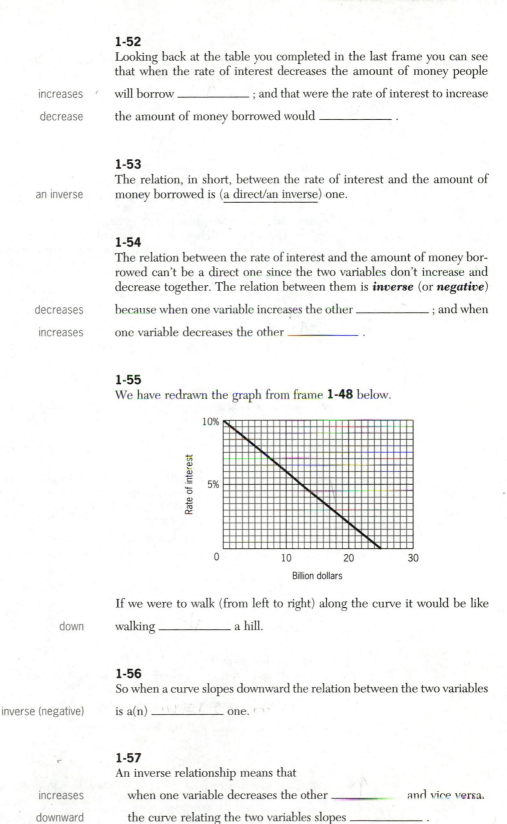

If we were to walk (from left to right) along the curve it would be like

down — walking __________ a hill.

1-56

So when a curve slopes downward the relation between the two variables

inverse (negative) — is a(n) __________ one.

1-57

An inverse relationship means that

increases — when one variable decreases the other __________ and vice versa.

downward — the curve relating the two variables slopes __________ .

1-58

When two variables increase and decrease together, they are said to change in the same/opposite direction. And if when one variable increases the other decreases, they are said to change in the ______ direction.

same
opposite

1-59

Economists try to determine which variable is "cause" and which is "effect." The ***dependent variable*** is the "effect" or outcome. The ***independent variable***, then, is the ______. If economists always followed mathematical convention, they would always put the dependent variable on the vertical axis and the independent variable on the ______ axis.

cause
horizontal

1-60

If you will look back at frame **1-37** you will see that saving is on the ______ axis and income on the ______ axis. Since saving is the dependent/independent variable and income the ______ one, we are here following/not following mathematical convention.

vertical, horizontal
dependent, independent
following

1-61

In frame **1-49** we said "when the rate of interest is 6 percent people will borrow $10 billion." This implies that the rate of interest is cause/effect and the amount borrowed is ______. The rate of interest is on the ______ axis and the amount borrowed is on the ______ axis. Here we are/are not following mathematical convention. Does it matter?° ______.

cause
effect
vertical, horizontal
are not
not to economists! Choice of axis is a matter of convention or convenience

1-62 Review Frame

Before we look a little more closely at curves and their slopes we should review what we have just learned about them.

If two variables increase and decrease together the relation between them is ______ and the curve showing this relationship slopes ______.

direct (positive)
upward

But if one variable increases while the other decreases the relation is ______ and the curve slopes ______.

inverse (negative), downward

1-63 Review Frame

Were the variables *X* and *Y* inversely related, an increase in *Y* would

decrease — result in a(n) __________ in *X*. Were the variables *V* and *W* directly

decrease — related, a decrease in *V* would bring about a(n) __________ in *W*.

1-64

Look at the two curves on the graph below.

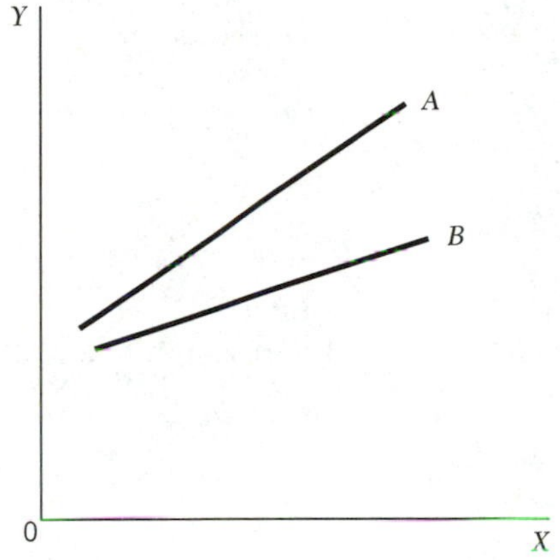

upward — Both curves slope __________. The two curves show that the relation

X, *Y* (either order) — between the variables __________ and __________ is

direct (positive) — __________.

1-65

more — But it is plain to see that the curve labeled *A* is (more/less) steep than the one labeled *B*.

1-66

On the graph below,

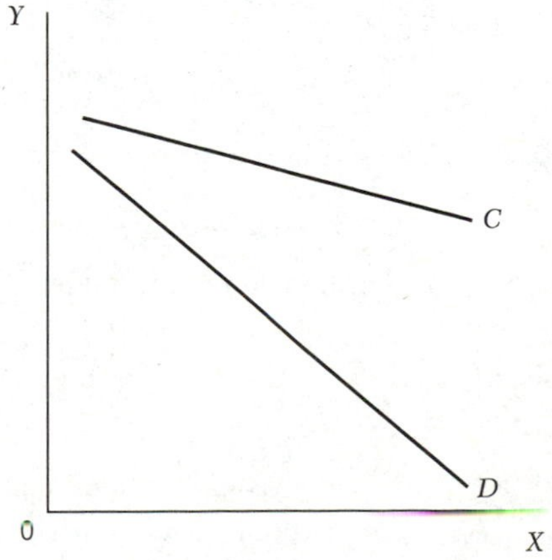

downward — the two curves slope __________ , the relation between X and Y is

inverse (negative), less — __________ , and curve C is __________ steep than curve D.

1-67

The naked eye will usually tell us which curve is more or less steep than another. Suppose, however, we want to measure the steepness of a curve precisely. How would we do this? If we were highway engineers measuring the steepness (or grade) of an uphill road we might say that the road rises 50 feet per 1,000 feet. This would mean that as we move *along*

up — the road 1,000 feet we move 50 feet __________ -ward.

1-68

The steepness of a road going downhill 100 feet per 1,000 feet means

1,000 — that when we move along the road __________ feet we move

100 — __________ feet down the hill.

1-69

We can measure the steepness of a curve between two points on the curve in exactly the same way. Let's look again at the curve you drew in frame **1-37** relating saving and income. We have redrawn this curve below.

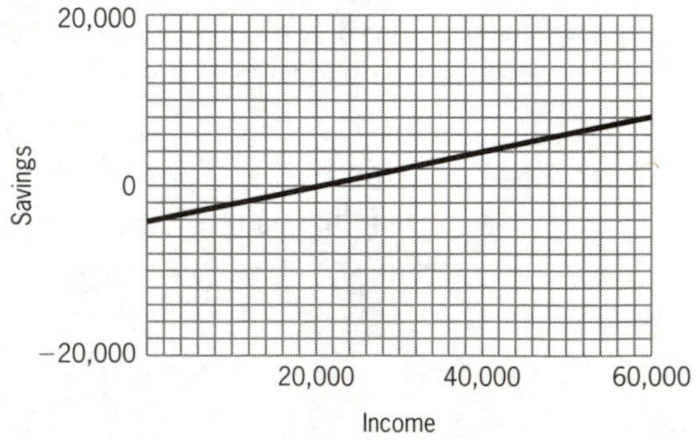

If we move along this curve—from left to right, always—by $20,000, the

increases, $4,000 — amount of saving done (increases/decreases) by $ __________ .

1-70

The slope of a curve between two points is equal to the distance moved vertically divided by the distance moved horizontally. When income in-

+ — creases by $20,000 the change in saving is a (+/−) $4,000.

1-71

So the distance moved vertically is a +$4,000; and the distance moved horizontally is a +$20,000. And +$4,000 divided by +$20,000 is equal

+⅕ (or + 0.2) to __________ .

1-72

The slope of the curve relating saving and income is +⅕ because +$4,000 divided by +$20,000 is *plus* (+) ⅕. This curve, we can see, has an upward slope. We may conclude, therefore, that curves with up-

\+ ward slopes have a slope that is (+/−).

1-73

Let's measure the slope of the curve relating the rate of interest and the amount borrowed.

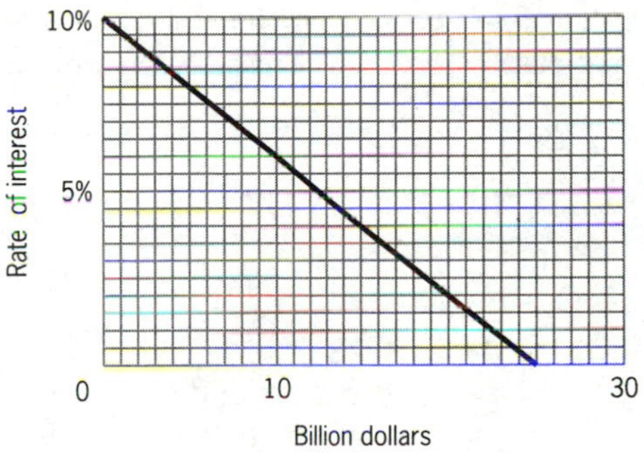

If we move horizontally along the curve by $10 billion, the rate of interest

decreases, 4 (increases/decreases) by __________ percentage points.

1-74

When the amount of money borrowed changes by +$10 billion, it is

− because the rate of interest has changed by a (+/−) 4 percent.

1-75

The distance moved vertically divided by the distance moved horizontally

−4, +$10 is equal to __________ percent divided by $ __________ billion,

− which is equal to (+/−) 4⁄10 or ⅖.

1-76

The slope of the curve in frame **1-73** is −⅖ since −4 percent divided by +$10 billion equals −⅖. Because this curve has a downward slope

− we may conclude that curves sloping downward have a (+/−) slope.

1-77

Look at the curve below.

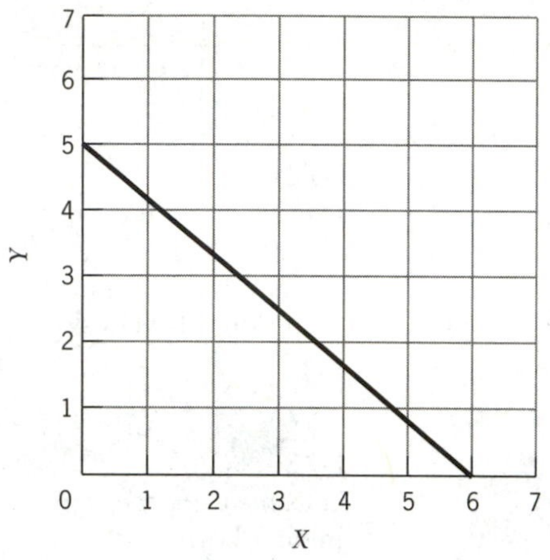

negative
decreases
−5, +6
−⅚

This curve has a (positive/negative) slope. When X increases from 0 to 6, Y (increases/decreases) from 5 to 0. The slope of the curve is therefore equal to ________ divided by ________, or ________.

1-78

The curve in the diagram below

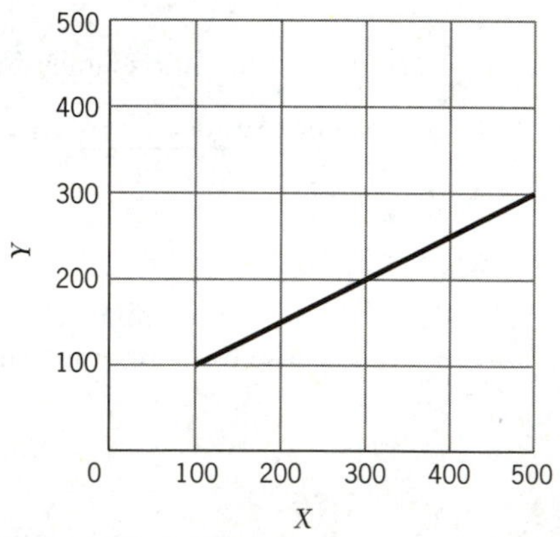

positive
+200

has a ________ slope. When X changes by +400 Y changes by ________.

1-79

+200
+400, +½

The slope of the curve in the frame above is equal to ________ divided by ________ or ________.

1-80 Review Frame

vertical
horizontal

We can find the slope of a curve between two points by dividing the (vertical/horizontal) difference between the two points by the (vertical/horizontal) difference.

1-81 Review Frame

A curve that slopes

positive, direct — upward has a __________ slope and shows a(n) __________ relationship between the two variables.

negative, inverse — downward has a __________ slope and shows a(n) __________ relationship between the two variables.

1-82 Review Frame

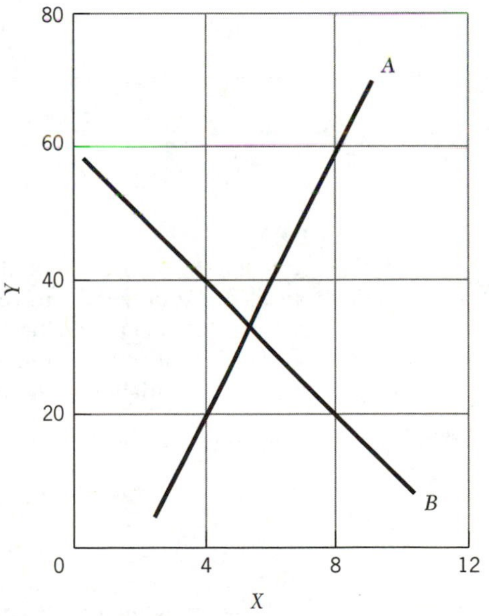

+10 — Curve *A* above has a slope of __________ .

−5 — Curve *B* has a slope of __________ .

1-83

Below is a graph which relates consumption to income. As income in-

increases, 50 — creases by $100, consumption increases/decreases by $ __________ . The

$50/$100 or ½ — slope of this ***consumption line*** is ________ . When income is $0, con-

50 — sumption is $ _____ .

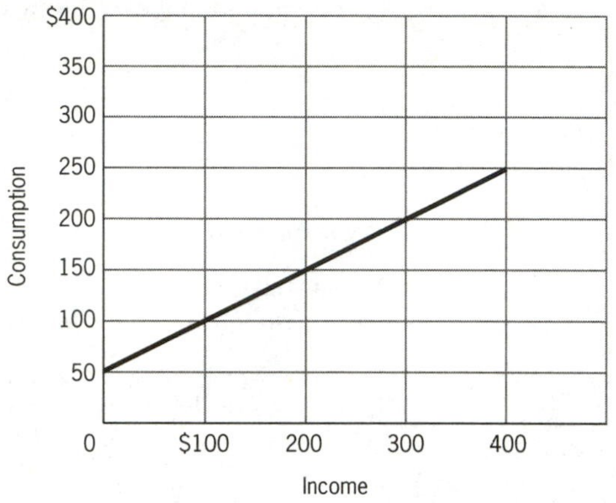

1-84

When income is $0, consumption is $50. How is this possible? *

By dissaving, selling of assets, borrowing — ____________________________________ .

1-85

50 — Note that the consumption line meets the vertical axis at $ _____ . This is called the ***vertical intercept***. Knowing this and the slope, we can describe the line in equation form: $y = a + bx$, where y is the variable on the vertical axis, a is the vertical intercept, b is the slope of the line, and x is the variable on the horizontal axis. Therefore, designating con-

$C = \$50 + ½(\$100)$ — sumption as C, the equation of our line is: * ____________________ .

1-86

With this equation we can determine consumption at any level of income. For example, at the income level of $200, consumption is:

150 = 50 + ½($200) — $ _____ = $ _____ + _____ .

1-87

All the curves we have looked at so far have been straight lines or *linear*. Not all relations between two economic variables can be described by linear curves. Some relationships can only be described by lines that are curvilinear or *nonlinear*. Below, for example,

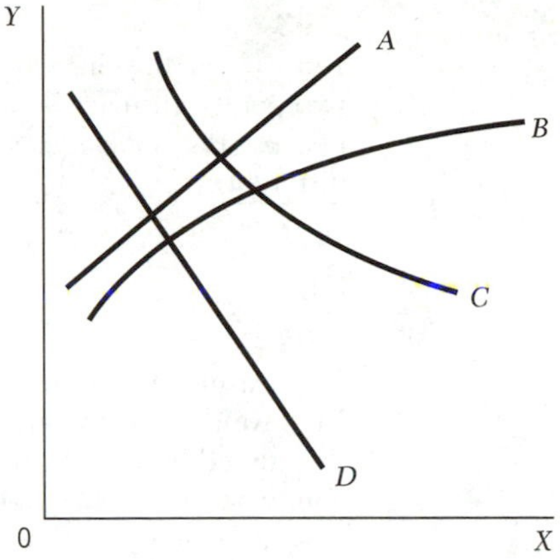

A, *D* (either order) — the linear lines are the ones labeled ________ and ________

B, *C* (either order) — and the nonlinear lines are ________ and ________ .

1-88

Like linear lines, nonlinear lines may slope either upward or downward. When they slope upward the relation between the two variables is direct and the curve has a positive slope; and when they slope downward the relation is inverse and the slope is negative. Thus, in frame **1-87** curves

direct — *A* and *B* both show a(n) ________ relation and curves *C* and *D* show

inverse — a(n) ________ relation between *X* and *Y*.

1-89

positive — Look first at curve *B* in frame **1-87**. This curve has a ________ slope.

increases — This means that when *X* increases, *Y* ________ .

1-90

Still looking at curve *B*, we can see that the slope of the curve is positive

is not — and that the slope (is/is not) the same at all points along the curve.

1-91

In fact, as we move along the curve (from left to right, as always) the

decreases — slope of the curve (increases/decreases).

1-92

Earlier we learned how to measure the slope of a linear curve *between two points* by dividing the vertical difference between the two points by the horizontal difference. And because the curve was a straight line the

the same — slope of the curve was (the same/different) at all points along the curve.

1-93

different — But we won't even try to measure the slope of a nonlinear line between two points. Instead we will measure the slope *at points* along the curve because the slope at each point along a nonlinear line will be (the same/different).

1-94

To measure the slope of a curved line at any point is relatively simple. First we draw a straight line ***tangent*** to the curved line at the point on the curved line at which we measure the slope. The straight line is tangent when it touches the curved line at one and only one point. In the diagram below,

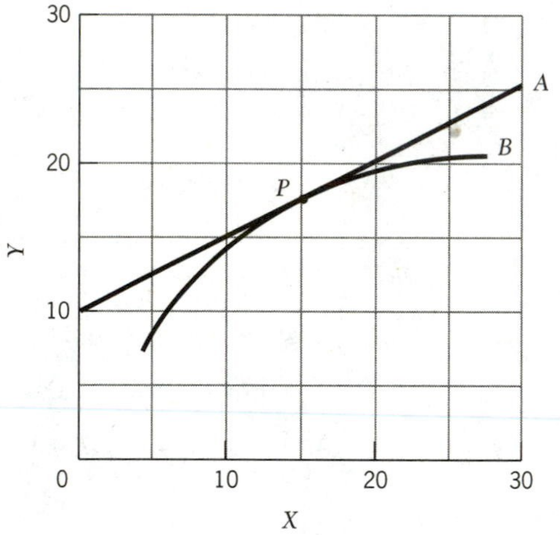

A — the straight line labeled ________ is tangent to the curved line

B, P — labeled ________ at point ________ .

1-95

After we have drawn a straight line tangent to the curved line at a single point we can then measure the slope of the curved line at that point by measuring the slope of the straight line. In the diagram in frame **1-94** we can see that as we move along the straight line *A* which is tangent to the curved line *B* at point *P*, when *X* increases by 30, *Y* increases by

15 — ________ .

1-96

15 — The slope of the straight line in frame **1-94** equals ________ divided

30, $+\frac{1}{2}$ — by ________ and is equal to ________ .

The slope of the nonlinear line *B* at point *P* is therefore equal to

$+\frac{1}{2}$ — ________ .

1-97

Suppose we wanted to measure the slope of the curve *C* at point *P* in the diagram below.

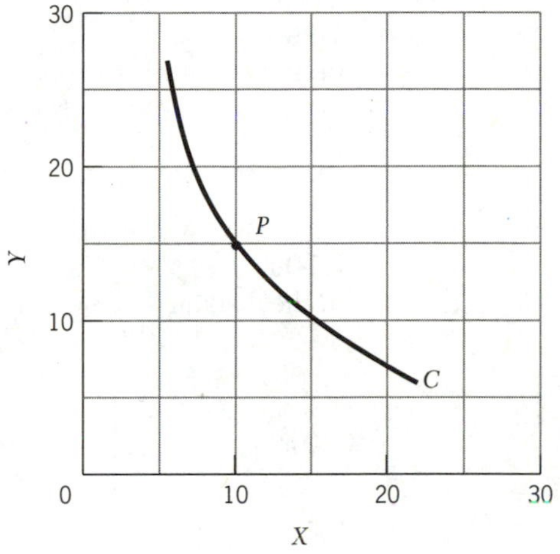

tangent

We would first draw a straight line __________ to curve *C* at point *P*.

the slope of the straight line tangent to curve *C* at point *P*

The slope of the curve *C* at point *P* would be equal to * __________ __________.

1-98

We have drawn a straight line tangent to curve *C* at point *P* in the diagram below.

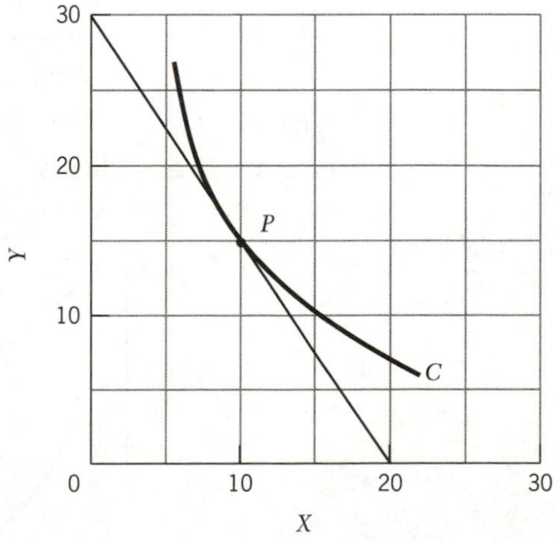

decreases, 30

We can see that along the straight line as *X* increases by 20, *Y* __________ by __________.

−1½ The slope of the straight line is ________ .

−1½ The slope of curve C at point P is ________ .

1-99

In describing what happens to the slope of a nonlinear line as we move along the curve we always describe what happens as we move from

left, right ________ to ________ .

1-100

In the diagram below,

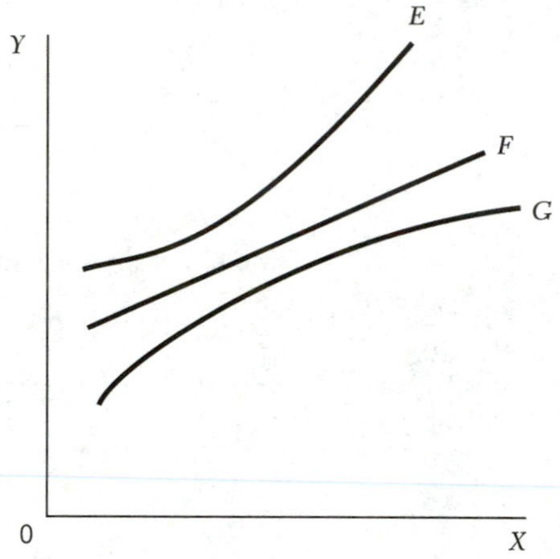

positive we can see that three curves have ________ slopes. But in moving along the curves we can see that the slope of

increases Curve E (increases/decreases/remains constant),

remains constant Curve F * ________ ,

decreases Curve G * ________ .

1-101

And in the diagram below

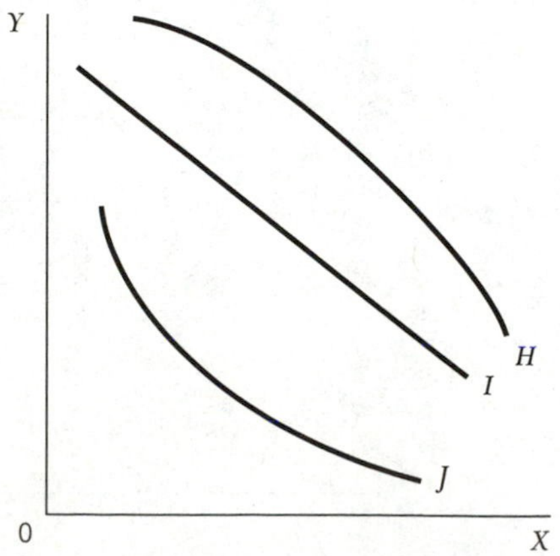

negative — all three curves have ________ slopes but the slope of

increases — Curve *H* * ________________,

remains constant — Curve *I* * ________________,

decreases — Curve *J* * ________________.

1-102

Take a look at the two curves in the figure below

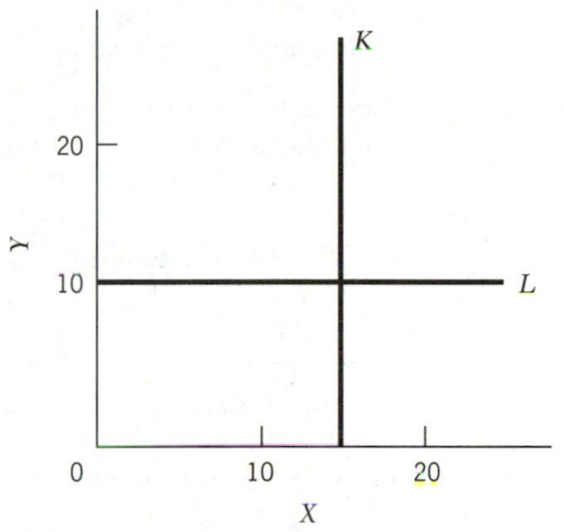

As we move along curve *L*, when *X* increases by 10, *Y* increases by 0.

0, 10 — The slope of this curve is equal to ________ divided by ________

0 — and is, therefore, equal to ________.

As we move along curve *K*, when *Y* increases by 10, *X* increases by 0.

10 — We should say that the slope of this curve equals ________ divided

0 — by ________.

1-103

Since mathematicians won't allow us to divide by zero, the slope of curve *K* really has no measurement. We will say that a curve like *K* has a slope of ***infinity***. So in the diagram below

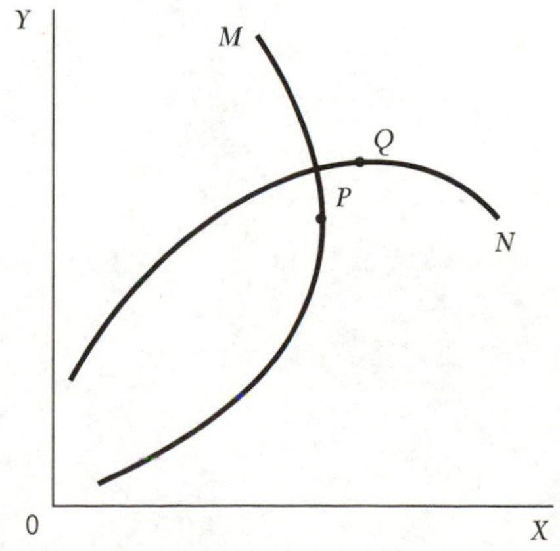

infinity
0

the slope of curve M at point P is ________ and the slope of curve N at point Q is ________ .

1-104 Review Frame

linear
nonlinear
positive
negative
different
increases, decreases (either order)

Straight line curves are said to be ________ while curved ones are called ________ .

Curved lines sloping uphill have ________ slopes and curved lines sloping downhill have ________ slopes.

Nonlinear lines have a ________ slope at every point along the curve and the slope either ________ or ________ as we move along the curve.

1-105 Review Frame

straight, tangent
the slope of the straight line which is tangent to the curved line at that point

To measure the slope of a nonlinear line at a point we must draw a ________ line which is ________ to the point on the curved line. The slope of the curved line at that point is equal to * ________ ________.

1-106 Review Frame

infinity
zero

The slope of a vertical line is equal to ________ and the slope of a horizontal line is equal to ________ .

Now take the Review Test for Section 1 at the back of the book.

Scarcity

section 2

The name of the economics game is scarcity. If there were no scarcity there would be no subject called economics, no textbooks in economics, no economics courses, and no professors of economics. But scarcity isn't going to go away and neither is economics. No matter how affluent we become, scarcity will remain.

Let's see if we can't find out what scarcity is, what it is that is scarce, and why it is scarce. Once we learn these things we can go on to find out what economics is.

THE ECONOMIC PROBLEM

2-1

Everyone in the world, rich and poor, is aware of scarcity. Take Alice Adams, for example. Adams is a college student. Excluding her tuition and books (for which her parents will pay), Adams has $300 a month to spend; and she believes she must spend the following amounts each month.

Food	$110
Housing	100
Clothing	30
Recreation	40
Laundry and Dry Cleaning	30
Miscellaneous	20

What is the total amount Adams feels she must spend each month?

330 $____________ .

less Adams has an economic problem: her resources are (greater/less) than the amount she thinks she must spend.

2-2

The personal problem confronting Adams is not at all unusual. The re-

scarce sources available to her are (scarce/abundant) relative to her wants.

2-3

Why does Adams have an economic problem? Because her wants tend to be unlimited. No matter how large an amount she has available to spend, she will always find that the amount she wants to spend is

greater (greater/less) than the amount available to her.

2-4

unlimited — The world is made up entirely of people like Adams. Their wants are (limited/unlimited) and, as a result, their resources are always

scarce — ______________ compared with their wants.

2-5

The personal economic problem facing Adams (and everybody else in

resources — the world) is that her ______________ are scarce relative to her unlim-

wants — ited ______________ .

2-6

The economic problem of every society is similar to the personal problem facing Adams and the rest of the world. The wants of society

unlimited, scarce — are ______________ and its resources, therefore, are ______________ .

2-7

Unlike Adams, a society's resources are *not* the amounts of money it has to spend. Its resources are the amounts of labor, land (or natural resources), capital goods, and entrepreneurial ability which it can employ to produce the things people want. But no matter how many resources a society has, resources will be scarce compared with the

wants — ____________ of society.

2-8

Society uses its resources to produce the goods and services people want. The only difference between a good and a service is that goods are tangible and services are intangible. An item such as a loaf of bread, for

good — example, is a (good/service) while having a dentist clean your teeth is a

service — (good/service).

2-9

At any particular time there are just so many economic resources available to society. The quantities of resources are limited; and so the quan-

goods, services (either order) — tities of ______________ and ______________ society (or the economy) is able to produce are also limited.

2-10

Economics is the social science concerned with scarcity. This means that economics is the subject that studies how society uses or employs its

resources — scarce ______________ to produce goods and services in order to satisfy

wants — human ____________ .

2-11

The basic or central economic problem of every society, then, is that its resources are ________ compared with its ________ wants. But the more resources a society has the (more/fewer) goods and services it can produce and the (more/fewer) wants it can satisfy.

scarce, unlimited
more
more

2-12

Assuming an economy has fixed amounts of resources, the more *efficient* an economy is the (more/fewer) goods and services it can produce and wants it can satisfy. No economy, however, can satisfy all human wants because * ________________________ .

more
human wants are unlimited

2-13

An economy is not so efficient as it can be unless all of its resources are employed. Resources that remain unemployed are not used to produce the goods and services that satisfy human wants; and so wants that could have been satisfied remain ________________ .

unsatisfied

2-14

For an economy to be efficient and to satisfy as many wants as possible it must, first of all, employ ________ of its ________ .

all, resources

2-15

But to be efficient an economy must do more than just employ all of its resources. If the American economy, for example, employed some of its labor resources to produce automobiles and each automobile worker toiled alone in a garage with only a hammer and a hacksaw, the economy would not be using its resources efficiently. The economy would be using its labor resources inefficiently because the best method of producing automobiles (has/has not) been employed.

has not

2-16

An efficient economy is one in which there is *both* full production and full employment.

Full production means that the economy employs the best available methods to produce goods and services.

Full employment means that the economy employs * ________ ________ to produce goods and services.

all of its
resources

2-17

The methods an economy uses to convert resources into goods and services are referred to as its ***technology***. So if there is to be full production an economy must employ the ________ available technology.

best

2-18

employment
production
(either order)

Economic efficiency, in short, requires both full ______________ and full ______________ .

2-19

technology
(methods)

Full employment is achieved when the economy employs all of its resources and full production is achieved when the economy uses the best available ____________________ to produce goods and services.

2-20 Review Frame

We have already learned quite a bit about scarcity and economics. But let's take two frames to review what we have just learned.

resources

the wants of society are unlimited

Every society finds that its ______________ are scarce because * ____ .

goods, services
(either order)
satisfy

Economics is the social science that studies how society uses its scarce resources to produce the ____________________ and ____________________ that ____________ human wants.

2-21 Review Frame

full employment

full production
(either order)

the economy employs all its resources

it uses the best methods (technology) to produce goods and services

For an economy to be efficient there must be both ______________ ______________ and ______________ ______________ in the economy.

Full employment means that * ____ .

Full production means that * ____ .

2-22

We can throw a little more light on scarcity and the problems it creates by examining the table below.

	Combinations										
Goods	**A**	**B**	**C**	**D**	**E**	**F**	**G**	**H**	**I**	**J**	**K**
Food	0	1	2	3	4	5	6	7	8	9	10
Clothing	100	99	96	91	84	75	64	51	36	19	0

This table shows the different combinations of two goods it is possible to produce when there are both full employment and full production in a hypothetical economy whose resources and technology remain un-

food | changed. The two goods this economy is able to produce are ________

clothing (either order) | and ____________ .

2-23

We have supposed this economy is capable of producing only food and clothing to keep our illustration simple.

We already know what full employment and full production mean.

Assuming that the economy's resources and technology do not change means that the numbers in the table are fixed—they do not change while we are talking about them.

Looking at the table, we can see that there are eleven different

combinations | ____________ of food and clothing this economy can produce.

2-24

This table is called a production possibilities table because it shows the different combinations of food and clothing it is possible to produce. One of these is combination *D*. If the economy produces combination *D* it produces 3 units of food and 91 units of clothing. Were the economy

6 | to produce combination *G* it would produce ____________ units of

64 | food and ____________ units of clothing.

2-25

Should the economy decide to produce 5 units of food it could produce

75 | ____________ units of clothing. And were it to produce 19 units of

9 | clothing it could produce ____________ units of food.

2-26

Combination *C* is another combination of food and clothing it is

possible, produce | (possible/necessary) for this economy to ____________ with its fixed

full employment | resources and technology when it achieves both ________________

full production (either order) | ________________ and ____________ ____________ .

2-27

impossible | The economy finds it's (possible/impossible) to produce 3 food and 96 clothing or 2 food and 99 clothing. It cannot produce these combinations

fixed | because its resources and technology are ____________ .

2-28

production possibilities

decrease

One of the things we notice in this ______ ______ table is that when the economy increases its production of food it must (increase/decrease) its production of clothing.

2-29

increase

increase

Were the economy to decrease its production of food it would be able to ______ its production of clothing. And should it decrease its production of clothing it could ______ its production of food.

2-30

fewer

decrease

Why must the economy decrease its production of one good to be able to increase its production of the other good? To produce more food the economy must use more of its fixed quantity of resources on food production. And if it uses more resources to produce food there are (more/fewer) resources available to produce clothing.

When fewer resources are devoted to clothing production the production of clothing must ______ .

2-31

decrease

more

increase

Put the other way around, were the economy to use fewer resources to produce food, its production of food would ______ .

With fewer resources used to produce food, there are ______ resources available to produce clothing and the production of clothing can ______ .

2-32

decrease

Our production possibilities table reveals something important about an economy in which there are both full employment and full production: to increase the production of one good requires that the production of the other good ______ .

2-33

more

Is this generalization of any practical significance in the world of reality? Economists think so. Assuming full employment and production and fixed resources and technology, the only way we can, for example, produce more low-cost housing is to produce less of something else. And if we were to produce fewer military goods we could produce ______ of such other things as low-cost housing.

2-34

produce less of something else

Given our assumptions, the only way we can produce more of anything is to * ______ .

2-35

A production possibilities table such as the one in frame **2-22** does *not* tell us which combination the economy should produce. What the economy should produce depends upon what the people in that economy
cannot — want produced. Said another way, we (can/cannot) determine from the table whether combination *C* is better or worse than combination *D*.

2-36

If our hypothetical economy were located on an island in the South
clothing — Pacific it would probably want to produce very little (food/clothing)
food — and so would produce a lot of (food/clothing). But if it were located above the Arctic Circle its people want to produce a considerable amount
clothing, food — of ______ and not quite so much ______ .

2-37

But which combination people will actually choose to produce the pro-
does not — duction possibilities table (does/does not) tell us.

2-38

While the table does not tell us which combination they will choose, it does tell us that economy must make a choice: it must choose which
combination — ______ of food and clothing to produce.

2-39

The production possibilities table, though it does not tell us which combination the economy will produce, *does* tell us the *cost* of producing food and clothing. Cost, in economics, means the sacrifice that must be made (or what must be done without) in order to produce a good. To produce more food, in the table in frame **2-22**, requires that the econ-
clothing — omy do without or sacrifice the production of some ______ .

2-40

The cost of producing more food is the clothing the economy must
sacrifice — ______ or do without. Similarly, the cost of producing more
food — clothing is the ______ the economy must give up in order to produce the clothing.

2-41

The amount of food that must be sacrificed in order to produce additional clothing is called the ***opportunity cost*** of producing clothing. If our hypothetical economy, whose production possibilities table is reprinted below, wished to increase its production of food from 3 to 4 it
7 — would have to decrease its production of clothing by ______ .

	Combinations										
Goods	A	B	C	D	E	F	G	H	I	J	K
Food	0	1	2	3	4	5	6	7	8	9	10
Clothing	100	99	96	91	84	75	64	51	36	19	0

7 The opportunity cost, therefore, of the fourth unit of food is ______
clothing unit(s) of ______ .

2-42
Should the economy wish to increase its production of food from 4 to 5
9 it would have to do without ______ units(s) of clothing.
We would call the 9 units of clothing the economy has to do without
opportunity in order to increase its production of food from 4 to 5 the ______ cost of producing this additional food.

2-43
When the economy is producing 4 units of food the opportunity cost of producing a fifth unit of food is 9 units of clothing; but if it is already producing 5 units of food the opportunity cost of another unit of food is
11 ______ units of clothing. We see that the more food the econ-
greater omy produces the (greater/less) is the opportunity cost of producing additional food.

2-44
Put another way, as the production of food increases the opportunity
increase cost of producing food will ______ .

2-45
Suppose this economy wished to increase its production of *clothing*
1 from 36 to 51. It would have to do without ______ unit(s) of
food ______ . The unit of food the economy must sacrifice in order to increase its production of clothing from 36 to 51 is the
opportunity cost ______ ______ of the 15 additional units of clothing.

2-46
Does the opportunity cost of producing clothing also increase as the production of clothing increases? We can see that it does. Increasing the production of clothing from 36 to 51 costs the economy 1 unit of food. *Each* of the 15 units of clothing, therefore, costs $\frac{1}{15}$ of a unit of food. And increasing the production of clothing from 51 to 64 requires the economy go without another unit of food. Each of the 13 additional units
$\frac{1}{13}$ of clothing costs ______ of a unit of food.

2-47

Regardless, therefore, of whether we are talking about food or clothing the opportunity cost increases as the production of the good

increases ______________ .

2-48

This tendency for the opportunity cost of producing a good to increase as the production of that good increases is known in economics as ***the law of increasing opportunity costs***. All it means is that the more an economy produces of any good or service, the (greater/smaller) is the opportunity cost of producing an additional unit of that good or service.

greater

2-49 Review Frame

So in summary the opportunity cost of producing a good is

the amount of other goods that must be sacrificed * ____

and as the production of a good increases, the opportunity cost of producing it ______________ .

increases

2-50

It is a fair question to ask *why* the opportunity cost of producing a good should increase when the production of the good increases. Let's see if we can't use the production of food and clothing to find the reason behind the law of increasing opportunity costs.

For simplicity, suppose that the only resources needed to produce food are tractors and workers; and that the only resources required in the production of clothing are sewing machines and workers. But whenever we draw up a production possibilities table we assume that the quantity of each of these resources available to the economy is

fixed ______________ .

2-51

To increase food production the economy must shift resources from the production of ______________ to the production of ______________ .

clothing, food

Inasmuch as tractors aren't used to produce clothing and sewing machines can't be used to produce food, to increase the production of food requires that ______________ be shifted out of clothing and into food production.

workers

2-52

As the number of workers employed in food production increases, the number of available tractors remains fixed. The result of increasing the number of workers engaged in food production is a(n) (increasing/decreasing) number of workers *per tractor* and a(n) (increasing/decreasing) number of tractors *per worker*.

increasing

decreasing

2-53

The effects of increasing the number of workers engaged in food production and of decreasing the number of tractors per worker are shown in the table below.

Number of workers	Production of food
0	0
1	8
2	15
3	21
4	26
5	30

It is clear that as the number of workers employed in food production

increases — increases, the production of food ______________ .

2-54

But look at what happens to the size of the increase in food production as each new worker is shifted into the production of food. Increasing the number of workers from zero to 1 increases food production from zero to

8, 8 — ______________ ; and this is an increase of ______________ units of food.

2-55

When the number of workers employed in the production of food increases from

7 — 1 to 2, food production increases by __________ .

6 — 2 to 3, food production increases by __________ .

5 — 3 to 4, food production increases by __________ .

4 — 4 to 5, food production increases by __________ .

2-56

We can see in the table that as the number of workers employed in the production of food increases, food production increases and the additional food produced by each additional worker (increases/decreases).

decreases

2-57

What has this got to do with the increasing opportunity cost of producing food? Let's take another look at the table in frame **2-53**. To increase food production from zero to 15 required that (1/2/3/4) additional worker(s) be employed. But to increase food production by *another* 15 (from 15 to 30) requires that __________ new workers be employed.

2

3

2-58

Each new worker employed in the production of food increases the amount of food produced by decreasing amounts. This means that to increase food production by any given amount—such as by 15 units—

increasing — requires a(n) (increasing/decreasing) number of additional workers.

2-59

To see why the opportunity cost of producing food increases as the production of food increases, let's look at what happens to the production of *clothing* when the number of workers employed to produce clothing changes. In the table we can see that as the number of workers employed in the production of clothing increases, the

increases — production of clothing ______________ and the extra clothing that re-

decreases — sults from each added worker ______________ .

Number of workers	Production of clothing
0	0
1	50
2	90
3	120
4	140
5	150

2-60

To understand why the extra clothing produced by each new worker employed in the production of clothing should decrease, we need to recall that the number of sewing machines in the economy is fixed. And, therefore, as the number of workers employed in clothing production increases, the number of workers per sewing machine

increases — (increases/decreases) and the number of sewing machines per worker

decreases — ______________ .

2-61

Looking back at frame **2-57**, we found that to increase the production of *food* from zero to 15 required 2 additional workers and that to increase the production of food another 15 units required 3 additional workers. If we look at the table in frame **2-59** we can discover what happens to the production of clothing if we decrease the number of workers engaged in clothing production.

Decreasing the number of workers employed in clothing from 5 to 3

30 — will decrease the production of clothing by ______________ .

Decreasing the number of workers employed in clothing from 3 to

120 — zero will decrease clothing production by ______________ .

2-62

Now let's put it all together. (Consult frames **2-57** and **2-59** if you like.) When the first 2 workers went into the production of food, food production increased by 15; but reducing the number of workers engaged in the production of clothing from 5 to 3 decreased the production of clothing by 30. The opportunity cost, therefore, of the first 15 units of

30 food was ________ units of clothing.

2-63

But to increase food production by *another* 15 units required 3 additional workers. And when these 3 workers were taken away from the production of clothing, the output of clothing decreased by 120. So the opportunity

120 cost of the second 15 units of food was ________ units of clothing.

2-64

Now what is the real cause of the increasing opportunity cost of producing food? Perhaps you have already figured it out. What do you think

If you said the decreasing extra production that results from adding workers you have found the real reason. the real reason for increasing costs is? * ____.

2-65

Opportunity costs increase as the output of a good increases because the extra output that results from using more resources (workers in this case) decreases. To be sure that you understand the reason behind the law of increasing opportunity costs, look again at frame **2-59**. Suppose we wished to increase the production of clothing from 90 to 120. To do this

1 we would require (how many) ________ additional worker(s)?

2-66

But to obtain this additional worker we would have to decrease the number of workers engaged in the production of food from 3 to 2. Looking at the table in frame **2-53** we can see that this would reduce the pro-

6 duction of food by ________ .

The opportunity cost of these additional 30 units of clothing is, therefore,

6 ________ units of food.

2-67

Should we wish to increase the output of clothing by another 30 units

2 from 120 to 150, we would need to employ (how many) ______ more worker(s).

But this would reduce the number of workers engaged in the production

15 of food from 2 to zero and decrease the production of food by ______ units of food.

15 And so the opportunity cost of these 30 extra units of clothing is ______ units of food.

2-68 Review Frame

To review,

the law of increasing opportunity costs is the tendency for the

opportunity ______ cost of producing a good to increase when the produc-

increases tion of that good ______ ;

the opportunity cost increases because as additional resources are em-

decreases ployed the extra output that is produced ______ ; and the extra output produced decreases because the additional resources are em-

fixed ployed along with ______ quantities of other resources.

2-69

Let's put the production possibilities table of our hypothetical economy on a graph.

food On one axis we will want to measure the quantity of ______

clothing (either order) and on the other axis the quantity of ______ the economy is able to produce.

2-70

Here, once more, is the production possibilities table for our hypothetical economy.

	Combinations										
Goods	**A**	**B**	**C**	**D**	**E**	**F**	**G**	**H**	**I**	**J**	**K**
Food	0	1	2	3	4	5	6	7	8	9	10
Clothing	100	99	96	91	84	75	64	51	36	19	0

For no particular reason, let's measure food along the horizontal axis and clothing along the vertical axis.

We have plotted combination *F* for you. Plot the ten other combinations of food and clothing the economy is able to produce on the graph.

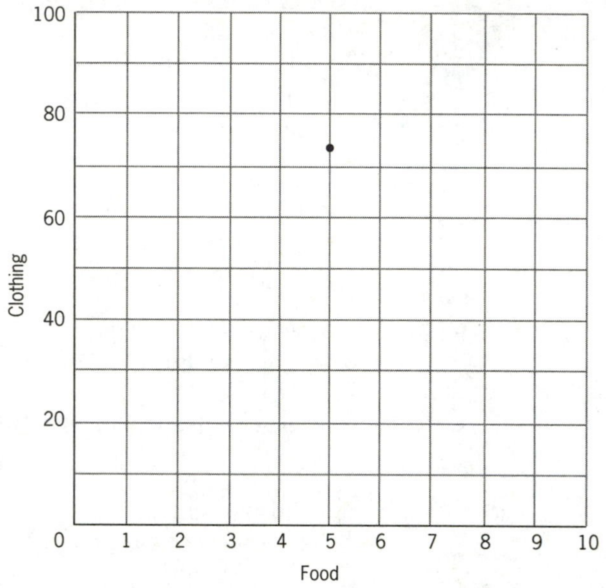

See the next frame for a picture of how the graph you drew should look.

Now draw a curved line through the eleven points.

2-71

The curve you drew in frame **2-70** should look like this.

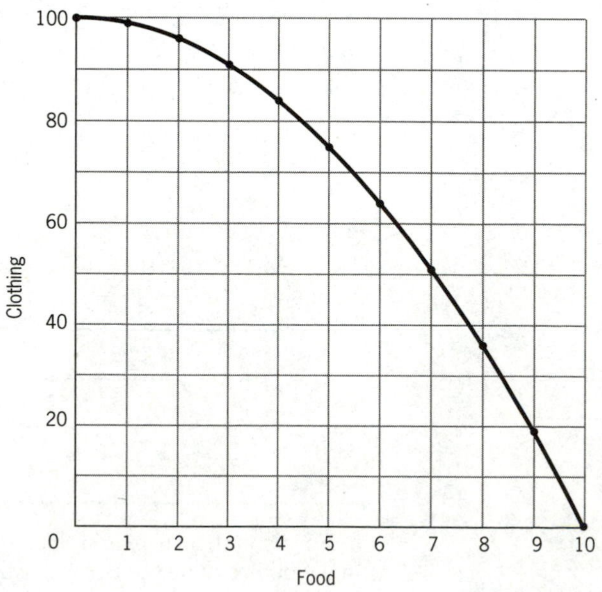

negative

increases (if you put down wrong answers here you should review frames 1-43 to 1-101)

From what you learned in Section 1 about graphs, you can see that this curve has a (positive/negative/zero) slope and that this slope (increases/decreases/remains constant) as we move along it from left to right.

2-72

The negative slope of this production possibilities curve is nothing more than a graphical way of saying that if food production is to increase, the

decrease

production of clothing must ______________ ; and that if clothing

decrease

production is to increase food production must ______________ .

2-73

The increasing slope of the production possibilities curve is the graphical

increases

way of saying that the opportunity cost of producing food __________ as the production of food increases; and that the opportunity cost

increases

of producing clothing ____________ when clothing production increases.

2-74

We have redrawn the production possibilities curve you drew in frame **2-70** on the graph below. To the graph you drew we have added two new points: points *L* and *M*.

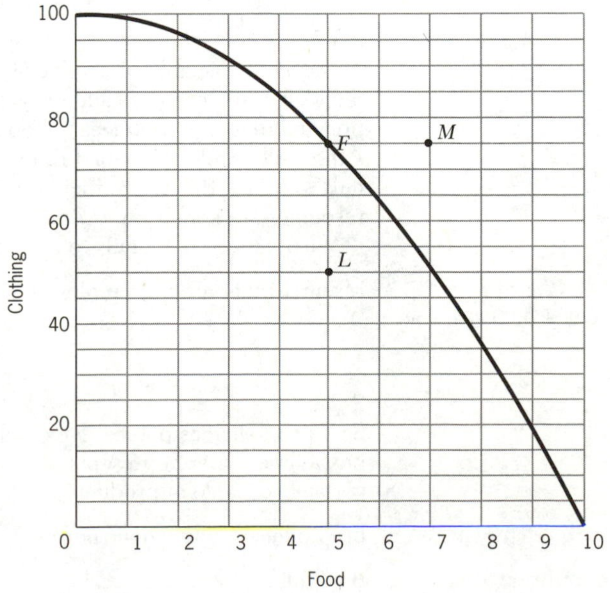

are not — Without even looking very closely at these new points you can see that they (are/are not) located on the production possibilities curve.

Looking more closely, you can see that point *L* represents a combination that includes ________ units of food and ________ units of clothing.

5, 50

Point *M* is a combination of ________ food and ________ clothing.

7,75

2-75

Compare combination *L* (5 food and 50 clothing) with the combination of food and clothing that lies directly above it *on* the production possibilities curve. This is combination *F* which contains ________ food and ________ clothing.

5

75

Do you think the economy is *able* to produce combination *L*? (Yes/No)

Yes is what you should say.

2-76

An economy that is able to produce 5 food and as much as 75 clothing when it employs all of its resources and utilizes the most efficient production methods is certainly capable of producing a combination that includes 5 food and only 50 clothing.

In your opinion, what conditions prevail in an economy that produces only 5 food and 50 clothing when it is capable of producing 5 food and 75 clothing? * ____

____.

We asked for your opinion. To see if yours is the same as ours, go on to the next frame.

2-77

An economy capable of producing 5 food and 75 clothing when it employs all of its resources and uses the most efficient methods of production and that only produces 5 food and 50 clothing has failed to achieve either full employment or full production or both. When an economy fails to utilize the most efficient methods of production we say that its resources are *under*employed.

When an economy fails to employ all of its resources we say that the resources that are not employed at all are ____________.

unemployed (not underemployed)

2-78

So a point such as point *L* lying below (or to the left of) the production possibilities curve represents a combination of goods that an economy is certainly capable of producing. But it represents a combination that will be produced only when there is less than full ____________ or less than full ____________ in the economy.

employment

production (either order)

2-79

Put another way, a point such as *L* on the graph in frame **2-74** means that resources are either ________ or ________ in this economy.

unemployed, underemployed (either order)

This means that some of the economy's resources are * ________ ________ or that the economy is not using * ________.

not employed

the most efficient production methods

2-80

Suppose the economy were actually producing at point *L* (5 food and 50 clothing) and then, by eliminating unemployment and underemployment, was able to move to point *F* (5 food and 75 clothing).

It would have been able to increase the production of clothing by ________ units and its production of food would have * ________ ________.

25

remained changed

The opportunity cost of this additional clothing production was ________ units of food.

zero

2-81

So one way an economy can increase its production of a good at no cost is to eliminate * ________ ________ in the economy.

unemployment and underemployment

2-82

Take another look at the graph in frame **2-74**. Given the amount of resources available to this economy and its technology, do you think it is able to produce the combination of food and clothing represented by point *M*? (Yes/No)

You should say no.

2-83

To be able to produce combination *M* the economy would have to expand its production possibilities. This means that it would have to push its production possibilities curve to the (right/left) or (upward/downward).

right, upward

2-84

An economy can expand its production possibilities either by increasing the amount of resources available to produce goods and services or by improving its technology (or by doing both).

Suppose the economy does one or both of these things and that it moves its production possibilities curve so that it goes through points *S*, *M*, and *T*. Draw in a new production possibilities curve on the graph from frame **2-74** reprinted at the top of the next page.

2-85

If the economy were originally producing combination *H* (7 food and 51 clothing) and now, because it has increased its production possibilities, produces combination *M* (7 food and 75 clothing) it has increased its

24 production of clothing by __________ units while its production of

remained unchanged food * __________________________.

By expanding its production possibilities it was able to increase its production of clothing and the opportunity cost of this increased production

zero of clothing was __________ .

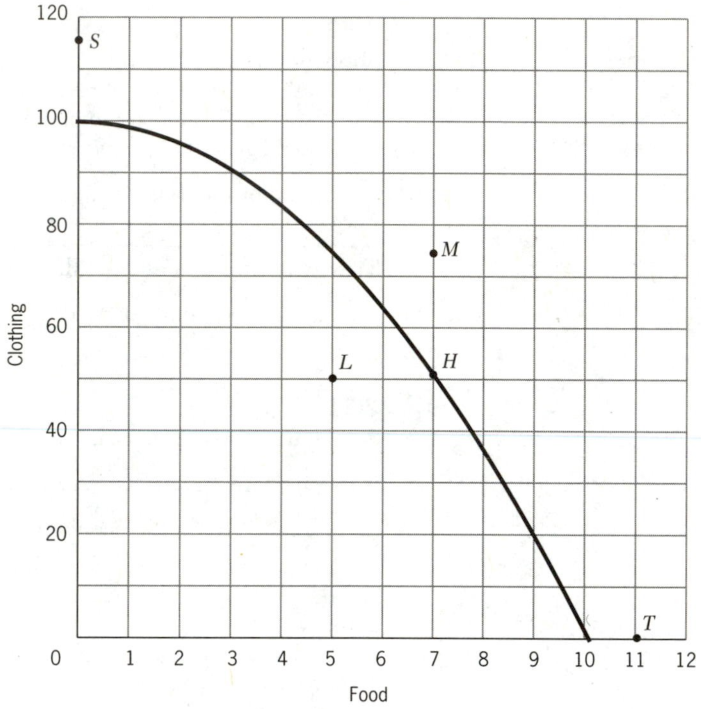

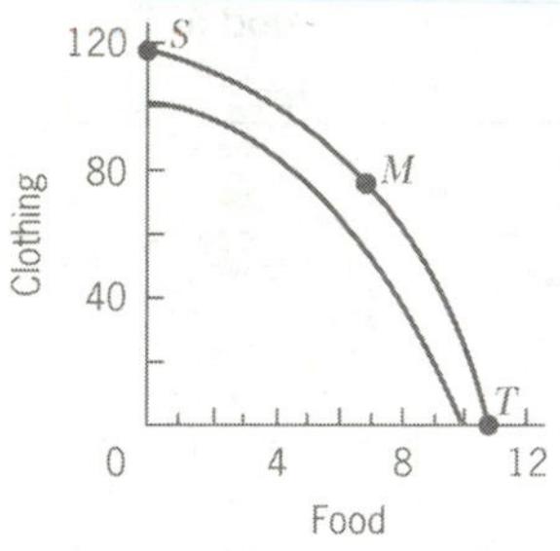

2-86

But an economy can expand its production possibilities and so produce

resources more clothing or more food only if it increases the __________

technology available to produce food and clothing or improves its __________ .

2-87

If this economy were originally producing combination *G* (6 food and 64 clothing) and if it then expanded its production possibilities and produced combination *M* (7 food and 75 clothing) it would have, in fact,

both food and clothing increased its production of (food/clothing/both food and clothing).

2-88 Review Frame

A point that lies to the right (or above) an economy's production possibilities curve represents a combination of goods that the economy (can/cannot) produce with its fixed resources and technology. — cannot

A point that lies to the left (or below) its production possibilities curve represents a combination of goods it __________ produce. — can

2-89 Review Frame

A point to the

left of the production possibilities curve represents a combination that is produced when there is * __________ or * __________ in the economy.

unemployment (less than full employment)
underemployment (less than full production)
(either order)

right of the curve represents a combination that cannot be produced unless the economy * __________ or * __________ .

increase its resources
improves its technology
(either order)

2-90 Review Frame

Eliminating the underemployment or unemployment of resources enables an economy to increase its production of a good at an opportunity cost of __________ . Increasing its resources or improving its technology enables it to increase the production of a good at an opportunity cost of __________ .

zero

zero

FIVE FUNDAMENTAL ECONOMIC QUESTIONS

We have found that human wants tend to be unlimited; and that because wants are unlimited, resources and the goods and services that satisfy wants are scarce. Every society has a big economic problem: there aren't enough resources to satisfy all its wants. Some wants are going to remain unsatisfied.

Faced with this central or basic economic problem of scarcity, every society is going to have to make some decisions. It must come up with answers to fundamental questions about the use of its scarce resources and the satisfaction of wants.

There are at least five of these Fundamental Economic Questions that every society must answer. These questions are:

What to produce
How to produce
For whom to produce
What must be done to ensure the *full employment* of resources
How to provide for *flexibility* in the economy

Let's look now at each of these five Questions.

2-91

In examining the production possibilities table and curve we encountered the first of the Five Fundamental Economic Questions: *what* to produce. We saw that our hypothetical economy had to decide

combination — what ________________ of food and clothing to produce.

2-92

Put another way, our hypothetical economy had to decide what amount of food and what amount of clothing to produce with its scarce resources.

In real world economies there are more than just two goods and services the economy can produce. There are hundreds of thousands of different things these economies are able to produce. But these economies,

what — like our hypothetical one, must also decide ________ amount of each good and of each service to produce.

2-93

Different economies decide what goods and services to produce in different ways. The American economy, by and large, tries to let the individual members of society decide what they want produced. It allows society to tell the producers of goods and services which of their wants are most pressing and how much of each item they want produced.

But no matter what system or method is employed to make the de-

what to produce — cision, all societies must decide * ________________________________

____ .

2-94

Imagine that our hypothetical economy decided that the combination of food and clothing it wanted produced was combination *F* (5 food and 75 clothing) in its production possibilities table (in frame **2-70**). To produce

some — combination *F* (all/some/none) of its resources would have to be used to

some — produce food and ________________ of its resources would have to be employed to produce clothing.

2-95

Were too many of our hypothetical economy's resources used to produce food (and too few employed to produce clothing) it might end up producing combination *G* instead of *F*. Should this happen it would have to

decrease — (increase/decrease) the amount of its resources used to produce food

increase — and (increase/decrease) the quantity of resources employed in producing clothing.

2-96

Similarly, too many of the economy's resources might be used to produce clothing and too few might be employed to produce food; and the economy might end up producing combination *E*. If the economy is to produce combination *F* it would have to shift or reallocate resources
from, to (from/to) the production of clothing (from/to) food production.

2-97

The second Fundamental Economic Question every society must answer is *how* to produce. This means that society must decide how to organize production so that it produces what society says it wants produced. In our example the question of how to produce is a question of getting the
resources right amount of ____________ employed in the production of food and the right amount employed in the production of clothing.

2-98

There is, however, a little more to the question of how to produce what society wants produced than just getting the right amounts of its total resources employed in the production of food and clothing. Imagine that the economy could produce the 5 food and the 75 clothing society wants by using one-half of all its resources in food production and one-half in clothing production.

But suppose that the one-half of the total resources employed in food production were the economy's sewing machines; and the one-half assigned to clothing production were its tractors. The economy
would not (would/would not) be able to produce the 5 food and 75 clothing it wants
is not because this (is/is not) the most efficient method it can utilize to produce food and clothing.

2-99

To produce any combination of food and clothing in its production possibilities table, the economy must employ the most efficient methods of production. This means that it must utilize the resources that are
more (more/less) efficient in producing food to produce food; and the re-
more sources that are (more/less) efficient in producing clothing to produce clothing.

2-100

what The first Fundamental Economic Question was ____________ to pro-
how duce and the second is ____________ to produce it. Answering the second Question requires that the economy determine

efficient which of its resources are more ____________ in the production of a particular good or service;

proportion what is the right ____________ of its total resources to be employed in the production of each good and service.

2-101

Assume our hypothetical economy decides it wants 5 food and 75 clothing produced and that it manages to get the right amount and the most efficient resources assigned to the production of food and clothing.

There are in this economy, let us assume, five families. Each of these families would like to have as much food and as much clothing as it can

unlimited — get because its wants are ______________ .

2-102

If one of the five families received 3 units of food and 50 of clothing

2, 25 — there would be ___________ food and ___________ clothing for the other four families.

Or if each family were to receive equal amounts of food and clothing,

1, 15 — there would be ___________ food and ___________ clothing for each family.

2-103

There is no one way of deciding which of these two distributions of the total production of food and clothing is better. But having produced the 5 food and 75 clothing this economy has somehow to answer the question: How will we divide up (or distribute) the total? This is the third Fundamental Economic Question of *for whom* to produce the output.

food, clothing — For whom, in our example, means how much ______________ and how

(either order) — much ______________ each family will receive?

2-104

There are an extremely large number of possible answers to the for whom question. An economy always finds that there are billions of different ways it can divide up or distribute the total output of goods and services among its citizens. No matter how it decides to distribute total output no one is going to be satisfied because everyone would like a

larger, smaller — (larger/smaller) share and no one wants a (larger/smaller) share of the total output.

2-105

what — The first Fundamental Economic Question was ______________ to pro-

how — duce, the second was ______________ to produce, and the third

for whom — is _________ _________ to produce these goods and services. Answering the third question requires that the economy decide how to

divide (distribute) — ______________ its total production among the families or people who live in that economy.

2-106

The fourth Fundamental Economic Question leads us back to point *L* on the figure in frame **2-74**. If our economy were to produce the combination of 5 food and 50 clothing represented by point *L*, we learned earlier, there would be either underemployed resources or

unemployed — ______________ resources in the economy.

2-107

The production of any combination of food and clothing *on* the production possibilities curve requires both full production and full employment of the economy's resources.

Full employment means that all resources that want (or are willing) to be employed are in fact employed. If, for example, any economy had 100 laborers and 20 of these workers did not want to work, there would

80 — be full employment of labor when (20/80/100) workers were employed.

But if only 75 workers could find jobs there would be (how many)

5, unemployed — __________ workers in the economy who are ______________ .

2-108

Quite often in the world of real economies and real people, workers who want jobs can't find them. More than this, owners of natural resources (land) and owners of machinery (capital) can't find employment for their resources. And when resources that want employment are not employed,

less than — the economy ends up producing an output that is (less than/equal to) what it is capable of producing.

2-109

So if an economy is to produce as much as it is capable of producing and to satisfy as many wants as it is capable of satisfying it must find

full employment — some means of ensuring the ______________ ______________ of its resources.

2-110

The first Fundamental Economic Question was what to produce, the

for whom — second was how to produce it, the third was __________ __________ to produce, and the fourth is what must be done to bring about the full

resources — employment of the economy's ______________ .

2-111

We can illustrate the fifth Fundamental Economic Question by again looking at the production possibilities table in frame **2-70**.

Suppose society had decided it wanted combination *F* (5 food and 75 clothing) produced; and then changed its collective mind and wanted the economy to produce combination *G* (6 food and 64 clothing).

To do this the economy would have to alter its use of resources and

clothing — shift resources *from* the production of ______________ *to* the produc-

food — tion of ______________ .

2-112

Societies do change their minds about what they want produced and how they want the economy's resources used. But if the economy is to respond to society when it changes its mind it must be *flexible*. This means that it must be capable of moving resources (into/away from) the production of the things society wants more of and (into/away from) the production of those items society wants less of.

into
away from

2-113

To be able to change the answer to the *what to produce* question and to decrease its production of clothing from 75 to 64 while it increases its production of food from 5 to 6 requires that the economy ________ resources out of the production of clothing and to the production of food.

shift (move)

When an economy is able to do this we say that it is ________ .

flexible

2-114

But in addition to being able to adapt to changes about what it wants produced society often finds that its production possibilities curve has moved. We know from earlier frames that the production possibilities curve moves to the right (or upward) when the resources available to the economy (increase/decrease) or when ________ improves.

increase, technology

2-115

Look now at the two production possibilities curves below.

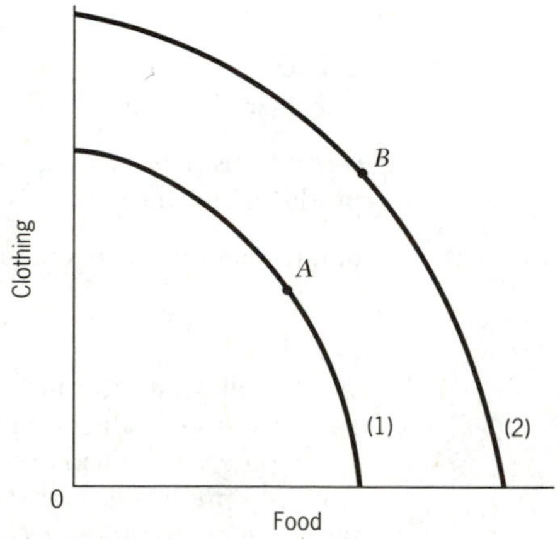

A shift in the curve from (1) to (2) means that the economy has either increased its available ________ or ________ its technology or both.

resources, improved

2-116

If an economy is able to change or alter the way it employs its resources

flexible — when wants change it must be __________ .

It must also, if it is to be flexible, be able to adjust to changes in the availability of resources and to changes in technology.

Were the economy's production possibilities curve to shift from (1) to (2) in frame **2-115** and the economy continued to produce combination *A* we would have to say that this economy was (flexible/inflexible) because it (has/has not) adapted its output of goods and services to the change in its production possibilities curve.

inflexible, has not

2-117

But if, when the curve moves from (1) to (2), the economy changes the combination of food and clothing it produces from *A* to *B* we

flexible — would say that the economy was __________ because it has

adapted — __________ its output to take account of the new production possibilities curve.

2-118 Review Frame

We have now encountered all five of the Fundamental Economic Questions for which every society must find answers. A society must decide

what — __________ to produce

how — __________ to produce it

for whom — __________ __________ to produce these goods and services

full employment — what it needs to do to ensure the __________ __________ of its resources

flexible — what it must do if the economy is to be __________

THE CIRCULAR FLOW

We have looked at the five Fundamental Economic Questions every society must answer. But we have not explained the different methods (or economic systems) various societies use to determine their answers to these questions.

An explanation of the system the American economy employs to find answers to the five Fundamental Economic Questions would be an entire course in economics. We can, however, lay the groundwork for understanding American capitalism by constructing a simplified picture of its operation.

2-119

In the space below we have drawn two boxes.

households
business firms

You can see that one of these boxes is labeled ______________ and the other is labeled ______________ ______________ .

2-120

unlimited
business firms

The households of the American economy include all the families and individuals who live in the economy. These households have wants that tend to be ______________ . In addition, these households own the economy's resources: labor, land (or natural resources), capital goods (machinery and buildings), and entrepreneurial ability (the taking of risks).

Most of these resources, instead of being employed by the households themselves, are employed by the ______________ ______________ in the economy.

2-121

households

The business firms that employ these resources use them to produce goods and services that satisfy human wants. The goods and services which the firms produce are sold to the ______________ of the economy.

2-122

To show the *flows* of resources and goods and services between the business firms and households of the economy, let's put some arrows into our diagram. It now looks like this.

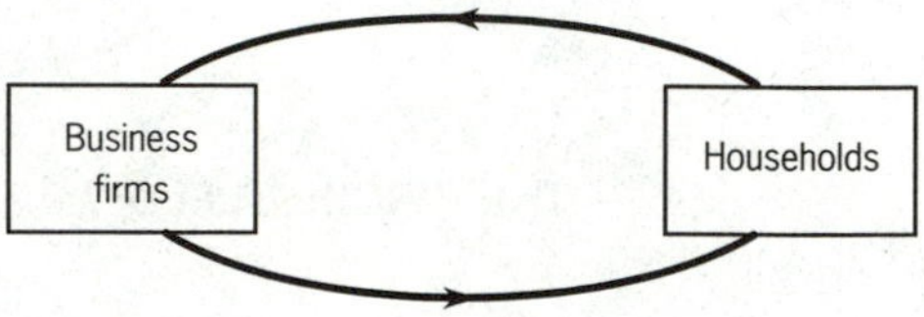

resources
households
business firms
goods, services
business firms, households

The upper arrow shows the flow of (resources/goods and services) from the ______________ in the economy to the economy's ______________ ______________ . The lower arrow represents the flow of ______________ and ______________ from the ______________ ______________ to the ______________ .

2-123

Households furnish business firms with resources and receive something in return. In fact, if they didn't receive something in return for their resources they wouldn't provide firms with the resources needed to produce goods and services.

For example, people wouldn't work for a firm (that is, provide the firm with labor resources) unless in return they received:

(a) the thanks of their employer
(b) some of the goods and services produced by their employer
(c) money

(c), to be realistic, is what workers get in return

Which one? ______________________

2-124

Business firms which produce and sell goods and services also receive

money

__________ in return from the households.

2-125

So in addition to the flow of resources and goods and services through the economy there is also a flow of money. Money flows from households

goods and services

to firms in return for * ______________ and money flows from

resources

firms to households in return for ______________________ .

2-126

Let's put this money flow into the diagram we drew in frame **2-122**. The diagram now looks like this.

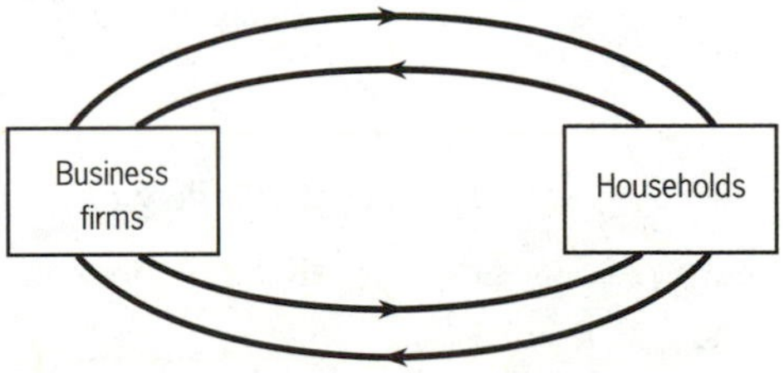

business firms

The uppermost arrow shows the flow of money from __________

households

______________ to ________________ in return for the

households

flow of resources provided by the ______________________

business firms

to the __________ __________ of the economy.

households

The lowermost arrow represents the flow of money from ________

business firms

____________________ to __________ __________ in

business firms

return for the flow of goods and services provided by __________

households

________________ to ________________ .

2-127

We can see why the diagram in the last frame might very well be called the ***circular flow*** diagram. We can also see that there are two different *kinds* of flows in the economy.

One of these flows is called the ***real*** flow. This is the flow of resources and of goods and services.

money — The other flow is a flow of ______________ . Not too surprisingly this

money — flow is called the ______________ flow.

2-128

The circular flow diagram helps us to understand the dual roles played by business firms and households in our economy.

employ / produce — Business firms play a dual role because they (employ/produce) the economy's resources and (employ/produce) the goods and services that satisfy human wants.

provide / use — Households play a dual role because they (provide/use) the resources and (provide/use) the goods and services.

2-129

resources — Put another way, in the American economy ______________ flow from

produce — households to business firms that use them to ______________ goods and services; these goods and services then flow to the households who

satisfy, wants — use them to ____________ their human ____________ .

real — This flow is called the (real/money) flow.

2-130

Looking at the flow of money we see that households use the money

resources — they receive for providing firms with ______________ to buy

goods and services — * ____________________ . Firms in turn use the money they receive

goods and services — for providing households with * ____________________ to pay for the

resources — ______________ they employ.

2-131

incomes / expenditures — The monies which households receive are their (incomes/expenditures) and the monies they exchange for goods and services are their (incomes/expenditures).

receipts / costs — The monies which firms receive are their (costs/receipts) and the monies which they exchange for resources are their (costs/receipts).

2-132

In short, and using the terms employed in the last frame, the expenditures of households are the ______ of business firms; and the incomes of households are the ______ of the business firms. Furthermore, the receipts of business firms are the ______ of households; and the costs of business firms become the ______ of households.

receipts
costs
expenditures
incomes

2-133

So households and business firms are both buyers and sellers in the economy: each obtains something by giving up money and each surrenders something in return for money.

Households (buy/sell) resources and (buy/sell) goods and services.

Firms ______ resources and ______ goods and services.

sell, buy
buy, sell

2-134

We might digress for a frame to ask why we have business firms. Who needs them? Instead of having firms which buy resources from households and then sell the goods and services they produce from these resources back to the households, why not skip the firm? Why not have each household use its own resources to produce its own goods and services?

Most firms produce only one or a very few goods or services. They ***specialize***. By specializing they are able to produce a greater quantity of goods and services with resources than the households could produce with the same resources. In short, were households to be jacks-and-jills-of-all-trades they would be quite inefficient in producing goods and services; but firms that ______ in the production of one or a few products are much more ______ at producing these goods and services.

specialize
efficient

2-135

Let's digress for another frame to ask why we use money. Do we need it? Instead of having firms pay for the resources they obtain from households with money, why don't they simply pay for these resources with some of the goods and services they produce? And instead of having households pay for the goods and services they obtain from firms with money, why don't they pay for these goods and services with some of the resources available to them? This would be most inconvenient! The firm buying resources would have to find a household with the resources the firm wants and is willing to take in return the good or service the firm produces. And the household buying a good or a service would have to find a firm that is willing to take the resources the household has in return. Most inconvenient!

We don't really need to use money. It is simply more ______ to use money than to swap or barter resources for goods and services.

convenient

2-136

Return now to households and firms as buyers and sellers. We saw that firms buy ° ______ and sell ° ______ while households buy ° ______ and sell° ______.

resources, goods and services
goods and services, resources

2-137

In the jargon of economics this means that firms are *demanders* of resources and *suppliers* of goods and services.

Households are (demanders/suppliers) of goods and services and (demanders/suppliers) of resources.

demanders
suppliers

2-138

The coming together of demanders and suppliers to buy and to sell is called a *market*. There are two principal types of markets in our economy. One type of market is the market for resources. In these markets the demanders are ______ and the suppliers are ______.

business firms
households

2-139

The other type of market is called the *product* market because the products (that is, goods and services) produced by ______ are sold in these markets to ______.

business firms
households

2-140

To put it all together:

Business firms are demanders in the ______ markets and suppliers in the ______ markets.

Households are demanders in the ______ markets and suppliers in the ______ markets.

resource
product
product
resource

2-141

The dual roles of households and firms we discussed earlier can also be seen in the markets of our economy. In these markets we see firms as ______ of resources and ______ of products; and households as ______ of resources and ______ of products.

demanders, suppliers
suppliers, demanders

2-142 Review Frame

We have finished looking at the circular flow diagram. Before going on in Section 3 to explain how demand and supply determine the quantity of a resource or product bought and sold in a market and the price at which it sells, let's review what we have learned about the overall operation of our economy.

In the circular flow diagram there are two groups represented and two flows shown.

households and business firms

The two groups are * ______________________.

real, money (either order)

The two flows are the __________ flow and the __________ flow.

2-143 Review Frame

resources, households, business firms

In the real flow ______________ flow from __________ __________ to ______________________

goods and services, business firms, households

and ______________ flow from ______________ __________ to ______________.

business firms

households

incomes

costs

In the money flow monies flow from __________ to ______________ in payment for resources; and the monies in this flow are the __________ of households and the __________ of firms.

households, business firms

expenditures, receipts

Monies flow from __________ to __________ in payment for goods and services; and the monies in this flow are the __________ of households and the __________ of firms.

2-144 Review Frame

The dual role of

to furnish resources and use goods and services

households is * ______________________.

to employ resources and produce goods and services

firms is * ______________________.

resource

product (either order)

The two types of markets in the economy are the __________ markets and the __________ markets.

2-145 Review Frame

demanders (buyers)

suppliers (sellers)

In the resource markets of the economy firms are the __________ and households are the __________.

suppliers (sellers)

demanders (buyers)

In the product markets of the economy firms are the __________ and households are the __________.

Now take the Review Test for Section 2 at the back of the book.

Fundamentals of Demand and Supply

section 3

Nearly everyone has heard about the Law of Supply and Demand. Very few people, however, know what supply and demand are, or what the Law of Supply and Demand is.

Demand and supply are basic thinking tools in the study of economics. Economists use them to help understand what causes the price of a good or service to be what it is and to explain what causes the price of a good or service to change. Demand and supply are important because together they determine the price of a commodity and the amount of that commodity that will be bought and sold.

Before we can use demand and supply to explain the price and the amount of a commodity bought and sold, we must know some important things about demand and about supply. To begin, we will examine demand and learn what is important to know about it. Then we will do the same for supply. Finally, we can use demand and supply together to explain what the price of a commodity will be, how much of the commodity will be bought and sold, when its price will change, and when the amount bought and sold will change.

When we have finished, we will not only understand the Law of Supply and Demand, but we will also have acquired some very useful thinking tools.

DEMAND

3-1

As economists use the term, ***demand is always expressed as a schedule***. Here is an example of a demand schedule.

Demand for milk
Week of June 8–14, 1992

Price (per quart)	Quantity demanded (quarts)
$1.30	1,300
1.20	1,400
1.10	1,500
1.00	1,600
0.90	1,700
0.80	1,800
0.70	1,900

This demand schedule and every demand schedule has two columns:

price, quantity demanded

the __________ column and the __________ __________ column.

3-2

Every demand schedule is for some specific period of time. If you will look at the schedule in frame **3-1** above, you will see that it is the demand

the week of June 8–14, 1992

schedule for* ______________________________ ,

______________________ .

3-3

The demand schedule in frame **3-1** shows the number of quarts of milk buyers in some area would purchase in the week of June 8–14, 1992, and the various prices that might be charged for a quart of milk. For example, if the price of milk were $1.30 a quart, they would buy 1,300 quarts. Likewise, if the price were 80 cents a quart, they would purchase

1,800

__________ quarts.

3-4

Still looking at the demand schedule in frame **3-1**, to get buyers to purchase 1,600 quarts of milk in the week of June 8–14, 1992, the price of

1.00

milk would have to be $__________ per quart.

3-5

Economists give very special meanings to certain terms.

demand for milk

The schedule which indicates the number of quarts of milk buyers will purchase in the week of June 8–14, 1992, at the various prices that might be charged for milk is called the (demand for milk/quantity of milk demanded).

quantity of milk demanded

The 1,700 quarts of milk that buyers of milk would purchase in the week of June 8–14, 1992, if the price of milk were $0.90 cents per quart is called the (demand for milk/quantity of milk demanded).

3-6

Using what we have said about the demand for milk, let's see if we can now define demand. We are agreed that demand is expressed as a __________ which indicates the __________ __________ of a commodity at various __________ during a specific __________ .

schedule, quantity demanded

prices

time (period, etc.)

3-7

Here is another example of demand.

Demand for cigarettes
Month of July, 1992

Price (per carton)	Quantity demanded (cartons)
$16	8,000
15	9,000
14	10,000
13	11,000
12	12,000
11	13,000
10	14,000
9	15,000

Just to make sure we have our terms correctly in our minds, when the price of cigarettes is $14 per carton, 10,000 cartons is the __________ __________ .

quantity demanded

3-8

If you look at the example of demand in frame **3-7** you will see that the lower the price charged for a carton of cigarettes, the (greater/smaller) is the quantity of cigarettes demanded and vice versa.

greater

3-9

Let's put what has come to be called the Law of Demand another way. In the typical demand schedule:

When the price of the commodity increases, the quantity demanded of the commodity will (increase/decrease), and

when the price of the commodity decreases, the quantity demanded of the commodity will (increase/decrease).

decrease

increase

3-10

The Law of Demand can be put very simply: There is an inverse (negative) relation between the price of a commodity and the quantity of that commodity demanded.

The demand schedule in frame **3-7** is an example of this inverse relationship: When the price of cigarettes changes, the quantity of cigarettes demanded changes in the (same/opposite) direction.

opposite

3-11

Are you certain that you know what the Law of Demand is? If the price of a commodity were to decrease, then, according to the Law of Demand, there would also be:

(a) an increase in the demand for the commodity
(b) an increase in the quantity demanded of the commodity.

Which one? ______

(b) If you put down (a) you have forgotten that demand means "demand schedule" and that a price change results in a "change in quantity demanded"—not in demand.

3-12

To summarize what we know about the Law of Demand: When the price of a commodity increases, the quantity demanded of it will ________ and vice versa. In other words, we say that the relationship between price and quantity demanded is ________ .

decrease
inverse (negative)

3-13

Common sense and observation convince us that a downsloping demand curve is realistic: people *do* buy more at lower prices and stores *do* have sales in recognition of this. Economists explain the law of demand in terms of the ***substitution*** and ***income effects***. If the price of steak were to go on sale at half price while hamburger's price did not change, some people, at least, would buy more steak/hamburger; that is, they would *substitute* ________ for ________ . This is the (substitution/income) effect.

steak
steak, hamburger
substitution

3-14

With the price of an important commodity such as steak at half price, people would feel (richer/poorer) and thus be able to buy (more/less) ________ while (giving up/not giving up) other commodities. This is called the ________ effect.

richer, more
steak, not giving up
income

3-15

The substitution effect is the tendency of people to buy (more/less) of a commodity when its price drops. The income effect is the tendency of people to buy ________ of a commodity when its price drops. The two effects (cancel each other out/reinforce each other) in explaining the Law of Demand.

more
more
reinforce each other

3-16

Here is still another example of demand.

Demand for sugar, 1992	
Price (per pound)	Quantity demanded (millions of pounds)
$.90	100
.84	200
.78	300
.72	400
.66	500
.60	600
.54	700

For convenience it is very often useful to have a graph of demand (see below). Let's measure price on the vertical axis and the quantity demanded on the horizontal axis. We call this graph of demand the ***demand curve***.

We have indicated with a point on the graph that when the price of sugar is 90 cents a pound, the quantity demanded is 100 million pounds. Complete this graph of the demand schedule by plotting the other six points and connect the seven points with a line.

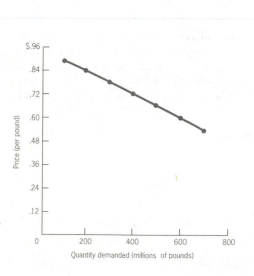

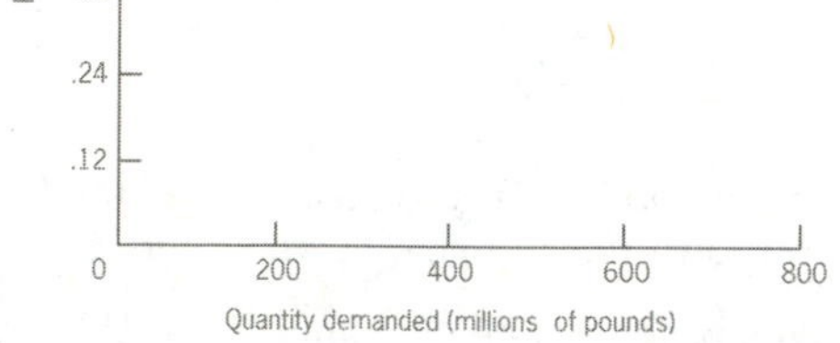

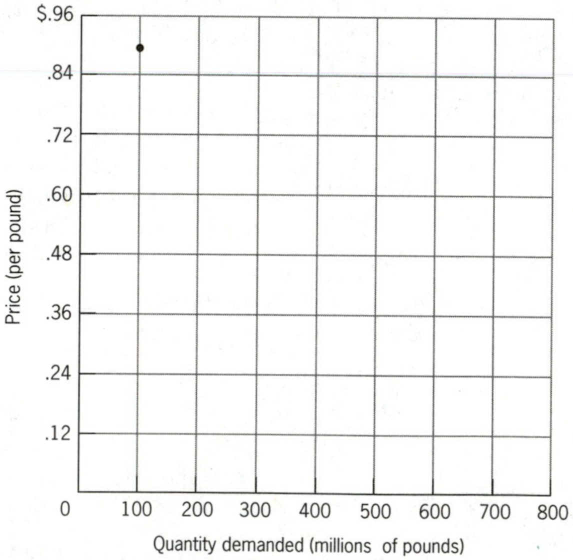

3-17

vertical

horizontal, demand

downward

Now look at the curve you plotted in frame **3-16**. In plotting the curve we put price on the (vertical/horizontal) axis and quantity demanded on the (vertical/horizontal) axis. This curve is called the __________ curve. From left to right the curve slopes (downward/upward).

3-18

Here is another example of a demand curve.

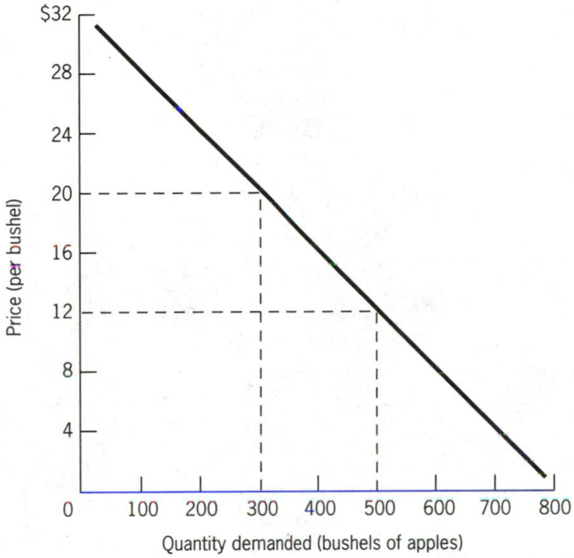

If you read the graph correctly you see that when the price of apples

300 is $20 per bushel, the quantity of apples demanded is __________ bushels; and if the quantity of apples demanded is 500 bushels, the price

12 of apples must be $______ per bushel.

3-19

The Law of Demand means that:

inverse The relation between price and quantity demanded is (direct/inverse), and

downward the demand curve slopes (downward/upward) from left to right.

3-20

Let's review what we learned about constructing a demand curve.

A demand curve is nothing more than a demand schedule plotted

graph on a __________ . In plotting demand we place price on the

vertical, horizontal __________ axis and quantity demanded on the __________ axis.

3-21

A frequent source of difficulty for students learning about demand is the important distinction between demand and quantity demanded.

The amount buyers will purchase at some particular price is the

quantity demanded of (demand for/quantity demanded of) a commodity.

The schedule or curve which indicates the amount of a commodity

demand for buyers will purchase at various prices is the (demand for/quantity demanded of) a commodity.

3-22

Based on this distinction between demand and quantity demanded, a ***change in demand*** means that the demand schedule (or curve) has changed in some way.

And a ***change in the quantity demanded*** means that the price of the commodity has changed and as a result the amount buyers wish to purchase has also changed.

Look at the demand schedule for pecans below.

Demand for pecans
Month of July, 1992

Price (per ounce)	Quantity demanded (ounces)
$1.00	4,000
.90	5,000
.80	6,000
.70	7,000
.60	8,000
.50	9,000
.40	10,000

If the price of pecans were to fall from 90 to 80 cents, and buyers increased their monthly purchase of pecans from 5,000 to 6,000 ounces we would call this a change in (demand/quantity demanded).

quantity demanded

If the price of pecans were 70 cents an ounce and buyers increased their purchase of pecans from 7,000 ounces in July to 7,500 ounces in August 1992, we would call this a change in (demand/quantity demanded).

demand

3-23

As we will see, there are a number of reasons why the demand for a commodity might change. There is, however, only one cause of a change in the quantity demanded of a commodity. Look again at the demand for pecans in frame **3-22**.

A change in the quantity of pecans demanded from 5,000 to 6,000 ounces is brought about by a change in the ________ of pecans. A change in the quantity of pecans demanded from 9,000 to 8,000 ounces is the result of a change in the ________ of pecans from ________ cents to ________ cents.

price

price

50, 60

3-24

When economists say that the only cause of a change in the quantity demanded of a commodity is a change in its price, they are also saying that: The one thing that *doesn't* cause a change in the demand for a commodity is a change in the price of that commodity.

In short, when the price of a commodity rises or falls, the quantity demanded (will/will not) change, but demand (will/will not) change.

will, will not

3-25

price
demand

To summarize this important distinction: A change in the ________ of a commodity will bring about a change in the quantity demanded, but will not result in a change in the ________ for the commodity.

3-26

We will explain shortly *why* the demand for a commodity might change. A change in demand may be either an increase or a decrease. To help us understand changes in demand, look at the following three demand schedules for pecans.

Demand for pecans
Months in 1992

	Quantity demanded		
Price	**July**	**August**	**September**
$1.00	4,000	4,500	3,500
.90	5,000	5,500	4,500
.80	6,000	6,500	5,500
.70	7,000	7,500	6,500
.60	8,000	8,500	7,500
.50	9,000	9,500	8,500
.40	10,000	10,500	9,500

You will see from these schedules that the quantity demanded at any price in August is different from the quantity demanded at that price in July. And the quantity demanded at any price in September is different from the quantity demanded at that price in August. We must conclude, therefore, that:

demand for — Between July and August there was a change in the (demand for/quantity demanded of) pecans.

demand for — Between August and September there was a change in the (demand for/quantity demanded of) pecans.

3-27

Just as the quantity demanded of pecans may increase or decrease, so may the demand.

increased
decreased

An *increase* in demand means that the quantity demanded at each price has (increased/decreased), while a *decrease* in demand means that the quantity demanded at each price has (increased/decreased).

3-28

As you can see on the demand schedules for pecans:

an increase — Between July and August there was (an increase/a decrease) in the demand for pecans.

a decrease — Between August and September there was (an increase/a decrease) in the demand for pecans.

a decrease — Between July and September there was (an increase/a decrease) in the demand for pecans.

3-29

Plot the three demand schedules in frame **3-26** on the graph below. Be sure to label each of the curves to indicate whether it is the demand in July, August, or September.

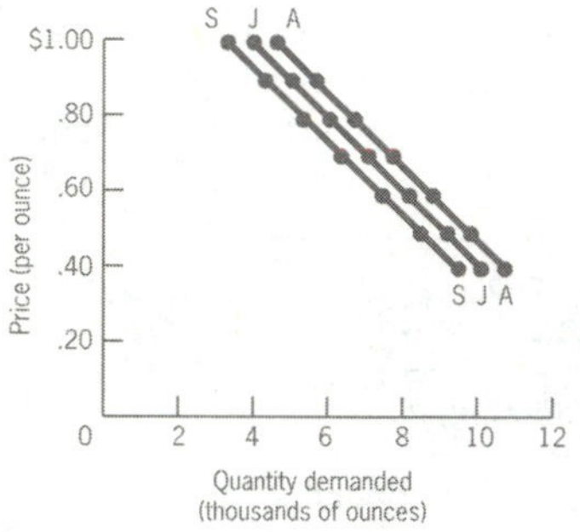

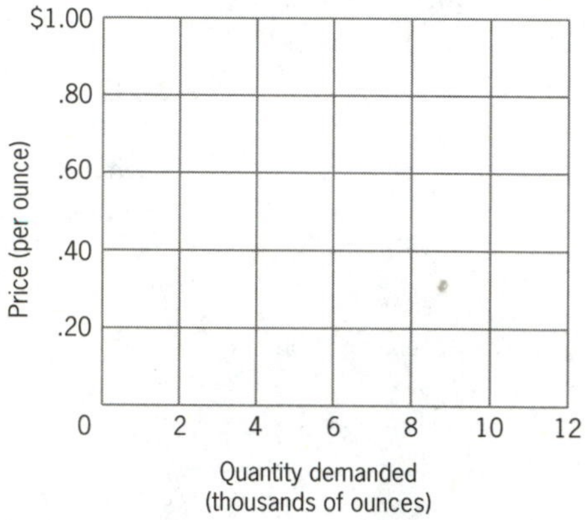

3-30

right

left

Between July and August the demand for pecans increased. The August demand curve lies to the (right/left) of the July demand curve.

Between August and September the demand for pecans decreased. The September demand curve is to the (right/left) of the August demand curve.

3-31

increased

decreased

When the demand curve for a commodity moves to the right, we know that the demand for that commodity has ________ . And when the demand curve moves to the left, the demand for the commodity has ________ .

3-32

increased

right

decreased

left

Let's summarize what we have learned about changes in demand.

An increase in demand means that the quantity demanded at each price in the demand schedule has ________ and that the demand curve has moved to the ________ . A decrease in demand means that the quantity demanded at each price in the demand schedule has ________ and that the demand curve has moved to the ________ .

3-33

is not

a change in the price of the commodity

We have also learned that a change in demand (is/is not) the same thing as a change in the quantity demanded. Changes in quantity demanded are the result of * ________________________ .

3-34

A change in quantity demanded is caused by a change in

price, is not

__________ . A change in demand (is/is not) caused by a change in price of the good or service in question. A change in demand is caused by a change in one or more of the ***determinants*** of demand. The five determinants of demand are: number of buyers, tastes, income, prices of related goods, and expectations. Let's examine each in turn.

3-35

If the number of buyers of a product increases we would expect the demand for the product to (increase/decrease) and the demand curve would shift to the __________ . This means that at each and every price (more/less) would be bought. Another way of expressing that is to say that any given quantity would be bought at a (higher/lower) price. If you are not convinced of this, examine the "August" demand curve you drew in frame **3-29**.

increase
right
more
higher

3-36

If people's tastes change in favor of a product, that is the same as saying they wish it (more/less) and that their demand for it has __________ .

more
increased

3-37

If people's incomes increase, we would expect their demand for most products to __________ . With higher incomes people will buy (more/less) steaks, video cassettes, and sunscreen. These are called ***superior*** or ***normal*** goods. However, there is a class of goods, such as potatoes, cabbage, or bread, that people may buy *less* of as their incomes rise, because they can now buy more high-protein foods. For these ***inferior*** goods, increased income causes a(n) __________ in demand.

increase, more
decrease

3-38

If the price of coffee rises sharply (say, because of a killing frost in Brazil) some people will buy (more/less) coffee: the (demand/quantity demanded) of coffee has __________ . Let's say coffee and tea are ***substitutes***. Since people are buying less coffee because its price has risen, they will buy (more/less) tea: the (demand/quantity demanded) of tea will __________ . And this will cause the price of tea to __________ .

less, quantity demanded
decreased
more, demand
increase
increase

	3-39
decrease quantity demanded, increase, demand increase	The increased price of coffee has led to a(n) (increase/decrease) in (demand/quantity demanded) of coffee *and* to a(n) (increase/decrease) in (demand/quantity demanded) of tea, which causes the price of tea to __________ .
	3-40
same	From this we see that the prices of substitutes tend to change in the (same/opposite) directions(s).
	3-41
quantity demanded decrease decrease, demand decrease	If the price of gasoline rises sharply (say, because of a renewed war in the Middle East), the (demand/quantity demanded) of gasoline will __________ . Cars and gasoline are ***complements***. The increased price of gasoline will __________ the (demand/quantity demanded) of large gas-guzzlers and the price of large cars will __________ .
	3-42
decreased quantity demanded, demand decrease, decreasing	The increased price of gasoline has led to its (increased/decreased) (demand/quantity demanded), causing the __________ for large cars to (increase/decrease) and this results in the price of large cars ________ .
	3-43
opposite	From this we see that the prices of complements tend to change in the (same/opposite) directions(s).
	3-44
increase demand increase less demand, less	If people expect prices to rise shortly, they will (increase/decrease) their *present* buying. In other words, their *present* (demand/quantity demanded) will __________ . If people know that a sale will start tomorrow, they will buy (more/less) today. That is, *today's* (demand/quantity demanded) will be __________ .
	3-45
determinants of demand	When we state that demand for a product is a schedule showing how much will be bought at various prices during a given time period, then, we are assuming that "other things are equal" or "other things do not change," these "other things" being the five categories we have been discussing and which are called the * ____________________ .

3-46 Review Frame
Before going on to supply, test your understanding of demand. In your own words:

A schedule showing the quantities demanded of a commodity at various prices during some specific period of time, assuming determinants do not change.

Explain what demand is: * ______________________________
____
____
____.

Price and quantity demanded are inversely related to each other (as price increases quantity demanded decreases and vice versa).

State the Law of Demand: * ______________________________
____
____
____
____.

A graph of demand (of the demand schedule).

Explain what a demand curve is: * ______________________________
____

Demand is the schedule or curve, while quantity demanded is the amount that will be purchased at some particular price in the schedule.

What is the difference between demand and quantity demanded?
* ____
____
____
____
____.

Supply

Demand alone never tells us what the price of a commodity will be or how much of the commodity will be bought and sold. Only demand and supply *together* give us answers to these questions.

We have looked at demand. Now let's look at the other side of the market: the supply side. Then we can put the two sides together and determine the price of a commodity and how much of it will be bought and sold.

3-47
In many ways supply and demand are alike. However, they do differ in several important ways. Below is an example of supply.

Supply of milk
Week of June 8–14, 1992

Price (per quart)	Quantity supplied (quarts)
$1.30	1,700
1.20	1,600
1.10	1,500
1.00	1,400
0.90	1,300
0.80	1,200
0.70	1,100

Supply is like demand in that supply refers to a specific period of

time, schedule ________ , and supply is expressed as a ________ which

two (2) has ________ columns.

3-48

one (1) The supply schedule above covers a period of ________ week. The

price two columns in the supply schedule are the ________ column and

quantity supplied the ________ ________ column.

3-49

A person reads a supply schedule in almost the same way that he reads a demand schedule. If the price of milk were $1.20 a quart, sellers would

1,600 offer to sell ________ quarts during the week of June 8–14, 1992. To get sellers to sell 1,300 quarts of milk in the week of June 8–14, 1992,

0.90 the price of milk would have to be $________ a quart.

3-50

The only difference between demand and supply we have found so far

demanded is this: The demand schedule has a price and a quantity ________

supplied column. The supply schedule has a price and a quantity ________ column.

3-51

Because demand and supply are so similar, our definitions of demand and supply are very much alike.

schedule, quantities Supply is expressed as a ________ of the ________

supplied, prices, period ________ at various ________ during a specific ________

time of ________ .

3-52

Economists are careful to distinguish between supply and quantity supplied. The 1,600 quarts of milk that suppliers would offer for sale during the week of June 8–14, 1992, if the price were $1.20 a quart is called the (supply of milk/quantity of milk supplied).

quantity of milk supplied

3-53

The schedule that tells us the number of quarts of milk sellers would offer for sale in the week of June 8–14, 1992, at the various prices that might be charged for milk is known as the (supply of milk/quantity of milk supplied).

supply of milk

3-54

Look at the example of supply below.

Supply of cigarettes
Month of July, 1992

Price (per carton)	Quantity supplied (cartons)
$16	12,000
15	11,000
14	10,000
13	9,000
12	8,000
11	7,000
10	6,000
9	5,000

The supply of cigarettes (is/is not) 10,000 cartons when the price of cigarettes is $14.

is not

The quantity of cigarettes supplied (is/is not) 8,000 cartons when the price of cigarettes is $12.

is

The supply of cigarettes (is/is not) the schedule showing the number of cartons of cigarettes that will be offered for sale at various prices during a specific period of time.

is

3-55

There is one more important difference between demand and supply. We discovered earlier that there is an inverse relationship between price and quantity demanded: When price decreases, the quantity demanded (decreases/increases) and vice versa. We named this inverse relationship the ***Law of*** ________ .

increases

Demand

3-56

If you will look at the supply schedule in frame **3-54**, you will discover the ***Law of Supply***.

decreases

increases

direct

When the price of cigarettes decreases, the quantity of cigarettes supplied (increases/decreases). When the price of cigarettes increases, the quantity of cigarettes supplied ________ . The relation between price and quantity supplied is (inverse/direct).

3-57

supplied

demanded

Applying both the Law of Demand and the Law of Supply, we see that when price increases, the quantity ________ will increase and the quantity ________ will decrease.

3-58 Review Frame

A schedule of the quantities supplied at various prices during a specific period of time.

The *direct* relation between price and quantity supplied (when price increases quantity supplied increases and vice versa).

Just for a minute, let's review what we have learned about supply and the Law of Supply. What, in your own words, is:

Supply: * ____

____

____ .

The Law of Supply: * ______________________________

____

____ .

3-59 Review Frame

Supply is a schedule and quantity supplied is the amount offered for sale at a particular price.

What, in your own words, is the difference between the supply and the quantity supplied of a commodity? * ________________________

____

____ .

3-60

supply curve

When we plotted the demand schedule on a graph, we called this graph the demand curve. Similarly, when we plot the supply schedule, we call the resulting graph the ________ ________ .

3-61

price When we graph the supply schedule we again place ________ on the vertical axis. But on the horizontal axis we plot the quantity

supplied ________ .

3-62

Here is still another example of supply.

Supply of sugar, 1992

Price (per pound)	Quantity supplied (millions of pounds)
$.90	1,100
.84	1,000
.78	900
.72	800
.66	700
.60	600
.54	500

On the graph below complete the plotting of the supply schedule. One point on the supply curve is already plotted. When you have finished plotting the other six points, connect the points with a line.

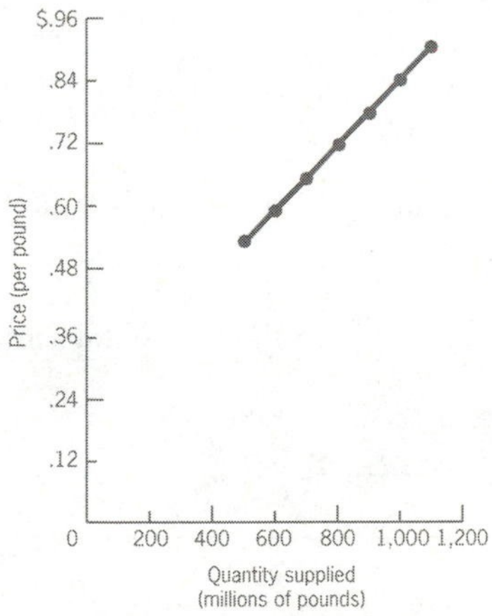

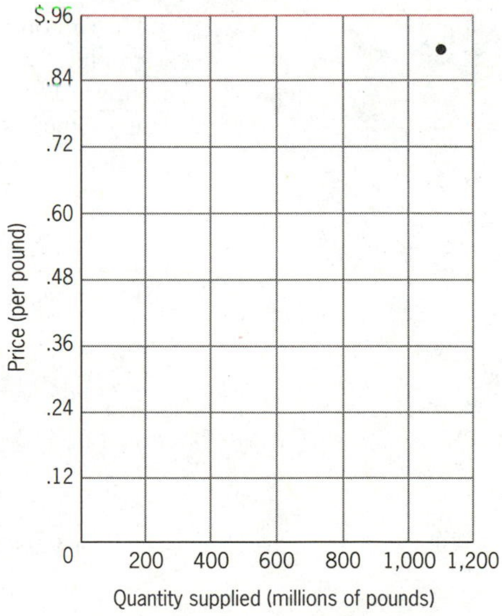

3-63

Look at the curve you plotted in the frame **3-62**. This curve is called the

upward supply curve. From left to right it slopes (upward/downward).

3-64

On the graph below is another supply curve.

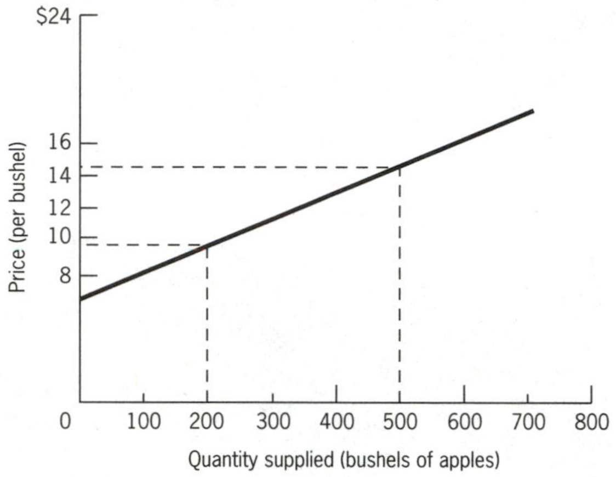

If you read this graph properly, you will see that when the price of apples is $9.60 a bushel, the quantity of apples supplied is

200 ___________ bushels. Similarly, if the quantity of apples supplied is 500

$14.40 bushels, the price of apples must be $ ___________ .

3-65

The upward-sloping supply curve is the Law of Supply expressed graphically. *Along the curve* the price of apples increases as we move

upward (upward/downward) and the quantity of apples supplied increases

right as we move to the (right/left).

3-66

To summarize what we know about the supply curve, it is a graph show-

schedule ing the supply ___________ .

price On the vertical axis we plot ___________ . On the horizontal axis

quantity supplied we plot ___________________________ .

upward From left to right the curve slopes ___________ .

Law of Supply This *slope* graphically expresses the * ______________________ .

3-67

We have been careful to distinguish between supply and quantity supplied. We must be equally careful to distinguish between a *change in supply* and a *change in the quantity supplied.*

As you know from studying the supply schedules shown, a change in

quantity supplied price is accompanied by a change in (supply/quantity supplied).

3-68

In contrast, a change in supply means that there has been a change in

supply schedule the ________ ________ .

3-69

Look at the schedule below.

Supply of pecans
Month of July, 1992

Price (per ounce)	Quantity supplied (ounces)
$1.00	8,000
.90	7,000
.80	6,000
.70	5,000
.60	4,000
.50	3,000
.40	2,000

If the price of pecans were to rise from 60 to 70 cents an ounce and sellers increased the amount of pecans they were willing to supply from 4,000 to 5,000 ounces a month, we would call this a change in the

quantity supplied (supply/quantity supplied) of pecans.

If the price were 80 cents an ounce and sellers increased the amount of pecans they were willing to offer for sale from 6,000 ounces in July to 7,000 ounces in August, we would call this a change in the

supply (supply/quantity supplied) of pecans.

3-70

We will explain shortly *why* the supply of a commodity might change. However, we can explain now why the quantity supplied will change. Look again at the supply of pecans in the frame **3-69**: The quantity of

price pecans supplied changes whenever there is a change in the ________ of pecans.

3-71

As we will see, there are a number of different reasons why the supply of a commodity might change. Economists say that the one thing that does *not* result in a change in supply is a change in the price of the

quantity commodity. When price changes, they say the ________

supplied, supply ________ changes, but the ________ does not change.

3-72

Like the changes in demand, a change in supply may be either an increase or a decrease. Look at the three supply schedules for pecans shown below.

Supply of pecans Months in 1992			
	Quantity supplied		
Price	**July**	**August**	**September**
$1.00	8,000	7,500	8,500
.90	7,000	6,500	7,500
.80	6,000	5,500	6,500
.70	5,000	4,500	5,500
.60	4,000	3,500	4,500
.50	3,000	2,500	3,500
.40	2,000	1,500	2,500

a decrease

an increase

Between July and August there was (an increase/a decrease) in the supply of pecans. Between August and September there was (an increase/a decrease) in the supply of pecans.

3-73

an increase

supply

When the quantity supplied at each price in the supply schedule increases, we may say that there has been (an increase/a decrease) in (supply/quantity supplied).

3-74

Now plot the three supply schedules in frame **3-72** on the graph below. For each supply curve, indicate whether it is for July, August, or September.

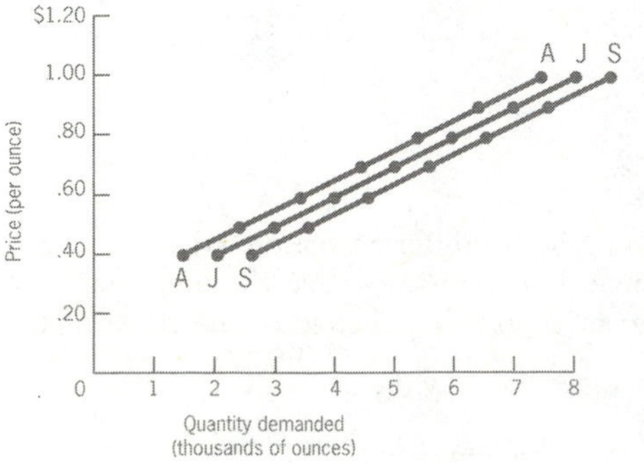

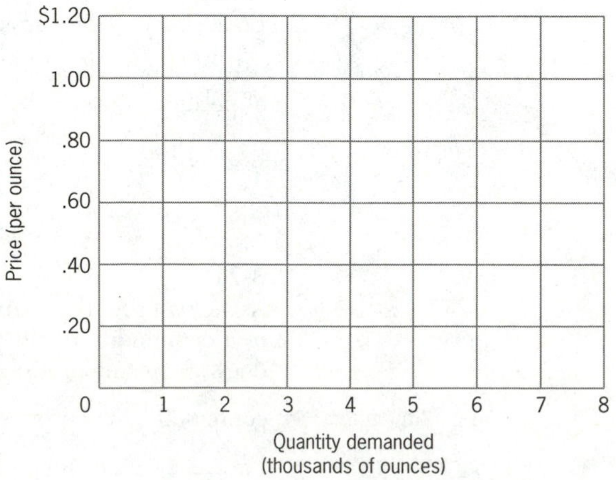

3-75

left
right

Between July and August, supply decreased and the supply curve shifted to the (right/left). Between August and September, supply increased and the supply curve moved to the (right/left).

3-76

increased
increased
right
right

Let's compare demand and supply again. An increase in demand means that the quantity demanded at each price in the demand schedule has ___________ . An increase in supply means that the quantity supplied at each price has ___________ . When demand increases, the demand curve moves to the ___________ . When supply increases, the supply curve moves to the ___________ .

3-77

Because the distinctions are so important, in your own words, explain the difference between:

Supply is the schedule (or curve), while quantity supplied is the amount offered for sale at a particular price.

Supply and quantity supplied. * ____

A change in supply is a change in the schedule (or curve), while a change in quantity supplied is the result of a price change.

A change in supply and a change in the quantity supplied. * ____

When supply increases (decreases), the quantities supplied at each price increase (decrease).

An increase and a decrease in supply. * ____

3-78

price
is not

A change in quantity supplied is caused by a change in ___________ . A change in supply (is/is not) caused by a change in price of the good or service in question. A change is supply is caused by a change in one or more of the ***determinants*** of supply. The six determinants of supply are: number of sellers, resource prices, technology, taxes and subsidies, prices of related goods, and expectations. Let's examine each in turn.

3-79

increase
right
more
lower

If the number of sellers of a product increases we would expect the supply of the product to (increase/decrease) and the supply curve would shift to the ________ . This means that at each and every price (more/less) would be sold. Another way of expressing this is to say that any given quantity would be sold at a (higher/lower) price. If you are not convinced of this, examine the "September" supply curve you drew in frame **3-74**.

3-80

decrease
lower, greater
supply, increase

If the prices a firm must pay for resources decrease, its production costs will (increase/decrease). This means the firm will be willing to sell a given quantity at a (higher/lower) price or a ________ quantity at the same price. In either case its (supply/quantity supplied) will ________ .

3-81

lower
increase, supply

Improved technology implies the ability to produce more efficiently, that is, at (higher/lower) cost per unit of output. Thus, improved technology causes a(n) (increase/decrease) in (supply/quantity supplied).

3-82

increase, supply
decrease
decrease, supply
increase

If taxes are increased on a business (for example, real estate taxes), production costs will ________ and (supply/quantity supplied) will ________ . On the other hand, if government subsidizes production, costs will ________ and (supply/quantity supplied) will ________ .

3-83

increase, supply
decrease

If the price of tea drops sharply (because of decreased demand), its producers will switch to producing, say, jute. The result will be a(n) (increase/decrease) in the (supply/quantity supplied) of jute and a(n) ________ in its price. (In this example, tea and jute are assumed to be "related goods" in the sense that producers can switch from producing one to the other.)

3-84

decrease
supply
decrease
more
supply, greater

If producers expect prices to rise shortly, they will (increase/decrease) their *present* offers to sell. In other words, their *present* (supply/quantity supplied) will ________ . If producers believe that prices are likely to drop soon, they will offer to sell (more/less) today. That is, *today's* (supply/quantity supplied) will be ________ .

3-85

When we state that supply of a product is a schedule showing how much will be offered for sale at various prices during a given time period, then, we are assuming that "other things are equal" or "other things do not change," these "other things" being the six categories we have been discussing and which are called the * ______________________.

determinants of supply

3-86

We are just about ready to put supply and demand together to determine the __________ of the commodity—whether it be sugar, cigarettes, apples, or pecans. We will also see what __________ of the commodity is going to be bought and sold. But first, let's review supply and demand very briefly.

price

quantity (amount)

3-87 Review Frame

Both demand and supply are expressed as schedules or curves. During a specific period of time the demand schedule indicates the __________ __________ and the supply schedule indicates the __________ __________ at various prices in the schedule.

Both demand and supply have their laws: between price and quantity demanded there is a(n) __________ relationship, and between price and quantity supplied there is a(n) __________ relationship.

Both demand and supply may be graphed. The demand curve slopes __________. The supply curve slopes __________.

Both demand and supply may change. An increase in demand or supply means that the quantities in the schedule have __________, causing their curves to move to the __________. A decrease in demand or supply means that the quantities in the schedule have __________, causing their curves to move to the __________.

quantity demanded

quantity supplied

inverse

direct

downward, upward

increased,

right

decreased

left

Equilibrium

We have looked at demand and at supply. Neither told us what the price of the commodity would be or how much of that commodity would be bought and sold. But when we use demand and supply together, we can find answers for both these questions. Demand and supply determine the *price* of a commodity and the *quantity* of the commodity bought and sold.

3-88
Here is a combined demand and supply schedule for milk in a certain area.

Demand and supply: Milk
Week of June 8–14, 1992

Quantity demanded (quarts)	Price (per quart)	Quantity supplied (quarts)
1,300	$1.30	1,700
1,400	1.20	1,600
1,500	1.10	1,500
1,600	1.00	1,400
1,700	0.90	1,300
1,800	0.80	1,200
1,900	0.70	1,100

There is only one price at which the quantity of milk demanded and

1.10 the quantity of milk supplied are equal: $________ per quart. At this price, the quantity demanded and the quantity supplied are each equal

1,500 to ________ quarts.

3-89
In a competitive market, the price of a commodity will tend to be that price at which quantity demanded and the quantity supplied are equal. Economists call this price the ***equilibrium price***. Similarly, the quantity demanded and the quantity supplied at the equilibrium price is called

equilibrium quantity the ________ ________.

3-90
Using the demand and supply schedules in frame **3-88**: $1.10 a quart is

equilibrium price the ________ ________ and 1,500 quarts is the ________

equilibrium quantity ________.

3-91
Here is another set of demand and supply schedules.

Demand and supply: Cigarettes
Month of July, 1992

Quantity demanded (cartons)	Price (per carton)	Quantity supplied (cartons)
8,000	$16	12,000
9,000	15	11,000
10,000	14	10,000
11,000	13	9,000
12,000	12	8,000
13,000	11	7,000
14,000	10	6,000
15,000	9	5,000

14 — quantity demanded — quantity supplied (either order) — equilibrium quantity

The equilibrium price of cigarettes is $_______ per carton because at this price the ____________ ____________ of cigarettes is equal to the ____________ ____________ of cigarettes. In other words, 10,000 cartons is the ____________ .

3-92

less — greater

Look again at the demand and supply schedules in frame **3-91**.

At prices *above* the equilibrium price there will be a ***surplus*** of cigarettes because the quantity demanded is (greater/less) than the quantity supplied.

At prices *below* the equilibrium price there will be a ***shortage*** of cigarettes because the quantity demanded is (greater/less) than the quantity supplied.

3-93

surplus — shortage

In a competitive market, whenever there is a (shortage/surplus) of a commodity, *sellers* of that commodity will bid its price downward in order to sell what they could not sell at the higher price.

But when there is a (shortage/surplus) of a commodity in a competitive market, ***buyers*** of that commodity will bid its price upward to encourage sellers to supply them with the commodity.

3-94

lower — demanded, supplied

There is a shortage of a commodity whenever the price of that commodity is (higher/lower) than the equilibrium price, because the quantity (demanded/supplied) is greater than the quantity (demanded/supplied).

3-95

higher — supplied, demanded

There is a surplus of a commodity whenever the price of a commodity is (higher/lower) than the equilibrium price, because the quantity (demanded/supplied) is greater than the quantity (demanded/supplied).

3-96

fall — increase (rise) — decrease (fall)

At prices above the equilibrium price there exists a surplus of the commodity and its price will (rise/fall).

According to the Laws of Demand and of Supply, as the price of this commodity falls the quantity demanded will ____________ and the quantity supplied will ____________ .

3-97

decrease

These changes in the quantities demanded and supplied will cause the size of the surplus to (increase/decrease).

3-98

When the price of the commodity is below its equilibrium price, there is a shortage of the commodity and the price of the commodity will rise. The Laws of Demand and of Supply tell us that as the price of the commodity increases, the quantity demanded will ____________ and the quantity supplied will ____________ .

decrease (fall), increase (rise)

3-99

As the price of the commodity increases, the changes in quantity demanded and quantity supplied will cause the amount of the shortage to (increase/decrease).

decrease

3-100

As long as there is *any* surplus of a commodity, (sellers/buyers) will bid its price downward. And *any* shortage of a commodity will induce (sellers/buyers) to bid its price upward.

sellers
buyers

3-101

But when the price of the commodity reaches the equilibrium price, there is neither a surplus nor a shortage. Sellers then have no reason to lower the price they charge. And buyers have no motive to increase the price they will pay.

The price of any commodity demanded and supplied in a competitive market will, therefore, tend to be the price at which there is neither a ____________ nor a ____________ of the commodity.

shortage, surplus (either order)

3-102

In your own words:

Define equilibrium price. * ____________________________________ .

The price at which the quantity demanded of a commodity equals the quantity supplied.

Define equilibrium quantity. * ____________________________________ .

The quantity demanded and the quantity supplied at the equilibrium price.

3-103

Let's review the reasons the price of any commodity will move toward its equilibrium price. As long as the price of this commodity is *above* the
surplus equilibrium price, there will be a (shortage/surplus) of the commodity
decrease which will cause the price of the commodity to ________ .

3-104

increase As price falls, the quantity demanded will ________ , the quantity
decrease supplied will ________ , and the difference between the quan-
decrease tities demanded and supplied will (increase/decrease).

3-105

Similarly, whenever the price of a commodity is *below* the equilibrium
shortage price, there is a (shortage/surplus) of the commodity which will cause
increase the price of the commodity to ________ .

3-106

decrease This causes the quantity demanded to ________ , the quantity
increase supplied to ________ , and the difference between the quantities
decrease demanded and supplied to (increase/decrease).

3-107

Here we have still another example of demand and supply.

Demand and supply: Sugar, 1992

Quantity demanded (millions of pounds)	Price (per pound)	Quantity supplied (millions of pounds)
100	$.90	1,100
200	.84	1,000
300	.78	900
400	.72	800
500	.66	700
600	.60	600
700	.54	500

Plot the demand schedule for sugar and the supply schedule for sugar on the graph below. Be sure to indicate on the graph which curve is the demand curve and which is the supply curve.

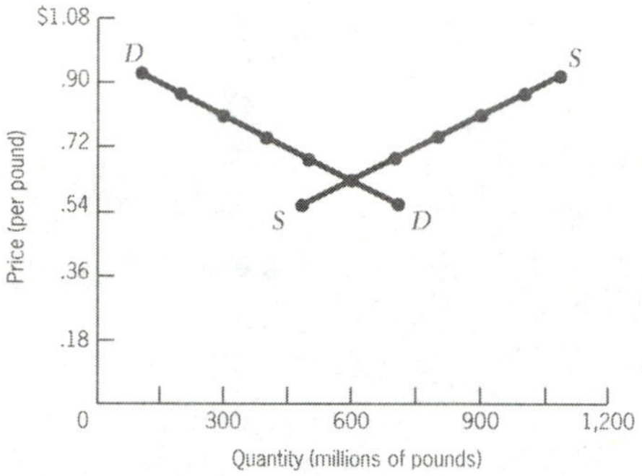

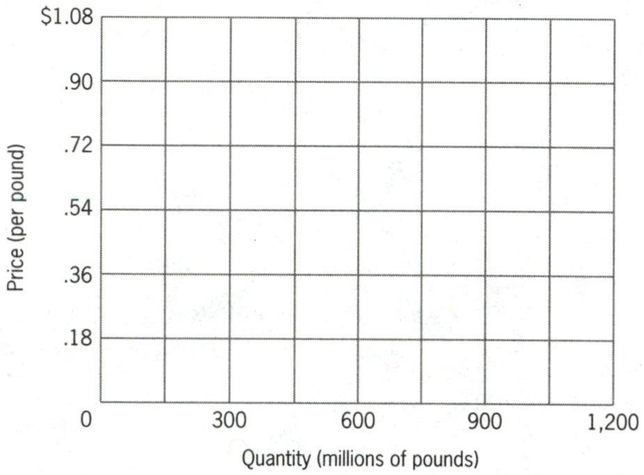

3-108

As you have just seen, the demand and supply curves cross each other. Draw a dashed line from the point where they cross to the price axis of the graph. Then draw another dashed line from the point where the curves cross to the quantity axis. Your graph will then look something like this:

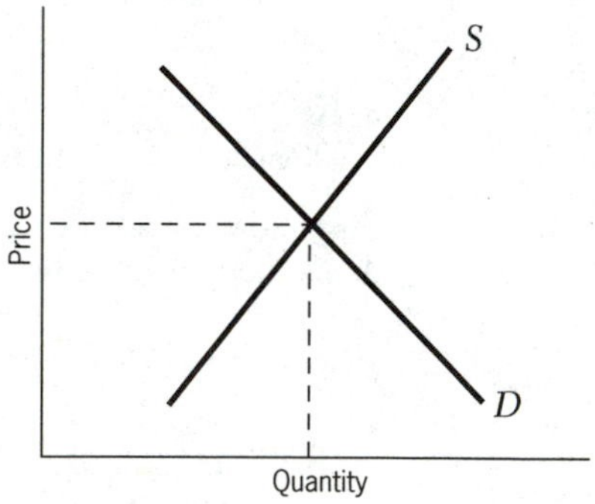

The line you drew to the price axis indicates that the price at which
60 the two curves cross is ________ cents. The line you drew to the quantity axis indicates that the quantity at which the two curves cross
600 is ________ million pounds.

3-109

If you plotted the demand and supply curves accurately, you found that they crossed at a price of 60 cents and at a quantity of 600 million pounds. Look back now to the demand and supply schedules in frame **3-107**.

60 The equilibrium price of sugar is ____________ cents. The equi-
600 librium quantity of sugar is ____________ million pounds.

3-110

We may conclude that the price at which the demand and supply curves cross is the ____________ price and the quantity at which the two curves cross is the ____________ quantity.

equilibrium

equilibrium

3-111

Below is another graph with the demand and supply curves for apples.

The graph indicates that the equilibrium price of apples is $______, and the equilibrium quantity is ________ bushels.

$12.80

500

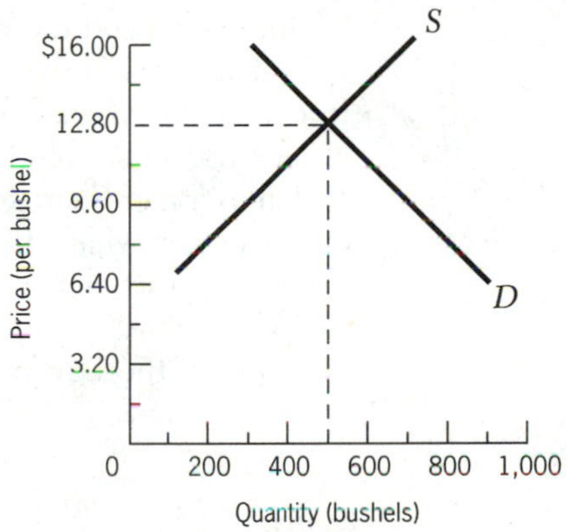

3-112 Review Frame

Demand and supply, we have discovered, determine what the price of a commodity will be and how much of that commodity will be bought and sold.

The price which will be charged for a commodity in a competitive market is called the ____________ price. The quantity of the commodity which will be bought and sold is called the ____________ quantity.

equilibrium

equilibrium

3-113 Review Frame

Suppose the actual price being charged for a commodity were not its equilibrium price. *Why* would the actual price of the commodity move toward its equilibrium price?

If this actual price started out *above* the equilibrium price, then * ______________________________.

there would be a surplus of the commodity and sellers would bid the price downward

If this actual price started out *below* the equilibrium price, then * ______________________________.

there would be a shortage of the commodity and buyers would bid the price upward.

3-114 Review Frame

If you plot demand and supply on a graph, what does the point where the two curves cross indicate? * ________________ ________________.

The equilibrium price and equilibrium quantity

Changes in Demand and Supply

As long as the demand for and the supply of a commodity do not change, the equilibrium price and quantity of the commodity will not change. But if either demand or supply changes, the equilibrium price and the equilibrium quantity will change.

Will an increase in demand raise or lower the equilibrium price? Will it increase or decrease the equilibrium quantity? Will a decrease in supply increase or decrease the equilibrium price and increase or decrease the equilibrium quantity? Let's see if we can discover what effects changes in demand and supply have upon the price charged and the amount of a commodity bought and sold. When we have found this out we will have learned the meaning of the Law of Supply and Demand.

3-115

To find the effects changes in demand and supply have on equilibrium price and quantity, we can use demand and supply curves. A demand curve and a supply curve appear below; their crossing point is circled.

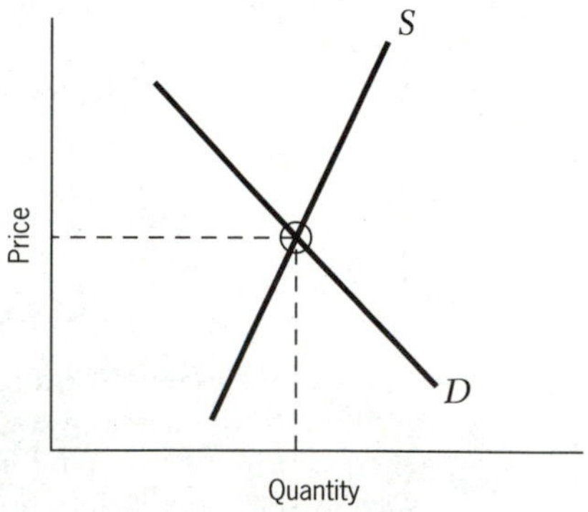

Now let's increase the demand for the commodity. This means we have to draw a *new* demand curve to the (right/left) of the demand curve on the graph.

right

3-116

Go ahead and draw this new demand curve and circle the point where the new demand curve crosses the supply curve. This new crossing point is at a (higher/lower) price, and at a (larger/smaller) quantity.

higher, larger

3-117

From what we did in frame **3-116** we can draw the following conclusion.

increase increase — An increase in demand will cause the equilibrium price to (increase/decrease) and the equilibrium quantity to (increase/decrease).

3-118

But what effects will a *decrease* in demand have? Let's find out. On the graph below is another set of demand and supply curves with their crossing point again circled. When we decrease demand, the

left — demand curve moves in what direction? To the ______ .

Draw this new demand curve on the graph and circle the new intersection.

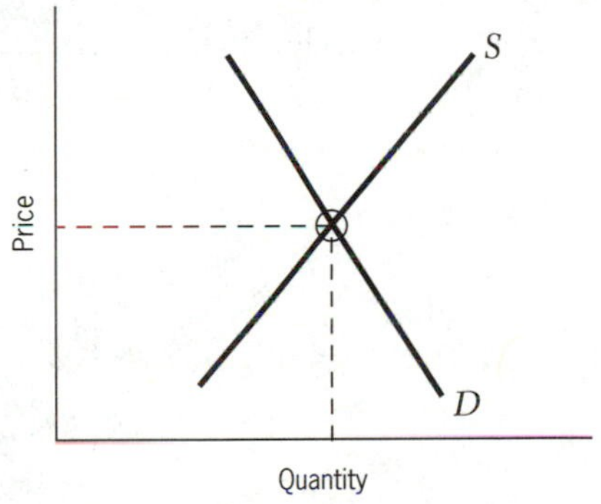

3-119

When you have drawn the new curve, you will see that the new inter-

lower, smaller — section is at a (higher/lower) price and a (larger/smaller) quantity.

We may conclude that a decrease in demand will cause the equi-

decrease — librium price to ______ and the equilibrium quantity to

decrease — ______ .

3-120

We have already learned something about the effects of changes in demand. An *increase* in demand brings about an increase in both equilibrium price and equilibrium quantity. And a *decrease* in demand causes decreases in both equilibrium price and quantity.

In short, a change in demand results in a change in equilibrium price

same — and equilibrium quantity in the (same/opposite) direction.

3-121

Putting it another way, the relation between a change in demand and a

direct — change in equilibrium price is (direct/inverse) and a change in demand

direct — and a change in equilibrium quantity is (direct/inverse).

Helpful Hint: To remember the effects of a change in demand on price and quantity, simply sketch a graph of demand and supply. Then increase or decrease demand to discover what happens to equilibrium price and quantity. Like the sea captain who couldn't remember the difference between port and starboard and who had to carry a note which read, "Port, left; starboard, right," some economists can't remember whether an increase in demand increases or decreases price without drawing a graph.

3-122

We can use the same graphical method to discover the effects of a change in supply upon equilibrium price and quantity. On the graph below demand and supply curves are shown and their intersection is circled.

Draw in a new *supply* curve which shows an *increase* in supply and

right — which is to the ____________ of the old supply curve.

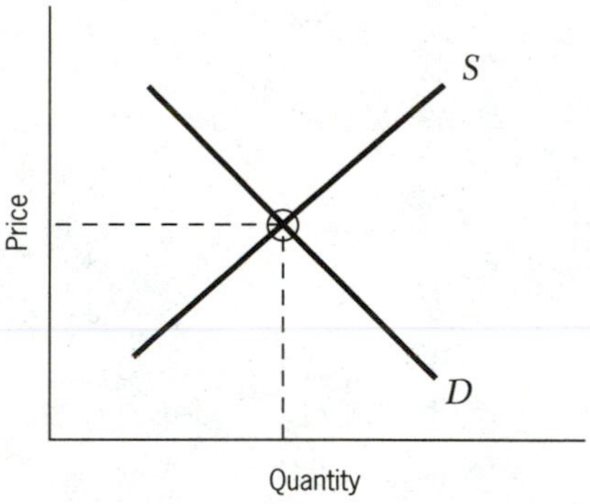

decrease — An increase in supply causes the equilibrium price to ____________

increase — and the equilibrium quantity to ____________ .

3-123

What about a *decrease* in supply? What are its effects on price and quantity? This time you figure it out for yourself. We'll give you a graph to start with.

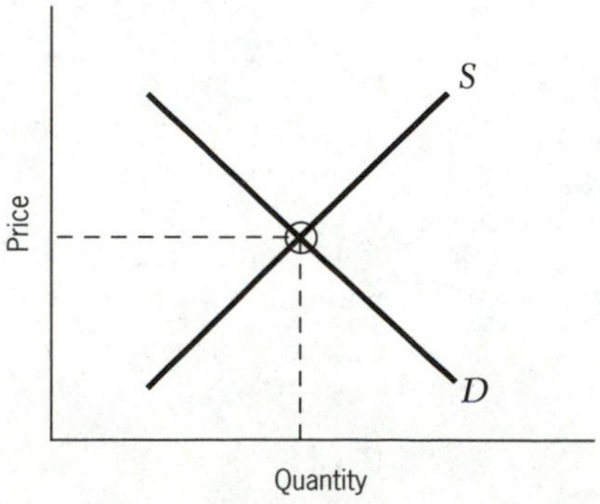

increase — A decrease in supply brings about a(n) ____________ in the equi-

decrease — librium price and a(n) ____________ in the equilibrium quantity.

3-124

opposite / same

To summarize what we have just discovered: When supply changes, equilibrium price changes in the (same/opposite) direction and equilibrium quantity changes in the (same/opposite) direction.

3-125

It will be useful—as we will see shortly—to have what we have just learned about the effects of changes in demand and supply in a summary table.

Fill in the blanks in the table with either + (for an increase) or − (for a decrease). If you have forgotten the effect of a change in demand or supply upon price and quantity, don't look back. There are two graphs below which you may use to help you rediscover whatever you may have forgotten.

		Upon equilibrium	
	Effect of:	**Price**	**Quantity**
+, +	An increase in demand	______	______
−, −	A decrease in demand	______	______
−, +	An increase in supply	______	______
+, −	A decrease in supply	______	______

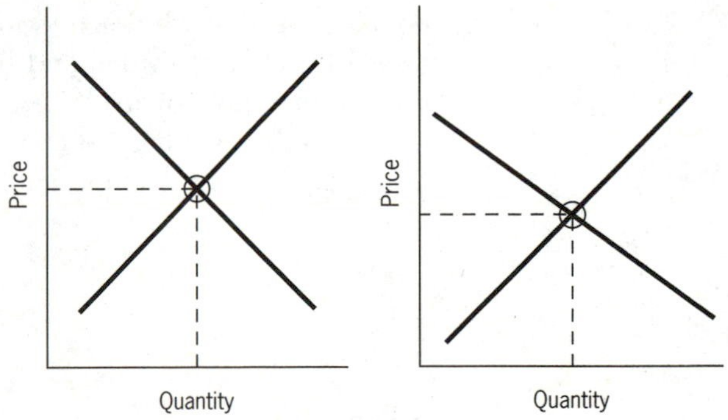

3-126

direct / direct / inverse / direct

The table in frame **3-125** shows that the relation between a change in *demand* and the resulting change in equilibrium price is (direct/inverse), and the resulting change in equilibrium quantity is ______________ .

Similarly, the relationship between a change in *supply* and the resulting change in equilibrium price is ______________ and the resulting change in equilibrium quantity is ______________ .

3-127

What have we found? There is *only* one inverse relationship. Just remember that all the relationships are direct except one: the relationship between a change in (demand/supply) and the change in equilibrium (price/quantity).

supply
price

When *either* the demand for *or* the supply of a commodity changes, the equilibrium price and the equilibrium quantity of the commodity will also change—as we have just seen. But it is quite possible for *both* the demand for *and* the supply of the commodity to change *at the same time*.

Simultaneous changes in demand and supply bring about changes in equilibrium price and quantity, just as changes in either demand or supply resulted in changes in price and quantity. What we want to do now is find out what effect these simultaneous changes in demand and supply have upon price and quantity. If demand and supply both increase, will equilibrium price rise or fall? Will the equilibrium quantity become larger or smaller? What happens to price and quantity if demand increases while supply decreases?

We must be very careful *not* to rely on demand and supply curves to discover the effects of simultaneous changes. If demand alone changes or supply alone changes, graphs will give us the right answers. But, as we will see, we cannot depend on demand and supply graphs for the answers to these questions when *both* demand and supply change.

What shall we use? The answer is quite simple. We will use the conclusions that we reached in the last few frames about the effects of a change in demand by itself and about the effects of a change in supply by itself.

Now let's see what we can learn about the effects of simultaneous changes in demand and supply.

3-128

We'll start with the conclusions which we summarized in frame **3-125**. These conclusions are reprinted in the table below. Again, the plus sign (+) means an increase and the minus sign (−) means a decrease.

	Upon equilibrium	
Effect of:	**Price**	**Quantity**
An increase in demand	+	+
A decrease in demand	−	−
An increase in supply	−	+
A decrease in supply	+	−

Now let's suppose that *both* demand and supply *increase*. Looking at the previous table we can see that the effect of the increase in demand is to ______________ equilibrium *quantity*, and the effect of the increase in supply is to ______________ equilibrium *quantity*.

increase
increase

3-129

Because the increase in demand and the increase in supply have the same effect upon the equilibrium quantity we may conclude that if both demand and supply increase, the equilibrium quantity will ______________ .

increase

3-130

What will be the effect of an increase in both demand and supply upon the equilibrium price? Here we run into a little difficulty because the effect of the increase in demand is *not* the same as the effect of the increase in supply upon the equilibrium price.

The effect of the increase in demand is to ______________ equilibrium price, and the effect of the increase in supply is to ______________ equilibrium price.

increase
decrease

3-131

What may we conclude about the effect about equilibrium price of increases in both demand and supply? Nothing! We have to say the effect is *indeterminate* (or unknown). Let's just say that our answer may be either + or − and call it a ?.

In summary, the effects of simultaneous increases in demand and supply are as follows:

Equilibrium price will (+/−/?).
Equilibrium quantity will (+/−/?).

?
+

3-132

Suppose demand and supply both *decrease*. Will equilibrium price increase or decrease or be indeterminate? Will the equilibrium quantity be larger or smaller or will we be unable to say which it will be? We must again refer to the summary table in frame **3-128**. The effect of the decrease in demand is to ______________ equilibrium price, and the effect of the decrease in supply is to ______________ equilibrium price.

The effect of the decrease in demand is to ______________ equilibrium quantity, and the effect of the decrease in supply is to ______________ equilibrium quantity.

decrease
increase
decrease
decrease

3-133

?, – Our conclusion is that when demand and supply both decrease equilibrium price will (+/–/?), and equilibrium quantity will (+/–/?).

3-134

? When demand and supply both increase, the equilibrium ***quantity increases***; and when they both decrease, the equilibrium ***quantity decreases***. The effect upon the equilibrium *price*, however, is (+/–/?) in both cases.

3-135

What would we have found if we had used graphs to discover the effects of simultaneous changes in demand and supply? Both graphs below indicate an increase in demand (from D_1 to D_2) accompanied by an increase in supply (from S_1 to S_2).

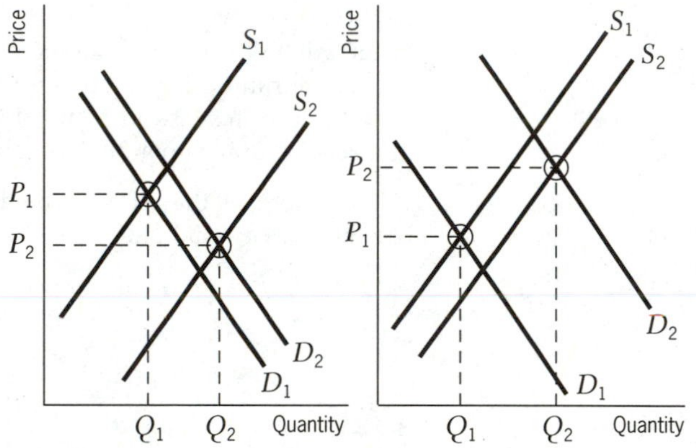

increase Both graphs indicate that the effect of these changes is to (increase/decrease) the equilibrium *quantity*.

3-136

decrease But the effects upon equilibrium price are conflicting: The graph on the left indicates that the equilibrium price will (increase/decrease), while the graph on the right indicates that the equilibrium price will
increase (increase/decrease).

3-137

large Equilibrium price fell in the left graph because the increase in supply was (large/small) compared with the increase in demand. Price rose in
smaller the right graph because the increase in supply was (larger/smaller) than the increase in demand.

3-138

Here's the point: Without specifying how large a change in demand and how large a simultaneous change in supply we are talking about, we can't come to any conclusions about their effect upon equilibrium

price ____________ .

3-139

If, for example, we know that the increase in demand is *greater* than the increase in supply, we can then conclude that the equilibrium price will (rise/fall).

rise

And if we know that the increase in demand is *smaller* than the increase in supply, we can then conclude that the equilibrium price will (rise/fall).

fall

(If you need help in answering these questions, draw a graph or look back to those in frame **3-135**.)

3-140

However, without knowing which increase is the larger, we can only say that the effect upon equilibrium price is ______________ .

indeterminate

3-141

Demand and supply may both increase or both decrease. But demand may increase while supply decreases, and demand may decrease as supply increases. These changes will also affect the equilibrium price and quantity. Let's see how. Refer back to the summary table in frame **3-128**.

Suppose demand increases and supply decreases. The increase in demand will (increase/decrease) the equilibrium *price*. And the decrease in supply will (increase/decrease) the equilibrium *price*.

increase
increase

3-142

Thus we may conclude that a simultaneous increase in demand and decrease in supply will ______________ the equilibrium price.

increase

3-143

However, the increase in demand will ______________ the equilibrium *quantity*, and the decrease in supply will ______________ the equilibrium *quantity*.

increase
decrease

And our conclusion is that when demand increases and supply decreases, the effect upon the equilibrium quantity is (+/−/?).

?

3-144

What about a simultaneous decrease in demand and increase in supply? Try this last one for yourself.

The effect upon equilibrium price is (+/−/?).

The effect upon equilibrium quantity is (+/−/?).

−
?

You may have observed that when demand and supply change in the opposite direction, the effect upon equilibrium quantity is indeterminate. This is always true unless we know how large the change in demand is, compared with the change in supply. When demand and supply changed in the same direction, it was the effect upon the equilibrium price that was indeterminate. Whenever there are simultaneous changes in demand and supply, the effect upon either price or quantity is indeterminate; and the effect upon the other is determinate. However, when we know how large the changes in demand and supply are, the effects on both price and quantity are determinate.

Before concluding our study of the fundamentals of supply and demand, let's review and summarize the effects of simultaneous changes in demand and supply.

3-145 Review Frame

Complete the table below, using either + (increase), − (decrease), or ? (indeterminate). Refer back to the table in frame **3-128** if you wish. Or, better still, work out for yourself the effects of changes in demand or supply, using the graphs provided below.

Answer	Effect of:	Upon equilibrium Price	Upon equilibrium Quantity
?, +	Increase in both demand and supply	______	______
?, −	Decrease in both demand and supply	______	______
+, ?	Increase in demand and decrease in supply	______	______
−, ?	Decrease in demand and increase in supply	______	______

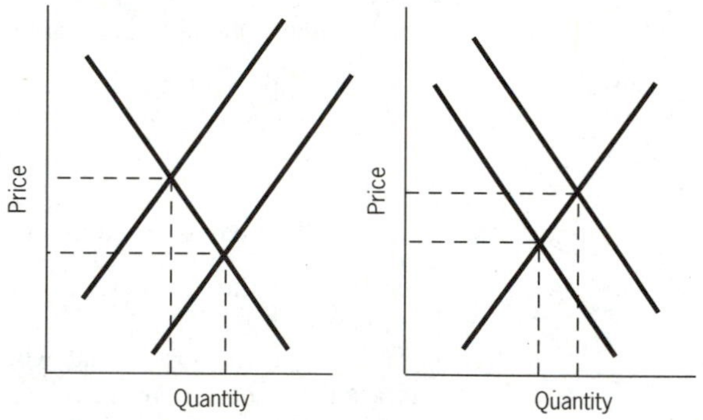

You now know most of what there is to know about the Law of Supply and Demand. This law deals with the effects upon price and quantity of changes in demand and supply. It may also refer to the causes of price and quantity changes. You have summarized the effects of demand and supply changes and the causes of price and quantity changes in frame **3-128** and in the table above. The Law of Supply and Demand may be a little complicated, but it should not be mysterious any longer.

Now take the Review Test for Section 3 at the back of the book.

National Income Accounting

section **4**

THE MEANING OF GDP

Managers of business firms hire accountants and keep books to find out how well or how poorly their firms have performed. These accounting records also help a firm to discover why it has been successful or unsuccessful. The records indicate whether the firm's performance has been getting better or worse over the years. They also suggest to management what might be done to improve its performance. Accounting, in short, is the means a business firm employs to calculate its profit or loss and to measure its success or failure.

As members of a free economy we are concerned with the profits and losses of business firms. We are also concerned with the successes and failures of the economy as a whole. To measure the performance of the entire economic system economists and accountants have devised a means of recording called ***national income accounting***.

The purpose of national income accounting is much like the purpose of business accounting. It enables us to find out how well or how poorly the economy has performed and why. National income accounting lets us know whether the economy's performance over the years has gotten better or worse; and it suggests means of improving its performance.

The economic well-being of the nation can generally be determined by calculating certain overall measures of economic performance. There are five of these measures of performance. In this chapter we will examine each of the five indicators, learn what each measures, and find out how each can be calculated. In the process of learning how to calculate, we will also come to understand a good deal about the operation of our economy.

4-1

The first of the five indicators of economic well-being which economists compute is called the ***gross domestic product***, and it is usually referred to by its initials: __________ .

GDP

4-2

Suppose we had a very small nation composed of just one completely self-sufficient farm family. All year this family utilizes its economic resources (land, labor, capital, and entrepreneurial ability) to produce various goods and services. At the end of the year the family lists the amounts of the various things produced during the year. This list of the quantities of all the goods and services produced by the farm family during the year would constitute this small economy's GDP.

goods — Thus, an economy's GDP consists of all the __________ and

services — __________ produced by the economy during a period of

one (a), year — __________ __________.

4-3

This farm family's GDP would consist of a *list* of the amounts of the various goods and services produced during a year. It would contain such items as:

8 pairs of shoes made and worn during the year
800 loaves of bread baked and eaten during the year
1 irrigation ditch built for the farm
30 cords of wood cut and stacked for the coming year
98 haircuts given to family members in the year
52 family washes done during the year

will not — As you can see, the family's GDP (will/will not) be one number which reflects total production, since—to borrow an old phrase—we

cannot — (can/cannot) add apples and oranges.

4-4

Now let's suppose that this family discovers that the things it produced for itself all have prices or *market* values in a neighboring community. Now the family *can* add up the goods and services it produced by

price (value) — attaching a __________ to each of them.

4-5

The table below indicates the amounts of the goods and services produced and the price or market value of each good or service. Complete the missing figures in the columns.

	Good or service	Amount produced	Price or market value	Total market value of each good or service
	Shoes	8	$20 a pair	$160
$400	Loaves	800	$.50 a loaf	$__________
$600	Ditches	1	$600 a ditch	$__________
$360	Cords of wood	30	$12 a cord	$__________
$384	Haircuts	96	$4 a haircut	$__________
$520	Family washes	52	$10 a wash	$__________

4-6

If these six items were the only goods and services produced by the family, its GDP would equal $__________ . This GDP figure represents the *total* __________ *value* of the goods and services produced during the year.

$2,424
market

4-7

After the list of goods and services and their market values was prepared by the family, one of the farmer's sons pointed out that the list was not complete. During the year the family grew *wheat* which it ground into *flour* to make the 800 loaves of *bread*. "Shouldn't the wheat and the flour be added to the list and their market values be included in the family GDP?" he asked.

What do *you* think? ____ .

(We asked what *you* think. To see what *we* think, read the next frame.)

4-8

Another son, who had read an economics textbook, rightfully argued that to count the wheat, the flour, and the bread would be *double counting*—counting the same thing more than once. The bread contained the flour, and the flour was made from the wheat. To count the bread, the flour, and the wheat would be to count the same thing three times.

Thus, the GDP of any community includes only the (intermediate/final) goods and services produced, such as the bread. GDP excludes the (intermediate/final) goods and services such as the flour and wheat.

final
intermediate

4-9

Of course, if some of the flour milled by the family had not been baked into bread, but put on the pantry shelf for future use, this flour would have been considered a __________ good. Thus, it would be (included/excluded) in the GDP.

final
included

4-10

Three important points to remember:

The market value of any good or service (is/is not) the same as its price.

GDP includes the final goods and services produced by the economy, and does not include the __________ goods and services produced.

For an economy to include in its GDP the market value of the steel it produced and the iron ore it mined and used to produce the steel would be an example of __________ __________ .

is
intermediate
double counting

4-11

Now you should be ready to define GDP. We'll start you: GDP is the total * ____ .

market value (price) of the final goods and services produced by an economy during one year

4-12

The total output of GDP of the self-sufficient farm family is the total amount of goods and services produced to satisfy the family's wants. For this reason we can also call it the family's *income*. Any economy's output (or production) and its income are simply two names for the same thing. Total output and total income are always ____________ .

equal (identical, the same)

4-13

For example, if a self-sufficient farm family had a GDP of $2,424, that family's total income would be equal to $____________ . And since the American economy in 1991 had a GDP of $5,672 billion, its total ____________ was also $5,672 billion.

$2,424

income

4-14

What can an economy do with its GDP or income? Our farm family did only two things with it. During the year some of this output was used up, or *consumed*. The remainder was kept for use in future years: it was *invested*. The irrigation ditch it dug will be used for several years to come and the wood it stacked will be used next year. The ditch and the wood represent the output that was ____________ while the shoes, bread, haircuts, and family washes are outputs that were ____________ during the year.

invested

consumed

4-15

When we add the total output that the economy consumed to the total output it invested, the sum is equal to:

(a) the economy's total output
(b) the economy's total income
(c) the economy's GDP
(d) all of the above
(e) none of the above

Which one? ____________

(d)

4-16

Any economy is made up of people. The small, self-sufficient farm family is composed of the members of the family. Their total output—or income, or GDP—was produced by them, and it belongs to them. This GDP may be divided up among them in any way they choose.

Regardless of how this division of income and output is made, if we add up the amounts received by each member of the family the sum will

GDP — be equal to the family's ________ . Other names for this sum are

output, income — the family's total ________ and its total ________ .

4-17 Review Frame

Now let's review some of the things we have learned so far about the self-sufficient farm family.

total market value of all the final goods and services produced during the year — Its GDP is the * ____

____

____ .

4-18 Review Frame

does, does — The family's GDP (does/does not) equal its total output of final goods and services and (does/does not) equal the family's total income.

4-19 Review Frame

consum- — Some of this GDP was output which the family ________-ed during

invest- — the year. The rest of the output was ________-ed for use during some later years. Adding up the incomes of all members of the family

GDP (or output or income) — tells us the size of the family's ________ .

4-20

Let's go on now and make this farm family a little more realistic. Most families have possessions which they own in common. No one member of the family owns them; the family as a whole owns them. The irrigation ditch that the family dug might be an example of this kind of possession. Let's call the family as a whole the family's *government*.

This means that part of the family's GDP will be produced for the government—for the family as a whole. Some will still be consumed by individual family members, some will still be invested for future use, and some will be utilized by the family's government. When we add the outputs consumed, invested, and used by government, the total is still

GDP — the family's ________ .

4-21

If some part of the family's GDP is utilized by the government of the family, the total portion left for the *individual* members of the family is (less than/greater than/equal to) the GDP.

less than

4-22

This means that the individual members of the family have turned over some portion of their income (their GDP and output) to their government. *Taxes* are the amounts of income which individuals are required to turn over to their ___________ .

government

4-23

When we add up the shares of the family's income received by each individual family member, the total will *not* equal the GDP because we have forgotten to include the amount of income handed over to the government. To determine the GDP of the family by totaling up incomes we must add each family member's ___________ and the amount collected by the governments as ___________ .

income

taxes

4-24

Very few, if any, families are self-sufficient. Most families and economies sell to and buy from other families and economies. *Exports* are the goods and services sent to others, and *imports* are the goods and services received from others. And, as you know from experience, the market value of exports and imports in any year (will/will not) necessarily be equal.

will not

4-25

The family may export some goods and services in return for the promises of others to pay for them in the future. And the family may import goods and services and promise to pay for them in the future. This is why imports and exports are often not ___________ in a given year.

equal

4-26

Net exports equal the family's exports *minus* its imports. The net exports of the family represent the family's output of goods and services that was sent to others *over* and *above* the goods and services received from these other families and economies.

Suppose a farm family received goods and services valued at $28 from others and sent goods and services whose market value was $40 to others.

Exports were equal to $___________ .

Imports were equal to $___________ .

Net exports were equal to $___________ .

$40

$28

$12

4-27

Assume a family had exports of $27 and imports of $33. Its net exports would equal $27 − $33 or a *minus* $6 (−$6). This negative net export figure means that $6 of the total amount of goods and services consumed, invested, and utilized by the family's government were goods

im- and services ________-ported and not paid for with goods and ser-

ex- vices ________-ported. It is the amount of goods and services bought on credit: not paid for with exports, but with promises to pay at some

future (later) ________ time.

4-28

There are, in short, four uses to which it can put its total output, of GDP. Assume that a family used the following amounts of GDP for these four purposes:

Consumption	$1,600
Investment	200
Government	400
Net exports	100

$2,300 The family's total output of GDP would equal $________ .

4-29

A family with a GDP of $2,300 would have a total income of $2,300. If taxes in this family amounted to $400, the individual family members

$1,900 would have a total income that amounted to $________ .

The family's GDP could be computed as follows:

$1,900	Income of family members	$________
$400	Taxes	$________
$2,300	GDP	$________

4-30

There are thus really *two* approaches an economist may employ to calculate any economy's GDP. One approach is to add up the amounts of final goods and services devoted to the four uses to which every economy may put its output:

consumed Some of its GDP is ________ by individuals during the year.

invested Some is ________ for future use.

exported Some is ________ to other economies.

government Some is utilized by the ________ of the economy to provide goods and services for the economy as a whole.

4-31

The second approach is to add up the incomes of all members of the economy to determine the GDP.

Some income goes to individual members of the economy. Some in-

taxes — come goes to the government and is called ______________ .

If we add up these two kinds of income, the total is the economy's

GDP — __________ .

4-32

Here are some scrambled figures for an economy.

Exports	$ 9	Invested	$ 4
Taxes	3	Government	7
Income of members of economy	23	Imports	7
		Consumed	13

Using the *first approach*, the economy's GDP would be the sum of the following four items and amounts.

	Item	*Amount*
consumed, 13	______________	$______
invested, 4	______________	______
goverment, 7	______________	______
exports minus imports, 2 (9 − 7) (any order)	______________	______

26 — The total, or GDP, is $__________ .

Using the second approach, GDP would be equal to the

income of members of economy, 23 — ______________________________ of $__________

taxes, 3 — plus the __________ of $__________ .

26 — The total, or GDP, is $__________ .

MEASURING THE GDP

As we have just seen, there are two ways to measure the GDP of an economy. The first approach involved adding up the market values of final goods and services produced for four different purposes. We call this the *expenditures approach* because we can determine the market value of the goods and services produced for each of these four purposes by finding out the amount of money spent, or expended, for that purpose. The market value of the final goods and services consumed, for example, is equal to the amount of money expended during the year for the goods and services which were consumed.

The second way to measure GDP is called the *income approach* and involves totaling the incomes of all persons and governments during the year. These two approaches give us the same GDP since the *market value* of the final goods and services produced in any economy during a year will be equal to:

the total *expenditures* for final goods and services.

the total *income* created by the production of these final goods and services.

The expenditures approach is usually considered to be the simpler of the two approaches because there are fewer things to add to compute the GDP. We will, therefore, first see what we have to add up in our modern and complex economy to determine GDP by the expenditures approach. Then we'll learn what kinds of income we must total to calculate GDP by the income approach.

4-33

We already have a pretty good idea of the figures we must add to find GDP by the expenditures method. An economy's

consumed, invested

GDP is either ________, ________, used by the

governments, exports

________ in the economy, or sent as ________ to other economies. The economy's GDP will equal the total amount ex-

four

pended to obtain final goods and services for these ________ purposes.

4-34

What we haven't yet learned are the particular names economists and national income accountants use for these four kinds of expenditures. The four classes of expenditures and the figure for each are shown in the table for a hypothetical economy.

Use of GDP	Name of expenditure	Amount (billions)
Consumed	Personal consumption expenditures (C)	\$237
Invested	Gross private domestic investment (I_g)	98
Used by government	Government purchases (G)	103
Sent to other economies	Net exports (X_n)	2

If we add these four kinds of expenditures we find that this hypo-

\$440

thetical economy's GDP is \$ ________ billion.

4-35

Assume another hypothetical economy had a GDP of \$612 billion. Of this total, the economy consumed \$418 billion, invested \$109 billion, used \$80 billion for government, and sent \$5 billion to other economies. The economist would say that:

$418 Personal consumption expenditures were $________ billion.

$80 Government purchases were $________ billion.

$109 Gross private domestic investment was $________ billion.

$5 Net exports were $________ billion.

4-36

Now look at the table below. You will find a list of national income accounting figures. There are many more figures there than you need to determine GDP by the expenditures method. Pick out the four you need. They are:

consumption — personal ________ expenditures,

gross private domestic investment — ________ ________ ________ ________ ,

government, exports — ________ purchases and net ________ .

Typical figures used in national income accounting

Interest	$ 19
Consumption of fixed capital	38
Exports	12
Net American income earned abroad	10
Compensation of employees	332
Undistributed corporate profits	8
Rents	9
Personal consumption expenditures	350
Dividends	17
Transfer payments	43
Indirect business taxes	49
Imports	7
Gross private domestic investment	75
Personal taxes	58
Proprietors' income	53
Corporate income taxes	25
Government purchases	110

4-37

GDP in this economy will be the sum of (refer to the table):

350 $________

75 ________

110 ________

5 ________

540 and will be equal to $________ .

4-38

In the table there is enough information to compute GDP by the

expenditures — __________ approach. But there are also sufficient data to determine

income — the GDP by using the __________ approach.

4-39

Nine kinds of income are received in the economy for producing the GDP. *Seven* of these incomes are the incomes earned by individuals.

two — The other __________ kinds of income are *not* earned by individuals; we call them *nonincome charges*. Finally, since GDP measures *domestic* production, net income received by Americans for the resources they

subtracted — own abroad must be (added/subtracted).

4-40

The two nonincome charges are: *consumption of fixed capital*, or *depreciation*, for short, and *indirect business taxes*.

In producing final goods and services every economy wears out or uses up some of its capital goods. *Depreciation* is the value of the capital used up or worn out to produce the GDP and belongs to those who supplied the economy with capital. Depreciation is best described as

reimbursement — (income/reimbursement).

4-41

Depreciation is *not income*; it is compensation for property used up. Suppose you let a friend borrow your brand-new copy of this book. When your friend later returns it to you all the blanks have been filled in. You find the book can't be used and can't be resold at the book store. You

wouldn't — (would/wouldn't) consider the payment by your friend of the full purchase price of the book to be income.

4-42

The other nonincome charge is *indirect business taxes*: such taxes as sales, excise, and business property taxes. Business firms must pay them to governments whether the firms earn a profit or not. They are a cost to businesses and are "passed on" to buyers in the price paid for goods

government(s) — and services. They are a source of income for the __________ but *not* for individuals who furnish the economy with economic resources. This

nonincome — is why we classify them as __________ charges.

4-43

The nonincome charges in the table in frame **4-36** will be equal to

\$38, \$49, \$87 — \$__________ + \$__________, and will total \$__________.

4-44

The seven items that make up the incomes earned by individuals are in the form of compensation of employees, rents, interest, and profits. Let's look at each.

The *compensation of employees* is the income earned by those who supply labor to the economy and is the sum of *wages and salaries* and *wage and salary supplements.*

The income which employees "receive" and out of which they pay their personal taxes is classified as __________ and __________ .

wages, salaries

The money which employers take from their own pockets and put into public and private pension, health, and welfare funds are classified as __________ and __________ __________ .

wage, salary supplements

4-45

Wage and salary supplements (are/are not) included in the compensation of employees since they represent income *earned* by labor. However, they are income which the worker does not receive because the __________ puts them directly into various funds.

are

employer

4-46

The money which employers deduct from the wages and salaries of their employees and put into public pension, health, and welfare funds is included in the *compensation of employees* item. We will see how they are treated later. In the table in frame **4-36** the compensation of employees is equal to $__________ .

$332

4-47

Before we go on to rents, interest, and profits, let's review what we have already learned about computing the GDP by the income approach.

We must add a total of (7/8/9/10) items. Two of these items are (income/nonincome) charges. The two nonincome charges are __________ and __________ __________ __________ . Net income earned abroad must then be __________ .

9

nonincome

depreciation, indirect business taxes

subtracted

4-48

The remaining seven items are the incomes (compensation of employees, rent, interest, and profits) earned by those who supply the economy with economic resources.

	Those who supply the economy with:	*Earn an income called:*
compensation of employees	Labor	° ____________
rents	Land	____________
interest	Capital	____________
profits	Entrepreneurial ability	____________

4-49

wages — salaries, wage and salary supplements

The compensation of employees is earned by those who supply the economy with labor and is the sum of *two* subitems: ___________ and ___________ and ° ________________________________ .

4-50

land — capital (money)

Rent is the income of those who furnish the economy with __________ (or property resources) and *interest* is the income of those who provide business firms with the use of ___________ .

4-51

rents — interest

Now look again at the table in frame **4-36**.

There is only *one* item which represents the income of suppliers of land. It amounts to \$9 and it is called ___________ . There is only *one* item which represents the income of suppliers of capital. It amounts to \$19 and it is called ___________ .

4-52

proprietors'

Profit income is the income of suppliers of entrepreneurial ability. It breaks down into four separate items. First there is the profit of *un*incorporated business firms. Because such firms are run by *proprietors*, we call this type of profit __________ income.

4-53

profits

The income of corporations constitutes the other three types of (rents/wages/profits/interest) that we've been discussing. Let's look at each.

4-54

government

Corporate income taxes must be paid before corporate profits are distributed. While this is part of the income earned by suppliers of entrepreneurial ability, it is turned over to the ___________ .

4-55

The corporations' profit that remains after the payment of these taxes may be paid out to the stockholders of the corporation as *dividends*. Or they may be retained by the firm as *undistributed corporate profits*. Again, using the figures in our table in frame **4-36**:

$25, $17, $8 (any order), $50 — corporate profits equal $_____ + $_____ + $_____, for a total of $_____;

proprietor — profits in the economy equal corporate profits + ________s'

$53, $103 — income of $_____, for a total of $_____.

4-56

Adding the seven income items gives us the *national income* earned by American-supplied resources both at home *and abroad*. Adding the two nonincome charges yields gross *national* product (abbreviated

GNP, domestic, GDP — ______), not gross ______ product (______). To get

subtract, abroad — GDP, we (add/subtract) American income earned (domestically/abroad)

add — and (add/subtract) income earned by foreigners in the United States.

American income earned abroad — The result is net * __________________.

$10, positive — This is shown in frame **4-36** as $_____. This being a (positive/

more — negative) amount means Americans earned (more/less) abroad than for-

subtracted from — eigners earned in the United States and must therefore be (added to/subtracted from) GNP to get GDP.

4-57 Review Frame

And that completes our discussion of how to measure GDP by means of

income — the (expenditures/income) approach. Let's review it.

9 — We must add ______ items to compute GDP. Two of these items do not represent the incomes of individuals who supply the econ-

nonincome — omy with resources. These two items are called ______ charges;

indirect business — they are *depreciation* and ______ ______ taxes. Finally, we

net American income earned abroad — must subtract one item, which is * __________________.

4-58 Review Frame

Seven of these items are the incomes earned by those who provide the economy with labor, land, capital, and entrepreneurial ability. The income of those who supply:

compensation of employees — Labor is called * __________________.

rents — Land is called ______.

interest — Capital is called ______.

profits — Entrepreneurial ability is called ______.

4-59 Review Frame

The compensation of employees, the income earned by labor, results in one of the items we add to measure GDP. This item is made up of two subitems: __________ and __________ ; and * __________ __________.

wages, salaries, wage and salary supplements

4-60 Review Frame

Profit, the income earned by entrepreneurial ability, falls into four categories. One of these four categories is the income of owners of business firms which are not corporations. This is called __________ __________.

proprietors' income

Three of these four categories make up the income of owners of business firms which are corporations. These three are __________ __________ __________, __________, and __________ __________ __________.

corporate income taxes, dividends, undistributed corporate profits

4-61

Using the figures in the table in frame **4-36**, we found that the nine items which are added and the one that is subtracted to determine GDP by the income approach can be arranged as follows:

Nonincome charges		$ 87
Depreciation	$38	
Indirect business taxes	49	
Compensation of employees		332
Rents		9
Interest		19
Profits		103
Proprietors' income	53	
Corporate income taxes	25	
Dividends	17	
Undistributed corporate profits	8	
less net American income earned abroad		10

$540 GDP in this economy thus comes to $__________.

4-62

Back in frame **4-37** we computed GDP for this economy by the (income/expenditures) approach (look back). We found that its GDP was $__________, the same figure we just arrived at in the last frame, using the __________ approach.

expenditures

$540

income

4-63

Now let's apply what you've just learned by calculating the GDP for the mythical nation of Atlantis. Again we have arranged in a random fashion the national income accounting figures for the economy of Atlantis. There are enough figures to compute the GDP using either the

income, expenditures

__________ approach or the __________ approach.

Atlantis: National income accounting figures

Dividends	$ 29
Rents	20
Net exports	14
Indirect business taxes	49
Undistributed corporate profits	22
Gross private domestic investment	82
Depreciation	46
Proprietors' income	48
Transfer payments	12
Personal consumption expenditures	473
Net Atlantis income earned abroad	15
Interest	16
Compensation of employees	462
Personal taxes	84
Government purchases	141
Corporate income taxes	33
Social security contributions	20

4-64

Pick out the four items you need to measure GDP by the expenditures approach. The names of these items and the amounts are:

personal consumption expenditures, $473

______________________________ $______

gross private domestic investment, $82

______________________________ $______

government purchases, $141

______________________________ $______

net exports, $14

______________________________ $______

$710

The economy of Atlantis has a GDP of $______ .

Suggestion: If you had trouble with the last frame, you had better review frames **4-34**, **4-35**, **4-36**, and **4-37**.

4-65

Now find the ten items you need to calculate GDP by the income approach. Write down the names and the amounts of the ten items and the total amount.

compensation of employees, $462	* ______________________	$______
rents, $20	* ______________________	$______
interest, $16	* ______________________	$______
proprietors' income, $48	* ______________________	$______
corporate income taxes, $33	* ______________________	$______
dividends, $29	* ______________________	$______
undistributed corporate profits, $22	* ______________________	$______
depreciation, $46	* ______________________	$______
indirect business taxes, $49	* ______________________	$______
less net American income earned abroad $15	* ______________________	$______
$710	Gross domestic product	$______

4-66

Computing GDP by the expenditures method, you found it to be $710. And you found that it was also $710 using the income approach. Why do you get the same answer regardless of which approach you use?

(a) This is an accident.
(b) The person who made up this problem had it come out this way.
(c) An economy's total income is always equal to its total expenditures.
(d) The Federal government follows policies that are designed to bring about this equality.

(c) Which one? __________

OTHER MEASURES OF PERFORMANCE

There are five measures of the overall performance or well-being of an economy. GDP is just one of these five and not necessarily the most important, but it is the most inclusive, the most basic. And GDP is always larger than the other four.

Having learned how to compute the GDP, we have learned most of what we need to know in order to understand and compute the four other indicators of an economy's performance.

The remaining four measures are net domestic product (NDP), national income (NI)—which we mentioned in frame **4-56**—personal income (PI), and disposable income (DI).

Again, we want to learn what each of these indicators measures and how each of them can be calculated.

4-67

Imagine a farmer who in the spring of the year sows 400 bushels of wheat as seed. In the fall he harvests 50,000 bushels of wheat. How much wheat did this farmer produce?

He harvested 50,000 bushels. This we call his *gross* production or output. But he started with 400 bushels of wheat for seed. Thus, he only produced 49,600 bushels over and above what he started with. This is his *net* production or output.

total output — *Gross* production refers to * ______________________ .

output *after* deducting what was used up to produce the total (gross) output — *Net* production refers to * ______________________ ______________________ .

4-68

Now suppose an entire economy has a *gross* domestic product of $605 billion. To produce this GDP, the economy had to consume or wear out fixed capital goods valued at $35 billion. We call this amount *depreciation*.

The economy produced final goods and services valued at

$605 — $__________ billion and in the process consumed, or depreciated,

$35 — $__________ billion worth of capital. It produced an output of

$570 — $__________ billion over and above the fixed capital consumed. We

net — call this latter amount the __________ domestic product.

4-69

The *net domestic product* (NDP) of any economy is the market value of its output of final goods and services during a year less the value of the fixed capital consumed during that year. This means that:

depreciation — The NDP equals the GDP minus __________ .

depreciation — The GDP equals the NDP plus __________ .

4-70

If you will look back to our table of figures for Atlantis (frame **4-63**) you will find that the GDP was $710. The NDP is equal to $710 minus

$46, $664 — $__________ , or $__________ .

4-71

Suppose economists started out to compute the NDP from scratch—without first computing the GDP. What would they add up to determine NDP? Regardless of whether they use the income approach or the expenditures approach to find the NDP, the principle they must apply is the same: add all of the items used to compute the GDP *except*

depreciation ___________ .

4-72

Suppose we use the income approach to compute NDP. Ten items were added or subtracted to find the GDP. To find the NDP, add or subtract *nine* of these items. The only item of the ten not added to determine

depreciation the NDP is ___________ .

4-73

Below is enough information to compute the NDP using the income approach.

Dividends	$17	Indirect business taxes	$ 49
Rents	9	Undistributed corporate profits	8
Net exports	5	Transfer payments	43
Interest	19	Personal consumption expenditures	350
Personal taxes	58	Compensation of employees	332
Depreciation	38	Government purchases	110
Proprietors' income	53		
Corporate income taxes	25		
Net American income earned abroad	10		

If you will pick out the items needed to compute NDP by the income

$502 approach, you find that the NDP is equal to $___________ . In this

$540 same economy, the GDP is equal to $___________ .

(If you failed to *subtract* net American income earned abroad, see frame **4-56**.)

4-74

Remember the farmer who sowed 400 bushels of wheat in the spring and harvested 50,000 bushels of wheat in the fall, and whose net production of wheat was 49,600 bushels?

Out of his gross production of 50,000 bushels he sold 49,000 bushels and set aside 1,000 bushels to be used for seed the following spring. His *gross* investment was 1,000 bushels. But his *net* investment was only 600

400 bushels of wheat because ___________ bushels must be counted as replacement for the wheat which he used up during the year.

Now suppose that our entire economy in a recent year had a GDP of $689 billion. Part of this total output of final goods and services consisted of the production of capital goods: buildings, machinery, tools, and additions to inventories. The total expenditure for these capital goods was $103 billion. During this same year the economy consumed capital goods valued at $42 billion.

4-75

gross — The economist would say that: $103 billion was the (gross/net) private

depreciation — domestic investment and $42 billion was the amount of __________ in the economy.

4-76

The *gross* output of capital goods was $103 billion and the economy used up $42 billion worth of capital goods during the year. Its *net* output of capital goods—its output of capital in excess of the capital it used up—

$61 — was $______ billion.

net — The economist would call this amount the __________ private domestic investment in the economy.

4-77

The net private domestic investment of any economy, as we just dis-

depreciation — covered, can be found by subtracting __________ from the

gross private domestic — __________ __________ __________

investment — __________ .

(Review frame **4-74** if you had difficulty in this frame.)

4-78

Assume that the national income accounting figures for our economy in another recent year were:

Personal consumption expenditures	$350
Gross private domestic investment	75
Government purchases	110
Net exports	5
Depreciation	38

$540 — GDP would be equal to $________ .

$38 — NDP would be equal to GDP minus $________ , which amounts

$502 — to $________ .

$75 — Net private domestic investment would be equal to $________

$38, $37 — minus $________ , which amounts to $________ .

4-79

We used the figures in frame **4-78** to determine the GDP first. Then we subtracted depreciation from the GDP to find that the NDP was $502.

Suppose we were to take the four items we added to find the GDP by the expenditures method and were to *substitute net* private domestic investment (NPDI) for *gross* private domestic investment (GPDI).

depreciation

NPDI is less than GPDI by the amount of ______________ in the economy.

The total of these four items will be less than the GDP by the amount

depreciation

of ______________ in the economy.

The total of these four items will, therefore, be the economy's

net domestic product

* ____ .

4-80

Using the figures in frame **4-78**, NDP is the sum of the following four items:

Personal consumption expenditures	$350
_______ private domestic investment	_____
Government purchases	110
Net exports	5

Net, $37

$502

NDP will be equal to __________ .

4-81

This is not too surprising a result!

Since NPDI is less than GPDI by depreciation, the sum of these four items will be less than the GDP by depreciation. We call this sum

NDP

______________ .

4-82

Let's review what you have learned about the NDP and its computation.

the market value of the final goods and services produced during a year less the capital used up during the year

The NDP is * ____

____

____

____

minus (less) depreciation

The NDP equals the GDP __________ __________ .

Using the *income* approach, what items do you add to find the NDP?

All items that are added to find the GDP except depreciation.

* ____

____

____

4-83 Review Frame

The capital goods produced during a year less the capital goods worn out.

What is net private domestic investment? * ____ .

minus (less) depreciation

NPDI equals GPDI __________ __________ .

Using the *expenditures* approach, what items do you add to find the

Personal consumption expenditures, net private domestic investment, government purchases, net exports.

NDP? * ____ .

4-84

The third of the five indicators of an economy's overall performance is called the *national income* (NI). (It is this measure of performance for which the kind of accounting we have been doing is named.) National income can be computed from scratch only by using the income approach. To find out what the NI is, let's look at the ten items we added

GDP, income

or subtracted earlier to find the __________ by the (income/expenditures) approach.

Depreciation	$ 38
Indirect business taxes	49
Compensation of employees	332
Rents	9
Interest	19
Proprietors' income	53
Corporate income taxes	25
Dividends	17
Undistributed corporate profits	8
less net American income earned abroad	10
Gross domestic product	$540

Two of these ten items added or subtracted to find the GDP are *not incomes earned* by those who supply the economy with economic resources. You should remember that economists call such items

nonincome charges

__________ __________ . The two items above which are not

depreciation, indirect business taxes

incomes earned by resource suppliers are __________ and __________ __________ .

4-85

NI is all income *earned* by American-owned resources located here or abroad (regardless of whether or not the resource suppliers ever actually receive this income). Remember that both depreciation and indirect business taxes (are/are not) incomes earned by resource suppliers.

are not

4-86

do not

Depreciation is not income at all; it is compensation for capital used up and worn out. Indirect business taxes are not the incomes of resource suppliers. They are a major source of income of governments. But governments (do/do not) provide the economy with economic resources.

4-87

is not, is not
is

Net American income earned abroad (is/is not) part of GDP, (is/is not) part of NDP, (is/is not) part of NI.

(Review frame **4-56** if you had difficulty in this frame.)

4-88

To compute NI using the income approach, we add all nine items used to determine the GDP *except* the two nonincome charges. The seven items we would add (refer to frame **4-84** if you need help) are:

compensation of employees | * ______
rents | * ______
interest | * ______
proprietors' income | * ______
corporate income taxes | * ______
dividends | * ______
undistributed corporate profits | * ______

We do *not* add in net American income earned abroad because it is already included in compensation of employees, rents, interest, proprietors' income, and profits.

4-89

If we had already computed either GDP or NDP using either of the two approaches, we could find the NI by deducting certain amounts from GDP or NDP and adding one amount.

depreciation
indirect business taxes
net American income earned abroad

To find the NI, from GDP we must deduct ______ and ______ ______ ______; and add * ______ ______.

indirect
business taxes
net American income earned abroad

To find the NI, from NDP we need only deduct ______ ______ ______; and add * ______ ______.

4-90

$463

Look back now to frame **4-84**. Using any means you choose, what is the size of the NI? $______

4-91
Here are the national income accounting figures which you saw in frame **4-63**.

Atlantis: National income accounting figures	
Dividends	$ 29
Rents	20
Net exports	14
Indirect business taxes	49
Undistributed corporate profits	22
Gross private domestic investment	82
Depreciation	46
Proprietors' income	48
Transfer payments	12
Personal consumption expenditures	473
Net Atlantis income earned abroad	15
Interest	16
Compensation of employees	462
Personal taxes	84
Government purchases	141
Corporate income taxes	33
Social security contributions	20

Recall that you calculated the GDP and found it was $710. The NDP is equal to $______ . The NI is equal to $______ .

$664 (=$710 − $46)
$630 (=$664 − $49 + $15)

4-92 Review Frame
Let's quickly review what you have just learned about national income.
NI is the income (earned/actually received) by those who provide the economy with economic ______ .
NDP equals GDP minus ______
NI equals NDP minus * ______
and plus * ______
NI can be computed via the income approach by adding (how many) ______ items.

earned
resources
depreciation
indirect business taxes
net American income earned abroad
seven

4-93 Review Frame
The items we add to find NI by the income approach include all of the nine we added to compute the GDP except those two which together are called ______ ______ .
These seven items which constitute the incomes earned by the four kinds of economic resources and the four incomes are called * ______ , ______ , ______ , and ______ .

nonincome charges
compensation of employees, rents, interest, profits

Economists are more interested in the incomes earned by the suppliers of economic resources than is the average citizen. Most people are not very much concerned with the national income at all. They are much more concerned with the income which they actually receive and the income left after paying taxes—their take-home pay.

The economist and national income accountant also have an interest in these kinds of income, and they have devised ways of computing them. It is now time for us to look at these two kinds of income which are of so much concern to both the typical citizen and the economist.

4-94

When we computed the NI back in frame **4-90**, we summed the following the items:

Compensation of employees	$462	Corporate income taxes	$33
Rents	20	Dividends	29
Interest	16	Undistributed corporate profits	22
Proprietors' income	48		

We found that the NI was $630—the total of these seven items.

Now look closely at these seven items again. All of them are incomes *earned* by resource suppliers. But some of this earned income was *not received* by those who earned it. Two of the seven were clearly not incomes received by those who provided resources to the economy.

The taxes on their incomes (or profits) which corporations paid to different governments were not received by the stockholders and are

corporate income

called ______ ______ taxes.

Similarly, the profits (or income) of corporations which were not paid as taxes to various governments or distributed as dividends to stockholders were not received by these stockholders and are called

undistributed corporate profits

______ ______ ______.

4-95

If we deduct corporate income taxes and undistributed corporate profits from the seven items we added to find the NI, five items remain. These are

Compensation of employees
Rents
Interest
Proprietors' income
Dividends

There is, sadly, another complication. This complication results from the method used in the United States to finance the public social security system. The social security system is financed by taxes (called "contributions") imposed on both employers and employees. These taxes are assumed to have been earned by the employees; but clearly they

are not

(are/are not) received by these employees.

4-96

earned

The wage and salary supplements in frame **4-95**, as you may recall from frame **4-44**—look back if you wish—are the funds which employers take from their own pockets and put into public and private pension, health, and welfare funds. The funds transferred by employers to these funds are assumed to be (earned/unearned) by the employees.

4-97

subtract

The way national income accountants do things, the portion of the wage and salary supplements paid as taxes (contributed) to the social security by employers are treated as income earned but not received by the employees (of course!) and are labeled *social security contributions*. So to find the income received by employees we must (add/subtract) the social security contributions of employers from the NI.

4-98

social security contributions

This means that if we are to find the income that was earned by employees and received by them we must subtract from the NI:

* ______________________________.

4-99

earned and received

If we deduct the social security contributions from the five remaining items in frame **4-95**, namely,

Compensation of employees
Rents
Interest
Proprietors' income
Dividends

what's left is the income which is (earned and not received/earned and received).

4-100

(Read the next frame for the answer.)

Do these five items add up to the income that individuals in the economy actually received? Not quite. The citizens and families of an economy have income that is *earned and not received* and income that is *earned and received*. But they also have income that is *received and not earned!* Where does this unearned income come from? Who pays it? And why is it received if it isn't earned by its recipients?

Care to take a guess before we tell you? * ______________________________.

4-101

Each year governments and private firms in the economy turn over monies to citizens in return for which the citizens provide the governments and firms with no economic resources *in that year*: no labor, no use of land or capital, and no entrepreneurial ability. These monies are "gifts" (or grants) and take many forms: aid to the needy, veterans' benefits, interest on the public debt, unemployment compensation, benefits to the aged and ill under the social security program, and payments from private pension and welfare funds. These gifts of money are incomes *not* earned by their recipients and are called ***transfer payments***.

The *earned and received* incomes are:

compensation of employees — * ______________________________,

rents — * ______________________________,

interest — * ______________________________,

proprietors' income — * ______________________________,

dividends — * ______________________________,

social security contributions — Less: * ______________________________

The one *received but not earned* item is:

transfer payments — * ______________________________.

4-102

When we add these seven items the total is called *personal income* (PI). This figure is the total income received in the economy.

Transfer payments are $12 and the social security contributions are $20. Using the figures in frame **4-94**, personal income is equal to

$567 (= $630 − $33 − $22 + $12 − $20) — $________. (Do not forget to subtract corporate income taxes and undistributed corporate profits.)

4-103

If you found (as you did in frame **4-90**) that the NI was $463 and you also knew that:

Social security contributions were	$ 9
Transfer payments were	43
Undistributed corporate profits were	8
Corporate income taxes were	25

Personal income is equal to:

The national income of $463

9 — minus $________

8 — minus $________

25 (any order) — minus $________

43 — plus $________

464 — PI would be equal to $________

4-104

expenditures

There is another method we might employ to determine the PI of an economy. The income method we just used had us add up the sources of PI. But if we knew the various things people did with their personal incomes we might total the amounts devoted to each of these different *uses* of PI to discover the economy's PI. This method of computing PI takes us back to the (expenditures/income) approach to national income accounting.

4-105

The table below shows the three things people do with their PI.

Personal taxes	$ 58
Personal consumption expenditures	350
Personal saving	46

personal

Out of their PI people must first pay their ________ taxes.

4-106

Personal taxes are personal income, personal property, and inheritance taxes. The table in frame **4-105** indicates that after these personal taxes have been paid people use the larger part of what remains of their PI

personal consumption expenditures

for ________ ________ ________ .

4-107

After people have paid their personal taxes and made their personal consumption expenditures, what remains of their PI is their ________

personal saving

________ .

4-108

An economist looking at the accounting figures in frame **4-105** would

personal

be able to say that the economy's ________ income was equal to

$454

$________ .

4-109 Review Frame

received
earned

PI is the income which is (earned/received); and NI, you should recall, is the income which is (earned/received).

4-110 Review Frame

PI can be calculated either by adding the following items:

compensation of employees ______

rents ______

interest ______

proprietors' income ______

dividends ______

transfer payments ______

less social security contributions (any order) ______

or by adding the following three items:

personal saving ______

personal taxes ______

personal consumption expenditures (any order) ______

social security contributions, corporate income taxes, undistributed corporate profits (any order)

PI can also be determined by subtracting * ______

______

______

______

transfer payments

from the NI and then adding ______.

4-111 Review Frame

To test your understanding of PI, let's use the following national income accounting data:

Transfer payments	$ 16	Social security contributions	$ 8
Undistributed corporate profits	16	Depreciation	21
Gross private domestic investment	72	Net exports	−6
		Dividends	17
Compensation of employees	404	Personal taxes	71
Indirect business taxes	14	Rents	11
Personal consumption expenditures	384	Proprietors' income	39
		Interest	7
Corporate income taxes	12	Net American income earned abroad	8
Government purchases	83		

Using the income approach, how much was PI in this economy?

$486 $______

(This next question will require you to make two subtractions from PI.)

$31 (= $486 − $384 − $71) How much was personal saving in the economy? $______

4-112

Look again at the figures in the last frame. Personal income was $486 and personal saving was $31. Suppose now we want to answer these two questions:

How much income do individuals have left to spend *after* they pay their personal taxes?

What was the total amount which was spent for personal consumption *and* saved in this economy?

By this stage of the game you can answer both these questions by yourself. And you find that the answers to these two questions are (the same/different).

the same

4-113

Economists call the answer to these questions the economy's *disposable income* (DI), the income left after personal taxes are paid. Make up an equation for finding DI. Use the symbols PI and PT (for personal taxes).

DI = PI − PT

______

4-114

Using the information and your answers in frames **4-111** and **4-113**, you can calculate DI in two ways.

$486, $71, $415

DI is equal to $______ minus $______, or $______.

$384, $31, $415

DI is also equal to $______ plus $______, or $______.

4-115

What there is to know about DI can be quickly summarized:

personal taxes

DI can be found by subtracting ______ ______

personal income

from ______ ______.

personal consumption expenditures

personal saving (either order)

People use DI in two ways: * ______

and * ______.

4-116 Review Frame

If you would like to test your own ability, try computing the first three of the five measures of the economic performance of a nation. Use the national income accounting figures in frames **4-111**. These three measures are:

$533 (= $384 + $72 + $83 − $6)

GDP $______

$512 (= $533 − $21)

NDP $______

$506 (= $512 − $14 + $8)

NI $______

4-117

To test your knowledge of PI and DI, look at frame **4-63**.

$567 PI was $________

$483 DI was $________

$10 Personal saving was $________

ADJUSTING THE GDP

For quite a few years now economists have collected statistical information about our economy and have used it to determine the GDP, NDP, NI, PI, and DI. The computation of these indicators has helped us to learn: *how* the economy performed, *why* it performed as it did in each of these years, and *what* we might do to improve its performance.

These measures of overall performance also enable us to compare the economy and its operation from one year to the next. Did the GDP rise or fall? Was investment larger or smaller? Were personal incomes higher or lower? In making these comparisons, however, we run into one major difficulty: the prices or market values of final goods and services have changed over the years. And these price changes make it hard for us to make direct comparisons of our outputs of goods and services in different years.

We want to learn now why price changes make comparisons difficult and what we must do to make such comparisons less difficult. That is, we must learn how to adjust the GDP before we make comparisons.

4-118

Suppose our economy had produced 1,000 bushels of kumquats last year. The price of kumquats last year was $40 a bushel.

This year our economy again grew 1,000 bushels of kumquats but the price of kumquats this year was $50 a bushel.

The total market value of all the kumquats produced in the economy

50,000 last year was $40,000 and this year was $__________ .

4-119

Between last year and this year:

did not change Our production of kumquats (increased/decreased/did not change).

increased The price of kumquats (increased/decreased/did not change).

increased The total market value of kumquats (increased/decreased/did not change).

4-120

The total market value of kumquats increased between last year and this year because:

(a) the production of kumquats increased.
(b) the price of kumquats increased.
(c) both (a) and (b).
(d) neither (a) nor (b).

(b) Which one? ________

4-121

If we were to look only at what happened to the dollar value of the kumquats produced, we might be led to a mistaken conclusion that our production of kumquats had increased. Actually this 25 percent rise in the total market value of the kumquats produced was the result of the

price 25 percent rise in the ________ of kumquats.

4-122

Total market value increased from $40,000 to $50,000. Price rose from $40 to $50 a bushel. If we had only the above information about kumquats, we could have determined whether or not the actual production of kumquats had changed:

Divide the total market value of the kumquats produced last year *by* last year's kumquat price. This would tell us that last year's production

1,000 of kumquats was ________ bushels.

Divide the total market value of kumquats this *year* by the price of kumquats *this year*. We would then know that the output of kumquats

1,000 this year was ________ bushels.

4-123

In this way we would have discovered that the actual production of

0 kumquats between this year and last increased by ________ bushels.

4-124

Let's look at another commodity. Suppose the total market values and the prices of a certain grade of steel in two different years were those shown in the table below.

Year	Total market value	Price (per ton)
1991	$6000	$100
1992	8400	120

To find the number of tons of steel produced in 1991 we divide $6000 by the price of $100 per ton.

60 In 1991 there were ________ tons of steel produced, but in 1992
70 there were ________ tons of steel produced.

In other words, between 1991 and 1992 the production of this grade
increased by 10 tons of steel * ______________________________ .

4-125

Look at what happened to the price of this steel between 1991 and 1992. Let's put this price information in percentage terms:

$20 is 20 percent of $100.
$120 is 120 percent of $100.

20 Between 1991 and 1992 the price of steel rose __________ percent,
120 making the price of this steel __________ percent of its price in 1991.

4-126

The expansion of the total market value of this steel was the result of:

(a) an increase in the price of steel
(b) an increase in the production of steel
(c) both (a) and (b)
(d) neither (a) nor (b)

(c) Which one? __________

4-127

Now let's look at the economy as a whole and see if what we have done for kumquats and steel we can also do for the entire economy.

The GDP of the American economy in 1929, 1933, 1941, and 1982 is given in the table below.

Year	GDP (billions)
1929	$ 103
1933	56
1939	91
1987	4,540

Can you tell from this table what happened between these years to
No our total output of final goods and services? ____________________ .

4-128

The prices used to compute the GDP in each of these four years were the prices paid for final goods and services *in that year!* Thus, before we can compare the outputs of the economy in the four years we must first
adjust (correct, alter, etc.) ______________ these GDP figures to take account of these changes in the average price of goods and services that occurred.

4-129

To adjust the total market values of steel and kumquats for changes in

market | the prices of steel and kumquats, we divided the total ______

value, price | ______ of the product by the ______ of the product.

Similarly, to adjust these GDP figures we must divide them by the

price | average ______ of the final goods and services.

4-130

How do we measure the average price of all the final goods and services included in the GDP? Do we add up the prices of each good and service and divide this total by the number of goods and services? This could be done. But economists do not use this method to measure the average price of a group of commodities. Instead they use a device called a *price index*.

Suppose the price of a package of cigarettes in 1933 was 20 cents and 24 cents in 1941.

4 | Between 1933 and 1941 the price of cigarettes rose ______

20 | cents a package and increased ______ *percent*. In 1941 the price

120 | of cigarettes was ______ percent of their price in 1933.

4-131

The price index for cigarettes in 1941 was 120 because the price of cigarettes in 1941 and 120 percent of the price of cigarettes in 1933. In

1933 | other words, we used the year ______ as our *base year*.

4-132

Let's take another example. The price of wheat in 1933 was 40 cents a bushel. In 1941, the price was 50 cents a bushel.

125 | The price of wheat in 1941 was ______ percent of the price of

base | wheat in 1933. So we know that 1933 was used as the ______

year, 125 | ______ . The price index for wheat in 1941 is ______ .

4-133

The base year may be any year we decide to select. If we are comparing prices in 1933 and 1941, we may use either 1933 or 1941 for the base

price index | year. The ______ ______ is always 100 in the base year.

4-134

Let's apply this to the price of milk in four different years, given in the table below. Use 1940 for the base year and compute the price index for each of the four years.

	Year	Price of milk (per quart)	Price index
100	1940	$.25	______
120	1945	.30	______
160	1950	.40	______
200	1955	.50	______

4-135

Statisticians compute the price index for almost every commodity bought and sold in the economy. They also figure out price indexes for such groups of commodities as the final goods and services included

price in the GDP. Economists can then use these ______

indexes, GDP ______ to adjust the ______ for changes in the general level of prices in the economy.

4-136

The price indexes economists use to adjust the GDP is *not* the same thing as the consumer price index (the CPI), which is often called the "cost of living" index. (In technical terms the index used by economists to adjust the GDP is called the "GDP deflator.")

total market value Let's go back to the GDP figures we looked at in frame **4-127**. These figures tell us only what happened to the economy's (production/total market value) of final goods and services.

4-137

These GDP figures appear in the table below, along with the price index for *all* final goods and services in each of the four years.

1987 The year used for the base year is ______ .

To adjust the GDP in each of these four years, divide the GDP in that year by the price index for that year, then multiply the result by 100.

Go ahead and adjust each of the four GDPs. Put the adjusted GDP figures in the table.

	Year	GDP (billions)	Price index	Adjusted GDP (billions)
837	1929	$ 103	12.3	$______
596	1933	56	9.4	______
850	1939	91	10.7	______
4,540	1987	4,540	100	______

4-138

The *adjusted GDP* is sometimes called the "real GDP" because these figures indicate what really happened to the output—not just to the market value—of all final goods and services from one year to another.

What we have done in adjusting the GDPs is to measure the total production of final goods and services in terms of the prices charged for commodities in the base year.

The adjusted GDP figures in frame **4-137** represent what the total market value of all final goods and services *would* have been if we had computed market values for each commodity by using the price

base charged for that commodity in 1987, the ______________

year ______________ .

4-139

Economists refer to a rise in the general level of prices as *inflation* and to a fall in the level of prices as *deflation*.

We see by examining the table in frame **4-137** that between 1929 and

deflation 1933 the economy experienced (inflation/deflation) and that between

inflation 1933 and 1941 it experienced (inflation/deflation).

4-140

Just to make sure we understand how to adjust GDP, let's take one more example. In the table below are some purely hypothetical GDP figures for five different years.

2 The base year is apparently year (1/2/3/4/5). Fill in the adjusted GDP figures, using the price indexes given.

	Year	GDP (billions)	Price index	Adjusted GDP (billions)
$400	1	$300	75	$______
300	2	300	100	______
300	3	360	120	______
400	4	320	80	______
300	5	450	150	______

4-141

Between years:

decreased 1 and 2 the economy's real GDP (increased/decreased/remained the same).

remained the same 2 and 3 real GDP (increased/decreased/remained the same).

increased 3 and 4 real GDP (increased/decreased/remained the same).

decreased 4 and 5 real GDP (increased/decreased/remained the same).

4-142

rose
fell

Between years 1 and 2 the economy suffered inflation because the level of prices in the economy (rose/fell); but between years 3 and 4 it experienced deflation because the price index (rose/fell).

4-143

market
value
2

The adjusted GDP figures indicate the total ________ ________ of the economy's output of final goods and services, using the prices that prevailed in year ________ to measure the market value of each good and service.

4-144 Review Frame

adjust
prices
price index
100

What we have discovered about GDP figures is that appearances are often deceiving. You just can't trust the GDP figures to tell you what happened to the economy's total output unless you first ________ these figures to take into account the changes that may have occurred in the level of ________ over the years. We do this by dividing the GDP by the ________ ________ for that year and then multiplying by ________ .

4-145 Review Frame

rise
fall, price

We also learned that inflation is a ________ and deflation is a ________ in the ________ level.

Now take the Review Test for Section 4 at the back of the book.

Macroeconomic Analysis: Aggregate Demand and Aggregate Supply

section **5**

In Section 4 we discovered how domestic output and income are measured and how a price index is constructed and used to convert nominal (money) GDP to real GDP. Now we will introduce some basic tools to help us analyze how and why real GDP and the price level are constantly changing.

In Section 3 we learned how *individual* prices and *individual* quantities are determined. But we did not learn why prices in *general* rise and fall. Nor have we yet learned why *total* production—real GDP—varies from one year to the next. To learn these two things, we must combine all the individual prices into an *aggregate* price level and all the individual quantities into *aggregate* real domestic output: real GDP.

5-1

Below is the type of graph we will be using. On the vertical axis we

price level — have placed the __________ __________ , whereas in Section 3, dealing with the market for individual commodities, on this axis we

price, real GDP — placed __________ . On the horizontal axis we have placed __________

quantity — __________ , whereas in Section 3 we had placed __________ of

one — how many different types of commodities? __________ .

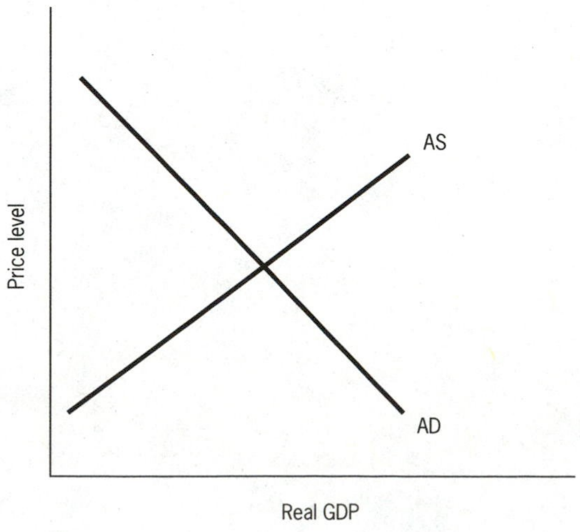

Aggregate Demand

5-2

From the graph in frame **5-1**, we can see that as the price level rises,
lower the (higher/lower) will be the real GDP purchased. And as the price
higher level drops, the __________ will be the real GDP purchased. Thus,
inverse the relationship between the price level and real GDP is (direct/inverse)
negative or (positive/negative).

5-3

We can see, then, that aggregate demand (AD) is a schedule, graphically
curve represented as a __________ , which shows the amounts of
real GDP __________ __________ that will be purchased at each possible
price level __________ __________ .

5-4

You will recall from Section 3 that the demand curve for an individual commodity sloped downward from left to right because of the
substitution, income __________ and the __________ effects. But these explanations do not apply when we are dealing with aggregates. In frame **5-1** as we move down the AD curve, prices in general are falling so the substitution effect (substituting a now cheaper product for one whose price
changed has not __________) cannot apply. Similarly, you will recall that while an individual's demand for a given product assumed a fixed income, movement along the AD curve assumes varying aggregate in-
GDP comes (varying real __________).

5-5

There are three reasons why the AD curve is downsloping. The first is the ***wealth*** or ***real-balances effect***. As the price level rises the pur-
decreases chasing power of one's money or other financial assets __________ .

5-6

If people are buying less because higher prices have reduced their pur-
decrease chasing power, there will be a(n) increase/decrease in the amount of real
GDP __________ demanded.

5-7

The second reason why the AD curve is downsloping is because of the ***interest rate effect***. With a given AD curve we assume the money supply
more is fixed. When the price level rises, people will need (more/less) money to buy commodities or run their businesses; that is, the demand for
increase money will (increase/decrease). And increased demand for a commodity
increases does what to its price? It __________ it.

5-8

What is the price of money? It's what you have to pay when you borrow it—and that's called ________ .

Answer: interest

5-9

As the cost of money—the interest rate—rises, the desire of people to borrow money for consumption or to invest in business will (increase/decrease).

Answer: decrease

5-10

A higher price level, then, by ________ the demand for money and, therefore, ________ the interest rate, leads to a(n) (increase/decrease) in the amount of real ________ demanded.

Answers: increasing; increasing; decrease, GDP

5-11

The third reason the AD curve slopes downward concerns the ***foreign-purchases effect***. As the American price level rises, American goods and services become relatively more expensive to foreigners, who therefore tend to import (more/less) from the United States: American exports (increase/decrease). At the same time, foreign goods and services become relatively (more expensive/cheaper) to Americans who therefore tend to import (more/less). Thus a rising American price level has a doubly (positive/negative) effect on American real net exports and thus on aggregate demand.

Answers: less; decrease; cheaper; more; negative

5-12 Review Frame

When the price level falls, real balances (rise/fall), consumers and firms find themselves (richer/poorer), and (increase/decrease) their spending; and the real GDP (increases/decreases); and vice versa.

When the price level falls, the demand for money (rises/falls), the rate of interest (increases/decreases), spending sensitive to changes in the rate of interest (expands/contracts), and the real GDP (increases/decreases); and vice versa.

When the price level falls, American goods and services become relatively (more expensive/cheaper) to foreigners and foreign goods and services become relatively (more expensive/cheaper) to Americans; thus net exports (increase/decrease), and the real GDP (increases/decreases); and vice versa.

Answers: rise; richer, increase; increases; falls; decreases; expands, increases; cheaper; more expensive; increase, increases

5-13

We have seen that changes in the price level cause changes in spending such that real GDP will change in the (opposite/same) direction to that of the change in the price level. That is, an increase in the price level, *other things equal*, will cause a(n) ________ in the amount of real output demanded, while a decrease in the price level will cause a(n)

Answers: opposite; decrease

increase
movements along

________ in the amount of real output demanded. These changes are shown graphically by (movements of/movements along) the AD curve.

5-14

made

price level

In Section 3 in discussing single product demand curves, we (made/did not make) a distinction between a change in demand and a change in quantity demanded. In analyzing changes in real domestic output we need to make a similar distinction between ***changes in the quantity of real output demanded*** caused by changes in the ______ ______ and changes in one or more of the ***determinants of aggregate demand***.

5-15

consumption

investment, government, net exports

C, I_g, G, X_n

Recall from Section 4 that total or aggregate expenditures (AE) in an economy are made up of four aggregates, which are: ________ , ________ , ________ , and ________ ________ .

In symbols AE = ____ + ____ + ____ + ____ .
A change in any one of these will shift the AD curve to the right or to the left, as shown in the graph below. We will examine in turn how each of the four determinants of AD affects the AD curve.

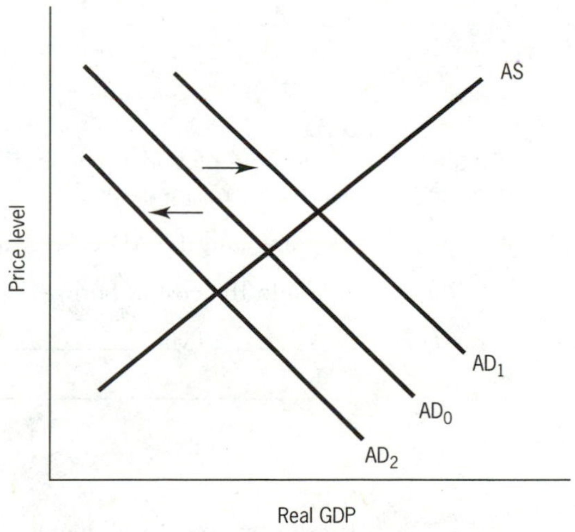

5-16

more

right

An increase in real consumer wealth will make the consumer (more/less) willing to buy and thus shift the AD curve to the ________ . (Note: We are *not* talking here of the "wealth effect" caused by a change in the price level. In the present case, the increase in real wealth occurs with *no* change in the price level. Example: coming into one's inheritance.)

5-17

If consumers expect their real incomes to rise in the near future, they will tend to spend (more/less) now and the AD curve will * ________ ____ _____ __________ .

more, shift to the right

5-18

If consumers have become heavily indebted, they will tend to (increase/decrease) present spending and the AD curve will * ______________ __________ .

decrease, shift to the left

5-19

A decrease in personal income tax rates will (increase/decrease) take home pay and will tend to __________ consumer spending and the AD curve will * ______________________ .

increase
increase
shift to the right

5-20

The second determinant of AD is investment spending—the purchase of capital goods. An increase in investment spending will shift the AD curve to the ________ and a decrease will shift the AD curve to the ________ .

right
left

5-21

If the cost of borrowing money, that is, the real __________ rate, decreases, businesses will tend to (increase/decrease) their investment spending and the AD curve will * ____________________ . An increase in the cost of borrowing money, that is, the ______________ ________ , will __________ investment and the AD curve will * ______________________ .

interest
increase
shift to the right
real
interest rate, decrease
shift to the left

5-22

If expectation of profit increases, investment will __________ and the AD curve will * ______________________ .

increase
shift to the right

5-23

An increase in business taxes will __________ after-tax profits on business investment and will therefore tend to __________ investment spending, and the AD curve will * ________________ .

decrease
decrease
shift to the left

5-24

New technologies—for example, continued improvements in the speed and power of computers—lead to __________ investment and the AD curve will * ____________________.

increased
shift to the right

5-25

During a deep recession factories tend to have (much/little) excess capacity. Investment will, therefore, tend to be (high/low) and the AD curve will * ____________________.

much
low
shift to the left

5-26

The third determinant of AD is government spending. When government increases its spending, the AD curve will * ____________________ ____________________, assuming government (does/does not) increase taxes at the same time and provided interest rates (increase/do not increase).

shift to the right, does not
do not increase

5-27

If the government increases its spending and taxes simultaneously and if real interest rates also increase, which would tend to (increase/decrease) consumption and investment expenditures, then we (can/cannot) be sure in which direction the AD curve will shift.

decrease
cannot

5-28

The fourth and final determinant of AD is net export spending. When foreigners change their buying of American goods and services and Americans change their buying of imports, *both for reasons other than changes in the American price level*, then the AD curve will shift. If the cause of the change in net exports is a change in the American price level, then AD (will/will not) shift.

will not

5-29

If you got the last one wrong, review frame **5-11**. When the American price level changes, we are confronted with the __________–__________ effect. A change in the American price level will cause movement (along/of) the AD curve. It is similar in effect to what we analyzed in Section 3 where a change in price of a single commodity caused a change in the (demand for/quantity demanded of) that commodity.

foreign-purchases
along
quantity demanded of

5-30

If national incomes change abroad, there will tend to be (a change/no change) in the demand for American exports. With increasing foreign incomes we can expect __________ demand for our exports and

a change
increased

right | the AD curve will shift to the _____ . With recession abroad, we can
decreased | expect __________ demand for our exports and the AD curve will
shift to the left | * ____________________ .

5-31

If American real interest rates rise relative to foreign real interest rates, we can expect foreign demand to buy American bonds, which now pay a higher return than foreign bonds, to __________ . American bonds must be paid for in American dollars. Therefore the demand for American dollars will also __________ .

increase
increase

5-32

When the demand for a normal good increases, its price __________ . The American dollar is a normal good; therefore when foreigners demand more American dollars to buy more American bonds, the price of the American dollar to foreigners will __________ , that is the price, or ***exchange rate***, of the American dollar in terms of foreign currencies will ***appreciate***.

increases
increase

5-33

Foreigners having to pay more for American dollars means that, in terms of their own currencies, they will have to pay (more/less) for our goods and services. Therefore, they will buy _____ .

more
less

5-34

When foreigners have to pay more for American dollars, Americans will pay (more/less) for foreign currencies, which will have ***depreciated*** in proportion to the appreciation of the American dollar. Thus Americans will find that foreign goods and services, in terms of the American dollar, cost _____ . Therefore we will tend to import _____ .

less
less, more

5-35

If foreigners are buying fewer American exports because the American dollar has (appreciated/depreciated) and Americans are importing more because foreign currencies have __________ , American net exports will __________ and our AD curve will * ____________________ .

appreciated
depreciated
decrease, shift to the left

5-36 Review Frame

The factors that influence the amount of real output that consumers, businesses, governments, and foreigners wish to buy *at each price level* are called the * ______________________________ .

determinants of demand

5-37 Review Frame

shift of

Changes in spending caused by a change in one or more of the determinants of demand lead to (movement along/shift of) the AD curve.

5-38 Review Frame

right

An increase in spending shifts the AD curve to the ________ .

left
was not

A decrease in spending shifts the AD curve to the ________ . In both cases, we are assuming that the change in spending (was/was not) caused by a change in the price level.

Aggregate Supply

5-39

The aggregate-supply curve usually looks like the one drawn below.

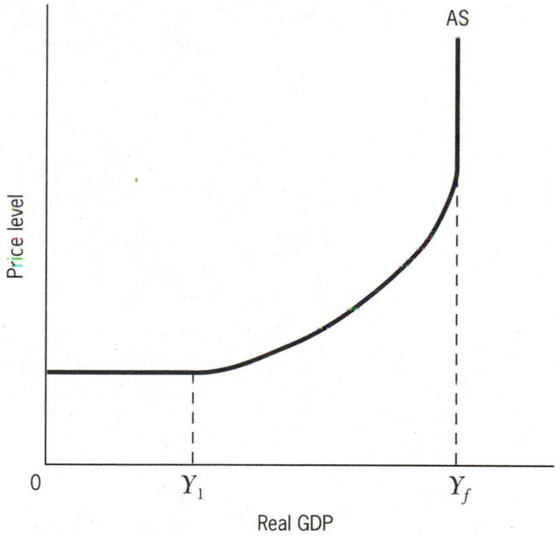

horizontal

Between outputs of zero and Y_1 the curve is (horizontal/vertical/upsloping).

upsloping

But between Y_1 and Y_f it is ________ .

vertical

And at output Y_f it is ________ .

5-40

The aggregate-supply curve is horizontal at low levels of real GDP: when the economy is in a severe recession or a depression. This horizontal range of the aggregate-supply curve is called the *Keynesian range* (because John Maynard Keynes, the British economist for whom the Keynesian theory which we will study in Section 6 was named, was concerned with the causes of and the remedies for unemployment and depression).

unnecessary

In this range to induce business firms to increase the quantities of final goods and services they are willing to supply (produce) it is (necessary/unnecessary) for the price level to rise.

5-41

need not | need not | remain constant

In a severe recession or depression many workers are unemployed and to induce them to take a job employers (producers) (must/need not) pay them a wage rate higher than the going wage rate.

And most business firms are producing less than they are capable of producing and they (must/need not) be paid a higher price for their products to induce them to expand their production.

In short, as real GDP increases in the Keynesian range the prices producers are willing to accept (rise/fall/remain constant).

5-42

cannot

At Y_f the aggregate-supply curve is vertical. Y_f is the full-employment output of the economy: the maximum output the economy is able to produce at this time (and the subscript f stands for full employment).

This vertical range on the aggregate-supply curve is called the *classical range* (because the so-called classical economists believed the economy would tend to produce its full-employment output).

In this range along the aggregate-supply curve an increase in the price level (will/cannot) increase the aggregate quantity of final goods and services produced in the economy.

5-43

necessary

Between Y_1 and Y_f the aggregate-supply curve is upsloping. And because it lies between the Keynesian and classical ranges, this range along the aggregate-supply curve is called the *intermediate range*.

The upward slope of aggregate supply in the intermediate range means that to induce producers to provide (produce) larger quantities of final goods and services it is (necessary/unnecessary) for the price level to rise.

5-44

upward | increase | higher | raises

There are two reasons business firms must receive higher prices for their products if they are to produce larger outputs.

First: As the economy's output expands shortages of *certain types* of labor develop. As firms (to increase output) compete for such labor, the wage rates received by these workers are bid (upward/downward) and the costs of producing the goods and services for which these types of labor are required will (increase/decrease). Merely to break even the firms concerned must obtain (higher/lower) prices for their products. Similarly, some firms may experience shortages of materials or other production bottlenecks.

The expansion of output, therefore, (raises/lowers) the price level.

5-45

increases | higher | raises

Second: As unemployment in the economy *decreases* (as the output of the economy *increases*) some firms will be forced to use older and less efficient machinery and hire less efficient workers. This also (increases/decreases) the costs of producing goods and services and makes it necessary for firms to charge (higher/lower) prices for their products. This (raises/lowers) the price level.

5-46 Review Frame

In summary:

3 There are along the aggregate-supply curve (1/2/3/4) ranges.

horizontal In the Keynesian range the curve is ______________ .

vertical In the classical range it is ______________ .

upsloping And in the intermediate range it is ______________ .

5-47 Review Frame

in a severe recession or depression The aggregate-supply curve is horizontal when the economy is (at full employment/in a severe recession or depression/between these two extremes).

at full employment It is vertical when the economy is * ______________ .

between these two extremes And it is upsloping when the economy is * ______________ .

5-48

increases We have seen that as we move from left to right through the Keynesian and intermediate ranges *along* the aggregate supply (AS) curve, real output (increases/decreases). Note that we stressed *along*. Any given AS curve shows the relationship between the price level and real domestic output (GDP), *other things equal*. These "other things" are called the ***determinants of aggregate supply***. A change in one or more of these will shift AS, as shown in the graph below.

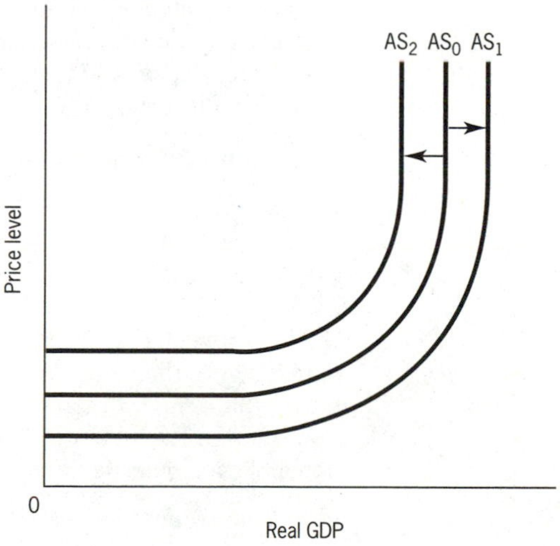

5-49

increase, more From what you learned about individual supply in Section 3, you can probably tell that a shift from AS_0 to AS_1 in the above graph indicates a(n) (increase/decrease) in AS, meaning that (more/less) will be supplied by business at each price level. A shift from AS_0 to AS_2 indicates

decrease, less a(n) __________ in AS, meaning __________ will be supplied at each price level.

5-50

There are three broad categories of determinants of AS. They all have one thing in common: when they change, per unit costs of production change at each price level. A decrease in per unit costs of production at each price level shifts the AS curve ______ ward. An increase in per unit costs at each price level shifts the AS curve __________ ward.

right
left

5-51

The first category is ***input prices***. Its first subcategory is domestic resource availability. If a discovery is made of a new, easily accessible source of an important natural resource ("land"), for example, oil, then per unit production costs will tend to __________ and the AS curve will * ________________________ .

decrease
shift to the right

5-52

Other subcategories of domestic resources are: labor, capital, and entrepreneurship. An increase in any of these *at a constant general price level* will __________ unit costs of production and shift the * ________________________________ .

decrease
AS curve to the right

5-53

Another subcategory of input prices is prices of imported resources. Suppose the dollar *appreciates* against foreign currencies, meaning that foreign goods and services now cost (more/less) in terms of the dollar. To the extent that imports are used in American production, our per unit costs of production will __________ and the AS curve will * ____ .

less
decrease
shift to the right

5-54

The final subcategory of input prices is market power: the ability to set a price higher than would occur in a competitive situation. A reduction in trade barriers, for example, would force domestic monopolies to face more foreign competition and lower their prices. To the extent these monopolistic domestic firms supply inputs to other domestic firms these other firms would now have ________ per unit costs and the AS curve would * ____ .

lower
shift to the right

5-55

Productivity is the second broad category of determinants of AS. Productivity is the amount of output obtained from a given amount of input. An increase in productivity means greater output per unit of input. Therefore, an increase in productivity results in ________ per unit costs of production and a ________ ward shift of the AS curve.

lower
right

5-56

The final broad category of determinants of AS is the ***legal-institutional environment***. The first subcategory is business taxes and subsidies. An increase in taxes will have the effect of an increase/decrease in per unit costs and will shift the AS curve to the ________ . An increase in subsidies will have (the same/the opposite) effect and will shift the AS curve to the ________ .

increase
left
the opposite
right

5-57

The second subcategory within the legal-institutional environment is government regulation. An increase in government regulation of business will ________ per unit costs of production and the AS curve will ________________ . Deregulation will ________ per unit costs of production and shift the AS curve ________ ward.

increase
shift to the left
decrease
right

Equilibrium

5-58

The real GDP along the aggregate-supply curve (or schedule) the economy will produce and the economy's price level depend upon the aggregate-demand curve (or schedule). The economy will tend to produce the real GDP at which the real GDP demanded equals the real GDP supplied for reasons made clear by using aggregate-demand and aggregate-supply curves.

Suppose aggregate demand is AD and aggregate supply is AS in the graph below.

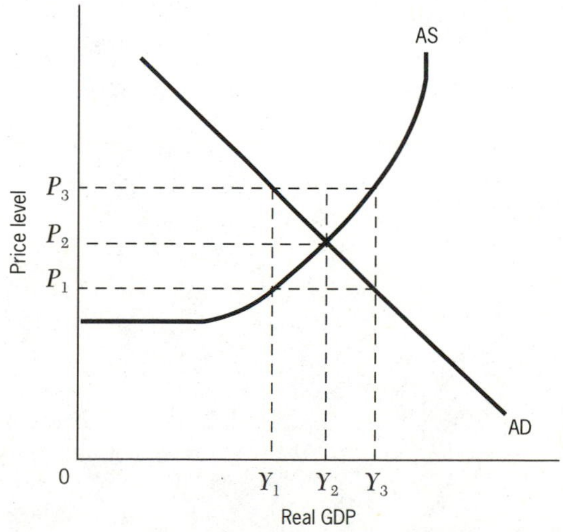

The equilibrium price level is ($P_1/P_2/P_3$) and the equilibrium real GDP is ($Y_1/Y_2/Y_3$).

But if the price level were P_1 the real GDP demanded (purchased) would be ($Y_1/Y_2/Y_3$) and the real GDP supplied (produced) would be ($Y_1/Y_2/Y_3$). At this price level (P_1) there would be a (shortage/surplus) of final goods and services equal to Y_3-Y_1.

P_2
Y_2
Y_3
Y_1, shortage

5-59

When there is a shortage of goods and services in the economy buyers bid the prices of goods and services (upward/downward). As the prices of goods and services are bid upward, producers will (increase/decrease) the quantities they supply (produce) and buyers will (increase/decrease) the quantities they demand (purchase); and the shortage will grow (larger/smaller).

upward
increase
decrease
smaller

5-60

When the price level has been bid upward to P_2 the shortage of final goods and services will have been eliminated.

But what if the price level had started at P_3? At this price level the real GDP supplied is ________ and the real GDP demanded is ________ ; and there is a (shortage/surplus) of goods and services equal to Y_3-Y_1.

Y_3
Y_1, surplus

5-61

A surplus of real GDP (more produced than purchased) may have one of two results.

Case I: Sellers of final goods and services may bid the price level (upward/downward). If this happens the real GDP demanded will (rise/fall), the real GDP supplied will (rise/fall), and the surplus will grow (larger/smaller).

When the price level has been bid downward to P_2, the surplus will have been eliminated and the real GDP demanded and the real GDP supplied will both equal ________ .

downward
rise, fall
smaller
Y_2

5-62

Case II: A surplus of real GDP may not induce sellers to lower their prices. Producers may decide to keep their prices at the existing level; and the price level will, therefore, remain at P_3.

At P_3 the real GDP demanded (purchased) will equal (Y_1/Y_2/Y_3) and to avoid producing more than they can sell the suppliers of final goods and services will reduce their output to (Y_1/Y_2/Y_3).

In this case the *equilibrium* real GDP is ________ .

Y_1
Y_1
Y_1

5-63

The fact that (in the United States, at least) the price level *rises* when there are shortages of final goods and services (when the real GDP demanded exceeds the real GDP supplied) and *does not fall* (to any great extent) when there are surpluses of final goods and services is called the ***ratchet effect***.

We'll have occasion later to look at the consequences of the irreversibility problem—of the ratchet effect.

For the moment, however, all we need to recall is that the ratchet effect means that the price level is (flexible/inflexible) *upward* but is (flexible/inflexible) *downward*.

flexible
inflexible

INFLATION AND UNEMPLOYMENT

Inflation is a rise in the price level in the economy. From Section 3 you learned what causes the price of a particular product to rise: an increase in demand *or* a decrease in supply. The same economic principle applies to the price level of an economy. An increase in aggregate demand or a decrease in aggregate supply may cause inflation.

There are, therefore, two kinds of inflation: demand-pull and cost-push inflation. Let's look at each of them in turn.

5-64

On the graph below is an aggregate-supply curve (AS) and an aggregate-demand curve (AD_1).

The aggregate-demand and aggregate-supply curves intersect in the

Keynesian ______________ range along the aggregate-supply curve.

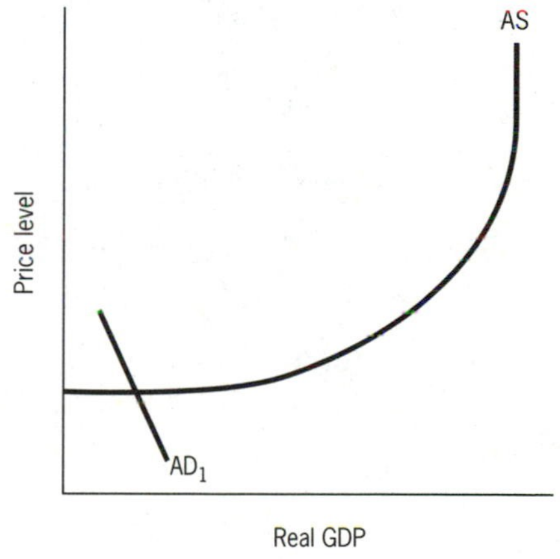

5-65

Draw in on the graph in frame **5-64** an aggregate-demand curve which lies to the right of AD_1 but still intersects AS in the Keynesian range. You may label this new aggregate-demand curve AD_2.

increase — The movement of aggregate demand from AD_1 to AD_2 is a(n) (increase/decrease) in aggregate demand.

left unchanged — This increase in aggregate demand has (increased/decreased/left unchanged) the equilibrium price level and has

increased ______________ the equilibrium real GDP.

5-66

has not — The increase in aggregate demand from AD_1 to AD_2 (has/has not) resulted in inflation because the increase in aggregate demand (was/was

was not — not) large enough to take the economy out of the Keynesian range.

It did, however, increase the real GDP and so resulted in a(n)

decrease — (increase/decrease/no change) in the amount of *un*employment in the economy.

5-67

But suppose aggregate demand had increased from AD_3 to AD_4, on the graph below.

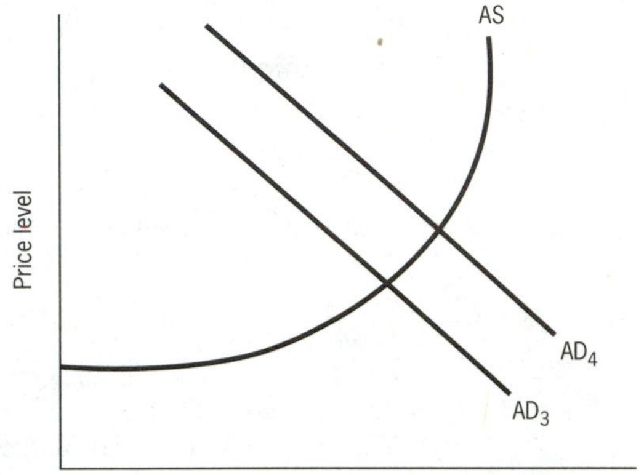

Regardless of whether aggregate demand is AD_3 or AD_4, the economy will produce in the ______________ range along the aggregate-supply curve.

intermediate

The increase in aggregate demand from AD_3 to AD_4, has (increased/decreased/left unchanged) the price level and (has/has not) been inflationary. It has also ______________ the real GDP.

increased, has

increased

5-68

Suppose on the graph below aggregate demand increases from AD_5 to AD_6.

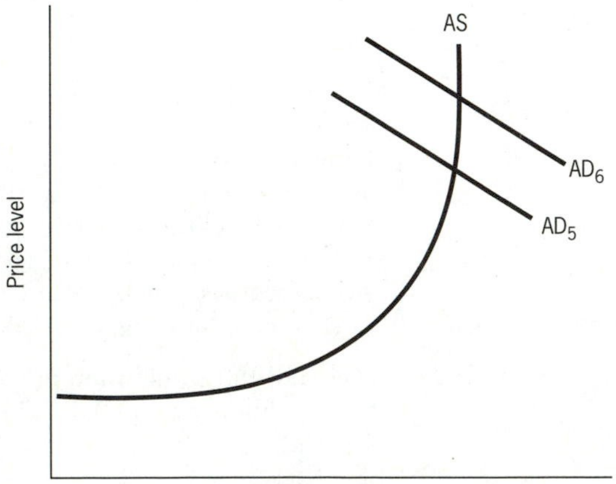

The price level will (rise/fall/remain constant) and this increase in aggregate demand (will/will not) be inflationary.

rise

will

The equilibrium real GDP has (risen/fallen/remained constant) because both aggregate-demand curves intersect along the aggregate-supply curve's ______________ range.

remained constant

classical

equal to

No matter whether aggregate demand is AD_5 or AD_6, the economy will produce an output which is (less than/equal to) its full-employment output.

5-69

Let's summarize what we have learned about the effects of increases in aggregate demand on the price level and the real GDP. On the graph below we have the aggregate-supply curve and all six of the aggregate-demand curves we drew in frames **5-64**, **5-67**, and **5-68**.

An increase in aggregate demand will increase the price level and be inflationary when the economy is producing in:

(a) the Keynesian range
(b) the intermediate range
(c) the classical range
(d) either the intermediate or classical range

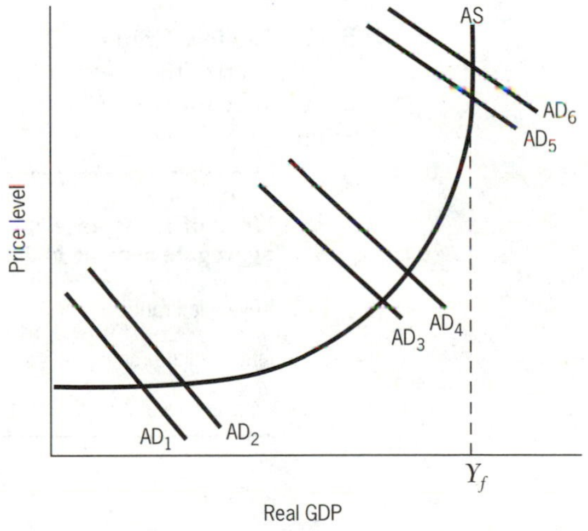

(d)

Which one? ____________

But an increase in aggregate demand will not be inflationary when the

Keynesian

economy continues to produce in the ____________ range.

5-70

An increase in aggregate demand will also increase the real GDP and reduce unemployment in the economy when the economy is producing in:

(a) the Keynesian range
(b) the intermediate range
(c) the classical range
(d) either the Keynesian or intermediate range

(d) Which one? ____________

But an increase in aggregate demand will not expand real GDP and reduce unemployment if the economy is already producing in the

classical ____________ range.

5-71

In short: An increase in aggregate demand in the Keynesian range

real GDP will increase the (price level/real GDP) and have no effect on the

price level ____________ ____________ ;

the price level and in the intermediate range will increase both ____________

the real GDP ____________ ;

price level in the classical range will increase the ____________ ____________

real GDP and have no effect on the ____________ ____________ .

5-72 Review Frame

To summarize the effects of increases in aggregate demand, complete the table below. Use + to mean increase, − to mean decrease, and 0 to mean no change.

	Effect of an increase in aggregate demand in the	On the Price level	On the Real GDP
0, +	Keynesian range	______	______
+, +	Intermediate range	______	______
+, 0	Classical range	______	______

5-73 Review Frame

No matter what you said, go on. Do you know what causes an increase in aggregate demand? (Yes/No)

5-74 Review Frame

If you said "Yes," good! But if you said "No," you have just forgotten the things you learned in frames **5-16** to **5-38**. Let's take several frames to review what you learned there.

An increase in total or aggregate spending *at any price level* will increase the real GDP the spenders in the economy wish to have produced.

Total spending $= C + I_g + G + X_n$

C Therefore, the real GDP demanded will increase when ____________ ,

I_g, G, X_n (any order) or ____________ , or ____________ , or ____________ increase; and vice versa.

5-75 Review Frame

What might cause C to increase? If the wealth of consumers increases they will spend (more/less) for C.

If personal taxes increase, take-home income (increases/decreases) and C will (increase/decrease).

But if personal taxes decrease, take-home income ____________ and C will ____________.

more
decreases
decrease
increases
increase

5-76 Review Frame

What might cause I to increase? I (spending for additional capital goods) is (directly/inversely) related to the rate of interest.

I will (increase/decrease) when profit expectations increase.

But even if profit expectations don't change, I will increase when the rate of interest (rises/falls) and decrease when the rate of interest ____________.

inversely
increase
falls
rises

5-77 Review Frame

Total spending and the real GDP demanded at any price level will increase as a result of any one of the following.

A(n) (increase/decrease) in taxes

A(n) ____________ in investment (I_g)

A(n) ____________ in G

A(n) ____________ in X_n

A(n) ____________ in the rate of interest

decrease
increase
increase
increase
decrease

5-78 Review Frame

The principal causes of increases in total spending and the real GDP demanded are increases in ____________, ____________, ____________, and ____________ and decreases in * ____________________.

C, I_g, G
X_n (any order), the rate of interest

This completes our review of the causes of increases in aggregate demand and our examination of demand-pull inflation and unemployment.

5-79

An increase in the price of a particular good or service may be the result of an increase in the demand for that good or service.

But an increase in its price may also be the result of a(n) (increase/decrease) in the supply of the good or service.

When aggregate supply decreases the price level will (rise/fall).

This kind of inflation is called (demand-pull/cost-push) inflation.

decrease
rise
cost-push

5-80

On the graph below are two aggregate-supply and three aggregate-demand curves. The leftward movement of the aggregate-supply curve from AS_1 to AS_2 is a decrease in aggregate supply.

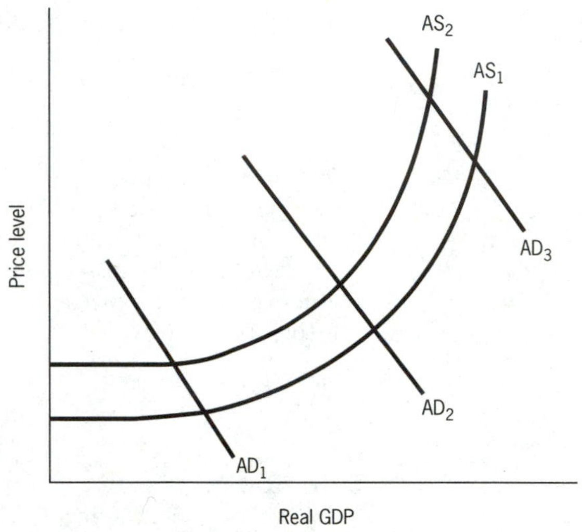

smaller

At every price level the quantity of final goods and services (real GDP) that producers will make available has become (larger/smaller).

higher

The prices which producers must receive to induce them to produce any given real GDP have become (higher/lower).

raise, contract

Regardless of the level of aggregate demand, the decrease in aggregate supply from AS_1 to AS_2 will (raise/lower) the price level and (expand/contract) the real GDP.

5-81

Aggregate supply in the American economy decreased during the 1970s for a number of reasons which we won't explore in detail.

increased

Increases in the prices charged by OPEC for oil, higher prices for agricultural products that resulted from poor harvests throughout the world, rises in the prices of goods and services imported from abroad, and expected inflation all decreased aggregate supply because they all (increased/decreased) the costs of producing goods and services in the United States.

5-82

decrease, price level, real GDP

In short, increases in the costs of producing goods and services (increase/decrease) aggregate supply and tend to increase the (price level/real GDP) and to decrease the ______________ ______________ .

will, will

Said another way, increases in costs (a decrease in aggregate supply) (will/will not) be inflationary and (will/will not) lead to more *un*employment in the economy.

5-83

Let's focus our attention on the intermediate range along the aggregate-supply curve (because this is the range in which the American economy has operated in recent years). Along this range:

increase — An increase in aggregate demand will (increase/decrease) the price

increase — level and ____________ the real GDP.

increase — But a decrease in aggregate supply will ____________ the price

decrease — level and ____________ the real GDP.

5-84

When inflation is the result of an increase in aggregate demand real GDP

expand — and employment will (expand/contract); but when inflation is the result of a decrease in aggregate supply real GDP and employment will

contract — ____________ .

5-85

Inflation accompanied by rising real GDP and employment is the result

increases, demand — of ____________ in aggregate ____________ , and inflation accom-

decreases — panied by falling real GDP and employment is the result of ____________

supply — in aggregate ____________ .

5-86

The inflation accompanied by falling real GDP and employment is called *stagflation* and is the result of * ______________________________

decreases in aggregate supply (increases in costs) — ______________________________ .

5-87

Stagflation has only been a problem in the American economy since the 1970s. Before then higher prices were mostly accompanied by higher levels of real GDP and employment and were the result of

increases, aggregate demand — (increases/decreases) in ____________ ____________ .

5-88

But since the 1970s and until the early 1980s—and again in 1990—the higher price levels were accompanied by lower levels of real GDP and

stagflation — employment. This is called ____________ and was the consequence

decreases, aggregate supply — of ____________ in ____________ ____________ .

5-89 Review Frame

Let's review the differences between the two kinds of inflation.

an increase in aggregate demand, | Demand-pull inflation is the result of * ______________________

real GDP and employment | and is accompanied by rising * ______________________ .

a decrease in aggregate supply, | Cost-push inflation is the result of * ______________________

real GDP and employment | and is accompanied by falling * ______________________ .

5-90 Review Frame

Suppose the economy is producing in the intermediate range along the aggregate-supply curve. Use + (for increase), − (for decrease) and 0 (for no change) to complete the following table.

Answer	Effect of	On price level	On real GDP
+, +	Increase in aggregate demand	______	______
+, −	Decrease in aggregate supply	______	______

5-91 Review Frame

Either an increase in aggregate demand or a decrease in aggregate supply will result in inflation. When, however, the inflation is demand-

increase | pull inflation the real GDP and employment will ____________ but when the inflation is cost-push inflation the real GDP and employment

decrease | will ____________ .

Now take the Review Test for Section 5 at the back of the book.

National Income Analysis

section 6

DOMESTIC OUTPUT AND AGGREGATE EXPENDITURES

Economists employ national income accounting to *measure* the overall performance of an economy. The most all-inclusive figure they calculate is GDP.

But economists do more than just measure the GDP. They also *explain* what determines how large a GDP the economy will tend to produce in any given year. The GDP produced in any year is called the economy's ***domestic output***. In this section we will define the economy's domestic output as its *real* GDP.

This explanation of what determines the size of an economy's real GDP or domestic output is called ***national income analysis***, or national income theory. Sometimes it is called the theory of employment because the explanation of what determines the domestic output or real GDP is also used to explain how many workers will be employed and unemployed in the nation.

In this section we want to examine this explanation of our GDP and learn two principal things: *First*, what determines the size of our real GDP; and *second*, why real GDP changes from year to year. This theory or explanation is called the Keynesian theory because it is based upon (and has its origins in) the writings of the British economist, John Maynard Keynes.

6-1

The quantity of final goods and services an economy produces in any year is its domestic output.

We have agreed in this section to call the economy's domestic output

GDP — its real ___________ .

6-2

To reduce the number of words we use in our explanation of what determines the size of the economy's domestic output or real GDP, let's drop the word *real* and refer simply to the GDP of the economy.

But where you see the term GDP, you will recall that we are talking

real — about the ___________ GDP.

has — And you will remember (from Section 4) that this means that the GDP (has/had not) been adjusted for any changes that may have taken place in the price level in the economy.

6-3

The GDP produced by an economy in any year depends upon how much money people spend for goods and services in that year.

larger — The greater the amount of total spending in the economy, the (larger/lower) will be the economy's GDP. But the smaller the total spending,

lower — the (larger/lower) is its GDP.

6-4

direct — In short, the relationship between total spending and the GDP is (direct/inverse).

6-5

Economists have a special name for the total amount people want to spend for the economy's output of final goods and services. They call this amount ***aggregate expenditures*** (AE).

The economy's output of final goods and services is its domestic output

GDP — or ______________ .

larger — The higher the level of AE the (smaller/larger) will be the domestic output. Similarly, a fall in AE will cause the domestic output to (rise/

fall — fall).

6-6

Who buys the final goods and services produced in an economy? What groups spend for the GDP? Total spending for the GDP of the American economy in 1991 is shown in the table.

Class of expenditure	Amount (billions)
Personal consumption expenditures	$3,887
Gross private domestic investment	725
Government purchases	1,087
Net exports	− 27
Total spending	$5,672

four — You can see that there were (how many) ______________ kinds of spending that added up to the total spending for the GDP, which was

5,672 — $______________ billion.

6-7

Each of the four kinds of spending is done by a different group. These groups are:

Consumers whose spending is called *consumption* (C)
Business firms whose spending is called *gross investment* (I_g)
Governments whose spending is called *government purchases* (G)
Foreigners whose spending is called *net exports* (X_n)

AE | Complete the formula: $C + I_g + G + X_n =$ ________ .

6-8
The total spending done in the economy is done entirely by these four groups of spenders. If you will look at the spending figures in frame **6-6** you will see that:

governments | $1,087 billion was the amount spent by ________
consumers | $3,887 billion was the amount spent by ________
foreigners | $27 billion was the amount spent by ________
business firms | $725 billion was the amount spent by ________

6-9
Because there are only four kinds of spending and four groups of spenders in the economy, AE has only four components:

$$AE = C + I_g + G + X_n$$

C represents the spending of consumers and is called * ________
consumption | ________ .
gross | I_g is the spending done by firms and is called * ________
investment | ________ .
government | G is what is spent by governments and is called * ________
purchases | ________ .
net | X_n is the spending done by foreigners and is called * ________
exports | ________ .

6-10
To summarize:

direct | There is a(n) (direct/inverse) relationship between AE and GDP.

consumption, gross investment, government purchases, net exports | AE has only four components: * ________
____
________ .

CONSUMPTION AND SAVING

6-11
Now, let's turn our attention to what determines the amount each of the four groups of spenders is going to spend for final goods and services.

Let's start with the biggest group of spenders in the economy, the group that spends over twice as much as the other three groups combined. Can you guess which group this is? ______

consumers

In order to simplify our discussion of what determines the amount consumers spend, let's make four unrealistic assumptions about the economy:

1. Governments collect *no taxes* of any kind.
2. Firms and governments make *no transfer payments*.
3. There are *no undistributed corporate profits*. Corporations pay out as dividends all their profits to stockholders.
4. Consumption of fixed capital (depreciation) and net American income earned abroad are *both zero*.

What are the relationships between GDP, NDP, NI, PI, and DI in such a hypothetical economy? Look at the national income accounting figures for this kind of economy in the table.

Gross domestic product (GDP)	$600
Minus: Consumption of fixed capital	−0
Net domestic product (NDP)	$600
Plus: Net American income earned abroad	+0
Minus: Indirect business taxes	−0
National income (NI)	$600
Minus: Social security contributions	−0
Minus: Corporate income taxes	−0
Minus: Undistributed corporate profits	−0
Plus: Transfer payments	+0
Personal income (PI)	$600
Minus: Personal taxes	−0
Disposable income (DI)	$600

The four assumptions we have made simply mean that the GDP, NDP, NI, PI, and DI are all the same. When we speak of the GDP we are also talking about DI and when we say DI we mean the GDP too.

6-12

The amount that consumers spend in any year depends upon a great many things; but the most important is the amount of DI they have to spend.

The relationship between DI and consumption spending (C) is shown in a ***consumption schedule:***

DI (=GDP)	C
$400	$400
410	408
420	416
430	424
440	432
450	440
460	448
470	456

more
smaller
direct

As you can see, the more DI consumers have, the (more/less) they spend for consumption and the smaller their DI, the (larger/smaller) is their consumption spending. In short, the relation between DI and *C* is (direct/inverse).

6-13

You may recall from what you learned about national income accounting that there are only two things people can do with DI: spend it (for goods and services) or save it. We can find out how much consumers save of

C, DI

each DI by subtracting __________ from __________ .

6-14

Saving (*S*) is simply DI not spent for *C*. Using the consumption schedule in frame **6-12**, determine how much consumers save at each of the eight levels of DI.

	DI (=GDP)	C	S
$ 0	$400	$400	$______
2	410	408	______
4	420	416	______
6	430	424	______
8	440	432	______
10	450	440	______
12	460	448	______
14	470	456	______

6-15

Look now at the DI and *S* columns in the preceding frame. The DI and *S* columns together are called the ***saving schedule***.

increases
direct

You will observe that as DI increases, *S* (increases/decreases), and vice versa; and the relation between *S* and DI is (direct/inverse).

6-16

To review: The most important factor determining how much consumers

disposable
income

will spend and save is the amount of their ______________________ __________ .

consumption
saving

The schedule which indicates how much consumers will spend at various levels of DI is called the __________ schedule, and how much they will save at various levels of DI is called the __________ schedule.

6-17

Continuing our review:

consumption — Saving is equal to DI minus ______. When DI increases, both

in- — C and S ______-crease, and vice versa. The relationship between

direct — DI and C is ______. The relationship between DI and S is

direct — ______.

6-18

A picture is often worth a thousand words, and economists find it very useful to have graphical pictures of the consumption and saving schedules. So let's plot this consumption schedule on the graph below. Connect the dots with a line.

DI (=GDP)	C	S
$ 50	$ 60	−$10
100	100	0
150	140	10
200	180	20
250	220	30
300	260	40
350	300	50
400	340	60

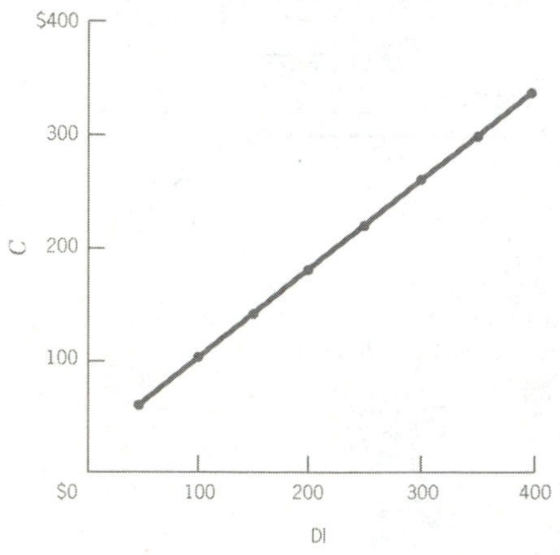

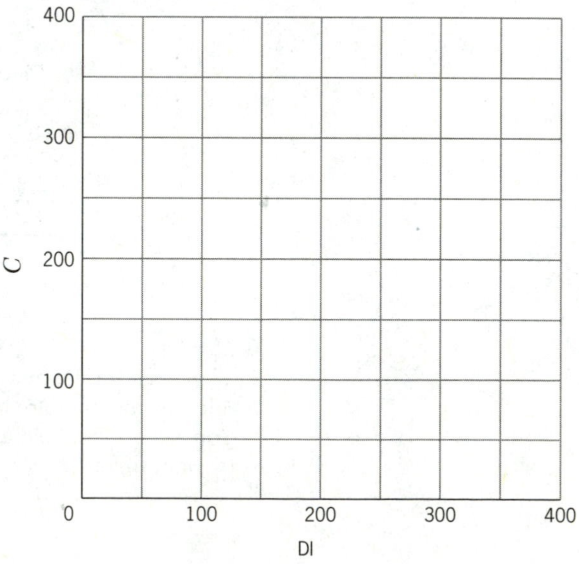

6-19

From the way this graph is set up, you can see that the economist plots

vertical, horizontal — C along the (vertical/horizontal) axis and DI along the ______ axis. By connecting the eight points you plotted with a line, you drew a ***consumption curve***. Because the relation between C and DI is a direct one,

upward — the consumption curve slopes (upward/downward) from left to right.

6-20

Let's look back at the consumption and saving schedules in frame **6-18**.

We already know that saving is simply DI not spent for consumption: S = DI − C.

greater

S turns out to be a negative (or minus) amount whenever C is (greater/less) than DI.

low

S tends to be negative at relatively (high/low) levels of DI.

less
high

Similarly, S is a positive amount whenever C is (greater/less) than DI, which happens at relatively (high/low) levels of DI.

6-21

Suppose DI is $100 (refer to frame **6-18**).

zero
equal

S will be (positive/negative/zero) because C and DI are ________ .

6-22

Just as we can put C and DI on a graph and call it the consumption curve, we can also put S and DI on a graph.

horizontal
vertical

We again plot DI on the ________ axis, and put S on the ________ axis.

6-23

Now plot the saving schedule in frame **6-18** on the graph below.

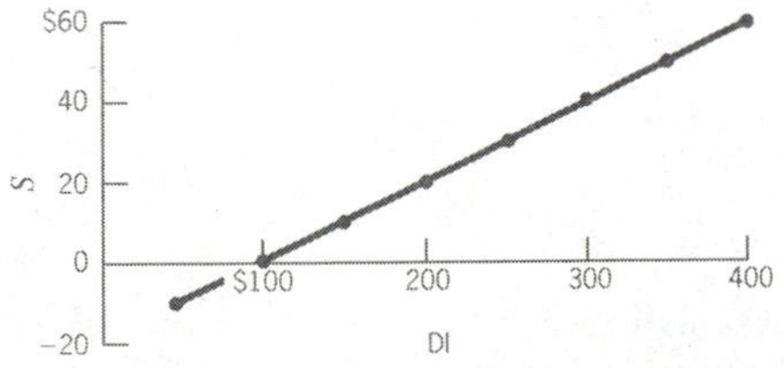

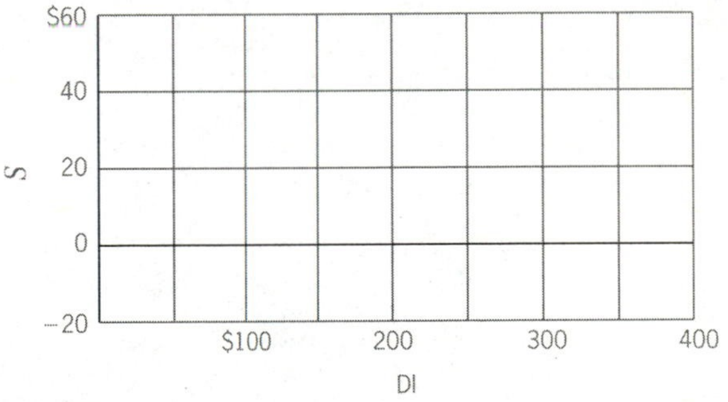

6-24

By connecting the eight points from the saving schedule which you just plotted, you will obtain a curve.

saving
upward
direct

We call this the ________ curve. This curve slopes (upward/downward) from left to right because the relation between S and DI is (direct/inverse).

6-25

On the following graph is plotted a consumption curve. Also plotted on this graph is a second curve which is labeled $C + S$.

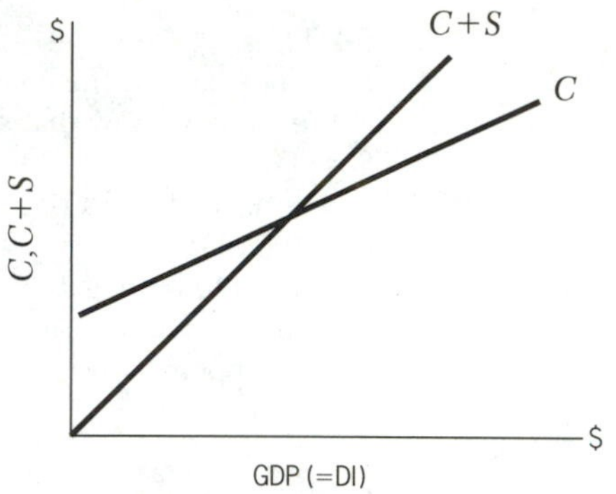

The $C + S$ curve indicates the amount spent on consumption *plus* the amount saved at each DI (or GDP). Because there are only two things people can do with their DI, whatever the level of their disposable

equal — income, $C + S$ and DI are always ________ .

6-26

A $C + S$ *schedule* would indicate the total amount of consumption *and* saving at various levels of DI. Complete the following schedule.

(answer)	DI	C + S
$ 40	$ 40	$______
80	80	______
120	120	______
160	160	______
200	200	______
240	240	______
280	280	______

6-27

The $C + S$ curve or schedule seems like rather a silly thing to bother with because all it says is that regardless of how much DI is, $C + S$ will equal it. But the $C + S$ curve does have several uses. Our discussion of the use to which we can put the $C + S$ curve will have to wait until later on in this section.

For the present we can observe that the vertical distance between the C and the $C + S$ curves *is* S. And where the $C + S$ curve:

positive — is above the C curve, S is (positive/negative zero),

negative — is below the C curve, S is (positive/negative/zero),

zero — crosses the C curve, S is (positive/negative/zero).

6-28

Just to be sure you understand how we can use the $C + S$ curve, look at the graph that follows:

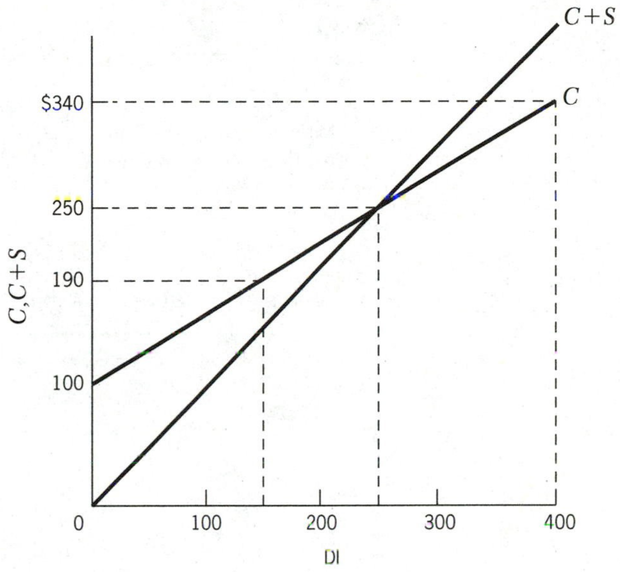

When C is:

–$40 $190, S is equal to $________,

$0 $250, S is equal to $________,

$60 $340, S is equal to $________.

6-29

If you would like to test yourself, sketch in on the blank graph: a C curve, an S curve, and a $C + S$ curve. Make sure that the C and the S curves show saving is zero at the *same* DI.

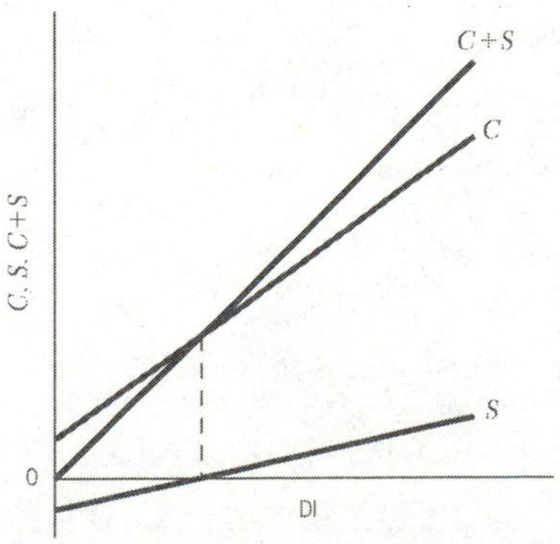

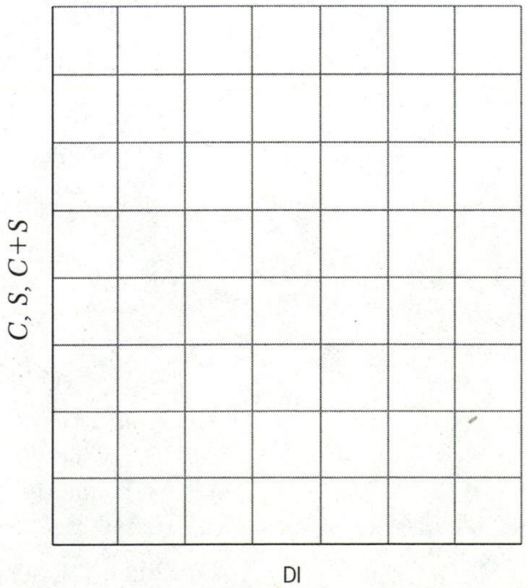

up- The C curve you have drawn should slope ________-ward, as should the S curve.

6-30

$0 The *C* curve crosses the *C* + *S* curve when *S* is equal to $________

DI (disposable income) and *C* is equal to ________ .

negative When *C* is greater than DI, *S* is (positive/negative), and when *C* is less

positive then DI, *S* is (positive/negative).

6-31

Below is another set of consumption and saving schedules.

DI (=GDP)	C	S
$100	$110	−$10
150	150	0
200	190	10
250	230	20
300	270	30
350	310	40
400	350	50
450	390	60

You can see that there are no savings when DI and *C* are equal at

$150, 100 $________ . At this level, ________ percent of the DI is spent for consumption.

6-32

Economists call the percentage (or fraction) of DI spent for consumption the ***average propensity to consume*** (APC). The percentage (or fraction) of DI saved is called the ***average propensity to save*** (APS). When

0 DI is $150, the percentage of DI saved is ________ percent.

6-33

If you spent 75 percent of your DI for consumption and saved the

average other 25 percent, 75 percent would be your ________

propensity ________ to consume, and 25 percent would be your

average propensity ________ ________ to save.

6-34

To find the APC, *divide* the amount of consumption by the DI.

To find the APS, *divide* the amount of saving by the DI.

When you look back at the schedules in frame **6-31** you find that

90 when DI is $300, the APC is ________ percent, the APS is

10 ________ percent, and the APC *plus* the APS is equal to

100 ________ percent.

6-35

The APC and the APS are sometimes expressed as decimals: an APC of 90 percent is expressed as 0.90, and an APS of 10 percent becomes 0.10.

Still using the schedules in frame **6-31**: 87½ percent of the $400 DI is consumed and 12½ percent is saved.

Expressed in decimals:

0.875 The APC is ________ .

0.125 The APS is ________ .

1.000 The sum of the APC and the APS is ________ .

6-36

Here are the same consumption and saving schedules with the APC and the APS at each DI also given:

DI (=GDP)	C	APC	S	APS
$100	$110	1.10	−$10	−0.10
150	150	1.00	0	0.00
200	190	.95	10	.05
250	230	.92	20	.08
300	270	.90	30	.10
350	310	.886	40	.114
400	350	.875	50	.125
450	390	.867	60	.133

smaller, larger As you can see, the larger the DI, the (larger/smaller) is the APC, and the (larger/smaller) is the APS.

6-37

rises, falls; opposite When DI falls the APC (rises/falls) and the APS (rises/falls). If DI changes, the APC and the APS move in the (same/opposite) direction,

1.00, 100 but the APC plus the APS always equal ________ , or ________ percent.

6-38

People with low incomes tend to spend a larger percentage of their incomes and to save a smaller percentage than do people with higher incomes. In fact, at very low incomes consumers sometimes spend amounts which are greater than their incomes.

negative, greater; less Whenever consumers spend more than their incomes we find that the amount they save is (positive/negative), their APC is (greater/less) than 1.0, and their APS is (greater/less) than 0.0.

6-39

Let's examine another set of consumption and saving schedules:

DI (=GDP)	C	S
$300	$300	$ 0
320	319	1
340	337	3
360	354	6
380	370	10
400	385	15
420	399	21
440	412	28

When the DI of consumers changes, both *C* and *S* also change. The change in *C* is never so large as the change in DI.

For example, if DI increases from $320 to $340, *C* increases from

$319, $337, $20 $________ to $________. The increase in DI is $________,

$18 but the increase in C is only $________.

6-40

When DI changes, the change in *S* is also never so large as the change in DI.

Assume DI decreases from $440 to $420: *S* will decrease from

$28, $21 $________ to $________. The change in DI is $20, but the

$7 change in *S* is only $________.

6-41

When DI increased by $20 from $320 to $340, *C* increased by $18, an amount equal to 90 percent of the increase in DI.

Economists call the *percentage* of any change in DI by which *C* changes, the ***marginal propensity to consume*** (MPC).

To find the MPC we *divide* the change in *C* by the change in DI. For example, when DI changes between $420 and $440, the MPC is equal to

$$\frac{\text{the change in } C}{\text{the change in DI}} = \frac{\$13}{\$20} = 65 \text{ percent}$$

And when DI changes between $360 and $380 the MPC is equal to

80 ________ percent.

6-42

Economists likewise call the percentage of any change in DI by which *S* changes the ***marginal propensity to save*** (MPS). To compute the MPS they *divide* the change in *S* *by* the change in DI. If the DI changes between \$420 and \$440, the MPS is equal to

$$\frac{\text{the change in } S}{\text{the change in DI}} = \frac{\$\ 7}{\$20} = 35 \text{ percent}$$

20 Between the DIs of \$360 and \$380, the MPS is ________ percent.

6-43

Look at the schedules in frame **6-39** once more. Between the DIs of

85 \$340 and \$360, the MPC is ________ percent, the MPS is

15, 100 ________ percent, and the MPC plus the MPS is ________ percent.

6-44

For simplicity, economists usually express the MPC and the MPS not as percentages but as decimals. An MPC of 70 percent is written 0.70 and MPS of 30 percent is written 0.30.

Between the DIs of \$360 and \$380, expressed in decimals, the MPC

0.80, 0.20 is ________ , the MPS is ________ , and the MPC + MPS is

1.00 ________ .

6-45

You may have noticed that the MPC plus the MPS is always 100 percent, or 1.00. Why? Because there are only two things consumers can do with their DIs or with any increases in their DIs: spend or save. And the percentage they consume plus the percentage they save have to add up to the total of 100 percent. Knowing this will save you a little time.

If you know that the MPC is 0.60, you almost automatically know that

0.40 the MPS is ________ , or if you know that the MPS is 0.15, you will

0.85 also know that the MPC is ________ .

6-46

de- Earlier we discovered that when DI increases, the APC ________-creases

in- and the APS ________-creases, and vice versa.

What about the MPC and the MPS? Do they change as DI rises and falls? Perhaps they do, and in the examples we have employed the MPC either decreased or remained the same as the DI increased. And the MPS either increased or remained constant as DI increased.

But because it isn't too far from the truth and because it makes things easier for us, let's just assume that the MPC and the MPS *do not change* when DI changes.

6-47 Review Frame

Now let's briefly review what we have just learned about the "propensities." You can test yourself and discover if you understand them.

In your own words, how would you define or compute:

A percentage or fraction of DI spent for *C* (divide *C* by DI).

The APC: * ______________________________

A percentage or fraction of DI saved (divide *S* by DI).

The APS: * ______________________________

A percentage or fraction of change in DI spent for consumption (divide change in *C* by change in DI).

The MPC: * ______________________________

A percentage or fraction of change in DI saved (divide change in *S* by change in DI).

The MPS: * ______________________________

6-48 Review Frame

decrease — rise — 100 — 100

The APC tends to (increase/decrease) as DI increases, and vice versa. The APS tends to (rise/fall) as the DI rises, and vice versa. The APC plus the APS are equal to __________ percent. The MPC plus the MPS are equal to __________ percent.

6-49 Review Frame

can — less — more

The APC (can/cannot) be greater than 1.00. The APS is less than zero when the amount of *S* is (more/less) than zero. The APC is greater than 1.00 when *C* is (more/less) than DI.

The most important determinant of the amount consumers spend and the amount they save is the level of DI. But there are determinants other than DI which affect *C* and *S*. These other determinants are called the ***nonincome determinants*** of *C* and *S*.

These factors are familiar to us from our discussion of them in Section 5 in a slightly different context when analyzing the factors that shift the aggregate demand curve. Our interest now is in how these factors affect the *C*-DI and the *S*-DI relationships.

6-50

less — decreases — increases — down, up

The more ***wealth*** people have, the (more/less) they feel the need to save. Thus, as wealth increases, *S* (increases/decreases) as a percentage of DI and *C* __________. Alternatively expressed an increase in wealth shifts the *S* schedule (up/down) and the *C* schedule __________.

6-51

down
decreases

An increase in the ***price level*** tends to shift the *C* schedule (up/down) ward because an increase in the price level (increases/decreases) the real value or purchasing power of financial assets (such as bonds) whose values are fixed in nominal (money) terms. This is the ________ effect of Section 5.

wealth

6-52

increase
decrease
increase
decrease

Expectations are the third nonincome determinant of *C* and *S*. If consumers expect prices to rise in the near future they will (increase/decrease) their present spending and ________ their present *S*. If incomes are expected to rise shortly, *C* will ________ now and *S* will ________ .

6-53

less
up

Indebtedness is the fourth nonincome determinant of *C* and *S*. The more consumers are in debt the (more/less) they will consume now. Thus, high consumer indebtedness will shift the *S* schedule ________ ward.

6-54

decrease

Since disposable income (DI) is personal income (PI) *after* payment of ***personal taxes***, an increase in such taxes will (increase/decrease) DI. The effect this will have on *C* and *S* will be analyzed later in this section.

6-55

In the following table are two sets of schedules for consumption and saving.

Set number 1			Set number 2		
DI	C	S	DI	C	S
$100	$110	−$10	$100	$120	−$20
150	150	0	150	160	− 10
200	190	10	200	200	0
250	230	20	250	240	10
300	270	30	300	280	20

more
less

At every level of DI in set number 2, *C* is (more/less) than it is in set number 1, and *S* is (more/less) than it is in set number 1.

6-56

increased
decreased

If the consumption and saving schedules changed from those in set number 1 to those in set number 2, economists would say that the consumption schedule has (increased/decreased), and the saving schedule has (increased/decreased).

6-57

So an increase in the consumption schedule simply means that C at every level of DI has ________-creased. A decrease in the consumption schedule means that C at every DI has ________-creased.

in-
de-

6-58

Likewise, when the saving schedule increases, S at every DI (increases/decreases); when it decreases, S at every DI (increases/decreases).

increases
decreases

6-59

If you will look back at the two sets of schedules in frame **6-55**, you will see that whenever the C schedule increases, the S schedule (increases/decreases), and vice versa; and whenever the S schedule increases, the C schedule (increases/decreases).

In other words, when the two schedules change, they change in the (same/opposite) direction.

decreases
decreases
opposite

6-60

Because consumption and saving curves are simply graphs of the consumption and saving schedules, changes in the schedules bring about changes in the curves.

On the graphs below are two consumption and two saving curves.

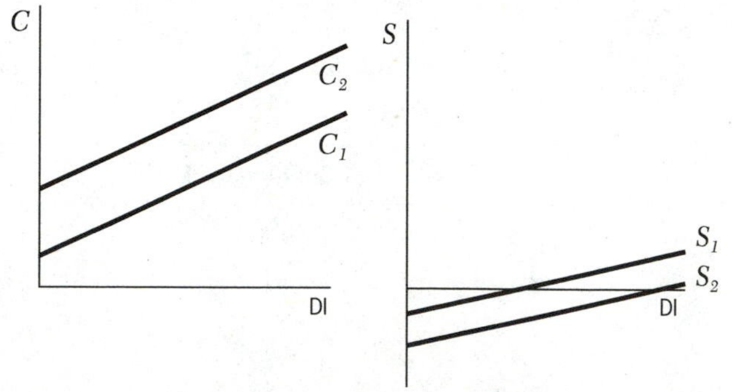

Consumption at every DI on C_2 is (greater/less) than it is on C_1. When the consumption schedule increases, the consumption curve moves (upward/downward).

greater
upward

6-61

If the saving curve were to move from S_1 to S_2, saving at every level of DI would (rise/fall). A decrease in the saving curve means that it moves (upward/downward).

fall
downward

6-62

In brief: When the consumption curve moves upward, the consumption schedule has (increased/decreased), and vice versa.

increased

When the saving curve moves upward, the saving schedule has (increased/decreased), and vice versa. If the saving curve were to move downward, the consumption curve would move ________-ward and vice versa.

increased

up-

6-63

When the consumer moves from one point to another on a stable *C* schedule, this is caused by a (change in disposable income/change in a nonincome determinant of consumption) and this is called a (change in consumption/change in amount consumed).

change in disposable income

change in amount consumed

6-64

When there is a shift up or down of an entire *C* schedule, this is caused by a (change in a disposable income/change in a nonincome determinant of consumption) and this is called a (change in consumption/change in amount consumed).

change in a nonincome determinant of consumption, change in consumption

6-65

The distinction in the previous frames between a "change in consumption" and "a change in amount consumed" (is/is not) similar to the distinction in Section 3 between a "change in demand" and a "change in quantity demanded."

is

INVESTMENT

The total amount of final goods and services an economy will produce in any year (GDP) depends upon the aggregate expenditures for these goods and services (AE). We have just examined consumption, the first of the four components of aggregate expenditures.

The second component of AE we are going to study is *gross investment* (I_g). *Investment* means spending by business firms for capital goods. Capital goods, or simply capital, include: *buildings*—homes, factories, stores, apartment houses, and offices; *equipment*—tools and machinery used by business firms to produce goods and services; *inventories*—goods which businesses keep in their warehouses and on their shelves.

Net investment spending is spending for additional capital. It *excludes* the spending for capital goods which merely replace other capital goods worn out or depreciated during the year.

Now let's find out how much money business firms will plan to spend for capital goods in any year: let's look at the determinants of I_g. After we have done this, we can then see how large the economy's output of final goods and services is going to be.

6-66

Business executives try to earn profits for their firms; they purchase additional capital for the firm only when they expect to earn a profit by buying it.

A firm is considering the purchase of a new drill press which it expects will yield an additional profit of $800. It is also considering the purchase of a new stamping machine which it expects would result in a loss of $600.

would
would not

The firm (would/would not) purchase the drill press and (would/would not) purchase the stamping machine.

6-67

Another firm that manufactures buttons is contemplating the acquisition of a new machine at a cost of $1,000. During the machine's estimated life span, the new machine will enable the firm to produce and sell more buttons, bringing in an additional $2,300 of revenue. To do this, the firm must spend an extra $1,100 for the plastics, labor, and electricity needed to produce the additional buttons. By purchasing the new machine, the firm expects to earn an additional profit of ($2,300/1,200/1,100/200) during the life span of the machine.

$200

$$\begin{array}{r} \$2,300 \\ -1,100 \\ \hline \$1,200 \\ -1,000 \\ \hline = \$200 \end{array}$$

6-68

expects to
profit
will

This additional profit of $200 is the extra profit the firm (does/expects to) earn. Since the new machine is expected to produce a (profit/loss), the firm probably (will/will not) buy this machine.

6-69

By putting up a new building that costs $5 million, a manufacturer of automobile bumpers expects to have additional sales revenue of $14 million; additional expenses for labor and materials will come to $10 million.

loss

The firm's expected (profit/loss) from the construction of this building

$1, would not

is $________ million. The firm (would/would not) add this building to its facilities.

6-70

Businesses never know for certain whether the purchase of additional capital will result in a future profit or a loss. Their decision to buy or not to buy the capital good must depend upon the profit or loss which they

expect (estimate forecast, etc.)

______________ .

6-71

Firms will buy a capital good if they believe the purchase will result in

profit

a ______________ . And they will not purchase capital if they believe it

loss

will result in a ______________ .

6-72

A department store is planning to spend $100,000 to increase its inventory of furniture and appliances. The store expects to be able to sell this inventory for $130,000. But it believes it will have to hire additional salespeople at a cost of $20,000 to help it dispose of the inventory.

The firm will choose to acquire this inventory because the expected

profit | ______________ from its acquisition is $10,000.

6-73

But if the cost of the inventory were to increase to $120,000, the firm's

loss, $10,000 | expected (profit/loss) would be $______________ and the firm (would/
would not | would not) acquire it.

Similarly, if the cost of the inventory were to decrease to $90,000, the

$20,000 | expected profit would be $______________ and the firm (would/would
would | not) buy it.

6-74

Suppose the cost of the inventory were $100,000 and the expected revenue from the sale of the inventory were to change.

If it fell from $130,000 to $115,000, the expected profit would (rise/
fall, would not | fall) and the firm (would/would not) purchase the inventory. And if it rose from $130,000 to $135,000, the firm would still purchase the inven-
$15,000 | tory but its expected profit would be $______________ instead of $10,000.

6-75

In deciding whether to invest in additional capital, a business firm con-
expected | siders the (actual/expected) profit from the extra capital.
decrease | Any *increase* in its anticipated expenses will (increase/decrease) this
increase | profit, and any *increase* in the anticipated revenue will (increase/decrease) this profit.

in- | Decreases in anticipated expenses ________-crease this profit, and de-
de- | creases in anticipated revenue ________-crease this profit.

6-76

Many factors influence the profits expected by a business firm from the purchase of more capital goods. One of the factors which has an important influence on a firm's expected profit is the price it has to *pay* for the use of money. The price a firm pays for the use of money is called
interest rate | the (interest rate/tax rate).

6-77

costs | When the interest rate, or *i*, increases, a firm's expected (costs/revenues)
fall | also increase and its expected profit will (rise/fall). But if *i* decreases, a
decrease | firm's expected costs will (increase/decrease) and its expected profit will
rise | (rise/fall).

6-78

lower

In short, the higher the interest rate, the (higher/lower) are a firm's expected profits, and vice versa.

6-79

The *rate* of interest is always expressed as a *percentage*. For example, suppose a firm can borrow $100 and must pay $3 a year interest for the use of the $100. The rate of interest is said to be 3 percent.

And if a firm could borrow $500 for a year and had to pay $25 for the use of this money, the rate of interest would be ________ percent.

5

6-80

The ABC Corp. wishes to buy capital goods worth $10,000. It may *either* borrow the $10,000 to pay for this capital, *or* use $10,000 of its own reserves.

Suppose the ABC Corp. *borrows* the $10,000 for a year. It will have to pay interest to the lender for the ____________ of the money. If the amount of interest it pays the lender is $400, then 4 percent is the ____________ ____________ ____________ .

use

rate of interest (*not* interest alone)

6-81

A firm may not need to borrow to pay for capital goods. It may have and *use its own money* for this purpose. But even when a firm uses its own money, it must "pay" for the use of this money.

A firm with $10,000 might lend it to others rather than use it to acquire capital goods. If the *rate* of interest it can obtain when it lends $10,000 to others is 6 percent, the *amount* of interest it can earn by lending it to others is $________ . If it uses its own $10,000 to purchase capital goods, the amount of interest it has to sacrifice and thus the price it has to pay to use this money is also $________ .

$600

$600

6-82

So regardless of whether a firm borrows or uses its own money to purchase capital goods, one of the costs of investing is an interest cost, and the rate of interest determines how large the interest cost is going to be.

From these two simple facts we may conclude that the higher the rate of interest, the (greater/less) will be the costs and the (greater/less) the expected profits from investment. The lower the rate of interest, the (greater/less) will be the costs and the (greater/less) the expected profits from investment.

greater, less

less, greater

6-83

In other words, the rate of interest affects costs and expected profits from investing in this way: Investments which are profitable at one i may become unprofitable when the rate of interest ______________ .

increases (rises, etc.)

6-84

Thus: The higher the i in the economy, the (more/fewer) are the investments which are profitable and which will be undertaken by business firms; and the lower the i, the (more/fewer) are the investments which are profitable and therefore undertaken.

fewer

more

6-85

The kind of relation that exists between i and I_g is illustrated in the following table.

Annual investment	
***i*(%)**	**I_g(billions)**
8	$10
7	15
6	19
5	22
4	24
3	25
2	25½

This table tells us that as the rate of interest decreases, the amount of investment in the economy (increases/decreases). As the interest rate increases, the amount of investment in the economy (increases/decreases).

increases

decreases

6-86

In short, for the economy as a whole, there is an inverse relationship between ______________________________ and ______________________ .

the rate of interest

investment (either order)

6-87

Suppose you could control the rate of interest in the economy. (Refer to the table in frame **6-85**.)

If you wished to increase I_g, you would have to (raise/lower) i. If you wished to have just $24 billion spent for additional capital, you would set i at ________ percent. If you set i at 7 percent, there would be $________ spent annually for investment.

lower

4

$15

6-88

If we plotted the data in frame **6-85** it would look like this.

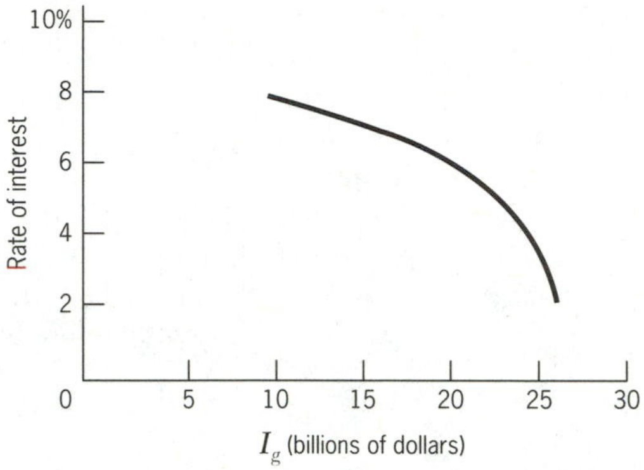

I_g On the horizontal axis we have measured ________ and on the ver-

i tical axis we have measured ________ .

down The curve relating these two variables slopes ________ward.

6-89

Because it shows the quantity of additional capital goods that would be demanded (or I_g) at different i's (the price for the use of money) the curve in frame **6-88** is called the ***investment demand curve***.

Like other demand curves, the curve slopes downward. This down-

inverse ward slope means that there is a(n) (direct/inverse) relationship between I_g and i.

6-90

And like other demand curves:

If the investment demand curve were to shift to the right we would

increased say that demand has (increased/decreased). And if the investment demand curve were to move to the left we would say that demand

decreased had ________________ .

6-91

An increase in investment demand means that at each i there will

more be (more/less) I_g; and a decrease in investment demand means that

at each i there will be less I_g ____ .

6-92

There is another important factor which affects investment spending in the economy.

GDP — On the graph below is plotted an ***investment schedule*** which indicates the amount of I_g at different levels of ________ .

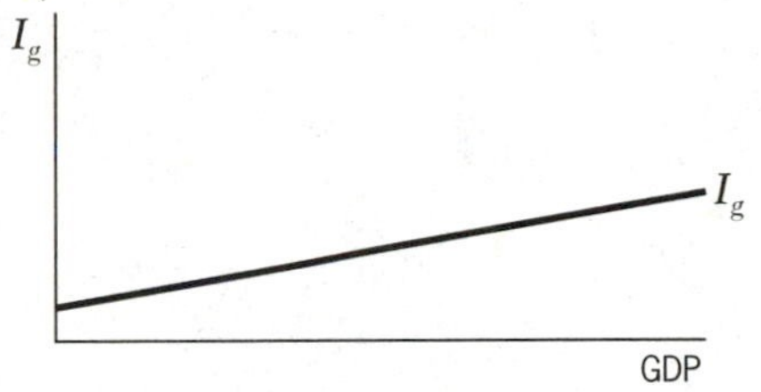

investment
domestic product

This graph tells us that ________ depends upon the size of the economy's ________ ________ .

6-93

decreases
smaller
direct

From the graph of the investment schedule in frame **6-92**, you can see that when GDP increases, I_g (increases/decreases); if GDP decreases I_g will become (larger/smaller); and the relationship between I_g and GDP is (direct/inverse)

6-94

more

When I_g depends directly upon the economy's GDP, economists say that investment is *induced*. Higher GDPs induce (more/less) I_g and vice versa.

6-95

rise
induce

The reason is clear: The greater the GDP, the larger will be the revenues which business firms expect to earn from any investment they undertake, and vice versa.

So if GDP rises, the expected profits from investment (rise/fall), which tends to ________ more investments.

6-96

fall (decrease)
fall (decrease)

But when GDP declines, the expected profitability of any investment will ________ , and the number of profitable investments will ________ .

6-97

Here is another graph of an investment schedule.

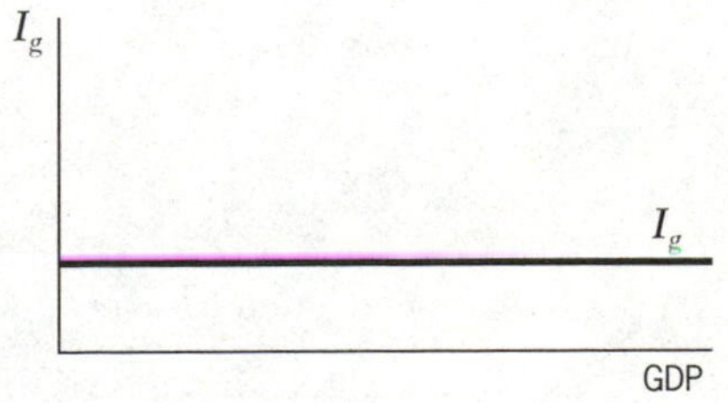

remain constant
remain constant
is not

If GDP were to increase I_g would (rise/fall/remain constant). If GDP were to decrease I_g would (rise/fall/remain constant). In other words, the graph indicates that I_g (is/is not) induced.

6-98

independent of

When the amount of I_g is not affected by the level of GDP, economists say that investment is ***autonomous***. Autonomous investment refers to investment that is (dependent on/independent of) the size of the economy's GDP.

6-99

Consider two investment schedules:

Investment schedule A	
GDP	I_g
$100	$25
200	25
300	25
400	25
500	25

Investment schedule B	
GDP	I_g
$100	$25
200	30
300	35
400	40
500	45

autonomous
induced

Investment in schedule A is (autonomous/induced).
Investment in schedule B is (autonomous/induced).

6-100

Before we conclude our discussion of the investment spending component of aggregate expenditures, we need to point out that there are many economic factors other than *i* and GDP that affect the amount of I_g in the economy.

You should be prepared to analyze these other factors and their effect upon aggregate expenditures for yourself:

Anything that influences the expected costs or revenues of a firm also

profits

affects its expected ______________ , which in turn helps the business executive to decide whether the firm will or will not invest in more

capital (capital goods, equipment, etc.)

______________ .

6-101

decline
rise

When expected costs rise or expected revenues fall, expected profits (rise/decline). And when expected costs decline or expected revenues increase, profit expectations (rise/decline).

6-102

less

In short: Lower profit expectations result in (more/less) investment spending in the economy, and higher profit expectations result in

more

______________ investment.

Now you can test yourself in the next four frames and see how much you have learned about investment.

6-103 Review Frame

use
money, cost
inversely

The rate of interest is the price paid for the ______________ of ______________ , is a (cost/revenue/profit) for a firm, and is (directly/ inversely) related to the amount of I_g.

6-104 Review Frame

does
does

When a firm:

Borrows money to spend for capital goods, it (does/does not) have an interest cost.

Uses its own money for more capital, it (does/does not) have to consider the cost of using its money to acquire capital.

6-105 Review Frame

decrease
fall (decrease)

I_g will ______________ in the economy when i increases, and vice versa.

To increase I_g, the rate of interest must ______________ .

6-106 Review Frame

induced
remain constant

If I_g increases when GDP increases, investment is said to be ______________ . If investment is autonomous, as GDP increases I_g will (increase/decrease/remain constant).

EQUILIBRIUM GDP

We have now looked at what determines the amount of consumer spending and investment spending in the economy.

Suppose there existed an economy in which there were only these two components of aggregate expenditures—an economy that had no government purchases and engaged in neither exporting nor importing. And suppose we continue to assume that in this economy there are no depreciation, no taxes or transfer payments and all corporate profits are distributed as dividends; GDP, NDP, NI, PI, and DI are still equal.

For this kind of hypothetical economy we want to discover two things: the size of the GDP the economy will tend to produce, and the effect of a change in AE upon the size of the GDP.

While this kind of economy is not completely realistic, studying it will help us to discover some important principles about the operation of our own economy. After we have examined this hypothetical economy, we can go on to examine a more realistic economy.

6-107

Imagine that the economy we are talking about has the following consumption and saving schedules (do not fill in the blanks yet):

GDP (=DI)	C	S	I_g	$C + I_g$
$300	$295	$ 5	$____	$____
325	315	10	____	____
350	335	15	____	____
375	355	20	____	____
400	375	25	____	____
425	395	30	____	____
450	415	35	____	____
475	435	40	____	____

Let's imagine also that investment spending (I_g) in this economy is entirely *autonomous*: profit expectations are such that the amount business firms want to spend for capital goods is $25.

Complete the *investment schedule* above by writing in the amount firms plan to spend for I_g at each level of GDP.

The amount is $25 at each of the eight GDPs.

6-108

Aggregate expenditures (AE) in this kind of economy is the sum of two components: C and I_g. We can draw up an *aggregate expenditure schedule* which shows the total amount consumers and business firms want to spend at the various levels of GDP. The last column of the table in frame **6-107** shows the ________________ for various GDPs shown in the first column.

aggregate expenditures

6-109

For example, when the GDP is $300:

Consumers will want to spend $________.

Business will want to spend $________.

Together consumers and business firms plan to spend $________.

$295

$25

$320

6-110

You can now compute $C + I_g$ at each of the eight levels of GDP. Go ahead and do it.

$320, $340, $360, $380, $400, $420, $440, $460

6-111

The first and last columns in the table represent the aggregate expenditures schedule; it tells us the total amount that will be spent for

consumption, investment

__________ and for __________ at different GDPs.

6-112

Look again at the schedules in frame **6-107**. There is *only one* GDP where $C + I_g$ and the GDP are equal. Economists refer to this GDP as the *equilibrium* GDP. In our schedule, the equilibrium GDP is

$400

$______ .

6-113

greater than
less than

When the GDP is $350, $C + I_g$ is (greater than/less than/equal to) the GDP. When the GDP is $450, $C + I_g$ is (greater than/less than/equal to) the GDP.

6-114

equal
equilibrium

But when the GDP is $400, the GDP and $C + I_g$ are __________ .

This GDP is called the __________ GDP.

6-115

C
I_g

The GDP an economy will *tend* to produce is its equilibrium GDP. Thus, we can discover the GDP the economy will tend to produce by finding the particular GDP that is equal to __________

\+ __________ .

6-116

Here is another set of schedules showing consumption, saving, investment, and aggregate expenditures for a hypothetical economy:

(1) GDP (= DI)	(2) C	(3) S	(4) I_g	(5) $C + I_g$	(6) Unintended $I(+)$ or Dis $I(-)$ in inventories
$400	$390	$10	$30	$420	$−20
420	406	14	30	436	−16
440	422	18	30	452	−12
460	438	22	30	468	− 8
480	454	26	30	484	− 4
500	470	30	30	500	0
520	486	34	30	516	+ 4
540	502	38	30	532	+ 8

The aggregate expenditures schedule consists of two columns: the

GDP(=DI)(first), $C + I_g$ (fifth) ______ column, and the ______ column.

6-117

$500 The equilibrium GDP is $______ because when GDP is this

$470, $30 amount, C is $______, I_g is $______, and $C + I_g$ is

$500 $______.

6-118

If you will look carefully at the schedules in frame **6-116** you will discover something interesting; at the equilibrium GDP, S is

$30, $30 $______, I_g is $______, and S and I_g are

equal ______.

6-119

Glance at the GDPs which are above and below the equilibrium GDP of $500. What do you find?

That at all GDPs *except* the equilibrium GDP

(a) S is equal to I_g.
(b) S is greater than I_g.
(c) S is less than I_g.
(d) S is either greater or less than I_g.

(d) Which one? ______

6-120

In other words, examination of the saving and investment schedules tells us we can find the equilibrium GDP by finding the GDP where

saving, investment ______ and ______ are equal.

6-121

What we have really discovered in this: There are *two* ways to find the

equilibrium ______ GDP.

Using the first approach, we look for the GDP at which

C, I_g ______ + ______ equals GDP.

Employing the second approach, we try to find the GDP at which

S, I_g ______ equals ______

6-122

An economy tends to produce its equilibrium GDP because producers of goods and services want to earn as large a profit as they can. To do this, business firms won't try to produce goods and services they can't sell, and business firms do try to produce all they can sell.

If we look back at the schedules in frame **6-116**, we find that when GDP is $420, the total production of goods and services is also

$420 $\$$______, but the total amount of goods and services which can be

$436 sold to customers and business firms is $______. The result is an unintended decrease or disinvestment in inventories of $16, as shown in the last column of the schedules in frame **6-116**. In seeking to build up these inventories again, producers will increase production and incomes until saving has increased to the point where it is ______

equal to ______ the intended or ***planned*** investment, namely,

I_g ______.

6-123

more
increase

Whenever the GDP is less than the AE for consumption and investment, business firms can sell (more/less) than they are actually producing. Therefore, they will (increase/decrease) their production and the GDP.

6-124

What if the actual GDP were $520? The total output of goods and serv-

$520, unintended ices produced is $______, resulting in (unintended invest-

investment, $+4 ment/disinvestment) in inventories of $______. Thus, produc-

reduce ers will want to (expand/reduce) their production.

6-125

At the equilibrium GDP of $500, producers discover that their total

equal
maintain

output will ______ the AE for goods and services. Under these conditions firms tend to (expand/reduce/maintain) production and the GDP. At the equilibrium GDP, there is no unintended investment or

inventories disinvestment in ______.

6-126

Any output above *or* below the equilibrium GDP is one which economists call a ***disequilibrium GDP***. At these outputs, the producers'

profit desire to operate at a ______ leads them either to

increase, decrease (either order) ______ or to ______ their production.

6-127

When actual GDP is greater than the equilibrium GDP, actual GDP is

greater, decrease ____________ than $C + I_g$ and firms ____________ their production to increase their profits.

When the actual GDP is less than the equilibrium GDP, actual GDP

less, increase is ____________ than $C + I_g$ and firms ____________ their outputs to increase their profits.

6-128

Looking back once more to the schedules in frame **6-116**, $500 is the equilibrium GDP. Other GDPs such as $480 and $520 are called

disequilibrium ____________ GDPs.

Before we discover what equilibrium and disequilibrium GDPs look like in terms of graphs, let's briefly review the more important things we have already learned about GDP.

6-129 Review Frame

The aggregate expenditures schedule indicates the total amount of

consumption, investment spending for ____________ and for ____________

GDP at various levels of ____________ .

6-130 Review Frame

The equilibrium GDP can be discovered either by finding the GDP at

GDP, $C + I_g$ which ____________ equals ____________ , or the GDP at which

S, I_g ____________ equals ____________ .

Because the GDP is another name for the domestic output of the economy and the total amount of spending in the economy are its aggregate expenditures for goods and services, when the economy pro-

domestic output duces its equilibrium GDP the ____________ ____________ is

aggregate expenditures equal to the ____________ ____________ made by consumers and business firms for goods and services.

6-131 Review Frame

greater At GDPs greater than the equilibrium GDP, GDP is ____________

greater than $C + I_g$, and S is ____________ than I_g.

less At GDPs less than the equilibrium GDP, GDP is ____________

less than $C + I_g$, and S is ____________ than I_g.

6-132 Review Frame

Business firms are motivated by their desire for profits. Therefore, when

increase — $C + I_g$ is greater than GDP, they will ______________ their production and the GDP.

GDP — Similarly, they will decrease their production and the ______________

C, I_g — whenever total spending for ______________ and ______________ is

less — (greater/less) than the GDP.

6-133

Now let's take the C and $C + I_g$ schedules from frame **6-116** and plot them on a graph. To make this graph easy to read we have not shown C and $C + I_g$ at GDPs all the way down to zero. GDP is plotted on the

horizontal — ______________ axis.

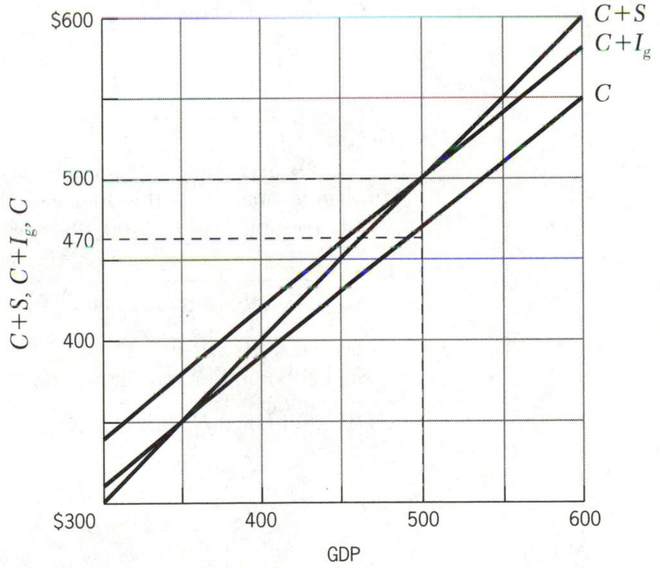

6-134

In addition to the C and $C + I_g$ curves on the graph, you will also find

$C + S$ — one labeled ______________ .

6-135

You have seen the $C + S$ curve and schedule earlier (in frames **6-25** through **6-30**). Just to review what we learned about them there, let's recall that in the kind of economy we have been talking about:

equal — GDP and DI are ______________ .

C, S — DI is equal to ______________ plus ______________ .

GDP — $C + S$ is, therefore, also equal to ______________ .

6-136

All this means is that $C + S$ is equal to GDP, and is therefore another way of measuring the GDP.

When the GDP is \$300, the total quantity of goods and services pro-

\$300 duced in the economy is also \$________ and the domestic output can

C, S be measured by calling it ________ plus ________ .

In short, when we measure the GDP along the horizontal axis, the vertical distance up to the $C + S$ curve is also equal to the

GDP ________ .

6-137

Because GDP and $C + S$ are equal at any GDP, the $C + S$ curve will cut the 90-degree angle formed by the axes of the graph exactly in half.

45 One-half of 90 degrees is ________ degrees.

6-138

The $C + S$ curve, for this reason, is called the 45-degree line or the 45-degree curve. All this means is that when GDP measured along the horizontal axis is \$400, the distance vertically to the 45-degree

\$400 line is \$________ .

And when the vertical distance to the 45-degree line is \$550, the GDP

\$550 measured horizontally is \$________ .

Said still another way, along the 45-degree line we can measure the

horizontal, vertical (either order) GDP on either the ________ or ________ axis.

6-139

vertical We can also find S and I_g on this graph. S turns out to be the (vertical/

C horizontal) distance between the $C + S$ and the ________ curve.

vertical I_g is the ________ distance between the $C + I_g$ curve and the

C ________ curve.

6-140

On the schedules from which we drew the $C + I_g$ curve, the equilibrium GDP was \$500.

Look again at the graph in frame **6-133**. At the equilibrium GDP

$C + I_g$ of \$500, we discover that the ________ curve *crosses* the

$C + S$ (either order) ________ curve.

6-141

45-degree
expenditures

Recall that $C + S$ is the ________ line and that $C + I_g$, as you learned in frame **6-108**, is the aggregate ________ curve.

6-142

equilibrium GDP

In other words, the 45-degree line crosses the aggregate expenditures curve at the ________ ________, which in our example is \$500.

6-143

$$C + I_g = C + S$$

If we subtract C from each side of the equation, we find that at the equilibrium GDP:

I_g, S

________ = ________

6-144

C, $C + S$ (either order)
\$30, C
$C + I_g$ (either order), \$30

Examine the graph in frame **6-133** again. At the equilibrium GDP of \$500, S and I_g *are* equal. S is the vertical distance between the ________ curve and the ________ curve, and is equal to \$________. I_g is the vertical distance between the ________ curve and the ________ curve, and is equal to \$________.

6-145

To test the conclusion that $S = I_g$ at the equilibrium GDP, let's put the S and I_g schedules on a graph by themselves.

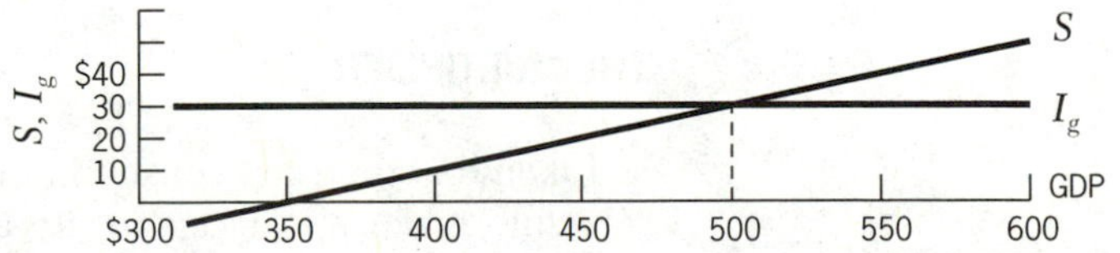

\$500

The two curves cross at the point where GDP = \$________.

6-146

aggregate expenditures
45-degree
S, I_g (either order)

Now we have two graphical ways of finding the equilibrium GDP (just as we had two ways of finding the equilibrium GDP from our schedules). Graphically we can find the equilibrium GDP either by finding the point at which the ________ ________ curve intersects the ________ line, or the point at which the ________ curve intersects the ________ curve.

Let's end this discussion of the equilibrium GDP with a self-test. Study the graph below, and then complete the two following review frames.

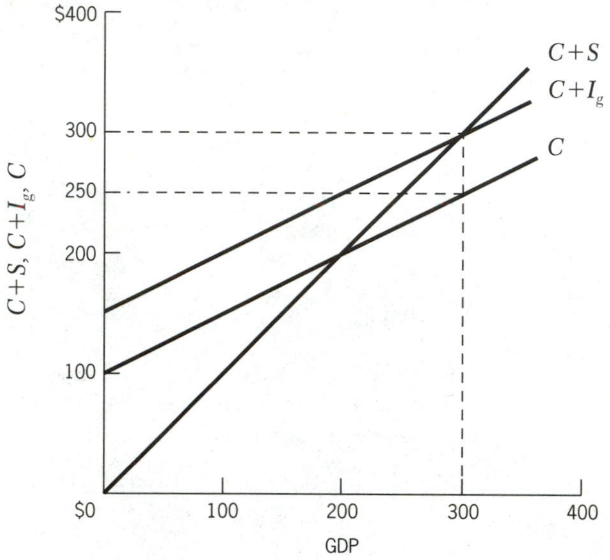

6-147 Review Frame

$C + I_g$ The aggregate expenditures curve is the one labeled ______________ ,

$C + S$ while the 45-degree line is the one called ______________ .

$300 These two curves cross at the GDP of $______________ .

6-148 Review Frame

equilibrium GDP This $300 is called the ______________ ______________ . At this GDP

$50 both S and I are equal to $______________ , and C is equal to

$250 $______________ .

THE MULTIPLIER

Taken together, the consumption schedule and the investment schedule make up the aggregate expenditures schedule. Aggregate expenditures determine how large a GDP the economy will tend to produce. But consumption and investment schedules sometimes change. Of the two, investment is the most apt to vary as time passes. If it changes, aggregate expenditures also change, and with it the equilibrium GDP.

What we have to do now is find out whether the equilibrium GDP increases or decreases when investment changes, and how much.

6-149

As a starting point, look at the schedules in the following table.

GDP	C	S	I_g	$C + I_g$	I'_g	$C + I'_g$
$500	$490	$10	$16	$506	$20	$510
510	498	12	16	514	20	518
520	506	14	16	522	20	526
530	514	16	16	530	20	534
540	522	18	16	538	20	542
550	530	20	16	546	20	550
560	538	22	16	554	20	558
570	546	24	16	462	20	566

With the consumption and investment schedules to the left of the double line, the equilibrium GDP is $530.

larger
rise

Suppose the amount of investment were to increase from $16 to $20, regardless of the GDP. Then $C + I_g$ at every GDP would be (larger/smaller), and the equilibrium GDP would tend to (rise/fall).

6-150

The columns to the right of the double line in the schedule above indicate the amounts of investment spending (I_g) and aggregate expenditures ($C + I_g$) after I_g has increased from $16 to $20.

$530
$550

The old equilibrium GDP was $________, but the new equilibrium GDP is $________.

6-151

increased
$20

As a result of the $4 increase in I_g, equilibrium GDP has (increased/decreased) by $________.

6-152

same, greater than

The $4 increase in investment has caused GDP to change in the (same/opposite) direction by an amount (greater than/less than/equal to) the change in I_g.

6-153

What would happen to the equilibrium GDP if I_g were now to decline from $20 to $10? The new investment and aggregate expenditures schedules are shown as I''_g and $C + I''_g$ in the following table.

GDP	C	S	I''_g	$C + I''_g$
$500	$490	$10	$10	$500
510	498	12	10	508
520	506	14	10	516
530	514	16	10	524
540	522	18	10	532
550	530	20	10	540
560	538	22	10	548
570	546	24	10	556

de- The equilibrium GDP would ________-crease from $550 to

$500 $________ .

6-154

The $10 decrease in I_g would bring about a change in the equilibrium

greater (larger, bigger, etc.) GDP. This change is ________ in size than the change in I_g.

same Moreover, the equilibrium GDP has changed in the ________ direction as the change in I_g.

6-155

When I_g was:	The equilibrium GDP was:
$10	$500
16	530
20	550

5 In every case shown, the change in GDP was (1/2/3/4/5) times larger than the change in investment. The relation between the change in I_g

direct and the change in equilibrium GDP is (direct/inverse).

6-156

The tendency for GDP to change in the same direction as any change in I_g by an amount greater than the change I_g is what economists call the ***multiplier effect***. The GDP changes by a multiple of the change in I_g. This multiple is greater than 1.0 and is called the *multiplier*. In frame

multiplier **6-155**, 5 was the ________ .

6-157

Suppose the multiplier were 7 and I_g increased by $4. In this case,

increase, 7 GDP would (increase/decrease) by ________ times $4, or

$28 $________ .

6-158

When the multiplier is 3 and I_g decreases by $6, the equilibrium GDP

fall, $18 will (rise/fall) by $________ as a result of the multiplier effect.

6-159

If an increase of $10 in I_g were to bring about a $40 increase in GDP,

multiplier effect we could say that the change in I_g had exerted a ________ ________

4 upon the GDP. The multiplier was (4/10/40).

6-160

When business firms spend an additional $10 on investment, they set off a chain reaction.

The output of final goods and services (the GDP) is increased by $10 and people find themselves with $10 more income (DI), which leads them to (increase/decrease) their own expenditures for consumption (*C*).

increase

6-161

When consumers obtain additional income, the *amount* by which they increase their own consumption expenditures depends upon two things: the size of the income increase and their MPC. For example, if the MPC were 0.8 and DI were to increase by $10, consumers would increase their consumption expenditures by ________ multiplied by $10, or $________ .

0.8

$8

6-162

When these consumers spend this additional $8 for consumption, they do two things: they increase the GDP by another $8, and they increase the DIs of other consumers by $8. The other consumers will in turn increase their expenditures for consumption by $8 multiplied by the ________ .

MPC (0.8 in this example)

6-163

Supposing that these other consumers also have an MPC of 0.8, they will increase their consumption by 0.8 times $8, or $6.40, resulting in an increase of $6.40 in the economy's ________ and in the consumers' ________ .

GDP

DI

6-164

This $6.40 increase in GDP and DI will bring about yet another increase in consumption, resulting in a further increase in GDP and DI. Is there any end to this chain reaction?

As we have seen in the preceding frames, the increases in GDP that occur become progressively (larger/smaller), and each increase in *C* is always (greater than/less than) the previous consumption increase.

smaller

less than

After the chain reaction has progressed for a number of "rounds," the increases in GDP and *C* become very small. They become so small that the GDP never increases beyond a certain amount. The limit is reached when the increased production (GDP) has resulted in income increasing enough to increase saving to the level where it is again equal to the increased investment that started the chain reaction. Only then will there no longer be unintended disinvestment in inventories (see frame **6-116**). To demonstrate this so that the working of the multiplier through to the limit becomes obvious, we will assume that MPC and MPS = ½. As we now know this results in a multiplier of ________ . We will also assume that, with GDP initially in equilibrium, we now have an increase in autonomous investment of $1 billion. The result will be a(n) ________ in GDP to $________ billion, as follows.

$\frac{1}{\frac{1}{2}} = 2$

increase, $2

(All figures in $billions)
INITIAL INCREASE IN I_g of $1 RESULTS IN:

Round	Increase in GDP	Resulting increase in:		Cumulative increase in both *C* and *S*
		C	*S*	
Initial	$1	$½	$½	$½
2nd	½	¼	¼	¾
3rd	¼	⅛	⅛	⅞
4th	⅛	1/16	1/16	15/16
5th	1/16	1/32	1/32	31/32

Looking at the right-hand column, it is clear that, at the limit, savings
$1 and consumption will both have increased by $________
equal and that then the increase in saving will be precisely ________
I_g to the increased ________ that started the process.

6-165

In an earlier example, we discovered that when the MPC was 0.8 the multiplier was 5. If the MPC were 0.6 we would find that the multiplier was equal to 2½. From this we may conclude that the smaller the MPC is, the (larger/smaller) the multiplier will be and vice versa.

smaller

6-166

There is, in fact, a precise relationship between the MPC and the multiplier. Mathematical friends tell us that

$$\text{the multiplier is equal to } \frac{1}{1 - \text{MPC}}$$

And because the MPS is always equal to 1 − MPC we can say that

$$\text{the multiplier is also equal to } \frac{1}{\text{MPS}}$$

This would mean that if the MPC were 0.9, the MPS would equal
0.1, 10 ________ and the multiplier would be equal to ________ .

6-167

Here are a few more MPCs. Just for practice, figure out the MPS and the multiplier in each case.

	MPC	MPS	Multiplier
0.3, 3⅓	0.7	______	______
⅙, 6	5/6	______	______
0.25, 4	0.75	______	______
0.5, 2	0.5	______	______

Now let's take five frames to review what you have learned about the multiplier.

6-168 Review Frame

increase, more
fall
more

When I_g increases by \$3, GDP will (increase/decrease) by (more/less) than \$3. And were I_g to decrease by \$5, GDP would (rise/fall) by (more/less) than \$5.

6-169 Review Frame

multiplier
effect

This tendency for GDP to change in the same direction as the change in I_g, although by a greater amount, is called the ________ ________________.

6-170 Review Frame

MPS
1 − MPC
(either order)

The size of the multiplier is equal to 1 divided by either ____________ or ______________.

6-171 Review Frame

\$80

If the multiplier were 4 and I_g were to rise by \$20, the GDP would expand by \$______________.

6-172 Review Frame

fallen (decreased, etc.),
\$25

When the multiplier is 3, a \$75 fall in GDP tells us that investment has ______________ by \$______________.

EXPORTS AND IMPORTS

So far we have been discussing a *closed* economy. We will now *open* the economy by bringing in exports and imports. Aggregate expenditures will still determine equilibrium GDP. However, with an open economy, aggregate expenditures will also be affected by exports and imports.

6-173

Foreign spending for American final goods and services (X) adds a third component to the aggregate expenditures for the economy's output. In other words, our equation expands to:

C, I_g

AE = ______________ + ______________ + X.

6-174

In the following table we show the consumption schedule *and* the total amount of spending for consumption and investment at several levels of GDP.

GDP	C	$C + I_g$
450	432	452
460	440	460
470	448	468
490	464	484
510	480	500
530	496	516
550	512	532
570	528	548
590	544	564
610	560	580
630	576	586

We have assumed that I_g is independent, or autonomous, and is
$20 equal to $______ . Without any spending by foreigners in this
$460 economy, the equilibrium GDP would be $______ , be-
C, I_g cause here, and only here, aggregate expenditures, ______ +
GDP ______ are equal to ______ .

6-175

The volume of spending by foreigners, American exports, will depend primarily upon the levels of incomes in foreign nations. For simplicity, we will assume exports are *entirely* dependent upon foreign incomes and independent of American domestic GDP. Suppose foreign nations decide to spend $30 for American final goods and services. Looking back at the schedules in the frame above:

When the GDP is $450, $C + I_g$ is $452 and $C + I_g + X$ is equal
$482 to $______ . And when GDP is $460, $C + I_g + X$ is
$490 $______ .

6-176

$C + I_g + X$ when X is $30 is shown in the following table.

GDP	C	$C + I_g$	X	$C + I_g + X$
$450	432	452	30	482
460	440	460	30	490
470	448	468	30	498
490	464	484	30	514
510	480	500	30	530
530	496	516	30	546
550	512	532	30	562
570	528	548	30	578
590	544	564	30	594
610	560	580	30	610
630	576	596	30	626

When there was no spending by foreigners, the GDP column was the total production column, and the ______ column was the aggregate expenditures schedule. But when there are exports, the aggregate expenditures schedule is expressed by the ______ column while the total production is still the ______ column.

$C + I_g$

$C + I_g + X$

GDP

6-177

In other words, aggregate expenditures at any level of GDP now equal ______ + ______ + ______.

C, I_g, X

6-178

Using the schedules in frame **6-176**, GDP and AE are equal when GDP is $(460/510/610/630); this GDP is the ______ GDP.

$610, equilibrium

6-179

Look at the equilibrium GDP of $610 in frame **6-176**. At this GDP, C is $560. Since $C + S$ are equal to GDP, S must be equal to $______.

$50

6-180

At the equilibrium GDP of $610, total production = AE. In other words, ______ + ______ = ______ + ______ + ______.

C, S, C, I_g, X

6-181

When the equilibrium GDP at $610 is produced, we find that S is $50, I_g is $20, X is $30, so $I_g + X$ is $______, which is (greater than/less than/equal to) S.

$50, equal to

6-182

Let's do a little more simple algebra. At the equilibrium GDP, $C + S = C + I_g + X$.

Subtracting C from each side, we arrive at the equation:

______ = ______ + ______.

S, I_g, X

6-183

Without exports of $30, the equilibrium GDP was $460. But when exports are $30, the equilibrium GDP became $610. The $30 increase in X caused the equilibrium GDP to (increase/decrease) by an amount (greater/less) than the increase in X.

increase
greater

6-184

As a result of a $30 increase in X, equilibrium GDP increased by $150.
5 The increase in GDP was (2/3/4/5) times the increase in X. This suggests
multiplier that, like changes in I_g, changes in X also have a ________ effect upon the equilibrium GDP.

6-185

The multiplier turned out to be 5 in our example because in the consumption schedule that we used earlier, 0.8 was the MPC. The MPS
0.2 must therefore be equal to ________.
MPS The multiplier always equals 1 divided by the (MPC/MPS), which comes out to 5.

6-186

2½ Were the MPC equal to 0.6, the multiplier would be equal to ____.
rise An $8 increase in X would cause the equilibrium GDP to (rise/fall) by
$20 $________, while a $12 decrease in X would cause the equilib-
decrease, $30 rium GDP to (increase/decrease) by $________.

6-187 Review Frame

When there is foreign spending for American goods and services, the
expenditures equilibrium GDP is the GDP at which aggregate ________ and
production total ________ are equal.

6-188 Review Frame

C, I_g, X At the equilibrium GDP, GDP equals ____ + ____ + ____.
S, C, I_g, X C + ____ are also equal to ____ + ____ + ____. There-
I_g, X fore S equals ____ + ____.

6-189 Review Frame

3⅓ When the MPC is 0.7, the multiplier is equal to ________, and
fall a $9 decrease in X will cause the equilibrium GDP to (rise/fall) by
$30 $________.

6-190

A country that exports also imports. Indeed, it is through exports that a country earns the foreign exchange (foreign currency) to be able to import. Now, unlike exports, imports (M) *are* related to the domestic GDP. And this relationship is similar to that between C and GDP. As GDP
increases rises, C (increases/decreases/remains the same). In the same way, when
increases GDP rises, M ________.

6-191

The following table is based on the table of frame **6-176**, with the following changes:

1. the *import schedule* (M) has been added;
2. a column headed X_n has been added; it shows *net exports* = $X - M$.
3. $C + I_g + X_n$ replaces $C + I_g + X$.

GDP	C	$C + I_g$	X	M	X_n	$C + I_g + X_n$
450	432	452	30	27	+ 3	455
460	440	460	30	30	0	460
470	448	468	30	33	− 3	465
480	456	476	30	36	− 6	470
490	464	484	30	39	− 9	475
500	472	492	30	42	−12	480
510	480	500	30	45	−15	485
530	496	516	30	51	−21	495
550	512	532	30	57	−27	505
570	528	548	30	63	−33	515
590	544	564	30	69	−39	525
610	560	580	30	75	−45	535
630	576	596	30	81	−51	545

When there was exporting but no importing, the aggregate expenditures schedule was ________ + ________ + ________ . When importing occurs, all spending on M must be subtracted from AE, for such spending is for the goods and services of (one's own economy/other economies). Thus the new AE schedule is $C + I_g + X - M$. Since $X - M$ is expressed as X_n, the open economy (without government) AE is: ________ + ________ + ________ . The total production column is, as always, the ________ column, and is equal to C + ________ , as before.

$C + I_g + X$

other economies

C, I_g, X_n

GDP

S

6-192

Using the schedules in frame **6-191**, GDP and AE are equal when GDP is $(460/505/535/610); this GDP is the ________ GDP.

\$460, equilibrium

6-193

No doubt you will have noticed that this equilibrium GDP is (the same as/different from) the equilibrium GDP of frame **6-174**, when the economy was still closed to foreign trade. This occurs because at the equilibrium GDP of ________ , the added injection of \$30 into aggregate expenditures because of X is precisely balanced by the additional leakage of \$30 because of ________ . In other words, when X and M are equal, their net effect on aggregate expenditures is ________—which is what one would expect, for if X and M are equal, $X - M$ must equal ________ .

the same as

\$460

M

zero

zero

6-194

increases | $3

Examining the M schedule in the table in frame **6-191**, you will note that for every $10 increase in GDP, M (increases/decreases) by $________.

6-195

S | GDP | M | GDP

You will recall that the MPS is the change in ________ divided by the change in ________. In exactly the same way, the ***marginal propensity to import***, *MPM*, is the change in ________ divided by the change in ________.

6-196

0.3

Therefore, based on the result you obtained in frame **6-194**, in this economy the MPM is ________.

6-197

Suppose the I_g of the table in frame **6-191** increases from $20 to $30 at all levels of GDP, so that we now have a new table, as follows:

NNP	C	$C + I_g'$	X	M	X_n	$C + I_g' + X_n$
450	432	462	30	27	+ 3	465
460	440	470	30	30	0	470
470	448	478	30	33	− 3	475
480	456	486	30	36	− 6	480
490	464	494	30	39	− 9	485
500	472	502	30	42	−12	490

C, I_g' | X_n, GDP | $480

Aggregate expenditures = ________ + ________ + ________ are now equal to total production = ________ at $________.

6-198

$10 | $20, 2

Because of the increase in I_g of $________, equilibrium GDP has increased by $________. This implies a multiplier of ________.

6-199

5 | If not, read on.

Before the economy was opened to foreign trade, the multiplier was ________. Can you explain why it has been more than cut in half?

6-200

You will recall from frame **6-166** that *that* multiplier—which we will now call the simple, or closed economy, multiplier—was equal to

$\frac{1}{MPS}$ $\frac{1}{1 - \text{MPC}} =$ ______________ .

However, when we have an open economy, we have a third choice, namely M, added to the previous only two ways of disposing of income,

C, S namely ______________ and ______________ . Only income spent on *domestic* production has a multiplier effect on GDP. Income spent on M subtracts from spending on domestic production in precisely the same

S way as does ______________ . Therefore, to find the *open economy multiplier*, we add the two leakages together so that the multiplier is equal to $\frac{1}{(\text{MPS} + \text{MPM})}$.

6-201

Now that we have derived our new open economy multiplier (which will be the only one we will use from here on), let us see what will happen if, instead of having I_g increase by \$10, as in frame **6-197**, we have X

\$40 increase by \$10, from \$30 to \$______________ , at all levels of GDP so that we now have a new table, as follows:

GDP	C	$C + I_g$	X'	M	X'_n	$C + I_g + X'_n$
450	432	452	40	27	+13	465
460	440	460	40	30	+10	470
470	448	468	40	33	+ 7	475
480	456	476	40	36	+ 4	480
490	464	484	40	39	+ 1	485
500	472	492	40	42	− 2	490

6-202

C, I_g Equality of aggregate expenditures, ______________ + ______________

X'_n, GDP + ______________ , and of total output, ______________ , now exists

\$480 at a level of \$______________ .

6-203

the same as This is (higher than/lower than/the same as) the GDP found in frame

\$10 **6-197**, when I_g increased by \$______________ .

6-204

the same Thus, equal increases in I_g and X have (the same/a different) effect on equilibrium GDP.

6-205

$20 — In both cases equilibrium GDP increased by $________ as a re-

expenditures, $10 — sult of an increase in aggregate ________ of $________ ,

2 — revealing a multiplier of ________ .

6-206

Would a *decrease* in M of $10 at all levels of GDP have an identical effect? Let's see in the table below, where we are again using the table of frame **6-191**, with only M changed this time.

GDP	C	$C + I_g$	X'	M	X_n'	$C + I_g + X_n'$
450	432	452	30	17	+13	465
460	440	460	30	20	+10	470
470	448	468	30	23	+ 7	475
480	456	476	30	26	+ 4	480
490	464	484	30	29	+ 1	485
500	472	492	30	32	− 2	490

Comparing this table to the one in frame **6-201** it will be seen that

C, I_g — the aggregate expenditures column ________ + ________

X_n, the same — + ________ is (the same/different).

6-207

GDP / the same as — Since the total output ________ schedule also has not changed, it therefore follows that the equilibrium GDP will be (the same as/different from) the one derived in frame **6-202** when X increased by $10.

6-208

identical — We could have attained this result directly by comparing the X_n' columns of the tables in frames **6-201** and **6-206**. These two columns are (identical/different). This, of course, follows from the fact that $X -$

X_n — $M =$ ________ . Adding $10 to X or subtracting $10 from M at

increase, $10 / increase, the same — all levels of GDP will both (increase/decrease) X_n by $________ , and thus (increase/decrease) aggregate expenditures by (the same/a different) amount.

6-209

Suppose now, to complete the picture, we have C increase by $10 at all

S — levels of GDP. This is identical to having ________ decrease by $10 at all levels of GDP. Would the result be the same as having either I_g or X increase, or M decrease, by $10 at all levels of GDP?

We hope you answered yes. If not, see below.

6-210

The answer is to be found in the table to frame **6-197**. Recall that
I_g, $10 here we had ____________ increase by $____________ at all
GDP levels of __________ . Since we had not bothered to include an I_g
$30 column (which would have shown I_g increase from $20 to $ ____ at all levels of GDP), we showed the increase in I_g by adding $10 to the $C + I_g$ column at all levels of GDP. Would it make any difference if instead of adding $10 to $C + I_g$ because of an increase of $10 in I_g, we
of course not added $10 to $C + I_g$ because of an increase of $10 in C?

6-211

Thus we arrive at our overall rule: Equal increases (decreases) in aggregate expenditures caused by equal increases (decreases) in C or I_g
X, M or ______ or the same equal decreases (increases) in S or __________ ,
precisely the same, GDP have (precisely the same/different) effect on the equilibrium ________ .

6-212

And the effect on equilibrium GDP is equal to the change in aggregate
expenditures, open economy multiplier ____________ times the * __________ __________ __________ .

6-213

I_g, X Recall from frame **6-182** that S = ____________ + ____________
M at the equilibrium GDP. That was before we added ____________ as another means of disposing of income.

6-214

Look back at the table of frame **6-191**. At the equilibrium GDP of
$460, $20, $30 $____________ , I_g = ____________ , X = ____________ ,
$20, $30 S = ____________ , and M = ____________ . [I_g, X, and M we can read off the table; but why does S = $20? Because $C + S$ =
GDP ____________ (see frame **6-179**); therefore S = GDP − C, which
$440 at the $460 GDP level = $460 − ____________ =
$20 $____________ .]

6-215

From the figures of the preceding frame we see that $S + M = I_g + X$ for, of course, $20 + $30 = $20 + $30. But is this a special case,
I_g caused by the fact that individually S = ____________ and X =
M ____________ ?

6-216

We will find the answer in frame **6-201**. Here, equilibrium GDP is

\$480, C, \$24 — \$__________ ; S = GDP − __________ = __________ ; I_g =

\$20, \$40, \$36 — __________ ; X = __________ ; and M = __________ .

6-217

\$60 — Therefore, $S + M = \$24 + \$36 =$ __________ ; and $I_g + X =$

\$60, GDP — \$20 + \$40 = __________ . Thus at the equilibrium __________ ,

always equal, is not — $S + M$ (always equal/do not equal) $I_g + X$ even when S (is/is not) equal

is not — to I_g and M (is/is not) equal to X.

6-218

Since at the equilibrium GDP, $S + M = I_g + X$, $S = I_g + X - M =$

X_n — I_g + __________ .

6-219 Review Frame

When an economy is opened to foreign trade, X is added to C and I as

expenditures — a new component of aggregate __________ , and M is added to S

leakage — as a new __________ from the income stream.

6-220 Review Frame

$\frac{1}{\text{MPS} + \text{MPM}}$ — The open economy multiplier = __________ . It has a value (higher

lower than — than/lower than/the same as) the closed economy multiplier because M,

a subtraction from spending on domestic production = a leakage — like S, is * ____________________

____________________ .

6-221 Review Frame

At the equilibrium level of GDP, that is, when total output equals

aggregate expenditures, I_g, X — __________ __________ , $S + M =$ __________ + __________

is not, is not, X — even when S (is/is not) equal to I_g and M (is/is not) equal to ________ .

GOVERNMENT AND THE ECONOMY

Talking about an economy where there are no governments to spend or tax has taught us several important things about the overall operation of the economy. But we can learn even more about the actual operation of our economy if we recognize two facts: first, how much governments purchase helps to determine what the equilibrium GDP will be; and second, the amount of taxes collected by governments also affects the economy's output of final goods and services.

We now have to incorporate these two facts into our explanation of how large a GDP the economy will tend to produce. The inclusion of government purchases and taxes in our explanation doesn't change the basic fact, however, that aggregate expenditures determine our equilibrium GDP. All it means is that government purchasing and taxing affect aggregate expenditures, and that we must modify our explanation of the equilibrium GDP by taking them into account.

We now want to find out how governmental purchases and the collection of taxes influence aggregate expenditures.

6-222

To keep the analysis of government purchases and taxation as straightforward as possible, we will assume that exports and imports are both equal to $10 billion at all levels of GDP. This means we are assuming
zero that net exports are __________ and that we are also assuming that imports, like exports and investment, are autonomous, that is, (independent of/dependent on) the level of GDP. The assumption means that
independent of
zero we are assuming the marginal propensity to import is ________ .

6-223

Government purchases of final goods and services (G) add a fourth component to the aggregate expenditures for the economy's output. In other words, our equation now expands to:

C, I_g, X_n

$$AE = \_\_\_\_\_\_ + \_\_\_\_\_\_ + \_\_\_\_\_\_ + G.$$

6-224

In the following table we show the consumption schedule *and* the total amount of spending for consumption, investment, and net exports at several levels of GDP.

GDP	C	$C + I_g + X_n$
$450	$432	$452
460	440	460
470	448	468
480	456	476
490	464	484
500	472	492
510	480	500
520	488	508

We have assumed that $I_g + X_n$ is independent, or autonomous, and
$20 is equal to $__________ . Without any government purchases in
$460 this economy, the equilibrium GDP would be $__________ .

6-225

Economists generally don't try to explain how much governments purchase. Governments do purchase, and the amount is largely the result of political decisions. Suppose governments in the economy decide to purchase $10 of final goods and services. Looking back at the schedules in the frame above:

When the GDP is $450, $C + I_g + X_n$ is $452 and $C + I_g + X_n +$

$462 G is equal to $__________ . And when the GDP is $460, $C +$

$470 $I_g + X_n + G$ is $__________ .

6-226

$C + I_g + X_n + G$ when G is $10 is shown in the following table.

GDP	C	$C + I_g + X_n$	$C + I_g + X_n + G$
$450	$432	$452	$462
460	440	460	470
470	448	468	478
480	456	476	486
490	464	484	494
500	472	492	502
510	480	500	510
520	488	508	518

When there was no government purchasing, the GDP column and

$C + I_g + X_n$ the __________ column were the aggregate expenditures schedule. But when there are government purchases, the aggregate expen-

GDP, $C + I_g + X_n + G$ ditures schedule is expressed by the __________ column and the

(either order) __________ column.

6-227

C, In other words, aggregate expenditures at any GDP now equal ______

I_g, X_n, G plus __________ plus __________ plus __________ .

6-228

Using the schedules in frame **6-226** above, GDP and AE are equal when

$510, equilibrium GDP is $(460/490/500/510); this GDP is the __________ GDP.

6-229

Look at the equilibrium GDP of $510 in frame **6-226**. At this GDP, C

$30 is $480, S is equal to $__________ , so $C + S$ must be equal to

$510 $__________ .

6-230

From the facts in the preceding frame, we discover that at the equilibrium GDP of $510 ______ + ______ = ______ + ______ + ______ + ______.

C, S, C
I_g, X_n, *G*

6-231

When the equilibrium GDP of $510 is produced, we find that *S* is $30, I_g is $20, X_n is 0, *G* is $10, $I_g + X_n + G$ is $______, which is (greater than/less than/equal to) *S*.

$30
equal to

6-232

Let's do a little more simple algebra. At the equilibrium GDP,

$$C + S = C + I_g + X_n + G$$

Subtracting *C* from each side, we arrive at the equation:

______ = ______ + ______ + ______.

S, I_g, X_n, *G*

6-233

Without the government expenditures of $10, the equilibrium GDP was $460. But when the governments spent $10, the equilibrium GDP became $510. The $10 increase in *G* caused the equilibrium GDP to (increase/decrease) by an amount (greater/less) than the increase in *G*.

increase, greater

6-234

As a result of a $10 increase in *G*, equilibrium GDP increased by $50. The increase in equilibrium GDP was (2/3/4/5) times the increase in *G*. This suggests that, like changes in I_g, changes in *G* also have a ______ effect upon the equilibrium GDP.

5
multiplier

6-235

The multiplier turned out to be 5 in our example because in the consumption schedule that we used earlier, 0.8 was the MPC. The MPS must, therefore, be equal to ______.

The multiplier always equals 1 divided by the (MPC/MPS), which comes out to 5.

0.2
MPS

6-236

Were the MPC equal to 0.6, the multiplier would be equal to ______. An $8 increase in *G* would cause the equilibrium GDP to (rise/fall) by $______, while a $12 decrease in *G* would cause the equilibrium GDP to (increase/decrease) by $______.

2½
rise, $20
decrease, $30

6-237

Now suppose that the equilibrium GDP is \$550 and the MPC is 0.9. Assume that at this GDP there is considerable unemployment in the economy and the government would like the equilibrium GDP to rise to \$600.

To bring this about, the government would have to (increase/decrease) its purchases of goods and services by \$(5/10/25/50).

increase
\$5 (1 − .9 = .1 = MPS. 1/.1 = 10 = the multiplier. 10 × \$5 = \$50, the difference between \$550 and \$600)

6-238

What if the equilibrium GDP were \$700, the MPC were 0.5, and the government would like the equilibrium GDP to fall to \$650? It would have to (increase/decrease) *G* by \$(10/12½/20/25).

decrease, \$25 (1 − .5 = .5 = MPS. 1/.5 = 2 = the multiplier. 2 × \$25 = \$50, the difference between \$700 and \$650)

But let's not forget that governments don't just purchase; they also collect taxes. We'll get to taxes shortly. First, let's take four frames to review what you've learned about *G* and the equilibrium GDP.

6-239 Review Frame

When there is government purchasing of goods and services, the equilibrium GDP is the GDP at which aggregate ____________ and ____________ are equal.

expenditures
GDP

6-240 Review Frame

At the equilibrium GDP, GDP equals ________ + ________ + ________ + ________. *C* + ________ are also equal to ________ + ________ + ________ + ________. Therefore *S* equals ________ + ________ + ________.

C, I_g
X_n, G, S
C, I_g, X_n, G
I_g, X_n, G

6-241 Review Frame

When *G* increases, GDP will (increase/decrease) by an amount (greater/less) than the increase in *G*.

increase
greater

6-242 Review Frame

3⅓ When the MPC is 0.7, the multiplier is equal to ____________ , and
fall a $20 decrease in G will cause the equilibrium GDP to (rise/fall) by
$66⅔ $____________ .

6-243

Now let's see how taxes affect aggregate expenditures and the equilibrium GDP. Just to keep things simple, we shall assume that the only taxes governments collect are *personal taxes*. When governments collect taxes from their citizens, these citizens are left with less disposable in-
C (consumption), S (saving) come to use for ____________ and ____________ .

6-244

For example, if the GDP were $450 and governments collected taxes of
$420 $30, consumers would have a DI of only $____________ to spend on consumption and to save.

6-245

There are now three things consumers do with the GDP: pay their taxes, spend for consumption, and save.

Suppose that taxes are $25, C is $280, and S is $20. The GDP
$325 must equal $____________ , but the DI of consumers is only
$300 $____________ .

6-246

Consumers now have a smaller DI than they would have if no taxes were collected in the economy. The collection of taxes by governments means
decrease that consumers have to (increase/decrease) the total amount they spend for consumption and save.

6-247

If governments were to *decrease* the amount of taxes they collect by $35,
increase, $35 DI would (increase/decrease) by $____________ . In other words,
increase, $35 $C + S$ would have to (increase/decrease) by $____________ .

6-248

The levying of taxes forces consumers to reduce their $C + S$ by the amount of taxes levied. Taxes mean less DI for consumers. And when
less DI decreases, consumers tend to spend (more/less) for C and to save
less (more/less).

6-249

Suppose there were no taxes and the consumption and savings schedules were those shown below.

GDP	C	S
$500	$480	$20
510	486	24
520	492	28
530	498	32
540	504	36
550	510	40
560	516	44
570	522	48

Examination of these schedules reveals that for each change in GDP,

0.6 the MPC is equal to ____________ , and the MPS is equal to

0.4 ____________ .

6-250

Now suppose governments levy taxes of $10. At every GDP, consumers will have $10 less for *C* and *S*. And when the DI of consumers decreases by $10, they will decrease their *C* by $10 *multiplied* by the MPC, and their *S* by $10 *multiplied* by the MPS.

In short, at every level of GDP, consumers will reduce their *C* by

$6, $4 $____________ , their *S* by $____________ , and their *C* + *S* by

$10 $____________ .

6-251

Imagine that the MPC is 0.8 and the GDP is $580. The amounts spent for consumption and saved at this GDP are:

GDP	C	S
$580	$550	$30

If governments now levy taxes of $30, *C* will decrease by

$24, $6 $____________ and *S* will decrease by $____________ .

6-252

At the GDP of $580, taxes will be $30. Thus, DI will be only

$550 $____________ . Breaking DI down still further, *C* will now be

$526, $24 $____________ and *S* will be only $____________ .

6-253

decrease
decrease

The effect of taxes is to (increase/decrease) DI by the amount of the taxes. This will have two effects: C will (increase/decrease) by the amount

consume
decrease

of the taxes multiplied by the marginal propensity to ______________ , and S will (increase/decrease) by the amount of the taxes multiplied by

save

the marginal propensity to ______________ .

6-254

In the following table the consumption and saving schedules are reprinted from frame **6-249**. Taxes (T) of \$10 were levied, and the levels to which consumption (C_a) and saving (S_a) fell for each GDP are shown. (C_a and S_a mean C and S after taxes.)

	Before taxes		After taxes		
GDP	**C**	**S**	**C_a**	**S_a**	**T**
\$500	\$480	\$20	\$474	\$16	\$10
510	\$486	24	480	20	10
520	492	28	486	24	10
530	498	32	492	28	10
540	504	36	498	32	10
550	510	40	504	36	10
560	516	44	510	40	10
570	522	48	516	44	10

At any level of GDP, we see that:

C, S

Before taxes, GDP equals __________ + __________ .

C_a, S_a, T

After taxes, GDP equals __________ + __________ + __________ .

6-255

Now suppose that taxes were to increase from \$10 to \$15. The MPC is still 0.6.

The effect of the \$5 tax increase will be to reduce C at every GDP by

\$3, \$2

\$______________ , and reduce S at every GDP by \$______________ .

6-256

If governments *reduced* taxes by \$8 at every GDP, the MPC remaining

\$4.80

at 0.6, C at every GDP would rise by \$______________ , and S at every

\$3.20

GDP would rise by \$______________ .

6-257

Let's go back to the schedules in frame **6-254**

GDP	C_a	S_a	T	$S_a + T$	$I_g + X_n + G$	$C_a + I_g + X_n + G$
\$500	\$474	\$16	\$10	\$26	\$34	\$508
510	480	20	10	30	34	514
520	486	24	10	34	34	520
530	492	28	10	38	34	526
540	498	32	10	42	34	532
550	504	36	10	46	34	538
560	510	40	10	50	34	544
570	516	44	10	54	34	550

In this economy, suppose $I_g + X_n$ were \$16 and G were \$18; $I_g + X_n + G$ would be \$34. The aggregate expenditures ($C_a + I_g + X_n + G$) at the various GDPs are shown in the table.

\$520 GDP and AE are equal at \$________ . This figure is the

equilibrium ________ GDP.

6-258

At the equilibrium GDP of \$520, which statement is true?

(a) $S_a = I_g$
(b) $S_a = I_g + X_n + G$
(c) $S_a + T = I_g = X_n$
(d) $S_a + T = I_g + X_n + G$

(d) Only statement (__) is true.

6-259

Recall that there are only three things people who receive the GDP can do with this income: spend for C, save, and pay taxes. In other words,

C_a, S_a, T GDP = ________ + ________ + ________ .

6-260

So at the equilibrium GDP, $C_a + S_a + T$ equals GDP, which also equals $C_a + I_g + X_n + G$.

expenditures $C_a + I_g + X_n + G$ is called aggregate ________ . And $C_a +$

GDP $S_a + T$ is the ________ .

6-261

To discover the equilibrium GDP in any economy in which governments spend for goods and services and collect taxes, we can look for the GDP at which aggregate expenditures and GDP are equal.

In symbolic terms, this means the GDP where

C_a, S_a, T, C_a, ________ + ________ + ________ = ________

I_g, X_n, G + ________ + ________ + ________

or, simplifying the equation,

S_a, T, I_g, X_n, ________ + ________ = ________ + ________

G + ________ .

6-262

The schedules from frame **6-257** are reprinted below.

GDP	C_a	S_a	T	$S_a + T$	$I_g + X_n + G$	$C_a + I_g + X_n + G$
\$500	\$474	\$16	\$10	\$26	\$34	\$508
510	480	20	10	30	34	514
520	486	24	10	34	34	520
530	492	28	10	38	34	526
540	498	32	10	42	34	532
550	504	36	10	46	34	538
560	510	40	10	50	34	544
570	516	44	10	54	34	550

If I_g *or* X_n should increase from \$16 to \$20, $I_g + X_n + G$ would

\$38 increase from \$34 to \$________ , and the equilibrium GDP

increase, \$530 would (increase/decrease) from \$520 to \$________ .

And if G were to decrease from \$18 to \$10, $I_g + X_n + G$ would

\$26 decrease from \$34 to \$________ , and the equilibrium GDP

fall, \$500 would (rise/fall) to \$________ .

6-263

Changes in either I_g, X_n or G have a multiplier effect upon the economy. But changes in taxes also have a multiplier effect. The changes in taxes, however, *do not* have the same multiplier effect as do the changes in I_g, X_n or G.

0.6 In the examples in the last frame, the MPC was equal to ________

2½ and the multiplier was therefore equal to ________ .

6-264

Let's increase taxes from \$10 to \$20. C at every level of GDP would

\$6 decrease by \$________ .

6-265

A \$6 decrease in C at every GDP has the *same* effect on the equilibrium GDP as a \$6 decrease in either I_g, X_n or G: equilibrium GDP will

fall, \$15 (rise/fall) by \$__________ .

6-266

What have we discovered? That a \$10 change in taxes brought about a \$15 change in the equilibrium GDP. An increase in taxes caused the

opposite equilibrium GDP to change in the (same/opposite) direction. The change

1½ in GDP was __________ times the change in taxes.

6-267

The ***tax multiplier*** in the example was only 1½: GDP changed by 1½ times the change in taxes. The multiplier we used for changes in I_g, X_n or G was equal to 2½ because the MPS was 0.4.

From this example we can reach the conclusion that the tax multiplier

less is (greater/less) than the regular multiplier by an amount *exactly* equal

1 to (1/2/3/4).

6-268

Suppose the MPC were 0.8. The regular multiplier would be

5, 4 __________ and the tax multiplier would be __________ .

6-269

Using this tax multiplier, a \$20 increase in taxes would cause the equi-

de-, \$80 librium GDP to __________-crease by \$__________ , while a \$15 decrease in taxes would result in the equilibrium GDP

in-, 60 __________-creasing by \$__________ .

6-270

Imagine that the equilibrium GDP is \$500 and the MPC is 0.75. To raise

fall, \$20 GDP to \$560, taxes would have to (rise/fall) by \$(20/30/40).

6-271

Assume governments do two things simultaneously: increase taxes by \$20 and increase their expenditures for goods and services by \$20.

If the MPC is ⅔:

The increase in taxes *by itself* will *lower* the equilibrium GDP

\$40 by \$__________ .

The increase in G *by itself* will *raise* the equilibrium GDP by

\$60 \$__________ .

The net or combined effect of equal increases in taxes and G is to

raise, \$20 (raise/lower) the equilibrium GDP by \$__________ .

6-272

There is a principle here, too: Equal *increases* in G and T *increase* the GDP by the same amount that G and T increase, and vice versa.

fall This *balanced-budget multiplier* also works in reverse. If both G and T decreased by \$30, the equilibrium GDP would (rise/fall) by

\$30 \$__________.

6-273

When the changes in T and G are *not* equal or are *not* in the same direction, we can always find their combined effect by adding the effect that each has by itself on the GDP. For example, suppose MPC is 0.8, G increases by \$5, and T falls by \$6.

rise The increase in G alone would cause the GDP to __________

\$25 by \$__________.

rise The decrease in T alone would cause the GDP to __________

\$24 by \$__________.

rise Together they would cause the GDP to __________ by

\$49 \$__________.

So far we have ignored a second kind of government spending: the making of transfer payments. But the effect of this kind of spending on the equilibrium GDP can be easily understood if we will just remember that government transfer payments are simply taxes *in reverse*. When the governments collect taxes, they take money away from citizens and give them no good or service in return. And when governments make transfer payments, they give money to citizens and receive no good or service in return.

6-274

opposite In other words, the collection of \$40 in taxes and the making of \$40 in transfer payments have the (same/opposite) effect upon the equilibrium GDP.

6-275

Suppose the MPC is 0.75 and the governments in the economy make \$60 in transfer payments. The effect of making this \$60 payment will be the exact reverse of the effect of collecting \$60 in taxes: the \$60 transfer payment will (increase/decrease) C at every level of GDP. As a result, the economy's GDP will tend to (rise/fall) by \$(180/240).

increase

rise, \$180

6-276 Review Frame

Now let's review what we have learned about the equilibrium GDP and the multiplier. In reviewing we shall discover that we can use the multiplier *in place of* most of the various schedules and curves that we used earlier to find the equilibrium GDP.

We shall employ only the consumption and saving schedules in the following table.

GDP	C	S
$550	$500	$50
560	508	52
570	516	54
580	524	56

0.8 The MPC is equal to ______________ . The spending multiplier is,
5 therefore, equal to ______________ . If $I_g + X_n$ were $50, the equilib-
$550 rium GDP would be $______________ .

6-277 Review Frame

Now forget the schedules in the preceding frame. Remember only that the spending multiplier is 5 and that when $I_g + X_n$ is $50, the equilibrium GDP is $550. Step by step, let's put government into the picture.

If *G* rises from $0 to $30, the equilibrium GDP rises from $550 to
$700 $______________ .

6-278 Review Frame

Now suppose government levies taxes of $40. The equilibrium GDP will
$540 fall to $______________ .

6-279 Review Frame

Finally, let's have the government make transfer payments of $10. Equi-
$580 librium GDP will now be $______________ .

6-280 Review Frame

If the government believed the GDP of $580 was $40 *too high*, it could lower it to $540 in any of three ways:

raising, $10 by (raising/lowering) taxes by $______________ ,
lowering by (raising/lowering) its purchases of goods and services by
$8 $______________ ,
lowering, $10 or by (raising/lowering) its transfer payments by $______________ .

6-281

Before we go on in the next section to examine money and banking we need to be clear about what we have explained and what we have *not* explained in this section.

In this section we have seen how the aggregate expenditures of consumers, business firms, and governments determine the equilibrium *real* GDP or the *real* domestic output of the economy.

has

This means that the GDP or domestic output (has/has not) been adjusted for any changes in the price level that may have occurred in the economy.

have not

But in this section we (have/have not) explained how the government might try to influence the price level in the economy.

6-282

In examining the amount business firms wish to spend for capital we saw that I_g depends inversely upon the rate of ________ . But in this section we (did/did not) explain what determines this rate.

interest
did not

6-283

In short, we have left two "loose ends" in this chapter. We have not explained what determines the rate of interest or how the government might influence the ____________ level.

price

And the rate of interest is important because it determines how much gross ____________ spending by business firms will be and what, therefore, the size of the equilibrium real ____________ will tend to be.

investment
GDP

Now take the Review Test for Section 6 at the back of the book.

Money and Banking; Fiscal and Monetary Policy

section 7

Money fascinates people. They try to get their hands on as much of it as they can. Having gotten it, most people try to get rid of it. A few find pleasure and enjoyment simply in having money in their possession.

Money also interests economists. They have long known that unless we use money in our society, we must put up with all the inconveniences that go along with the primitive practice of barter. Money serves us as a *medium of exchange*: we exchange goods for money and money for goods instead of trading one good for another.

Economists are interested in money for other reasons. We also use money to save for the future. We store it up so that we have it to spend later: we use it as a *store of value*. And everyone knows that we employ money—dollars and cents—as a *measure of value*; it's the method we use to tell each other how much the price of a good or service is.

Money is important to our economy for an additional and even more important reason: How *much* money there is in the economy affects how large our GDP will be and how many workers will be employed and unemployed.

The facts here are quite simple. First, as we learned in Section 6, aggregate expenditures are the chief determinant of our levels of GDP and employment. Second, the rate of interest is inversely related to the amount of investment spending done by business firms and, therefore, affects the level of aggregate expenditures. Third, as we will learn in this section, the amount of money in the economy affects how high or low the rate of interest will be.

What we want to do first in this section is find out what money is and how to measure the supply of money. Then we can look at the demand for money and see how the demand for and the supply of money determine the rate of interest in the economy. Next we find out who is responsible for increases and decreases in the supply of money. Then we learn who controls or regulates those who are able to increase or decrease the money supply. By answering these questions we clear up one of the "loose ends" we left in the last section: what determines the interest rate.

Finally, we analyze fiscal and monetary policy to show how the central authorities try to achieve full employment with no inflation.

First, however, let's find out what money *is* and what we mean by the money supply.

THE MONEY SUPPLY

7-1

When you drop six quarters and a dime into a vending machine to obtain a package of cigarettes, you are using one kind of money. Economists call this kind of money *coins*. And when you pay $10 for a haircut, you are likely to give the barber or beautician a $10 bill. This second kind of

paper — money is made out of ______________ , and is, for this reason, called

paper — ______________ money.

7-2

Together these two kinds of money are classified as *currency*. One of the two major elements in our money supply is this currency. And

coin, paper — currency consists of both ______________s and ______________

money — ______________ .

7-3

Suppose an automobile manufacturer buys $91,285,192.25 worth of steel from the USX. To pay for the steel, the car maker could either:

(a) deliver $91,285,192.25 in currency to the steel company, or
(b) send USX a check for this amount.

(b) . . . of course — Which will the auto manufacturer probably do? (a/b)

7-4

In our economy there are two principal ways a person or a business may choose to pay for a good or a service. They may give the seller coins or

currency — paper money, which is called ______________ , or a written order to a bank (or other financial institution) to pay someone money. This written

check — order is called a ______________ .

7-5

Of course, before you can lawfully write a check, you must have a checking account at a bank or at some other financial institution. Economists have special names for checking accounts. They call them *checkable deposits*.

The *total* amount of money you have is equal to the size of your checkable deposits *plus* the amount of ______________ you possess. — currency

Most of the checkable deposits owned by Americans are deposits in commercial banks. But such other financial institutions as savings and loan associations, mutual savings banks, and credit unions also accept deposits against which checks may be written. These other financial institutions are often called thrift (or savings) institutions or, simply, *"thrifts."*

The commercial banks *and* thrifts that accept checkable deposits are defined as *depository institutions.*

7-6

The *money supply* is the name given to the total amount of money in the entire economy. This money supply consists of just two principal kinds of money: ____________ and ____________ ____________.

currency, checkable deposits

7-7

In the United States there was (during November of 1991) $261 billion in currency and $605 billion in checkable deposits at depository institutions. Together they amount to $____________ billion; this was the ____________ ____________ in the economy.

866

money supply

7-8

About 70 percent of our money supply was (currency/checkable deposits), and about 30 percent of the money supply was (currency/checkable deposits).

checkable deposits

currency

7-9

It is estimated that about 90 percent of the dollar amount of things purchased in the United States is paid for with checks. All in all it seems reasonable to conclude that currency is the (more/less) important component and checkable deposits are the (more/less) important component of the money supply in the United States.

less

more

7-10

Knowing all these facts about the money supply, suppose you took $5 in currency to your depository-institution and deposited it in your checking account there. There has been no change in the amount of currency in the economy, but the size of your checkable deposit has (increased/decreased) by $5. Therefore, it seems that the money supply has also (increased/decreased) by $5.

increased

increased

7-11

Does this simple deposit of $5 in a checking account actually increase our money supply by $5? Do you have $5 more money than you previously had? Of course not! You have $5 (more/less) of checkable-deposit money, and $5 (more/less) of currency.

more

less

7-12

Your depository institution, however, has a $5 bill it didn't previously have. But this $5 bill really isn't theirs, it belongs to you. You simply placed it there for safekeeping, and they must return it whenever you ask for it. Actually it is the *same* $5 that you have in your checking account; to count the $5 bill in the institution and the $5 in your checking account each as a part of the money supply is to count the same $5 twice. So in fact, the deposit of the $5 bill in your checking account has left the money supply (decreased by $5/unchanged/increased by $5).

unchanged

7-13

How then are we to account for the fact that the money supply doesn't change at all when people deposit currency in their checking accounts? After all, there is $5 *more* in checkable deposits and the same amount of currency in the economy when you deposit $5 in your account. Economists simply (include/exclude) all currency in depository institutions when calculating the money supply.

exclude

7-14

So when you deposited the $5 bill in your checking account: The checkable deposit part of the money supply (rose/fell) by $5, the currency component (increased/decreased) by $5, and the total money supply did not ______________ .

rose
decreased
change

7-15

Economists also *ex*clude from the money supply of the U.S. any money owned by the Federal government or the Federal Reserve Banks. (We will have more to say about the Federal Reserve Banks later in this section.) Why economists do this we won't explain here.

But these exclusions mean that the currency the Federal government and the Federal Reserve Banks have in their vaults (is/is not) a part of the money supply, and their checking accounts (are/are not) in the American money supply.

is not
are not

7-16

The money supply as we have defined it is called *M*1. In addition to the *M*1 money supply, economists at the Federal Reserve Banks have broader definitions of the money supply which they call *M*2 and *M*3. We won't be concerned with these broader definitions of the money supply.

When we talk about the money supply we will be talking of *M*1; and when we want to know the size of this money supply, we first add the amounts of currency and checkable deposits in the economy.

But from this total we have to *subtract* the ______________ ______________ of the Federal government and the Federal Reserve Banks and the amounts of ______________ owned by the Federal government, the Federal Reserve Banks, and depository institutions.

The remainder is called (*M*1/*M*2/*M*3).

checkable
deposits
currency
*M*1

7-17

Imagine now that we know the following things about our economy. (Figures are in billions.)

Total currency in the economy	$ 72
Total checkable deposits in the economy	208
Currency in depository institutions	11
Currency belonging to the Federal government and the Federal Reserve Banks	1
Checkable deposits of the Federal government and the Federal Reserve Banks	3

$72 To determine the money supply, we would first add $________
$208 billion and $________ billion; then we would subtract
$11, $1, $3 $________ billion, $________ billion, and $________
$265 billion; to discover that the money supply is $________ billion.

7-18 Review Frame

We now know what money and the money supply are. In the United
currency States the money supply consists of the ________ and the
checkable deposits ________ ________ that are not owned by the
depository institutions, government ________ ________, the Federal ________, and
Reserve the Federal ________ Banks.

THE DEMAND FOR MONEY AND THE RATE OF INTEREST

The rate of interest is the price paid for the use of money, and, like any other price, depends upon both supply and demand. Let's look next at the demand for money and then put the demand for and the supply of money together to explain the rate of interest.

7-19

Households and business firms use money as a medium of exchange: they use it to purchase goods and services. They also use money as a store of value; they set it aside for future use. Ralph Roberts, for example, works for a business firm and is paid every month. On the first day of every month he receives $2,500 from his employer. His average
$500 propensity to save is 0.2 and so he saves $________ and spends
$2,000 $________ for goods and services every month.

7-20

He spends all of the $2,000 he has decided to spend for consumer goods and services during the following month. Ignoring the $500 he has saved:

On the first of each month he has $2,000.

By the end of the month he has $0.

The *average* amount of the $2,000 he possessed during the month was

$1,000 ($2,000 + $0) divided by 2, or $__________ .

7-21

The $2,000 in money he spent for goods and services during the month

medium of exchange he used as a (medium of exchange/store of value). If he kept the $500 he saved in his checking account or in currency, this $500 was being used

store of value as a (medium of exchange/store of value).

7-22

Assume the take-home pay of Ralph Roberts increased from $2,500 to $3,000 a month. If his marginal propensity to consume is 0.8, he would increase his monthly spending for goods and services from $2,000 to

$2,400 $__________ .

The average amount of money he would hold as a medium of exchange is the average of this amount and $0. This average would be

$1,200 $__________ .

7-23

In this example, as the take-home income of Ralph Roberts increased from $2,500 to $3,000 a month the average amount of money he wished

increased to hold as a medium of exchange (increased/decreased).

7-24

Economists call the amount of money households and business firms wish to have in their possession to use as a medium of exchange the *transactions demand for money* (D_t). In our example the D_t of Ralph

$1,000 Roberts was $__________ when his income was $2,500 a month

$1,200 and was $__________ when his income was $3,000 a month.

7-25

directly In short, Roberts's D_t was (directly/inversely) related to his income.

7-26

What was true of Ralph Roberts in our example is also true of the economy as a whole.

The amount of money firms and persons wish to have in their posses-

transactions sion to use as a medium of exchange is the __________ demand for money; and it is directly related to the total (income/

income wealth) of the economy.

7-27

The total income of the economy can be measured (as we learned in Section 4) in a number of different ways. We can measure its income by computing the GDP, NDP, NI, PI, or DI. Each of these can be measured either before or after adjustments have been made for changes in the price level of the economy.

The best way, it seems, to predict how much money people want to hold for transactions is to use the *nominal* (money) GDP.

increase — So as nominal GDP increases, D_t will (increase/decrease); and as the

decrease — nominal GDP decreases, D_t will ______________ .

7-28

A transactions demand for money curve is shown on the graph below.

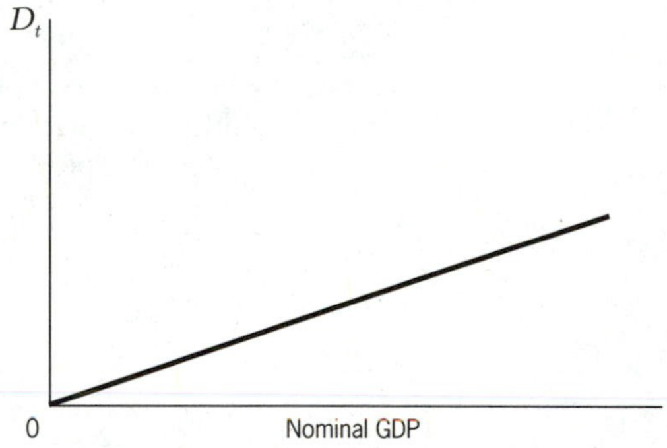

directly, nominal GDP — The curve slopes upward because D_t is ______________ related to the (real/nominal) (GDP/NDP).

7-29

To review: the transactions demand for money is the amount of money firms and households wish to have in their possession to use as a

medium, exchange — ______________ of ______________ and depends directly on the

nominal GDP — ______________ ______________ .

7-30

Remember the $500 Ralph Roberts saved every month when his monthly take-home income was $2,500 and the $600 he saved monthly when it was $3,000 a month? If he put his monthly saving in his checking account or kept currency in some safe place he was using this money as

store of value — a (medium of exchange/store of value).

7-31

Keeping your current and past saving in a checkbook account or in currency is not, however, the only way you can accumulate wealth or assets for future use. Money is only one type of asset that can be used as a store of value. Instead of holding money as a store of value, you might (for example) decide to hold a bond as a store of value. There is, however, this difference.

will not — If you hold currency as a store of value you (will/will not) earn any interest from your wealth.

not earn — And, like holding currency, if you hold a checking deposit as a store of value you will for all practical purposes (earn/not earn) interest from your wealth.

will — But if you hold a bond or a similar asset as a store of value you (will/will not) earn interest on your wealth.

7-32

As an example, suppose you had $40,000 which you could hold either as money or use to buy bonds. If the rate of interest on bonds were 8% per year and you chose to hold the $40,000 in money you would earn

$0 — $________ from your wealth each year; but if you purchased the

$3,200 — bonds you could earn $________ each year from your wealth.

And if the rate of interest were 9 percent per year and you bought the

3,600 — bonds you could earn $________ from your wealth each year.

7-33

Were you to decide to hold money rather than the bonds you would incur a *cost*. The cost of holding money is the income that you don't earn (that you go without or sacrifice). With $40,000:

when the rate of interest is 10%, the cost of holding your wealth in

$4,000 — money is $________ a year;

when the rate of interest is 7 percent, the cost of holding your wealth

$2,800 — in money is $________ a year.

7-34

greater — In short, the higher the rate of interest the (greater/smaller) is the cost of holding money and the lower the rate of interest the

smaller — ________ is the cost of holding money.

7-35

Because there is a cost to holding money as a store of value, it is surprising that anyone decides to keep any wealth in the form of money. There is, however, a benefit or advantage to having some of your wealth in money. If you decide you wish to use a part of your wealth to purchase a good (such as an automobile) or a service (such as a vacation in Las

can — Vegas) you will discover that you (can/cannot) use money to pay for the

cannot — good or service; but you (can/cannot) pay for them with the bond.

7-36

cost of

For this reason, households (and business firms, too) will almost always hold some of their wealth in money and some in such assets as bonds that earn interest. However, the higher the rate of interest the greater is the (cost of/income from) holding money, and vice versa.

7-37

less, more

When the rate of interest rises households and business firms find that the cost of holding money has increased. Like most other things, when the cost of holding money increases those with wealth will decide that they want to hold (more/less) of their wealth in money and (more/less) of it in bonds.

7-38

smaller

larger

Economists call the amount of money people wish to hold as a store of value the *asset demand for money* (D_a). As we saw above:

The higher the rate of interest, the greater is the cost of holding money as a store of value and the (larger/smaller) will be the quantity of money people want to hold as an asset.

And the lower the rate of interest, the smaller is the cost of holding money as a store of value and the ____________ will be the quantity of money people wish to hold as an asset.

7-39

downward

inverse, interest

On the graph below is a curve showing the asset demand for money. The curve slopes (upward/downward). This means that there is a(n) (direct/inverse) relationship between the rate of ____________ and the amount of money people wish to hold as assets.

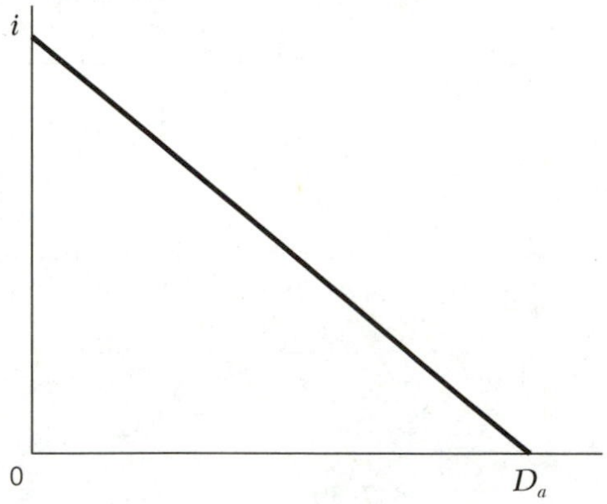

7-40

rise

fall

Put another way: when the rate of interest falls, the quantity of money people wish to hold as an asset or store of value will (rise/fall); and when the interest rate rises, the quantity of money they would like to have for this purpose will ____________ .

7-41

There is, along this curve a(n) ______ relationship between the * ______ and the * ______.

inverse
rate of interest
amount of money people wish to hold as a store of value (as an asset) (either order)

7-42

What we have found so far is that there are two demands for money (or two reasons why people want to have money in their possession). These two demands for money are the ______ demand and the ______ demand.

transactions
asset (either order)

7-43

The quantity of money demanded for transaction purposes is ______ related to the ______ ______. The amount of money demanded for asset purposes is ______ related to the ______ ______ ______.

directly, nominal GDP
inversely
rate of interest

7-44

The total demand for money is the sum of the transactions demand and the asset demand. The amount of money people will wish to hold will increase when the nominal GDP (rises/falls) or the rate of interest ______; and it will decrease if the nominal GDP ______ or the rate of interest ______.

rises
falls
falls, rises

7-45

We now have all the ingredients needed to explain what the rate of interest will be.

The rate of interest is the ______ paid for the use of money.

The rate of interest is determined by the money ______ and the ______ for money.

price
supply
demand

7-46

At any moment—such as at the end of a day, week, or month—a certain quantity of money exists in the economy.

The quantity of existing money is called the ______ ______.

All of this money (is/is not) owned by someone.

money
supply
is (If you know of some money that isn't owned by someone, write me. Then we'll go and get this unowned money and split it fifty-fifty.)

7-47

To the left of the double line in the table below is the transactions demand for money. The asset demand for money is to the right of the double line.

Nominal GDP	D_t	i	D_a
$ 900	$180	8%	$20
1,000	200	7	30
1,100	220	6	40
1,200	240	5	50
1,300	260	4	60
1,400	280	3	70
1,500	300	2	80

Suppose the nominal GDP were $1,000 and the rate of interest were 7%.

$200, $30 D_t would be $______ and D_a would be $______ .
The total or market demand for money (D_m) would be

$230 $______ .

7-48

Let's suppose that the nominal GDP is constant at $1,000, but that i can be anywhere between 8 percent and 2 percent. Complete the table below to show D_m—the total demand for money—at each of the seven rates of interest.

Answer	i	D_m
$220	8%	$______
$230	7	______
$240	6	______
$250	5	______
$260	4	______
$270	3	______
$280	2	______

7-49

Continue to assume the nominal GDP is $1,000. The total demand for money is as follows:

i	D_m
8%	$220
7	230
6	240
5	250
4	260
3	270
2	280

If the money supply (S_m) is \$250, for S_m to be equal to the amount of money people wish to hold (D_m), the rate of interest would have to be

5% equal to ________ percent.

7-50

Suppose the rate of interest were 6 percent.

less D_m would be (greater/less) than S_m.

\$240 People would want to have a quantity of money equal to \$________ ,

\$250 but the amount of money they actually have is \$________ .

more They have (more/less) money than they want to have.

And if the rate of interest were 4%:

greater D_m would be ________________ than S_m. People would want to have

\$260 a quantity of money equal to \$________ , but the amount of money

\$250, less they actually have is \$________ . They have ____________ than they want to have.

7-51

Just as in other competitive markets, the ***equilibrium rate*** of interest is the rate at which the amount of money demanded is equal to the quantity of money supplied.

If the quantity of money supplied—the money supply—is fixed at \$250, the equilibrium rate of interest is 5 percent because at this rate of

\$250 interest the quantity of money demanded is also \$________ . At lower

greater rates of interest the quantity of money demanded is (greater/less) than

rise the money supply and the rate of interest will (rise/fall). And at higher

less rates D_m is ________________ than S_m and the rate of interest will

fall ____________ .

7-52

Why does the rate of interest rise if it is below the equilibrium and fall if it is above the equilibrium rate of interest?

When the rate of interest is below the equilibrium rate of interest

shortage there is a (shortage/surplus) of money in the economy.

And when the rate is above the equilibrium rate there is a

surplus ______________ of money in the economy.

7-53

When there is a shortage of money in the economy those who want to hold more money than they have bid the interest rate—the price paid

upward for the use of money—(upward/downward). But if there is a surplus of money in the economy those who want to hold less than they actually

down have will bid the interest rate ______________-ward.

7-54

On the graph below are the D_t, D_a, and D_m curves and the S_m curve.

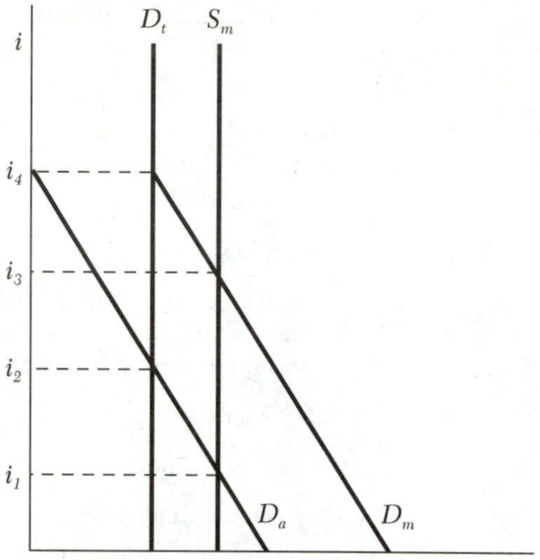

D_t is a vertical line because we have assumed that nominal GDP and the amount of money demanded for transactions is fixed. But if the nominal GDP were to increase the D_t curve would move to the (right/left); and if nominal GDP decreased the D_t curve would shift to the ____________ .

right | left

S_m is also a vertical line because at any time the money supply of the economy is fixed. But if S_m were to increase the money supply curve would shift to the (right/left) and if S_m decreased the money supply curve would move to the ____________ .

right | left

The D_a and D_m curves slope downward because as the rate of interest falls, the quantity of money demanded for asset purposes and the total quantity of money demanded will (increase/decrease).

increase

7-55

On the graph in frame **7-54** the equilibrium rate of interest is (i_1/i_2/i_3/i_4) because at this rate of interest

i_3

(a) $D_t = D_m$
(b) $D_m = S_m$
(c) $D_a = D_t$
(d) $D_a = S_m$

Which one? ____________

(b)

7-56

So we have learned what the rate of interest in the economy will tend to be. It will be the rate at which the money supply equals * ____________ ____________ .

the total quantity of money demanded for transactions and asset purposes

7-57

We can also use demand and supply to explain what causes the rate of interest to change.

fall — If the money supply were to increase, the rate of interest would (rise/fall) and if S_m were to decrease the rate of interest would

rise — ______________ .

inverse — There is, therefore, a(n) (direct/inverse) relationship between S_m and i.

7-58

Suppose the nominal GDP were to expand.

increase, increase — D_t would (increase/decrease) and D_m would ________________ .

rise — And the rate of interest would (rise/fall).

And if the nominal GDP were to contract, D_t and D_m would

decrease, fall — ______________ and the rate of interest would ______________ .

direct — There is, in short a(n) ________________ relation between nominal GDP and i, assuming no change in S_m.

7-59

Because the nominal GDP equals the real (or adjusted) GDP *multiplied* by the price level, D_t and D_m will increase when either the real GDP or

increase — the price level (or both) (increase/decrease) and this will cause the rate

rise — of interest to ______________ .

7-60

This is not too surprising a result of a rise in the price level. When the price level rises, the interest rate also rises. But, after all, the rate of

price — interest is nothing more than the ______________ paid for the use of money.

7-61

All this means that the two important determinants of the level of the interest rate in our economy are our money supply and our nominal GDP. As we saw in Section 6, the rate of interest is an important

investment — determinant of (consumption/investment/government) spending in the economy.

more, greater — And as we learned in Section 6, the lower the rate of interest the (more/less) investment spending there will be and the (greater/smaller) will be the real GDP produced in the economy.

7-62

So we have eliminated one of the "loose ends" we left in Section 6.

What determines the rate of interest is the money supply and the

demand — ______________ for money.

lower — The greater the money supply, the (higher/lower) will be the rate of

higher — interest, the (higher/lower) will be the amount of investment spending

higher — and the (higher/lower) will be the real GDP.

the higher will be the interest rate and the lower will *I* and real GDP be

But the smaller the money supply, * ______________________________ ______________________________.

Before we review, let's note that we have not explained what determines the money supply in the economy and who controls this money supply. This we will do in the next part of this section.

7-63 Review Frame

the money supply and the demand for money

The rate of interest is determined by * ______________________________ ______________________________.

transactions

asset (either order)

The total demand for money is the sum of the ______________ and the ______________ demand.

fixed

At any time the money supply is ______________.

7-64 Review Frame

directly

the nominal GDP

The transactions demand is ______________ related to * ______________ ______________.

inversely, the rate of interest

The asset demand is ______________ related to * ______________ ______________.

7-65 Review Frame

the money supply is equal to the quantity of money demanded

The equilibrium rate of interest is the rate at which * ______________ ______________________________.

decreases, increases

decrease

decrease

The equilibrium rate of interest will increase when either the money supply ____________ or the nominal GDP ______________. This increase in the rate of interest will tend to ____________ investment spending, and, therefore, to ______________ the real GDP produced in the economy.

the money supply increases, the nominal GDP decreases (either order)

increase both

A decrease in the rate of interest will occur when either * ______________________________ or * ______________ and this decrease in the rate of interest will have the following effects on investment and the real GDP: * ______________________________.

THE COMMERCIAL BANK

We have seen how to measure the money supply or *M*1 and learned that changes in the money supply affect the interest rate, investment spending, and the real GDP. In our economy the money supply does change. The American money supply is not the same year after year, month after month, or week after week. *M*1, for example, expanded from $825.4 billion at the end of 1990 to $896.7 by the end of 1991—an increase of $71.3 billion in one year. Between January and February of 1983, however, our money supply fell by $9 billion.

Where do the additional dollars in the economy come from when the money supply expands? And where do the dollars go when the money supply contracts? What causes the money supply to expand and to contract? These are the questions we want to answer next.

The plain facts about our money supply are these: money can be created and destroyed; the depository institutions in our economy are responsible for the creation and destruction of money; and depository institutions create money when they make loans and money is destroyed when loans are repaid.

The kind of money that is created and destroyed by depository institutions is not currency. It is the amount of *checkable-deposit* money which depository institutions expand and contract. The greater part—about two-thirds—of the checkable deposits in the American economy are *demand deposits* in *commercial banks*. Demand deposits are nothing more than checking accounts in commercial banks; and commercial banks are the depository institutions which we commonly call banks: the institutions which are not savings and loan associations, mutual savings banks, or credit unions.

Because such a larger portion of all checkable deposits are demand deposits in commercial banks, we are going to focus our attention on the commercial banks and the demand deposits they create and destroy. But whenever we say commercial bank, you may say depository institution instead; and when we use the expression demand deposit you may substitute checkable deposit.

Let's find out how and when commercial banks create money and whether there are limits on the amount of money they can create. The device which we will use to help us understand the creation and destruction of demand-deposit money is the *balance sheet*.

7-66

Here is the somewhat simplified balance sheet of a typical commercial bank. (For simplicity we have omitted the last six zeroes from all figures.)

Assets		Liabilities and net worth	
Cash	$ 100	Liabilities	
Deposits at the FRB	500	Demand deposits	$2,100
Loans	1,000	Time deposits	200
Securities	900	Net worth	200
Total	$2,500	Total	$2,500

You find that listed on the left side of the balance sheet are the bank's

assets, liabilities ______________ . The right side lists the bank's ______________

net worth and ______________ ______________ .

7-67

Assets are everything which the bank *owns* and which have a dollar and cents value. *Liabilities* are the amounts which the bank *owes*. *Net worth* shows us how much of the assets the bank's *stockholders own*.

This bank has:

$2,500 Assets worth $________

$2,300 Liabilities of $________

$200 A net worth of $________

7-68

Why is this called a balance sheet? Because the assets always equal or balance the liabilities *and* net worth. This means that the net worth is nothing more than the bank's assets *minus* its liabilities.

For example, if assets were $20,000 and liabilities were $17,000

$3,000 the net worth would be $______________ ; assets must equal liabilities

plus (plus/minus) net worth.

7-69

What are the principal assets of a commercial bank? *Cash* is the currency it has in its vaults. *Deposits at the FRB* is the dollar amount that the bank has on deposit at the Federal Reserve Bank (the bank's bank).

For simplicity let's put these two assets together and call them the bank's *reserves*. The commercial bank in frame **7-66** has reserves of

$600 $________ .

7-70

The other two assets of a commercial bank are loans and securities. *Loans* are nothing more than the IOUs the bank receives from borrowers when the bank lends them money. *Securities* are the United States government bonds which the bank owns.

We can lump loans and securities together and call them the bank's *other assets*. The commercial bank in frame **7-66** has other assets of

$1,900 $__________ .

7-71

Now we can simplify the assets side of the bank's balance sheet. In frame **7-66** there were four entries under *Assets*. There are now two. *Cash* and *Deposits at the FRB* that can be combined and called

reserves ______________ ; *Loans* and *Securities* can be combined and called

other assets ______________ ______________ .

Assets	
Reserves	$ 600
Other assets	1,900
Total	$2,500

7-72

Other assets are the income-earning assets of the bank. When banks make loans, they charge borrowers for the use of the borrowed money. The fee borrowers pay a bank for the use of money, as everyone knows, is called (rent/interest/profit).

interest

7-73

Securities are just engraved IOUs issued by borrowers of money. The securities owned by commercial banks are issued by the ______ ______ ______. The income earned by the owners of these fancy IOUs is also called ______.

United States government

interest

7-74

Reserves are *non-income-earning assets*. Currency in the bank's vault is not earning the bank any interest. Likewise, the Federal Reserve Bank does *not* pay interest on deposits the commercial bank has at the FRB.

In short, commercial banks earn income only from their (other assets/reserves).

other assets

7-75

We will discuss shortly why commercial banks choose to have assets which do not earn them any income. What we have learned, however, is that banks earn income from the ______ and ______ they own. The income resulting from the ownership of these assets is called ______.

loans, securities (either order)

interest

7-76

We already know what demand deposits are; now let's look at *time deposits*. Time deposits are those deposits on which checks *cannot* be written and which the bank need not pay to the depositor on demand; the bank *may* require the depositor to wait a period of time before the deposit is returned to him or her. Time deposits and demand deposits together are the two principal (assets/liabilities) of commercial banks.

liabilities

7-77

If you have a checking account, you have ______ *deposits* in the bank. If you have a noncheckable account, you have ______ *deposits* in the bank.

demand

time

7-78 Review Frame

To simplify our discussion of how banks create and destroy money, let's pretend that commercial banks *accept* only demand deposits. Our abbreviated balance sheet will now look like this (converting all former time deposits to demand deposits).

Assets		Liabilities and net worth	
Reserves	$ 600	Demand deposits	$2,300
Other assets	1,900	Net worth	200
Total	$2,500	Total	$2,500

Let's review briefly what these items on the balance sheet represent.

other assets — The assets which are income-earning are its (reserves/other assets),

reserves — and the assets which are non-income-earning are its (reserves/other assets).

7-79 Review Frame

loans — Continuing our review, other assets are the ______ and

securities (either order) — ______ which the bank owns. Reserves are the

currency, deposits (account) — ______ it has in its vaults and the ______ it has

Federal Reserve — at the ______ ______ Bank.

7-80

Now why would any commercial bank choose to own assets which do not earn any interest income for the bank? Because commercial banks are required by banking laws to have a reserve. This ***required reserve*** may be *either* currency in their vaults *or* deposits at the Federal Reserve Bank, or both.

Thus, commercial banks choose to keep some of their required reserve in the vault to satisfy the day-to-day needs of depositors who

checks — wish to cash ______. Commercial banks keep the remainder

reserves — of their ______ in their accounts at the Federal Reserve Banks.

7-81

The required reserve of any commercial bank depends upon the amount of deposits in the bank and the ***reserve ratio***, a percentage set by the Federal Reserve Banks in accordance with the Depository Institutions Deregulation and Monetary Control Act of 1980. A commercial bank's required reserve is equal to its deposits *multiplied by* the reserve ratio. For example, if there is $50,000 in deposits and the reserve ratio is 20

$10,000 — percent, the bank's required reserve is $______.

7-82

Suppose the reserve ratio were 25 percent for the bank whose balance sheet is given below:

Reserves	$ 30,000	Demand deposits	$100,000
Other assets	75,000	Net worth	5,000
	$105,000		$105,000

$25,000 The bank's *required* reserves would be $________ . The bank's

$30,000 ***actual reserves*** are $________ .

7-83

When a bank's actual reserves are greater than its required reserves, the bank has ***excess reserves***. The bank in frame **7-82** has excess reserves of $5,000 because its actual reserves exceed its required reserves by $5,000.

If the reserve ratio were 20 percent instead of 25 percent, its required

$20,000 reserves would be $________ , and excess reserves would be

$10,000 $________ .

7-84

Here is another balance sheet.

Reserves	$145,000	Demand deposits	$600,000
Other assets	480,000	Net worth	25,000
	$625,000		$625,000

Suppose the reserve ratio is 15 percent:

actual — $145,000 is the bank's (actual/required/excess) reserves.

required — $90,000 is the bank's (actual/required/excess) reserves.

excess — $55,000 is the bank's (actual/required/excess) reserves.

7-85

From time to time a commercial bank may find that it has *negative* excess reserves: that is, actual reserves are *less* than its required reserves. If a bank had the balance sheet in frame **7-84** and the reserve ratio were:

positive — 20 percent, it would have (positive/negative) excess reserves of

25,000 — $________ .

negative — 25 percent, it would have (positive/negative) excess reserves of

5,000 — $________ .

7-86

To find a bank's required reserves multiply its demand-deposit liability

reserve ratio — by the ________ ________ .

To find a bank's actual reserves look under *Assets* on the ________

balance sheet ________ .

required To find a bank's excess reserves subtract its ________ reserves

actual from its ________ reserves.

7-87

A commercial bank has *positive* excess reserves when its actual reserves

greater are (greater/less) than its required reserves and *negative* excess reserves

less when its actual reserves are (greater/less) than its required reserves.

7-88

Why do we take the trouble to examine the reserves of a commercial bank? Because the amount of additional money a single commercial bank can safely create is *equal* to its *excess* reserves. Consider this balance sheet and a reserve ratio of 25 percent:

Reserves	$140,000	Demand deposits	$500,000
Other assets	380,000	Net worth	20,000
	$520,000		$520,000

$15,000 This bank has excess reserves of $________ , and the bank can

$15,000 safely create $________ more money.

7-89

Banks create money by making new, or additional, loans. Thus, when a new loan for $15,000 is made, the bank acquires a new IOU for $15,000. The bank then puts $15,000 more in the demand-deposit account of the borrower. In other words, the bank increases the amount it owes the borrower by increasing the amount in his or her checking account.

Refer to the balance sheet in frame **7-88**. After the bank has made a

$395,000 $15,000 loan, its other assets will be equal to $________ ; demand

$515,000 deposits will be $________ .

7-90

Here is the bank's new balance sheet.

Reserves	$140,000	Demand deposits	$515,000
Other assets	395,000	Net worth	20,000
	$535,000		$535,000

increased As a result of the loan, demand deposits have (increased/decreased)

$15,000 by $________ .

increase The loan of $15,000 has caused the money supply to (increase/

$15,000 decrease) by $________ .

7-91

Look back to the balance sheet in frame **7-90**. If the reserve ratio is still

$128,750 25 percent, the bank's required reserves are now $________, and

$11,250 its excess reserves are now $________.

Why did the bank lend only $15,000 if it would still have excess reserves of $11,250 after making the loan? Why didn't it lend more? With excess reserves of $15,000 and a reserve ratio of 25 percent, it might have lent *$60,000* and still have had all the reserves required by law. The bank limited the loan to the amount of its excess reserves because:

People and business firms borrow from banks to have money to *spend*,

The borrower of the $15,000 will spend it shortly by *writing checks* for $15,000,

The lending bank must assume that the persons who receive checks written by borrowers will deposit them in *other* commercial banks in the economy (their own banks).

Now let's see what happens to the lending bank's balance sheet when the money it lent is spent by the borrower and deposited in other commercial banks.

7-92

Here is the bank's balance sheet after it made the loan.

Reserves	$140,000	Demand deposits	$515,000
Other assets	395,000	Net worth	20,000
	$535,000		$535,000

When the borrower spends the $15,000 by writing checks for that amount, the bank decreases the balance in his or her account by $15,000.

$500,000 Demand deposits in the bank will now be only $________.

7-93

When the checks are deposited in other commercial banks, the lending bank must pay $15,000 to the other banks. How does it pay them? By sending them currency? Not very likely. It pays them out of its checking account at the Federal Reserve Bank. When it pays the other banks, its balance at the FRB will decrease by $15,000. The lending bank's reserves

$125,000 will now be only $________.

7-94

After the checks for $15,000 are written, deposited in other banks, and the lending bank has paid the other banks, its balance sheet will be:

Reserves	$125,000	Demand deposits	$500,000
Other assets	395,000	Net worth	20,000
	$520,000		$520,000

If the reserve ratio is still 25 percent, the bank's excess reserves are

$0 — now $________. Therefore, it can safely make additional loans

$0 (Review frame 7-88 if you missed this.) — of $________.

7-95

The new loans a commercial bank can safely make are equal to its excess reserves because a lending bank must assume that it will (lose/regain) this amount of reserves and demand deposits to other commercial banks after the loan is made.

lose

Why? Because there are 14,000 commercial banks in the U.S., and the chances of having a borrower pay the money to someone who banks at the same bank that made the loan are rather (good/slim).

slim

7-96

Let's see what happens to a commercial bank that lends more than its excess reserves. Here is its balance sheet *before* it makes the loan.

Reserves	$ 90,000	Demand deposits	$400,000
Other assets	320,000	Net worth	10,000
	$410,000		$410,000

If the reserve requirement is 20 percent, the bank has excess reserves

$10,000 ($90,000–80,000) — of $________.

7-97

Because the excess reserves of $10,000 are 20 percent of $50,000, the bank decides to make $50,000 in additional loans. Write in the missing figures as they would appear in the balance sheet just after the bank has made new loans of $50,000.

Reserves	$90,000	Demand deposits	$______
Other assets	______	Net worth	10,000

$450,000

$370,000

7-98

Next, the $50,000 is spent by the borrowers. They write checks for this amount and give them to people and firms who deposit them in other banks. These checks must then "clear." That is, the FRB notifies the

$50,000 — lending bank that its account has been reduced by $________ and

$50,000 — that the other banks' accounts have been increased by $________.

7-99

Now let's look at the balance sheet of our lending bank (refer back to frame **7-97**):

$400,000 — Demand deposits will now be only $__________ . Reserves will be

$40,000 — only $__________ .

7-100

The bank's balance sheet now appears as:

Reserves	$ 40,000	Demand deposits	$400,000
Other assets	370,000	Net worth	10,000
	$410,000		$410,000

The reserve ratio is still 20 percent and the bank has an excess reserve

−$40,000 — of $__________ .

7-101

Because the bank lent $40,000 *more* than its excess reserves it now finds itself with *negative* excess reserves of $40,000. If a bank wishes to conform with the banking laws and never have negative excess reserves it must limit the new loans it makes to an amount equal to its

excess reserves — __________ __________ .

7-102

Commercial banks create demand-deposit money when they make loans. And when loans are repaid, just the opposite happens: money is *destroyed.*

Suppose a borrower repays a $5,000 loan from the bank by writing a check for $5,000 on his or her account in the bank. We'll ignore the interest paid the bank. The bank returns the borrower's IOU when the loan is repaid.

demand deposits — There will be a $5,000 decrease in __________ __________ .

other assets (either order) — There will also be a $5,000 decrease in __________ __________ .

7-103

Because demand deposits are money, as a result of the repayment of the

decreased, $5,000 — loan the money supply has (increased/decreased) by $__________ .

7-104

Suppose the borrower had repaid the loan at bank A by writing a check against his or her account at bank B. On bank B's balance sheet, demand

decreased, $5,000 — deposits would have (increased/decreased) by $__________ , and re-

decreased, $5,000 — serves would have (increased/decreased) by $__________ .

7-105

increased — On bank A's balance sheet, reserves would have (increased/decreased)

$5,000, decreased — by $________ , and other assets would have (increased/decreased)

$5,000 — by $________ .

7-106

As a result of the repayment of the loan, the money supply would have

decreased, $5,000 — ____________ by $________ .

7-107

If the borrower had repaid the loan in currency, there would be $5,000

less — (more/less) currency in the money supply.

7-108

In addition to creating money by making loans, commercial banks also create money whenever they *buy securities*—as long as those from whom they purchase the securities are *not* the Federal government or other banks. The amount of securities a bank can safely buy is again equal to the size of its excess reserves.

Consider the Milltown National Bank, a commercial bank with this balance sheet:

Reserves	$ 24,000	Demand deposits	$120,000
Other assets	101,000	Net worth	5,000
	$125,000		$125,000

If the reserve ratio is 15 percent, the bank has excess reserves of

$6,000, $6,000 — $________ . It can safely buy $________ worth of securities.

7-109

Suppose that the Milltown National Bank does purchase $6,000 in securities and gives the seller a check for this amount drawn on its *own account* in the Milltown National Bank (where else would you expect a bank to bank!). Its *other assets* and *demand deposits* will each increase by $6,000.

Demand deposits in the economy have increased by $6,000, and the

increased, $6,000 — money supply has ____________ by $________ .

7-110

A bank creates money when it buys securities from anyone but the Fed-

destroys — eral government or other banks; it ____________ money when it sells securities to anyone but the Federal government or other banks.

7-111

Imagine that a commercial bank with the following balance sheet *sells* $3,000 worth of securities to one of its own depositors.

Reserves	$ 6,000	Demand deposits	$30,000
Other assets	26,000	Net worth	2,000
	$32,000		$32,000

$23,000 Its other assets will now be $________ , its demand de-

$27,000 posits will be ________ , and the money supply will have

de-, $3,000 ________-creased by $________ .

7-112

The effect upon the money supply would have been the same if the purchaser of the securities had paid for them by writing a check on an account in another bank, because both the reserves and the

demand deposits ________ ________ in the other bank would have decreased by $3,000.

7-113

If the purchaser had paid for the securities with currency, the amount

decreased of currency in the money supply would have ________ by $3,000.

7-114 Review Frame

Now let's review what we have learned. Commercial banks create money

loans, securities when they make ________ or when they buy ________ from the

repaid public. Money is destroyed when loans are ________ or when

sell commercial banks ________ securities to the public.

7-115 Review Frame

The amount of new loans a bank can safely make and the amount of

excess securities it can safely buy are equal to its ________

reserves ________ .

7-116 Review Frame

its deposits times the reserve ratio A commercial bank's required reserves are equal to ________ ________ .

its actual reserves minus its required reserves Its excess reserves are equal to ________ ________ .

7-117 Review Frame

If a commercial bank lends *more* than the amount of its excess reserves, it may soon find itself with (positive/negative/zero) excess reserves. But if it limits itself to lending only the amount of its excess reserves, its excess reserves will never be (positive/negative/zero).

negative
negative

7-118 Review Frame

What happens to the size of the country's money supply if a commercial bank:

Sells $20,000 in securities to buyers other than the Federal government or other banks? * ____________________

It decreases by $20,000.

Accepts repayment of an $800 loan? * ____________________

It decreases by $800.

Makes a new loan of $1,500? * ____________________

It increases by $1,500.

Buys $12,000 of securities from sellers other then the Federal government or other banks? * ____________________

It increases by $12,000.

7-119 Review Frame

To *increase* the money supply, commercial banks must either make (more/fewer) loans or (buy/sell) securities from the public. And to *decrease* the money supply, banks should either make (more/fewer) loans or (buy/sell) securities to the public.

more, buy
fewer
sell

THE COMMERCIAL BANKING SYSTEM

We have seen that the amount by which any *individual* commercial bank can safely expand the money supply is equal to its excess reserves. For every dollar of excess reserves it has, a single bank is able to increase the supply of money by just one dollar. It might seem reasonable, therefore, to conclude that the money supply can increase by one dollar for every dollar of excess reserves in all the banks in the economy.

But one of the peculiar characteristics of the banking *system*—of all commercial banks as a group—is that it can expand the money supply by several times the amount of its excess reserves. Even though no individual commercial bank ever increases the money supply by more than its excess reserves, the banking *system* is able to expand the money supply by several times its excess reserves.

This *multiple-deposit expansion*—the multiple creation of money—is based on several simple facts:

Each individual bank tends to increase the money supply by the amount of its excess reserves.

The single bank does not increase the money supply by more than its excess reserves, because if it did the bank would soon find itself with negative excess reserves.

Whenever one bank in the economy loses reserves, other banks in the economy *gain* an *equal* amount of reserves.

Let's see how this multiple expansion of the money supply takes place and how large the multiple will be.

7-120

Suppose that the reserve ratio is 20 percent and the *First* National Bank has this balance sheet:

Reserves	$ 2,000	Demand deposits	$ 9,500
Other assets	8,000	Net worth	500
	$10,000		$10,000

$100 The First National has an excess reserve of $__________. It can

$100 safely make additional loans of $__________.

7-121

After it has made additional loans of $100, the First National's balance sheet will be:

Reserves	$ 2,000	Demand deposits	$ 9,600
Other assets	8,100	Net worth	500
	$10,100		$10,100

increased As a result of these loans, the money supply has (increased/decreased)

$100 by $__________.

7-122

After the borrowers spend the $100 by writing checks, and after these checks are deposited in *other* banks, the First National's balance sheet will be:

Reserves	$ 1,900	Demand deposits	$ 9,500
Other assets	8,100	Net worth	500
	$10,000		$10,000

$0 The excess reserves are now equal to $__________.

7-123

For simplicity, suppose that the checks for $100 are all deposited in the *Second* National Bank. The Second National Bank has a reserve ratio which is also 20 percent. *Before* the checks were deposited, its balance sheet was:

Reserves	$1,000	Demand deposits	$5,000
Other assets	4,300	Net worth	300
	$5,300		$5,300

$0 Second National had excess reserves of $________, and could
$0 safely increase the supply of money by $________.

7-124

As soon as the checks totaling $100 are deposited in the Second National
reserves and it collects the $100 from the First National, its ________
demand deposits and its ________ ________ will each increase by
$100 $________.

7-125

The Second National's balance sheet will then be:

Reserves	$1,100	Demand deposits	$5,100
Other assets	4,300	Net worth	300
	$5,400		$5,400

$80 The bank now has excess reserves of $________ and can safely
$80 increase the supply of money by $________.

7-126

The Second National now goes ahead and makes new loans of $80, based on its excess reserves of $80. It will then have this balance sheet:

Reserves	$1,100	Demand deposits	$5,180
Other assets	4,380	Net worth	300
	$5,480		$5,480

As a result of these new loans, the economy's money supply has in-
$80 creased by another $________.

7-127

The *First* National had excess reserves of $100 to begin with, and was
$100 able to increase the money supply by $________. The *Second* National had *no* excess reserves *to start*, but it obtained excess reserves of $80 after the First National made loans totaling $100. As a result the Second National was able to increase the money supply by
$80 $________. Together these two banks have increased the supply
$180 of money by $________.

7-128

After the Second National had made loans totaling $80 and thus increased the money supply by $80, this money is spent by the borrowers. They write checks which are deposited in other banks—call them the *Third* National Bank. After the Second National pays the Third National, the *Second* National's balance sheet will be:

Reserves	$1,020	Demand deposits	$5,100
Other assets	4,380	Net worth	300
	$5,400		$5,400

$0 The Second National now has excess reserves of $__________ .

7-129

Before the $80 is deposited in the Third National and collected from the Second National, the Third National had this balance sheet:

Reserves	$1,200	Demand deposits	$6,000
Other assets	5,000	Net worth	200
	$6,200		$6,200

With the reserve ratio still at 20 percent, the Third National has excess

$0 reserves of __________ .

7-130

But when the $80 is deposited in the Third National and collected from the Second National, the Third National's balance sheet becomes:

Reserves	$1,280	Demand deposits	$6,080
Other assets	5,000	Net worth	200
	$6,280		$6,280

$64 The Third National's excess reserves are now $__________ , and

$64 it can safely make additional loans of $__________ .

7-131

When the Third National increases its loans by $64, its balance sheet becomes:

$6,144	Reserves	$1,280	Demand deposits	$______
$5,064	Other assets	______	Net worth	200

7-132

As a result of the new loans made by the Third National, the money

$64 supply has increased by another $__________ .

7-133

Now let's break the chain and see where we have been. Recall that when we started, the picture looked like this:

Bank	Excess reserves
First National	$100
Second National	0
Third National	0

In other words, the three banks among them had a total of
$100 $________ in excess reserves.

7-134

With just $100 in excess reserves among them at the start: the First National has increased the money supply by $100, the Second National has increased it by $80, and the Third National increased it by $64.

$244 In other words, the three banks have added $________ to the supply of money in the economy.

7-135

Look back at frame **7-131**. After it makes the $64 in new loans, the
$1,228.80 Third National has required reserves of $________, actual re-
$1,280.00, $51.20 serves of $________, and excess reserves of $________.

7-136

After the $64 lent by the Third National is spent by its borrowers, it will be deposited in still other banks in the economy. The other banks will
$64 find their demand deposits increased by $________ and their
$64 actual reserves increased by $________.

7-137

If their reserve ratio is 20 percent, the other banks find that their re-
$12.80 quired reserves increased by $________ and their excess reserves
$51.20 increased by $________.

With the new excess reserves of $51.20, these other commercial banks will continue the process of making new loans and further expanding the money supply. All this began with just $100 of excess reserves in the banks in the economy.

But where will it end? How much can the money supply increase if there was $100 in excess reserves in the banking system at the start?

7-138

Let's ask the question another way: With a reserve ratio of 20 percent, for how many more dollars of demand deposits will $100 serve as the required reserve for the banking system? For $500. Because the $100

$500 would be the 20 percent reserve required for $________ in demand deposits.

7-139

So with $100 in excess reserves and a 20 percent reserve ratio, the bank-

five (5) ing system can increase money supply by $500, or *by* ________ *times*

excess reserves *the amount of the* ________ ________ .

7-140

Starting with excess reserves of just $100 in the economy and a reserve ratio of 20 percent, if demand deposits increase by $500, the required

$100 reserves increase by $________ and the excess reserves (increase/

decrease, $100 decrease) by $________ .

7-141

Assume the balance sheet below is the *consolidated balance sheet* for the commercial banking system—for all the commercial banks in the economy as a group.

(The figures are in the billions of dollars.)

Reserves	$ 35	Demand deposits	$150
Other assets	120	Net worth	5
	$155		$155

With a reserve ratio of 20 percent, the commercial banking system has

$5 excess reserves of $________ billion.

7-142

The actual reserves are $35 billion, and $35 billion is 20 percent of

$175 $(160/175/200/225) billion.

7-143

Thus, the commercial banks can increase the money supply from $150 to $175 billion. Because there is $5 billion in excess reserves, the com-

$25 mercial banking system can expand the supply of money by $________ billion.

7-144

The demand-deposit multiplier or ***monetary multiplier*** is 5 in this example: for every $1 of excess reserves, the banking system can increase the money supply by $5. If the monetary multiplier were 4, and the banking system had excess reserves of $2 billion, it could expand the

$8 money supply by $______ billion.

7-145

What determines the size of the monetary multiplier? The size of the reserve ratio. When the reserve ratio is 20 percent, the monetary multiplier is 5 because 5 is:

(a) equal to 20 percent
(b) equal to 1 divided by 20 percent

(b) Which one? __________

7-146

There is a precise relationship between the reserve ratio and the monetary multiplier.

$$\text{the monetary multiplier equals } \frac{1}{\text{the reserve ratio}}$$

Suppose the reserve ratio were 25 percent. To find the monetary mul-

1, 25 tiplier we would divide __________ by __________ percent.

4 And the monetary multiplier would be equal to __________

7-147

The table below shows a series of reserve ratios. For each reserve ratio determine the size of the monetary multiplier.

	Reserve ratio %	Monetary multiplier
2½	40	______
3	33⅓	______
3⅓	30	______
	25	4
	20	5
6	16⅔	______
6⅔	15	______
10	10	______

7-148

From the table in frame **7-147** you can conclude that the smaller the
larger — reserve ratio, the (larger/smaller) is the monetary multiplier, and vice versa. You can also conclude that the relationship between the reserve
inverse — ratio and the monetary multiplier is (direct/inverse).

7-149

Here is another consolidated balance sheet for the banking system.

Reserves	$130	Demand deposits	$500
Other assets	380	Net worth	10
	$510		$510

If the reserve ratio were 25 percent, the banking system would have
$5 — excess reserves of $______ and could increase the money sup-
$20 — ply by $______.

If the reserve ratio were 20 percent, the banks would have excess
$30 — reserves of $______ and could expand the money supply by
$150 — $______.

7-150

As you can see, a relatively small change in the reserve ratio can produce
large — a relatively (small/large) change in the country's money supply.

7-151

Here is another consolidated balance sheet for the banking system. The reserve ratio is 10 percent.

Reserves	$ 75	Demand deposits	$800
Other assets	730	Net worth	5
	$805		$805

−$5 — The banks have excess reserves of $______.

7-152

With a 10 percent reserve ratio, the banking system has enough reserves
$750 — for demand deposits of only $______.

7-153

If the reserve ratio is 10 percent, the monetary multiplier is
10 — ______. This means that with excess reserves of −$5, the
decrease — banking system must (increase/decrease) the money supply by
$50 — $______.

7-154

Thus, the monetary multiplier works in both directions. Suppose the reserve ratio is 25 percent.

increase — If excess reserves are $40, the banking system can (increase/decrease)

$160 — the money supply by $________. If excess reserves are −$25,

decrease — the banking system must (increase/decrease) the supply of money by

$100 — $________.

7-155

When banks have excess reserves, they expand the supply of money by making new loans. But when their excess reserves are negative, they must reduce the money supply. How? As *old* loans are repaid, *no* new loans are made to replace the repaid loans.

Borrowers pay off old loans by writing checks on their demand-deposit accounts in commercial banks. They give these checks to the banks which lent them money. This decrease in the amount in the

money — demand-deposit accounts constitutes a decrease in the ________

supply — ________.

7-156

For example, suppose the reserve ratio is 20 percent and the banking system has this balance sheet:

Reserves	$ 18	Demand deposits	$100
Other assets	87	Net worth	5
	$105		$105

$2 — The banking system has negative excess reserves of $________.

5 — The monetary multiplier is ________, so the commercial banks

$10 — must reduce the money supply by $________.

7-157

When borrowers pay back $10 in loans as they become due, there

other assets — will be a $10 decrease in ________ ________ and

demand deposits (either order) — ________ ________ on the balance sheet.

7-158

The balance sheet will then be:

Reserves	$18	Demand deposits	$90
Other assets	77	Net worth	5
	$95		$95

$18 — Required reserves are now $________, and excess reserves

$0 — have risen from −$2 to $________.

7-159

In discussing *multiple expansion* and *multiple contraction* of the money supply, we have learned that commercial banks expand the money supply by making new ______ , and commercial banks contract the money supply by *not* making new ______ as old ones are repaid.

loans
loans

7-160

But commercial banks also *expand* the money supply by buying ______ from the general public and *contract* it by selling them. For all practical purposes, however, there is no difference as far as the money supply is concerned between making new loans and (buying/selling) securities; both serve to ______ the money supply.

securities
buying, expand (increase)

7-161

When the commercial banks have excess reserves, they may *either* make new loans *or* buy securities (or both) to expand the supply of money. The total amount they can lend and spend for securities still depends upon two factors: the amount they have in ______ ______ and the ______ ______ .

excess reserves
reserve ratio (monetary multiplier)

7-162

If the banking system has negative excess reserves, *either* it must not make new loans as old ones are repaid *or* it must sell securities (or both). The amount it must reduce the money supply still equals ______ times ______ .

the monetary multiplier
the negative excess reserve

7-163

In short, whenever we have said "make new loans," we might also have said, "______ ______," and whenever we said, "fail to make new loans as old ones are repaid," we might also have said, "______ ______."

buy securities
sell securities

7-164 Review Frame

For every dollar of excess reserves, an individual commercial bank can increase the money supply by (more than \$1/\$1), and the commercial banking system can increase the money supply by (more than \$1/\$1).

\$1
more than \$1

7-165 Review Frame

Whenever a single commercial bank *loses* $500 in reserves and demand deposits because borrowers have written checks which were deposited in other banks, the other banks gain * ______________________________ ______________________________.

$500 in reserves and demand deposits

7-166 Review Frame

The size of the monetary multiplier can be found by * ______________ ______________________________. The relationship between the reserve ratio and the monetary multiplier is one which is (direct/inverse).

dividing 1 by the reserve ratio

inverse

7-167 Review Frame

With the following reserve ratios and excess reserves, tell what will happen to the money supply.

Reserve ratio %	Excess reserves	Money supply will
16⅔	−$5	______________ by $________
33⅓	3	______________ by $________
25	8	______________ by $________
12½	− 4	______________ by $________

decrease, $30

increase, $9

increase, $32

decrease, $32

7-168 Review Frame

The commercial banking system expands the money supply when it * ______________________________ ______________________________ and reduces the money supply when it * ______________________________ ______________________________ ______________________________.

makes new loans or buys securities from the public

does not make new loans as old ones are repaid or sells securities to the public

THE FEDERAL RESERVE BANKS

The twelve Federal Reserve Banks perform a number of important functions for the American economy. But their most important function is to control the size of the money supply. By controlling the money supply they attempt to achieve two goals: full employment and stable prices in the economy. The method they use to control the size of the money supply is simple: they control the amount of excess reserves in the commercial banking system.

Let's see what *three* specific devices the Federal Reserve Banks use to increase or decrease excess reserves and thereby control the money supply.

7-169

Here is a hypothetical consolidated balance sheet for the commercial banking system. (All figures are in billions of dollars.)

Reserves	$100	Demand deposits	$400
Other assets	350	Net worth	50
	$450		$450

If the reserve ratio is 25 percent, the banking system has excess re-

$0 serves of $________ .

7-170

are not The commercial banks (are/are not) able to *increase* the money supply.
do not Commercial banks (do/do not) have to *decrease* the supply of money.

7-171

It is the Federal Reserve Banks—commonly called the "*Fed*"—which set the reserve ratio for commercial banks. If the Fed were to *decrease* the reserve ratio from 25 to 20 percent, the commercial banks would (refer back to the balance sheet in frame **7-169**) have excess reserves of

$20, increase $________ and be able to (increase/decrease) the amount of de-

$500 mand-deposit money from $400 to $________ .

7-172

Suppose the Fed were to *increase* the reserve ratio from 25 to 30 percent. The commercial banking system would then have excess reserves

−$20, decrease of $________ and have to (increase/decrease) demand deposits

$333⅓ from $400 to $________ .

7-173

The first control device the Fed can use to affect the money supply is a

reserve ratio change in the ________ ________ .

7-174

To create excess reserves and expand the money supply, the Fed must
lower (raise/lower) the reserve ratio. And to create a shortage of reserves and
raise thereby decrease the money supply, it must (raise/lower) the reserve ratio.

7-175

You will recall that the amount the banking system can expand the money supply is equal to its excess reserves multiplied by the monetary multiplier; and that the amount it must contract the supply of money equals its (negative) excess reserves times the monetary multiplier. The monetary multiplier, you will also recall, is equal to 1 divided by the

reserve ratio — ______ ______ .

7-176

Changing the reserve ratio not only changes the amount of excess reserves, but also changes the size of the monetary multiplier.

increase — A *decrease* in the reserve ratio from 25 to 20 percent will (increase/

5 — decrease) the monetary multiplier from 4 to ______ . And an *increase* in the reserve ratio from 25 to 30 percent will (increase/

decrease, $3\frac{1}{3}$ — decrease) the monetary multiplier from 4 to ______ .

7-177

In brief, when the Fed *increases* the reserve ratio, excess reserves

decrease, decreases — ______ , the monetary multiplier ______ , and the

decreases — money supply ______ . A decrease in the reserve ratio will

increase — serve to ______ the excess reserves, the monetary multiplier, and the money supply.

7-178

The relationship between the reserve ratio and:

inverse — the monetary multiplier is ______ ,

inverse — excess reserves is ______ ,

inverse — the money supply is ______ .

7-179

Now, under what conditions would the Fed wish to increase the money supply? The *larger* the economy's money supply, the *lower* is the rate of interest (you will recall), and the *more* total spending there is for final goods and services; and the *smaller* is the money supply, the

higher, less — ______ is the interest rate, and the ______ total spending there is in the economy. In short, the relationship between the

direct — money supply and total spending is (direct/inverse).

7-180

One of the causes of *inflation* is *too much* spending, just as a basic cause of *unemployment* is *too little* spending in the economy. Because the relationship between the money supply and total spending is direct, the Fed will wish to *expand* the money supply during periods of

unemployment — (inflation/unemployment) and *contract* the money supply during times

inflation — of (inflation/unemployment).

7-181

increase
decreasing

Thus, during periods of inflation, to reduce the money supply the Fed may (increase/decrease) the reserve ratio. In times of unemployment, it may expand the money supply by (increasing/decreasing) the ratio.

7-182

increases

But changing the reserve ratio is not the only device the Fed can use to control excess reserves and the supply of money. It may also change the *discount rate*: the rate of interest commercial banks pay when they borrow money from the Fed.

When the Fed raises the discount rate, this (increases/decreases) what it costs commercial banks to borrow at the Fed.

7-183

less
more

The relationship between the discount rate and the amounts banks borrow from the Fed tends to be an inverse one. When the Fed *raises* the discount rate, commercial banks borrow (more/less). When the Fed *lowers* the discount rate, commercial banks borrow (more/less).

7-184

increases
decreases

When commercial banks borrow from the Fed the amount they borrow is added to their deposits at the Federal Reserve Banks. Commercial banks repay these loans by reducing their deposits at the Fed.

Borrowing from the Fed, therefore, (increases/decreases) the reserves of commercial banks; and the repayment of loans (increases/decreases) commercial bank reserves.

7-185

Here is a consolidated balance sheet which includes a fact we have so far ignored: one of the *liabilities* of commercial banks is the amount they owe the Fed as a result of past borrowing.

Reserves	$100	Demand deposits	$500
Other assets	450	Loans from Fed	10
		Net worth	40
	$550		$550

falls

These loans from the Fed tend to increase when the discount rate (rises/falls), and vice versa.

7-186

$0

If the reserve ratio for this consolidated balance sheet were 20 percent, the commercial banking system would have excess reserves of $____________.

7-187

Suppose now the Fed *increases* the discount rate from 9 to 10 percent and, as a result, the amount commercial banks wish to borrow from the Fed decreases from $10 to $6. When the commercial banks repay this $4 to the Fed, their loans from the Fed (increase/decrease) by $4, and their reserves (increase/decrease) by $4.

decrease
decrease

7-188

The commercial banks' balance sheet will now be:

Reserves	$ 96	Demand deposits	$500
Other assets	450	Loans from Fed	6
		Net worth	40
	$546		$546

The reserve ratio is still 20 percent. The commercial banks now have excess reserves of $________, and will therefore (increase/decrease) the amount of demand-deposit money in the economy from $500 to $________.

– $4
decrease
$480

7-189

What if the Fed had *lowered* the discount rate from 9 to 8 percent and the commercial banks had increased their borrowings at the Fed from $10 to $13? The commercial banks' loans from the Fed would (increase/decrease) by $3, and reserves would (increase/decrease) by $3.

increase, increase

7-190

Now their balance sheet would look like this:

Reserves	$103	Demand deposits	$500
Other assets	450	Loans from Fed	13
		Net worth	40
	$553		$553

Because the reserve ratio is 20 percent, the commercial banks now have excess reserves of $________. Thus, they will (increase/decrease) demand deposits from $500 to $________.

$3, increase
$515

7-191

If the Fed raises the discount rate, commercial banks borrow less, their excess reserves will (rise/fall), and the money supply will ________. But if the Fed lowers the discount rate, commercial banks borrow more, their excess reserves will (rise/fall), and the money supply will ________.

fall
fall (decrease)
rise
rise (increase)

7-192

When there is unemployment in the economy, the Fed will want to ______________ the money supply by (raising/lowering) the discount rate. When there is inflation, it will want to ______________ the supply of money by (raising/lowering) the discount rate.

increase, lowering
decrease
raising

7-193

So far we've discussed two ways the Fed can control the money supply. It can vary either the ______________ ______________ or the ______________ ______________.

reserve ratio
discount rate
(either order)

7-194

The third and probably the most effective device the Fed can use to control the money supply is to engage in *open-market operations*: to buy and to sell government securities. The purpose of open-market operations is the same as the purpose of changes in the discount rate or in the reserve ratio: to expand the money supply during periods of ______________ and to reduce it during times of ______________.

unemployment, inflation

7-195

When the Fed buys government securities it purchases them from commercial banks or the general public (individuals and business firms). When it sells securities, the securities are purchased by the same two groups: ______________ ______________ and the ______________ ______________.

commercial banks
general public
(either order)

7-196

Here is a balance sheet for the commercial banking system. The reserve ratio is 25 percent. (We can now, for simplicity, ignore the commercial banks' loans from the Fed.)

Reserves	$150	Demand deposits	$600
Other assets	500	Net worth	50
	$650		$650

The banking system has excess reserves of $______________.

$0

7-197

Suppose the Fed *buys* securities from the *commercial banks* for $10. The other assets of the commercial banks will (increase/decrease) by $10; and the Fed will pay the commercial banks for these securities by (increasing/decreasing) their reserves by $10.

decrease
increasing

7-198
The balance sheet will now be:

Reserves	$160	Demand deposits	$600
Other assets	490	Net worth	50
	$650		$650

$10, increase
$40

Their excess reserves are now $________, and they can (increase/decrease) the money supply by $________.

7-199
Here is the same balance sheet we started in frame **7-196**. There are no excess reserves and the reserve ratio is still 25 percent.

Reserves	$150	Demand deposits	$600
Other assets	500	Net worth	50
	$650		$650

decrease
increase

If the Fed *sold* $8 worth of government securities to the commercial banks, there would be an $8 (increase/decrease) in the reserves of the commercial banks, and an $8 (increase/decrease) in their other assets.

7-200
The commercial banking system's balance sheet would now look like this:

Reserves	$142	Demand deposits	$600
Other assets	508	Net worth	50
	$650		$650

−$8, decrease
$32

The commercial banks find themselves with excess reserves of $________ and they will (increase/decrease) the money supply by $________.

7-201 Review Frame

increase
increases (expands)
decrease
decreases (contracts)

Here's what we have discovered: when the Fed *buys* securities from the commercial banks, their excess reserves ________ and the money supply ________; when the Fed *sells* securities to the commercial banks, their excess reserves ________ and the money supply ________.

7-202 Review Frame

sell
buy

When the Fed wishes to decrease the money supply, it must ________ securities; when it wishes to increase the money supply, it must ________ securities in the open market.

7-203

How does the Fed get the commercial banks to *sell* some of their securities? By the simple device of (raising/lowering) the price that the Fed will pay for these securities until the commercial banks find it sufficiently profitable to sell them.

raising

7-204

If the Fed wishes to have the commercial banks *buy* securities, it would (raise/lower) the price it charges for the securities until the commercial banks find the price so attractive that they buy.

lower

7-205

Commercial banks are not the only ones who buy securities from the Fed or sell securities to the Fed in the open market; securities are also bought and sold in the open market by the general ____________ .

public

7-206

Assume that this is the commercial banking system's balance sheet and that the reserve ratio is 25 percent. (This is the same balance sheet that appeared in frame **7-196**.)

Reserves	$150	Demand deposits	$600
Other assets	500	Net worth	50
	$650		$650

The excess reserves are $____________ .

$0

7-207

The Fed buys securities worth $10 from the general public and pays for them with a $10 check drawn on the Fed's own account in the Federal Reserve Banks. The public deposits this check in demand-deposit accounts in various commercial banks. Thus, demand deposits in commercial banks are now $____________ .

$610

7-208

Having increased their depositors' demand deposits by $10, the commercial banks collect the $10 from the Fed. The collection of the $10 (increases/decreases) the ____________ of commercial banks by $10.

increases, reserves

7-209

The commercial banks now have the following balance sheet.

Reserves	$160	Demand deposits	$610
Other assets	500	Net worth	50
	$660		$660

Compare this with the balance sheet in frame **7-206**. The money supply has already (increased/decreased) by $________.

increased, $10

7-210

With a 25 percent reserve ratio, the commercial banks have excess reserves of $________ and can (increase/decrease) the money supply by another $________.

$7.50, increase

$30

7-211

The *total* result of the purchase of $10 in securities from the public is a $________ increase in the money supply. This change in the money supply is (the same as/different from) the one that occurs when the Fed buys $10 in securities from commercial banks. (Look back at frame **7-198** if you need help.)

$40

the same as

7-212

Let's use the same commercial bank balance sheet and again assume the reserve ratio is 25 percent. Excess reserves are $0 at the start.

Reserves	$150	Demand deposits	$600
Other assets	500	Net worth	50
	$650		$650

The Fed sells $8 in securities to the public, which pays for the securities with checks written on accounts in commercial banks. The Fed collects the $8 from the commercial banks by (increasing/decreasing) commercial bank ________ by $8.

decreasing

reserves

7-213

The commercial bank balance sheet then reads:

Reserves	$142	Demand deposits	$592
Other assets	500	Net worth	50
	$642		$642

Compared with frame **7-212**, the money supply has already (increased/decreased) by $________.

decreased, $8

7-214

Commercial banks now have excess reserves of $________ and will (increase/decrease) the money supply by $________.

–$6

decrease, $24

7-215
The net effect of the sale of $8 in securities to the public is a

$32, contraction
the same as

$________ (expansion/contraction) in the money supply. The effect upon the money supply is (the same as/different from) the sale of $8 in securities to the commercial banks. (Look back to frame **7-200** for help if you need it.)

7-216 Review Frame
Now let's review this.

unemployment
expand
inflation, contract

In using open-market operations to achieve stable prices and full employment, the Fed *buys* securities in times of (inflation/unemployment) to (expand/contract) the money supply; and *sells* securities in periods of (inflation/unemployment) to (expand/contract) the money supply.

7-217 Review Frame
The Fed has three controls it can use to change the money supply:

reserve ratio

discount rate (either order), securities

it changes the ________ ________, it changes the ________ ________, and it buys or sells ________ in the open market.

7-218 Review Frame
In times of inflation, the Fed desires that the money supply

decrease, decrease

increase (raise)

increase (raise), sell

________ in order to ________ total spending in the economy. To do this it might ________ the reserve ratio, ________ the discount rate, or ________ securities in the open market.

7-219 Review Frame
When there is unemployment in the economy, the Fed wishes to

increase, increasing

decrease (lower)

decrease (lower), buy

________ total spending in the economy by ________ the money supply. To bring about this result, the Fed might ________ the reserve ratio, ________ the discount rate, or ________ securities in the open market.

7-220 Review Frame

decreases
decreases

In *raising* the reserve ratio, the Fed not only (increases/decreases) the amount of excess reserves, but also (increases/decreases) the size of the monetary multiplier.

7-221 Review Frame

little difference

In selling securities in the open market, it makes (little difference/a great deal of difference) as far as the total effect on the money supply is concerned whether the Fed sells to commercial banks or to the general public.

7-222 Review Frame

If the Fed wishes to buy securities in the open market, it will

raise ______ the price it is willing to pay for the securities.

7-223 Review Frame

When the supply of money increases, the rate of interest in the economy

fall will (rise/fall) and total spending—especially investment spending—will

expand (expand/contract); and vice versa.

7-224 Review Frame

By controlling the money supply, the Fed is also able to affect the rate

interest, decrease of ______ . To raise this rate, the Fed needs to ______

increase the supply of money; and to lower it the Fed must ______ the money supply.

7-225 Review Frame

increase And, finally, decreases in the rate of interest will ______ total

decrease spending and increases in the interest rate will ______ total spending.

FISCAL AND MONETARY POLICY

To complete our study of macroeconomics, we will analyze the policies governments can adopt to overcome unemployment and inflation. We will start by redoing the last three frames of Section 5.

7-226

The differences between the two kinds of inflation are:

an increase in aggregate demand — Demand-pull inflation is the result of * ______

real GDP and employment — and is accompanied by rising * ______ .

a decrease in aggregate supply — Cost-push inflation is the result of * ______

real GDP and employment — and is accompanied by falling * ______ .

7-227

Either an increase in aggregate demand or a decrease in aggregate supply will result in inflation. When, however, the inflation is demand-

increase pull inflation the real GDP and employment will ______ but when the inflation is cost-push inflation the real GDP and employment

decrease will ______ .

7-228

Suppose the economy is producing in the intermediate range along the aggregate-supply curve. Use + (for increase), − (for decrease) and 0 (for no change) to complete the following table.

	Effect of	On price level	On real GDP
+, +	Increase in aggregate demand	_______	_______
+, −	Decrease in aggregate supply	_______	_______

Knowing the causes of inflation and unemployment in the economy suggests the things government might do to reduce or eliminate them. The Federal government has two basic tools it may use to achieve full employment and stable prices.

It may, first of all, change G or T. This is called *fiscal policy*.

It may also change S_m. For obvious reasons, this is called *monetary policy*.

Both of these kinds of policies are *demand-management* policies because they affect aggregate demand in the economy.

7-229

Suppose aggregate supply is AS in the figure below and aggregate demand is AD_1. Y_f is the full-employment real GDP.

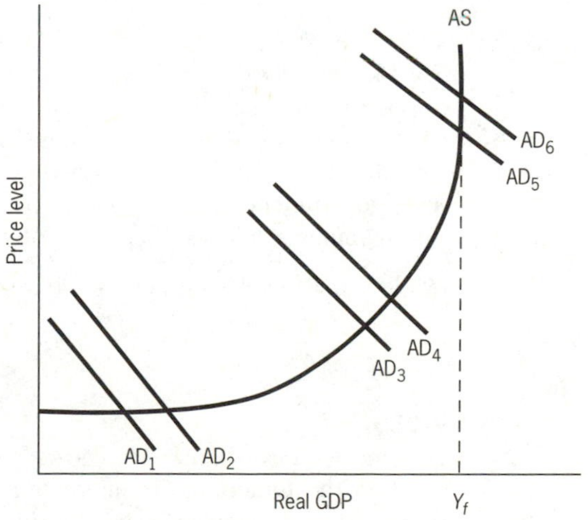

less than — The equilibrium real GDP is (less than/equal to) the full-employment real GDP.

increase — To increase the real GDP and employment in the economy the Federal government would want to (increase/decrease) aggregate demand.

increase, decrease, increase — To do this it might do any one or all three of the following: (increase/decrease) G, ____________ T, or ____________ S_m.

7-230

rise | remain constant

If these changes in G, T, and S_m increased aggregate demand to AD_2, real GDP and employment would (rise/fall) and the price level would * ______________________________ .

7-231

increasing G or S_m or decreasing T | rise, demand-pull

Were aggregate demand in the economy AD_3, government might increase it to AD_4 by * ______________________________ . Real GDP and employment would expand and the price level would ____________ . The result is ____________-____________ inflation.

7-232

reduce | rise

When the economy is operating in the intermediate range along the aggregate-supply curve an increase in aggregate demand will (reduce/increase) the *un*employment of labor in the economy; but the fall in the number of unemployed workers will be accompanied by a (rise/fall) in the price level.

7-233

price level | GDP, employment

If aggregate demand were at AD_5 the Federal government would in all likelihood not increase G or S_m or decrease T. Such an *expansionary* demand-management policy to increase aggregate demand to (say) AD_6 would result only in an increase in the ____________ ____________ and would not increase the real ____________ or ____________ in the economy.

7-234

decrease, increase | decrease

Suppose, however, the investment-demand of business firms (or the consumption schedule of consumers) is increasing and pushing aggregate demand toward AD_6. To prevent the rise in aggregate demand to AD_6 government might decide to pursue a *contractionary* demand-management policy. In the pursuit of such a policy it might do any one or all of the following: (increase/decrease) G, or ____________ T, or ____________ S_m.

7-235

decrease | remain constant | not affect | decrease

Imagine aggregate demand has already reached AD_6. To prevent further inflation the Federal government might employ one or several of the demand-management policies to reduce aggregate demand to AD_5.

If prices are *flexible* downward, the fall in demand from AD_6 to AD_5 will ____________ the price level and the real GDP and employment will * ____________ ____________ .

But if prices are *inflexible* downward, the decline in demand from AD_6 to AD_5 will (increase/decrease/not affect) the price level and both the real GDP and employment will (increase/decrease/remain constant).

7-236

To make sure you understand the important conclusion contained in frame **7-235**, we have drawn a graph below which contains only the classical range of the aggregate-supply curve, AS_1.

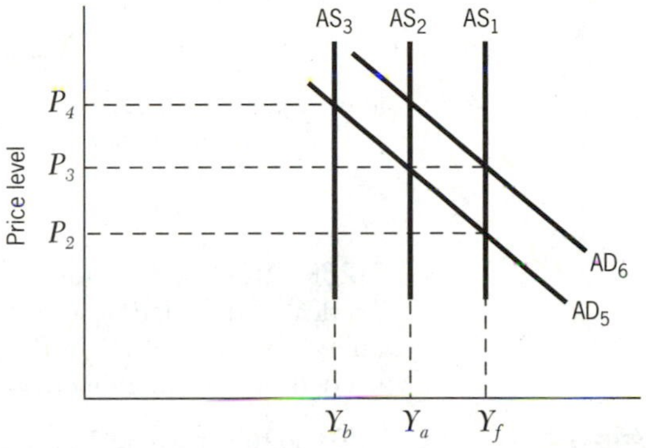

When prices are flexible downward and aggregate demand declines

P_3 from AD_6 to AD_5, the price level will fall from ______________ to

P_2, Y_f ______________ and the real GDP will remain at ______________ .

But if the price level is not flexible downward and demand falls

P_3 from AD_6 to AD_5, the price level will remain at ______________ . At

Y_a this price level the real GDP demanded is (Y_f/Y_a) and to avoid producing more goods and services than they can sell, business firms will

Y_a produce an output of ______________ , that is, aggregate supply has decreased to AS_2. To make matters worse, should the government decrease AD by increasing taxes and/or interest rates, the increasing costs brought about by these measures may shift AS all the way to AS_3, re-

P_4, Y_b sulting in a price level of ______________ and a real GDP of ________ —stagflation with a vengeance!

7-237

It would seem that having government reduce aggregate demand when prices are inflexible downward is not a good way to deal with inflation.

will not The price level (will/will not) decrease; but real GDP and employment

decline, rise will both ______________ ; that is, *un*employment will (rise/fall).

7-238 Review Frame

Demand-management policies are an effective way of increasing real GDP and employment when the economy is producing along the Keynesian range of the aggregate-supply curve. Government may in-

increasing G or S_m or decreasing T crease aggregate demand by * ______________________________ .

Real GDP and employment will rise and unemployment will therefore

fall, remain constant ______ ; and the price level will * ______

______ .

But when the economy is in the intermediate range, while an increase

increase in aggregate demand will ______ real GDP and employment

decrease, raise and ______ unemployment, it will also ______ the price level in the economy.

7-239 Review Frame

To deal with inflation when the economy is operating in the classical range, government might decrease aggregate demand or take the steps needed to prevent an increase in aggregate demand.

decrease G or S_m or increase T To do this it would * ______ .

price When prices are flexible downward, only the ______

level ______ would decline; but if prices are inflexible downward

real GDP the ______ ______ and employment would decline

rise and unemployment would ______ .

7-240

What, if anything, can government do about stagflation in the economy? Imagine that the economy is operating along the intermediate range of the aggregate-supply curve and aggregate supply decreases.

price level The decrease in aggregate supply will increase the (price level/real

real GDP GDP) and decrease the ______ ______ . It will also

increase (increase/decrease) unemployment in the economy.

This rise in the price level accompanied by a decline in real GDP and

is employment (is/is not) stagflation and has been caused by a decrease in

supply aggregate ______ .

7-241

If government were to follow an expansionary demand-management pol-

rise icy real GDP and employment would (rise/fall) and unemployment

decline, raise would ______ ; but such a policy would (raise/lower) the price level even more.

7-242

On the other hand, as long as prices are inflexible downward, a contractionary demand-management policy would prevent further rises in the

reduce price level; but such policy would also (reduce/increase) real GDP and

increase employment and ______ unemployment.

7-243

Government faces a dilemma: it can reduce unemployment by inflating the economy (driving the price level upward) *or* prevent further rises in the price level by increasing the amount of unemployment in the economy.

Demand-management policies are not an effective means of achieving both full employment and stable prices. To increase employment

rise — the price level must (rise/fall) and to prevent inflation employment must

fall — ______________ .

7-244

This dilemma has suggested another way of increasing employment toward the full-employment level without at the same time increasing the price level. The other way is often called *supply-side economics* or *supply-side fiscal policies*.

As its name suggests, to increase real GDP and employment (and decrease unemployment) without driving the price level upward, aggre-

increased — gate supply should be (increased/decreased).

7-245

On the graph below:

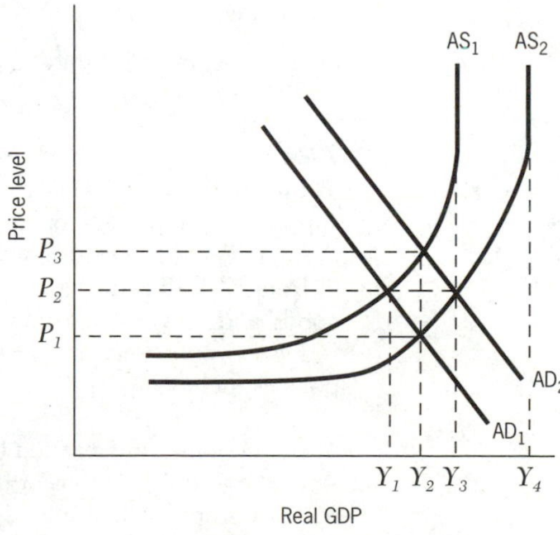

When aggregate demand is AD_1, and aggregate supply is AS_1, the real

Y_1, P_2 — GDP is ________ and the price level is ________ . The full-employ-

Y_3 — ment GDP is ________ ; and there are unemployed workers in the

less than — economy because the real GDP is ____________ ____________ the full-employment real GDP.

7-246

Government might use expansionary demand-management policies to increase aggregate demand from AD_1 to AD_2. This would (increase/decrease) the real GDP to ________ , ____________ unemployment, and ____________ the price level to ________ .

increase; Y_2, decrease; increase, P_3

7-247

Instead of using demand-management policies to increase aggregate demand, government might undertake various *supply-side policies* to increase aggregate supply from AS_1 to AS_2.

Any policy which induces producers of goods and services to offer each and every real GDP at a *lower* price (and to make a *larger* real GDP available at each and every price level) is a supply-side policy.

The movement of aggregate supply from AS_1 to AS_2 on the graph in frame **7-245** is an increase in aggregate supply that might result from the application of supply-side policies.

When aggregate demand is AD_1, the effect of the increase from AS_1 to AS_2 is to (increase/decrease) the real GDP to ________ , to ____________ unemployment, and to ____________ the price level to ________ .

increase, Y_2; decrease, decrease; P_1

7-248

Increasing aggregate demand and increasing aggregate supply both expand the real GDP and reduce unemployment. The important difference between these two methods of increasing output and employment is that increasing aggregate demand ____________ the price level and increasing aggregate supply ____________ it.

raises; lowers

7-249

There are three additional things to observe about increases in aggregate supply and supply-side policies intended to deal with stagflation.

First: The downward movement of aggregate supply from AS_1 to AS_2 in frame **7-245** is the result of a decrease in the costs of producing final goods and services; and any government policy that (sooner or later) reduces production costs is a supply-side policy. Examples of supply-side policies include:

- Reduction in the taxation of business firms
- Decreased regulations of business firms
- Tax reductions that increase incentives to work, save and invest, take risks, and develop improved methods of producing goods and services
- Decreased interest rates

Second: The increase in aggregate supply may well increase the full-employment real GDP of the economy. On the graph in frame **7-245** the increase in aggregate supply from AS_1 to AS_2 has increased the full-employment real GDP from ________ to ________ .

Y_3, Y_4

7-250

Third: A *decrease in aggregate demand* (as we learned in frame **7-236**) will probably not induce producers to lower their prices. An *increase in aggregate supply*, however, expresses the willingness of producers to accept lower prices. Producers are willing to produce (supply) the same quantities of final goods and services at a lower price level because their costs of producing these goods have fallen.

For example, if aggregate supply were AS_2 on the graph in frame **7-245** and aggregate demand decreased from AD_2 to AD_1, then, if prices were sticky downwards, causing aggregate supply to shift from AS_2 to AS_1, the price level (would/would not) fall from P_2 to P_1. But if aggregate demand were AD_1 and aggregate supply were to increase from AS_1 to AS_2, the price level (would/would not) decline from P_2 to P_1.

would not

would

7-251 Review Frame

Stagflation:

is * ______________________________

____

and is the result of * ______________________________ .

a rise in the price level accompanied by a fall in real GDP (a rise in unemployment)

a decrease in aggregate supply

7-252 Review Frame

To increase real GDP and reduce unemployment *without* increasing the price level government should:

seek to * ______________________________

and for this purpose utilize ____________-____________ policies.

increase aggregate supply

supply-side

7-253 Review Frame

A supply-side policy is a policy which reduces the ____________ of producing goods and services.

costs

Now take the Review Test for Section 7 at the back of the book.

Price Elasticity and Marginal Revenue

section **8**

The basic tools of the economist are demand and supply; and the fundamental laws of economics are the laws of demand and supply. Beyond what we have already learned about these tools and laws in Section 3 are two other tools which economists use and which are almost as important in studying economics as are demand and supply. These two tools are elasticity and marginal revenue.

Because we are going to need these tools ourselves in Sections 10 and 11, let's look at elasticity and marginal revenue and find out what they are, how they are related to each other, and how they are related to demand and supply.

ELASTICITY

8-1

Look at the following demand schedule for plastic ashtrays.

Demand for plastic ashtrays
Week of June 8–14, 1992

Price	Quantity demanded
$1.00	300
.90	400
.80	500
.70	600
.60	700
.50	800
.40	900
.30	1,000

When the price of ashtrays falls from $1 to 90 cents, 10 cents is the

price — change in the __________ of ashtrays and 100 ashtrays is the change

quantity demanded — in the __________ __________ .

8-2

If we wanted to measure the *percentage change* in the price of ashtrays we would divide 10 cents *by* $1. The percentage change in price is

10 — __________ percent.

8-3

In other words, to measure the percentage change in price we divide
change, price — the __________ in __________ by the price before the change.

8-4

Likewise, to calculate the *percentage change in the quantity* of ashtrays demanded we divide 100 by 300 ashtrays: 100 ashtrays is the
change, quantity — __________ in the __________ demanded, and 300 ashtrays is the
quantity demanded — __________ __________ before the price change.

8-5

$33\frac{1}{3}$ — The percentage change in the quantity demanded is __________ percent.

8-6

Suppose now that the price of ashtrays were 40 cents and then *rose* to 50 cents.

10 — The percentage change in price is equal to __________ cents
40, 25 — divided by __________ cents, or __________ percent.
100 — The percentage change in quantity demanded is equal to __________
900, $11\frac{1}{9}$ (11.11) — ashtrays divided by __________ ashtrays, or __________ percent.

8-7

But suppose the price of ashtrays were 50 cents and *fell* to 40 cents. The
20 — percentage change in price is now __________ percent. The percent-
$12\frac{1}{2}$ (12.5) — age change in quantity is __________ percent.

8-8

We have discovered something rather curious: When the price rises
25 — from 40 to 50 cents, the percentage change is __________ percent. But when the price *falls* from 50 to 40 cents, the percentage change
20 — is __________ percent.

8-9

Similarly, when the quantity demanded *falls* from 900 to 800 ashtrays,
$11\frac{1}{9}$ (11.11) — the percentage change is __________ percent. But if the quantity demanded rises from 800 to 900 ashtrays, the percentage change is
$12\frac{1}{2}$ (12.5) — __________ percent.

8-10

Shall we say that *between* 40 and 50 cents the percentage change in price is 20 or 25 percent? Let's compromise, as economists do, and calculate the percentage price change in this way: divide 10 cents (the change in price) by the *average* of 40 cents and 50 cents. Their average is

45 __________ cents.

8-11

If we measure in this way, the percentage price change is equal to

10, $22\frac{2}{9}$ (22.22) __________ cents divided by 45 cents, or __________ percent.

8-12

Economists compromise in the same way when they measure the percentage change in quantity. They divide the quantity change by the average of the two quantities involved. Between 40 and 50 cents, for example:

100 the change in quantity is __________ ashtrays,

850 the average of the two quantities is __________ ashtrays,

$11\frac{13}{17}$ (11.76) the percentage change in quantity is __________ percent.

8-13

Let's see if you have learned how economists compute percentage changes in price and quantity demanded. To test yourself, look at the demand schedule in frame **8-1** again. *Between* $1 and 90 cents

$10\frac{10}{19}$ (10.53) the percentage change in price is __________ percent and the

$28\frac{4}{7}$ (28.57) percentage change in quantity is __________ percent.

8-14

You know that when price changes, the quantity demanded also changes.

opposite The change in quantity is in the (same/opposite) direction as the price change.

8-15

But are the *percentage* changes in price and quantity always equal? From the examples we have used, you already know that the percentage

are not changes in price and quantity demanded (are/are not) always equal.

8-16

Sometimes a small percentage change in price brings about a large percentage change in quantity demanded. But sometimes just the

large opposite occurs: a __________ percentage change in price results

small in a __________ percentage change in quantity demanded.

8-17

When a small percentage price change brings about a large percentage change in quantity demanded, the quantity demanded is relatively *sensitive* to a price change. For example, if a 10 percent change in price brought about a 20 percent change in quantity demanded, we would
sensitive — have to say that quantity demanded is relatively (sensitive/insensitive) to the price change.

8-18

But suppose a 10 percent price change resulted in a 3 percent change
large — in quantity demanded. This is a (large/small) percentage price change
small — compared with a (large/small) percentage change in quantity. Quantity
insensitive — demanded is relatively (sensitive/insensitive) to the price change.

8-19

To measure this sensitivity, economists compare the percentage change in quantity with the percentage change in price. If the percentage change in quantity is:

Greater than the percentage price change, they say that quantity de-
sensitive — manded is relatively __________ to the price change;

Less than the percentage price change, they say that quantity de-
insensitive — manded is relatively __________ to the price change.

8-20

Economists have even developed a way to measure *how* sensitive (or insensitive) quantity demanded is to a price change. They *divide* the percentage change in quantity demanded *by* the percentage change in price and obtain a number which they call the *elasticity coefficient* (for demand).

As an example, when a 10 percent change in price brings about a 20 percent change in quantity demanded the elasticity coefficient is
20, 10 — equal to __________ percent divided by __________ percent,
2 — or __________ .

8-21

If a 3 percent change in quantity demanded were brought about by a 10 percent change in price, the elasticity coefficient would equal
3⁄10 (0.3) — __________ .

8-22

In summary, the elasticity coefficient is equal to the percentage change
quantity, price — in __________ divided by the percentage change in __________ .

8-23

Economists measure the percentage change in quantity by dividing the * ______________________________ by * ______________________________.

They measure the percentage change in price by dividing the * ______________________________ by * ______________________________.

change in quantity

the average of the two quantities involved

change in price

the average of the two prices involved

8-24

Now let's put a demand schedule, the percentage changes in price and quantity, and the elasticity coefficients into one table.

Price	Quantity demanded	Percent change in price	Percent change in quantity	Elasticity coefficient
$11	1			
		20	100	5
9	3			
		25	50	2
7	5			
		33⅓	33⅓	1
5	7			
		50	25	½
3	9			
		100	20	⅕
1	11			

The first thing we notice about the elasticity coefficients is that:

(a) they are greater than 1
(b) they are less than 1
(c) they are equal to 1
(d) they are greater than, less than, or equal to 1

Which one? __________

(d)

8-25

The elasticity coefficient is greater than 1 when the percentage change in quantity is (greater than/less than/equal to) the percentage change in price.

greater than

8-26

Why is this? Whenever we divide one number by *any smaller* number, the answer has to be some number larger than 1. So when we divide a percentage change in quantity by a smaller percentage change in price the __________ __________ will be larger than 1.

elasticity coefficient

8-27

In short, when the percentage change in quantity is greater than the percentage change in price, the elasticity coefficient will be * ____________________.

greater than 1

8-28

Looking at the table in frame **8-24**, we can also see that the elasticity coefficient is less than 1 whenever the percentage change in quantity is (greater than/less than/equal to) the percentage change in price.

less than

8-29

When we divide a percentage change in quantity by a *larger* percentage price change the coefficient of elasticity will always be less than ________ .

1

8-30

But is it possible for the elasticity coefficient to be equal to 1? Yes. This occurs when the percentage change in quantity and the percentage change in price are ________ .

equal (identical, the same)

8-31

Now let's summarize what we have learned about the elasticity coefficient. The coefficient can be ________ than, ________ than, or ________ to ________ .

greater, less (either order), equal, 1

8-32

A coefficient of less than 1 means that the percentage change in ________ is greater than the percentage change in ________ , while a coefficient of more than 1 means that the percentage change in ________ is larger than the percentage change in ________ .

price, quantity

quantity, price

8-33

Suppose the elasticity coefficient is 1 and the price of a commodity falls by 3 percent. The quantity demanded will rise by ________ percent.

3

8-34

Imagine that the coefficient is 2 and that we desire to increase the *quantity* demanded by 10 percent. We would have to lower the price by ________ percent. With a coefficient of 2, a 3 percent increase in price would decrease the quantity demanded by ________ percent.

$5\left(\frac{10\%}{5\%} = 2\right)$

$6\left(\frac{6\%}{3\%} = 2\right)$

8-35

Let's look back to the demand schedule and elasticity coefficients in frame **8-24**. You will notice that the coefficient is greater than 1 at the (higher/lower) prices and less than 1 at the (higher/lower) prices.

higher, lower

8-36

inelastic
elastic

Economists say that demand is price *elastic* when the coefficient is greater than 1 and price *inelastic* if the coefficient is less than 1. In general, at the relatively low prices, demand is price (elastic/inelastic) and price (elastic/inelastic) at relatively high prices.

8-37

greater
less

When the elasticity coefficient is equal to 1 (unity), economists say that demand is of *unit elasticity*. But demand is price elastic whenever the coefficient is (greater/less) than 1 and price inelastic when it is (greater/less) than 1.

8-38

greater than 1
1
less than 1

In summary, demand is price elastic when the coefficient is * ____________ ____________, of unit elasticity when the coefficient is ____________, price inelastic when the coefficient is * ____________.

8-39

$11

The demand schedule in frame **8-24** indicates that when the price of the commodity is $11, the quantity demanded is 1. This means that at this price buyers would be willing to spend $____________ for this commodity.

8-40

3
$27

If the price were reduced to $9, demanders would buy ____________ units, spending a total of $____________ for the commodity.

8-41

$27

When buyers spend $27 on a commodity the *total receipts* (or income, or revenue) of the sellers are also $____________.

8-42

price, quantity
demanded

The total receipts of sellers of a commodity are equal to the ____________ of the commodity multiplied by the ____________ ____________.

8-43

total receipts

The price of a commodity times the quantity demanded at that price is equal to the ____________ ____________ of sellers.

8-44

The following demand schedule together with the elasticity coefficient, is repeated from frame **8-24**. In the spaces provided, indicate the total receipts of sellers at each of the six prices in the demand schedule.

	Price	Quantity demanded	Elasticity coefficient	Total receipts
$11	$11	1		$______
			5	
$27	9	3		______
			2	
$35	7	5		______
			1	
$35	5	7		______
			½	
$27	3	9		______
			⅕	
$11	1	11		______

8-45

are not

You can see that the total receipts of sellers (are/are not) the same at all prices.

8-46

increase
decrease

When demand is elastic between any two prices, the coefficient of elasticity is greater than 1.

Between $11 and $9, for example, if the price of the commodity:
decreases, total receipts will (increase/decrease),
increases, total receipts will (increase/decrease).

8-47

decrease
increase

But between $3 and $1 demand is price inelastic. When the price:
decreases, total receipts will (increase/decrease),
increases, total receipts will (increase/decrease).

8-48

do not change (remain constant)
do not change (remain constant)

What if demand is of unit elasticity? When the price falls, total receipts * ________________, and when price rises, total receipts * ________________.

8-49

elastic
inelastic

Let's look at this in a somewhat different way. Suppose the price of a commodity *declines*. Total receipts will increase if demand is price (elastic/inelastic), and will decrease if demand is price (elastic/inelastic).

8-50

And when the price of a commodity *rises*, total receipts will rise if demand is price (elastic/inelastic), and will fall if demand is price (elastic/inelastic).

inelastic
elastic

8-51

Regardless of whether the price rises or falls, total receipts *will* not change if demand is * ______________ .

of unit elasticity

8-52

Is price elasticity of any practical importance? Let's see.

Suppose the wage rate (that is, the price of labor) declines. Employers will tend to employ more workers. But what will happen to the *total* wages paid by employers, which are the total receipts of workers? If the demand for labor is price elastic total wages paid will __________ . But if it is price inelastic, total wages paid will __________ .

increase
decrease

8-53

The demand for most agricultural products, such as wheat, is price inelastic. This means that the total receipts of wheat farmers rise when the price of wheat __________ but fall when the price of wheat __________ .

rises
falls

8-54

Let's look at another example of the importance of the elasticity of demand. The demand for color television sets is price elastic. Manufacturers of TV sets can only increase their total receipts by (raising/lowering) the price of sets. Their total receipts will decline if they (raise/lower) the price of sets.

lowering
raise

8-55

Why do total receipts increase when demand is price elastic and the price falls? Any decline in the price means that (more/less) will be demanded at the lower price.

more

8-56

But because demand is price elastic, the *percentage* increase in quantity demanded is (greater/less) than the percentage decrease in price.

greater

8-57

This means that a *small* price decline results in a relatively *large* increase in the amount of the product sold. As a result, the *additional revenue* the firms obtain from selling more sets is (greater/less) than their loss of revenue due to the fact that they are selling at a lower price.

greater

8-58

But when the demand is price *inelastic*, if the firms lower their price, the percentage increase in the quantity demanded is (greater/less) than the percentage decrease in price. The consequence is that the extra revenue that results from more sets being sold is (greater/less) than the loss of revenue that results from the lower price.

less
less

8-59 Review Frame

Now for a review of what we have learned about the elasticity of demand.

Using the method employed by economists and the following two lines from a demand schedule:

Price	Quantity demanded
$5.50	750
4.50	850

the percentage change in price is ____________ , and the percentage change in quantity is ____________ .

20
12½ (12.5)

8-60 Review Frame

To compute the elasticity of demand coefficient we must divide
* ______________________________ by
* ______________________________ .

the percentage change in quantity demanded
the percentage change in price

8-61 Review Frame

Demand is:

elastic when the coefficient is * ____________ ,
inelastic when the coefficient is * ____________ ,
unit elastic when the coefficient is * ____________ .

greater than 1
less than 1
equal to 1

8-62 Review Frame

For demand to be price elastic, the percentage change in quantity demanded must be ____________ than the percentage change in price. When the percentage change in quantity demanded is ____________ than the percentage change in price, demand is price inelastic.

greater
less

8-63 Review Frame

When demand is:

fall (decrease), rise (increase) — price elastic, total receipts ________ if price rises and ________ if price falls,

rise (increase), fall (decrease) — price inelastic, total receipts ________ if price rises and ________ if price falls,

do not change — unit elastic, total receipts * ________ when price rises or falls.

8-64

Before finishing our discussion of price elasticity, we should also talk about the elasticity of supply. Look at the following supply schedule.

Price	Quantity supplied
$11	3,100
9	2,900
7	2,500
5	1,900
3	1,100
1	0

Using the method employed by economists the percentage change in

100 — price between $1 and $3 is ________ , and the percentage change

200 — in the quantity *supplied* is ________ .

8-65

When we divide the percentage change in quantity *supplied* by the percentage change in price, we find that the elasticity of supply coefficient

2 — is equal to 200 percent divided by 100 percent, or ________ .

8-66

In other words, we find the coefficient of the elasticity of supply by

supplied — dividing the percentage change in the quantity ________ by the percentage change in price.

8-67

6.67 — Between $11 and $9, this coefficient is equal to ________ percent

20, 33⅓ — divided by ________ percent, or ________ .

8-68

Like the coefficient for the elasticity of demand, when supply is elastic the coefficient is ________ ________ 1, and the percentage change in quantity supplied is (greater/less) than the percentage change in price.

greater than
greater

8-69

And when the coefficient is less than 1, the percentage change in quantity supplied is ________ than the percentage change in price, and economists say that supply is ________ .

less
inelastic

8-70

When the percentage changes in quantity supplied and price are equal, the coefficient is ________ . Supply, in this case, is said to be of ________ ________ .

equal to 1
unit elasticity

8-71

Here are the same supply schedule and the elasticity of supply coefficients that we used in frame **8-64**. In the space provided, indicate the total receipts sellers would obtain if they sold the quantities they are willing to supply at each of the six prices.

	Price	Quantity supplied	Elasticity coefficient	Total receipts
$341	$11	31		$________
			.33	
$261	9	29		________
			.59	
$175	7	25		________
			.82	
$95	5	19		________
			1.07	
$33	3	11		________
			2.00	
$0	1	0		________

The coefficients tell us that supply is (elastic/inelastic) above the price of $5, and (elastic/inelastic) below $5.

inelastic
elastic

8-72

In other words, in this supply schedule supply is inelastic at the (higher/lower) prices and elastic at the (higher/lower) prices.

higher
lower

8-73

increase
decrease

But notice this: Regardless of whether supply is elastic or inelastic, when the price of the commodity increases, total receipts (increase/decrease), and when price decreases, total receipts (increase/decrease).

8-74

rises (increases)
rise (increase)

We can't tell if supply is elastic or inelastic by discovering what happens to total receipts when price rises and falls because when the price rises, the quantity supplied also __________ and since total receipts equal price times quantity supplied, they must also __________ .

8-75

fall (decrease)
fall (decrease)

And whenever price falls the quantity supplied will __________ ; this will cause total receipts to __________ .

8-76

increases, decreases

In short, when supply is either inelastic or elastic, total receipts increase when price __________ and decrease when it __________ .

8-77 Review Frame

To review what we have learned about the elasticity of supply, let's fill in the following table.

greater than 1, fall
less than 1, fall
equal to 1, fall

When supply is:	The elasticity (of supply) coefficient is:	And when price *falls*, total receipts:
Elastic	__________	__________
Inelastic	__________	__________
Unit elastic	__________	__________

8-78 Review Frame

greater
greater

For supply to be elastic, the percentage change in quantity supplied must be __________ than the percentage change in price. When supply is inelastic, the percentage change in price is __________ than the percentage change in quantity supplied.

MARGINAL REVENUE

Let's look now at demand from the viewpoint of the *individual seller* of a commodity. Demand is important to the seller because it tells the seller how much commodity it can sell at various prices.

8-79

Suppose that a firm selling garden hoes in a small town finds this is the weekly demand for hoes at its store

Demand for garden hoes (per week)	
Price	**Quantity demanded (hoes per week)**
$7.50	0
7.00	1
6.50	2
6.00	3
5.50	4
5.00	5
4.50	6
4.00	7
3.50	8
3.00	9
2.50	10

decrease (lower) To increase the number of hoes the firm sells weekly it must ______

increases (raises) their price. The number it sells will decline if it ______ their price.

8-80

Economists call this seller an *imperfectly competitive seller* because it

more has to lower the price of hoes to sell (more/fewer) hoes.

8-81

We'll put off for a while the question of what a *perfectly* competitive seller is. All we need to know for the moment is that any seller that must

imperfectly lower its price to sell more is called an ______

competitive ______ seller.

8-82

In other words, the relationship between the price an imperfectly competitive seller charges and the amount of a commodity it can sell is

inverse (inverse/direct).

8-83

If the seller of hoes in frame **8-79** charges a price of $7.50 for a hoe, it

0 is able to sell ______ hoes a week, and its weekly *total revenue*,

$0 or total receipts (TR), from the sale of hoes is $______ .

8-84

1 Were it to charge $7 per hoe, its weekly sales would be ______

$7 hoe(s) and its total revenue would be $______ .

8-85

By dropping the price of hoes from $7.50 to $7 it was able to increase its sale of hoes from 0 to 1 per week, and it was able to increase its weekly total revenue (TR) from $0 to $7. The sale of this hoe *increases*

$7 its TR by $__________ .

8-86

$6.50 To sell 2 hoes a week it would have to lower its price to $__________ .

$13 At this price its TR would be $__________ per week from the sale of hoes.

8-87

To increase its hoe sales from 1 to 2 a week it had to decrease its hoe price from $7 to $6.50. By selling one additional hoe it increased its TR

$6 by __________ .

8-88

The amount by which TR increases when the seller of hoes sells one more hoe is what economists call ***marginal revenue*** (MR). If its TR increases by $6 when it increases its sales of hoes from 1 to 2 per week,

$6 the MR from the sale of the 2d hoe is $__________ .

8-89

TR MR is defined as the amount by which __________ increases when a

one (1) seller sells __________ more unit of a commodity.

8-90

Here is the demand schedule for hoes again, along with a column showing the seller's TR at the various prices it might charge for hoes.

Demand and total revenue: Garden hoes (per week)

Price	Quantity demanded (hoes per week)	Total revenue
$7.50	0	$ 0
7.00	1	7
6.50	2	13
6.00	3	18
5.50	4	22
5.00	5	25
4.50	6	27
4.00	7	28
3.50	8	28
3.00	9	27
2.50	10	25

$5 The MR from the sale of the 3d hoe is $__________ .

8-91

You can see in these schedules that if the seller is to increase its weekly
$4 sale of hoes from 7 to 8 it must lower the price of hoes from $______
$3.50 to $______ .

8-92

$28, $28 Its TR at $4 was $______ , and its TR at $3.50 is $______ .

8-93

Thus its TR is unchanged and the MR from the sale of the 8th hoe per
$0 week is, therefore, $______ .

8-94

To increase sales of hoes from 8 to 9 a week the seller has to lower the
decreases price from $3.50 to $3. When it does this, TR (increases/decreases) from
$27 $28 to $______ .

8-95

In this case the change in TR is −$1 and the MR from the sale of the
−$1 9th hoe is equal to $______ .

8-96

Here are the demand schedule and TR figures once more. We've also put in the elasticity of demand coefficients. Fill in the last column to indicate the MR from the sale of the 1st through the 10th hoe.

	Price	Quantity demanded	Total revenue	Elasticity coefficient	Marginal revenue
	$7.50	0	$ 0		
				29	
$7	7.00	1	7		$______
				9	
$6	6.50	2	13		______
				5	
$5	6.00	3	18		______
				3.29	
$4	5.50	4	22		______
				2.33	
$3	5.00	5	25		______
				1.73	
$2	4.50	6	27		______
				1.31	
$1	4.00	7	28		______
				1.00	
$0	3.50	8	28		______
				.76	
−$1	3.00	9	27		______
				.58	
−$2	2.50	10	25		______

8-97

decreases

Now let's note three things about MR and elasticity. First, as price decreases and quantity demanded increases, MR (increases/decreases/remains constant).

8-98

decreases
increases
increases, decreases

In other words, MR *decreases* as price (increases/decreases) and as quantity demanded (increases/decreases). MR *increases* as price __________ and as quantity demanded __________ .

8-99

less

Second, with the exception of the 1st hoe, the MR from the sale of any hoe is (greater/less) than the price at which the hoe is sold.

8-100

greater

Put another way, except for the 1st hoe, the price at which an additional hoe can be sold is (greater/less) than the MR from the sale of the hoe.

8-101

positive
negative

Third, when demand is price elastic MR is (positive/negative/zero). But when demand is inelastic, MR is (positive/negative/zero).

8-102

1

MR is equal to zero when the price elasticity of demand is of unit elasticity and the elasticity coefficient is equal to __________ .

8-103

elastic
increases, greater

In short, demand is (elastic/inelastic) at the higher prices. This means that as price falls, TR (increases/decreases) and MR is (greater/less) than zero.

8-104

inelastic
decreases, less

At the lower prices demand is (elastic/inelastic). As price falls, TR __________ and MR is __________ than zero.

8-105

remain unchanged
zero

Somewhere between the higher and the lower prices, demand is of unit elasticity. At this point, a price decrease will cause TR to __________ and MR will then be equal to __________ .

8-106

Starting from the highest price and the most elastic demand, as the price is lowered TR at first will ________ and then will ________ as demand becomes inelastic; MR will at first be ________ than zero, but will become ________ than zero when demand is inelastic.

increase, decrease
greater
less

8-107

For all hoes except the first, MR is ________ than the price at which the hoe is sold.

less

8-108

Just to be sure we understand this the other way around, let's say that when MR is:

positive, demand is price (elastic/inelastic),

negative, demand is price ________ ,

zero, demand is * ________ .

elastic
inelastic
of unit elasticity

8-109

Let's plot price, TR, and MR at each quantity demanded, all on one graph.

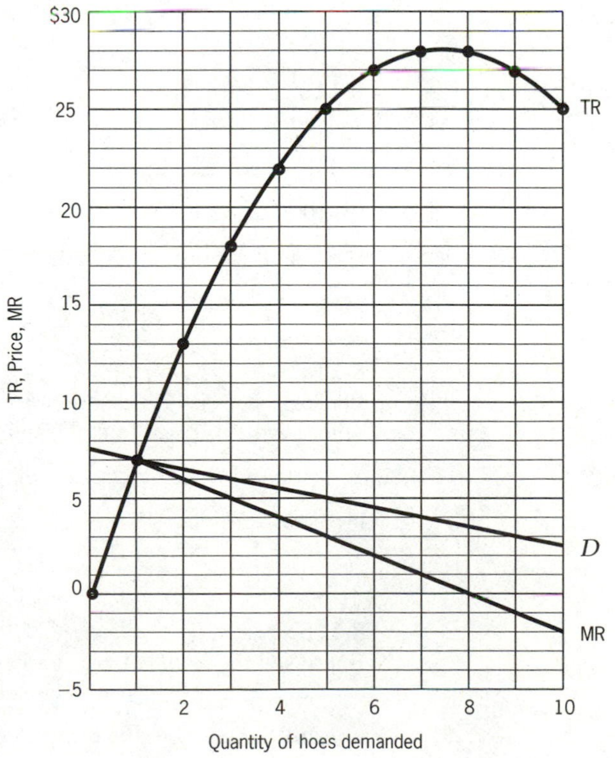

downward, MR
demand

You can see that both the demand and MR curves slope (upward/downward), but that the (demand/MR) curve is *below* the (demand/MR) curve.

8-110

increases
decreases
7, $4
8, $3.50

As the seller increases the number of hoes sold, TR at first (increases/decreases) and then (increases/decreases). TR is the greatest when the seller sells either __________ hoes, at a price of $__________ , or __________ hoes at a price of $__________ .

8-111

$0
1

The MR of the 8th hoe is equal to $__________ , and this means that between $4 and $3.50 the price elasticity of demand coefficient is equal to __________ .

8-112

increases
greater
elastic

Between 0 and 7 hoes, when the firm sells an additional hoe:
TR (increases/decreases),
MR is (greater/less) than zero,
demand is price __________ .

8-113

decreases
less
inelastic

When the firm sells the 9th or 10th hoe:
TR __________ ,
MR is __________ than zero,
demand is price __________ .

8-114

$6
$6

Looking back at the schedules in frame **8-96**, we can see that when the seller lowers its price from $6.50 to $6 it is able to sell an additional hoe at a price of $__________ . *By itself* the sale of this additional hoe increases the seller's TR by $__________ .

8-115

decreases, $1

But to sell this 3d hoe the seller has to *decrease* by 50 cents the price of each of the 2 hoes it had been selling at $6.50. *By itself* reducing the price of these 2 hoes (increases/decreases) TR by $__________ .

8-116

The 1 additional hoe sold *increased* TR by \$6. The decrease in the price of the 2 hoes *decreased* TR by \$1. Together the extra hoe and the price decrease necessary to sell the extra hoe (increased/decreased) TR by \$________. This change in TR is the ________ resulting from the sale of the 3d hoe.

increased

\$5, MR

8-117

Suppose the seller is already selling 9 hoes a week. To sell the 10th hoe it must lower the price of hoes to \$________. The sale of the 10th hoe by itself will increase TR by \$________.

\$2.50

\$2.50

8-118

Reducing by 50 cents the price of each of the 9 hoes it had been selling at \$3 will, by itself, (increase/decrease) TR by \$________.

decrease, \$4.50

8-119

Together the sale of the 1 extra hoe *plus* the reduced price of the 9 hoes (increases/decreases) TR by \$________, and thus the MR resulting from the sale of the ________th hoe is \$________.

decreases, \$2

10, −\$2

8-120

In summary, MR is positive whenever the increase in TR from the sale of an extra hoe is (greater/less) than the decrease in TR that results from the price decrease necessary to sell the extra hoe. This occurs whenever the demand for hoes is price (elastic/inelastic).

greater

elastic

8-121

When demand is price (elastic/inelastic), MR is negative because the increase in TR from the sale of the extra hoe is (greater/less) than the decrease in TR resulting from the price reduction necessary to sell the additional hoe.

inelastic

less

8-122 Review Frame

Now let's take four frames to review what we have learned about MR so far.

We have examined MR from the viewpoint of the individual (perfectly/imperfectly) competitive seller which finds that it must ________ the price charged in order to sell more of a commodity.

imperfectly, lower (decrease)

8-123 Review Frame

TR — MR is the amount by which __________ increases when the seller sells

1 — __________ more unit of the commodity. MR is:

elastic — a positive amount when demand is price __________ ,

inelastic — a negative amount when demand is price __________ ,

of unit elasticity — zero when demand is __________ .

8-124 Review Frame

less — Except for the first unit sold, MR is __________ than the price at which the commodity is sold. As the firm increases its sales, MR

decreases — __________ .

8-125 Review Frame

If demand is:

increase — price elastic and the firm sells an extra unit, TR will __________ ;

decrease — price inelastic and the firm sells an extra unit, TR will __________ ;

remain — unit elastic and the firm sells an extra unit, TR will __________

constant — __________ .

8-126

Following is the demand schedule for the Number 2 red wheat produced and sold by one *individual* farmer in North Dakota.

Demand for wheat produced by one farmer (1992)

Price (per 1,000 bushels)	Quantity demanded (thousands of bushels)
$4,200	0
4,200	1
4,200	2
4,200	3
4,200	4
4,200	5
4,200	6
4,200	7
4,200	8
4,200	9
4,200	10

does not / perfectly — To sell an additional 1,000 bushels of wheat this farmer (does/does not) have to lower the price. He is a(n) (perfectly/imperfectly) competitive seller.

8-127

Suppose we compute the elasticity of demand coefficient for this one farmer's wheat between 0 and 1,000 bushels of wheat. The *percentage change* in:

200 quantity demanded is ________ ,

0 price is ________ .

8-128

When we divide 200 percent by 0 percent the answer is positive and equal to infinity (∞). Between 0 and 1,000 bushels, therefore, the de-
elastic mand for this one seller's wheat is infinitely, or *perfectly*, price (elastic/inelastic).

8-129

Between 9,000 and 10,000 bushels of wheat the coefficient of elasticity
infinity, perfectly (infinitely) also is equal to ________ and demand is ________ price elastic.

8-130

In short, in a perfectly competitive market, the demand for a commodity produced by one individual seller is perfectly price elastic, and the seller
perfectly competitive is called a(n) ________ ________ seller.

8-131

Here again is the demand schedule facing this farmer. Compute his TR when he sells from 0 to 10,000 bushels of wheat and the MR from the sale of each additional thousand bushels.

	Price (per 1,000 bushels)	Quantity demanded (thousands of bushels)	Total revenue	Marginal revenue
$0	$4,200	0	$____	
$4,200, $4,200	4,200	1	____	$____
$8,400, $4,200	4,200	2	____	____
$12,600, $4,200	4,200	3	____	____
$16,800, $4,200	4,200	4	____	____
$21,000, $4,200	4,200	5	____	____
$25,200, $4,200	4,200	6	____	____
$29,400, $4,200	4,200	7	____	____
$33,600, $4,200	4,200	8	____	____
$37,800, $4,200	4,200	9	____	____
$42,000, $4,200	4,200	10	____	____

8-132

What can we discover about this perfectly competitive seller? Several
increases things. First, whenever he sells more wheat, his TR (increases/decreases/remains constant).

8-133

positive

elastic

In other words, the MR from the sale of additional wheat is always (positive/negative/zero) because the demand for his wheat is perfectly price ____________ .

8-134

remains constant

Second, as he increases his sales of wheat, MR (increases/decreases/remains constant).

8-135

equal

Third, not only is MR constant regardless of how little or how much wheat he sells, but the MR from the sale of an additional thousand bushels and the price at which he sells the thousand bushels are ____________ .

8-136

In brief, a perfectly competitive seller finds that:

price

It can sell as little or as much as it wishes at a ____________ that is contant.

MR

The ____________ from the sale of an additional unit of the commodity is also constant.

Price, MR (either order)

____________ and ____________ are equal.

8-137

Graphically, demand, TR, and MR look like this.

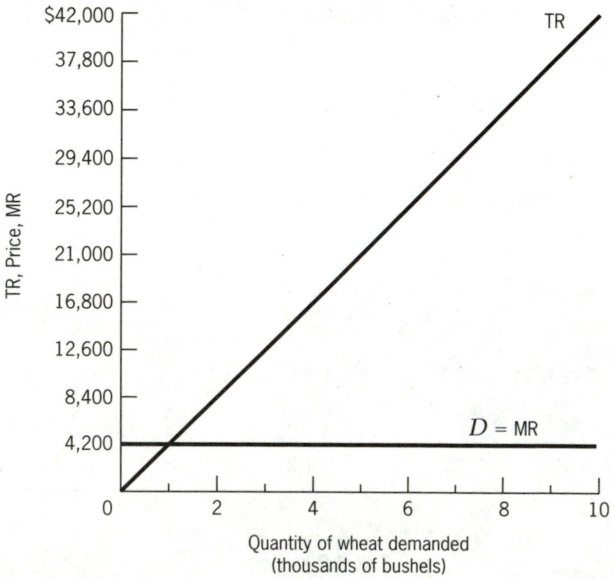

identical

The demand and MR curves are (identical/different).

8-138

The TR curve slopes:
(a) upward
(b) downward
(c) upward at first and then downward
(d) downward at first and then upward

(a) Which one? ______________

8-139

The demand and MR curves:
(a) slope upward
(b) slope downward
(c) are horizontal
(d) are vertical

(c) Which one? ______________

8-140

From this we can conclude that a horizontal demand curve shows demand which is ______________ price elastic.

perfectly

8-141

We can also conclude that the horizontal demand and MR curves would touch the *vertical* axis at the number of dollars which is equal to the ______________ at which the commodity can be sold.

price

8-142

In short:

Because demand is perfectly price elastic, the demand curve is ______________ .

horizontal

Because TR always increases when the seller sells more, the TR curve slopes ______________ .

upward

Because MR is constant, the MR curve is ______________ .

horizontal

Because price and MR are equal, the demand and MR curves are ______________ .

identical (the same)

8-143 Review Frame

Now let's review what we have learned about the perfectly competitive seller. It can sell as little or as much of a commodity as it wishes at a ______________ price because the demand for the commodity sold is ______________ ______________ .

constant (fixed)

perfectly elastic

8-144 Review Frame

As a result it finds that MR:

positive — is (positive/negative/zero)

is constant — (decreases/is constant) when sales increase

the price of the commodity — is equal to * ______________________ .

8-145 Review Frame

Whenever it sells an additional unit of the commodity TR

increases, price — ____________ by an amount which is equal to both ____________

MR — and ____________ .

Now take the Review Test for Section 8 at the back of the book.

The Costs of Production

section **9**

Business firms produce goods and services. They sell these goods and services in the product markets of the economy. Some of the product markets are competitive and some of them are noncompetitive, or monopolistic, markets. In both competitive and noncompetitive markets the price the firm is paid for its product and the amount of the product it produces and sells depend on the demand for the product and the cost of producing it.

So if we are to understand prices and outputs in competitive and noncompetitive markets it is essential that we know a few things about the costs of producing products. Before we start, however, it is a good idea to have a few basic facts.

1. There are several kinds of costs that are important to the business firm.
2. The cost of producing a product depends upon how much of the product the firm produces.
3. Cost also depends upon whether the firm does or does not have enough time to change the size of the plant in which it produces.

These are the things we are going to discuss. We are going to discover *how* and *why* the different kinds of costs vary as the firm adjusts its production in both the short run and long run. How these costs change will help us find out (in Sections 10 and 11) how much the firm will want to produce and what price it will obtain for its product.

ECONOMIC COSTS

9-1

You learned in Section 2 that costs in economies—economic costs—have to do with the forgoing of the opportunity to produce alternative goods

opportunity — and services and that they were therefore called ____________ costs.

9-2

economic

To a firm, __________ costs are those payments a firm must make, or incomes it must provide, to resource suppliers in order to attract these resources away from alternative lines of production. These payments may be either *explicit* or *implicit*.

9-3

nonowners

Explicit payments are those that must be made to "outsiders": those who supply labor services, materials, fuel, transportation, power, and so forth. Thus explicit costs are payments made to (owners/nonowners) of the firm.

9-4

$100

Implicit costs—or nonexpenditure costs—are those incurred by a firm using resources it owns. For example, when the rate of interest is 10 percent and a firm uses $1000 of its own money in its business, it is forgoing every year the $________ it could have made by lending the money.

9-5

is not
implicit, is

A person running his or her own business forgoes the payment he or she could have made working for someone else. The minimum required to keep a person content in his or her own business is called a ***normal profit***. Since a normal profit (must be/is not) paid out, it is an (implicit/explicit) cost. It (is/is not) an opportunity cost.

9-6 Review Frame

explicit, implicit (either order)
opportunity

All costs in economics include both __________ and __________ costs, for both are ______________ costs.

9-7

include
do

Implicit costs (include/do not include) a normal profit. When we say, then, that a firm is just covering its costs or breaking even, we (do/do not) mean that it is just making a normal profit.

9-8

more than
including

When a firm is making *more* than a normal profit, we say it is making a ***pure*** or ***economic profit***. Such a firm is (more than/less than/just) covering all its costs (including/not including) a normal profit.

SHORT-RUN COSTS

Total Costs

9-9

Here is a cost schedule for a firm producing instant coffee.

Short-run costs of production schedule
Pounds of instant coffee per hour

Output of instant coffee (100 lbs.)	Total fixed cost	Total variable cost	Total cost
0	$200	$ 0	$200
1	200	40	240
2	200	60	260
3	200	90	290
4	200	130	330
5	200	180	380
6	200	240	440
7	200	310	510
8	200	390	590

short-run

outputs (quantities, amounts)

This is a (short-run/long-run) cost schedule which indicates the costs of producing different ________ of instant coffee in an hour.

9-10

total

three (3)

In this short-run schedule we find the (average/total/marginal) costs of producing various quantities of instant coffee in an hour. There are (how many) ________ different kinds of cost shown in this short-run schedule.

9-11

cannot

fixed

During the short run some of the economic resources the firm uses to produce instant coffee are *fixed*. The firm (can/cannot) change the amount of these resources it employs, and the cost of employing these resources is called a ________ cost.

9-12

is

variable

Those resources which are *not* fixed are called *variable* resources. The firm (is/is not) able to change the amount of the variable resources it employs. Economists call the costs of such resources ________ costs.

9-13

fixed, variable (either order)

The *short run* is defined as any period of time in which some of the resources a firm uses are ________ and some are ________ .

fixed

variable (either order)

In the short run, therefore, some of the firm's costs are ________ and the remainder of its costs are ________ .

9-14

When the firm produces 200 pounds of instant coffee in an hour the total fixed cost (TFC) is $__________, and the total variable cost (TVC) is $__________.

$200

$60

9-15

Producing 200 pounds of instant coffee an hour, the firm finds that its total cost (TC) is $__________. TC can be determined by __________ TFC and TVC.

$260

adding (totaling, summing)

9-16

If the firm were to produce 300 pounds of instant coffee in an hour instead of 200 pounds, the TFC would be (the same as/different from) the TFC of producing 200 pounds per hour.

the same as

9-17

As the firm *increases* its production of coffee, TFC will (rise/fall/remain constant). And when the firm *decreases* its production, TFC will __________.

remain constant

remain constant (not change)

9-18

TFC is the cost of such fixed resources as the firm's *plant* (buildings and machinery), the size of which cannot be changed in the short run. If the firm wished to increase its production in the short run, it must use more of the __________ resources.

variable

9-19

Using more of such variable resources as labor, materials and fuel enables the firm to increase its production of instant coffee in the short run. But when the firm employs *more* of these variable resources, its TVC costs will (increase/decrease/remain constant). Were it to use fewer variable resources, the output would be (larger/smaller) and its TVC would be (larger/smaller/the same).

increase

smaller

smaller

9-20

Variable costs are variable not only because they are the cost of __________ resources, but also because they (are fixed/vary) when the firm changes its output.

variable, vary

9-21

fixed
do not change

Likewise, fixed costs are fixed because they are the cost of __________ resources and because they (change/do not change) when the firm changes its production.

9-22

total fixed
total variable
(either order)

Total cost (TC) is equal to __________ __________ cost plus __________ __________ cost.

9-23

increase, increase

As the firm increases its production, TFC remains constant, and TVC will __________ . And TC, therefore, will __________ .

9-24

total fixed
decrease

But when the firm *decreases* its output, __________ __________ costs remain constant, and TVC decreases. And this causes TC to __________ .

9-25

direct
neither
direct

In brief, the relationship between output and:
TVC is (inverse/direct/neither),
TFC is (inverse/direct/neither),
TC is (inverse/direct/neither).

9-26

costs
output (production)

Below is a graph of the cost schedules in frame **9-9**. When graphing costs in economics, it is customary to plot __________ on the vertical axis, and __________ on the horizontal axis.

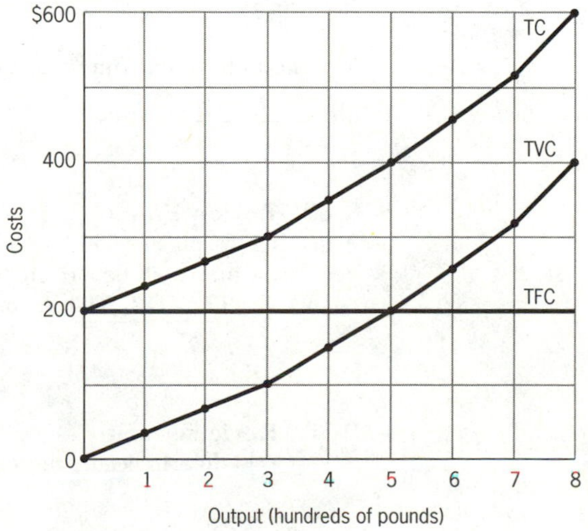

9-27

This graph tells us only a little more than the cost schedules in frame **9-6** told us. The graph tells us, for example, that when output is zero:

$0 — TVC = $________ ,

$200 — TFC = $________ ,

$200, TFC — TC = $________ and is equal to (TFC/TVC).

9-28

total / variable, total / total fixed

When production *increases*, there is an increase in both ____________ ____________________ and ____________ cost and no change in * ______________________ cost.

9-29

decrease, not change / decrease

As output decreases TVC will __________ , TFC will * __________ , and TC will __________ .

9-30

is, is not / is not

Looking more closely at the graph in frame **9-26**, you will see something that you probably didn't see in the schedules. The TFC curve (is/is not) a straight line, the TVC curve (is/is not) a straight line, and the TC curve (is/is not) a straight line.

9-31 Review Frame

That the TVC and TC curves are *not* straight lines is fairly obvious. What this means and why they are not straight lines we will discover shortly. Then we will be able to see it in the schedules too. Before we do this, however, let's review what you have already learned about costs.

The short run is defined as any period of time in which some of

variable, fixed (either order) / variable / fixed (either order)

the firm's resources are ___________ and some are ___________ . As a result, in the short run some costs are ___________ costs and the rest are ___________ costs.

9-32 Review Frame

total / TVC and TC / TFC / No

A firm's TVC plus its TFC is equal to its ___________ costs. As output *decreases*, there will be a decrease in [pick two] (TFC,TVC,TC) and no change in (TFC/TVC/TC). As output increases, will all three increase? (Yes/No).

9-33 Review Frame

A cost schedule indicates the costs of producing at different levels of

output (production) — ___________ .

9-34 Review Frame

output (production)
cost

In graphing cost schedules we plot __________ on the horizontal axis and __________ on the vertical axis.

Marginal Cost

9-35

Let's look back at the cost schedules in frame **9-9**.

Short-run costs of production schedule Pounds of instant coffee per hour		
Output of instant coffee (100 lbs.)	Total variable cost	Total cost
0	$ 0	$200
1	40	240
2	60	260
3	90	290
4	130	330
5	180	380
6	240	440
7	310	510
8	390	590

same
total variable, total

TFC need not be included in these schedules because it is the __________ at every level of output and can be found by subtracting __________ __________ cost from __________ cost.

9-36

$0, $40
$200, $240

When the firm increases its output from 0 to 100 pounds of coffee, TVC increases from $______ to $______ , and TC increases from $______ to $______ .

9-37

$40

Thus we see that when production increases from 0 to 100 pounds, *both* TVC and TC increase by $______ .

9-38

do not

When a firm expands its production, TVC and TC always increase by *equal* amounts. Why? Because increases in production during the short run (do/do not) bring about any change in the firm's TFC.

9-39

$40 It costs the firm an additional, or extra, $______ to produce an additional, or extra, 100 pounds of instant coffee when it increases its production from 0 to 100 pounds.

9-40

If TVC and TC increase by $40 when the firm produces an additional *100* pounds of instant coffee, how much extra does it cost *per pound* to

$0.40 (= $40 ÷ 100 pounds) increase production from 0 to 100 pounds? ______

9-41

Suppose the firm were to increase its production from 200 to 300 pounds

$30 of coffee; TVC and TC would increase by $______ . The additional

$0.30 cost of *each* additional pound of coffee would be ______ .

9-42

When a firm increases its production *by one unit* (here, 100 pounds of instant coffee), the amount TC and TVC increase is called the ***marginal cost*** (MC) of producing such a unit. The marginal cost of the third 100

$30 pounds is $______ .

9-43

Below is another set of cost schedules. Do not fill in the blanks until frame **9-44**.

Short-run costs of production schedule
Motorcycles per hour

Output of motorcycles	Total variable cost	Total cost	Marginal cost
0	$ 0	$ 400	
1	500	900	$______
2	900	1,300	$______
3	1,500	1,900	$______
4	2,400	2,800	$______
5	3,500	3,900	$______
6	4,800	5,200	$______
7	6,300	6,700	$______
8	8,000	8,400	$______

$400 The firm's TFC is $______ .

$500, $400, $600, $900, $1,100 $1,300, $1,500, $1,700

9-44
Compute the MC of each motorcycle and enter these figures in the table.

less than
greater than

9-45
What happens to MC as the firm increases the number of bikes that roll off the assembly line every hour? The MC of the second bike is (greater than/equal to/less than) the MC of the first bike. The MC of the fifth bike is (greater than/equal to/less than) the MC of the fourth bike.

decrease
increase

9-46
At first, as the firm increases its production MC will (increase/decrease); but after some level of production is reached, MC will start to (increase/decrease).

horizontal
vertical

9-47
Below are the MCs you computed in frame **9-44** and a graph on which to plot the eight points given by this MC schedule. You can see that you measure *output* on the (horizontal/vertical) axis and MC on the (horizontal/vertical) axis.

Plot the points given by this MC schedule on the graph.

Output	MC
1	$ 500
2	400
3	600
4	900
5	1,100
6	1,300
7	1,500
8	1,700

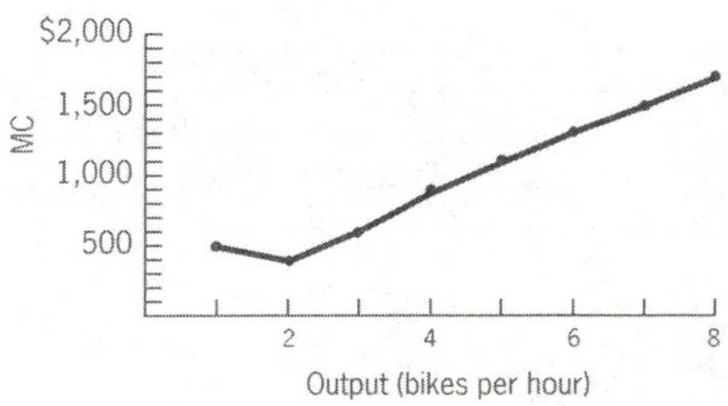

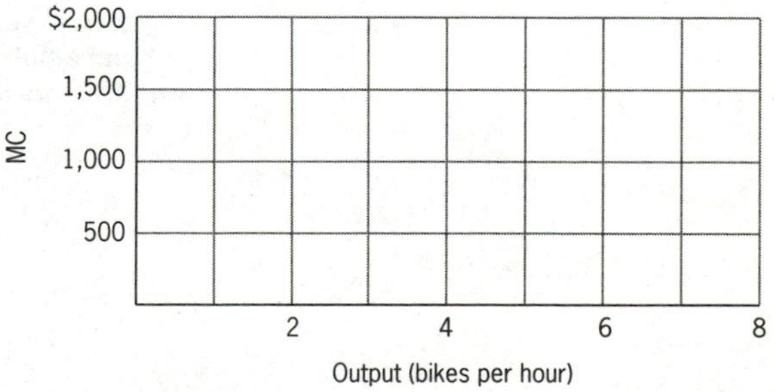

downward
upward

9-48
Connect the eight points you have just plotted with a line, or a curve. From left to right, this curve at first slopes (downward/upward), and afterward slopes (downward/upward).

9-49 Review Frame

In constructing a graph of MC, we use the horizontal axis to plot

output (production) ____________—just as we did when we graphed total costs. On the

marginal cost vertical axis we plot * ____________.

9-50 Review Frame

TVC or TC MC is the amount by which * ____________

output (production) increases when the firm increases its ____________ by (how much)

one additional unit * ____________.

9-51 Review Frame

As any firm expands its production in the short run, it finds that MC at

decreases, increases first ____________ and thereafter ____________. The MC curve at first

downward, upward slopes ____________ and thereafter slopes ____________.

9-52

It is reasonable to ask why MC should behave in this way as the firm increases its production. We already know that to produce *more* output

more in the short run, the firm must employ (more/less) of the (fixed/variable)

variable resources.

9-53

As a firm uses more of the variable resources—or inputs—total production will expand as it does in the following table.

Amount of variable input employed (worker-hours of labor)	Total output (100 lbs of crackers per hour)
0	0
1	5
2	11
3	18
4	24
5	29
6	33
7	36
8	38

When the firm increases the amount of the variable *input* employed

500 from 0 to 1 worker-hour, its total output will increase from 0 to ______ pounds of crackers per hour.

9-54

How much does production *increase* when the firm increases the amount
600 of the variable input from 1 to 2? __________ pounds of crackers per hour.

9-55

The amount by which total production, or output, increases when the firm uses *one more unit* of a variable input (such as a worker-hour of labor) is called the ***marginal product*** (MP) of that variable input. The
700 MP of the third worker-hour of labor is __________ pounds of crackers.

9-56

Below is another table showing the amounts of a variable input—bags of fertilizer—and total output—bales of cotton per year. Compute and enter in the table the MP of each bag of fertilizer for the farmer.

	Variable input (bags of fertilizer)	Total output (bales of cotton)	MP (bales of cotton)
	0	0	$______
2	1	2	______
5	2	7	______
6	3	13	______
5	4	18	______
4	5	22	______
3	6	25	______
2	7	27	______
1	8	28	______

9-57

In the table we see that as the farmer uses more and more of the variable input (along with whatever fixed resources—or inputs—he has), the
increases MP of the variable input at first (increases/decreases) and thereafter
decreases (increases/decreases).

9-58

This tendency for MP to rise at first and then to diminish, or decline, as the firm increases the amount of the variable input employed is called the ***Law of Diminishing Returns***: As more and more units of a (fixed/
variable, fixed variable) input are employed along with a constant amount of a (fixed/
marginal variable) input, the * ______________________________
product ______________ of the variable input after some point will decrease.

9-59

Now let's see what effect the Law of Diminishing Returns has upon the marginal costs of the firm in the short run. Suppose fertilizer is the only variable input, and the price the farmer must pay for *one* bag of fertilizer is $30; thus, if the farm used one bag of fertilizer, the TVC to the farmer would be $30. And if it employed two bags of fertilizer, TVC would be

$60 $__________ .

9-60

Assuming the price of a bag of fertilizer is $30, complete the TVC schedule in the following table. (This table is based upon the figures in frame **9-56**.)

	Variable input (bags of fertilizer)	Total output (bales of cotton)	MP (bales of cotton)	Total variable cost
$0	0	0		$______
$30	1	2	2	______
$60	2	7	5	______
$90	3	13	6	______
$120	4	18	5	______
$150	5	22	4	______
$180	6	25	3	______
$210	7	27	2	______
$240	8	28	1	______

9-61

When the farmer increases *output* from 0 to 2 bales of cotton, TVC

$30 increases by $__________ .

9-62

If it costs the farmer $30 more to produce 2 more bales of cotton, the MC of each of the 2 additional bales of cotton is $30 divided by 2 (bales

$15 of cotton), or $________ .

9-63

If the farmer were to increase production from 2 to 7 bales of cotton,

5 cotton production would increase by ______ bales, TVC would in-

$30 crease by $______, and the MC of each additional bale of cotton would

$6 be $______ .

9-64

You can now complete the following table by computing the MC of the additional bales of cotton.

	Variable input (bags)	Output (bales)	MP (bales)	TVC	MC (per bale)
	0	0		$ 0	
$15	1	2	2	30	$______
$6	2	7	5	60	______
$5	3	13	6	90	______
$6	4	18	5	120	______
$7.50	5	22	4	150	______
$10	6	25	3	180	______
$15	7	27	2	210	______
$30	8	28	1	240	______

9-65

Look at what happens to MC and MP as the farmer increases output of
decreases, increases cotton. MC at first ______ and then ______.
increases, decreases MP at first ______ and then ______.

9-66

In fact, we can observe that when MP is increasing, MC is (increasing/
decreasing, increasing decreasing), and when MP is decreasing, MC is (increasing/decreasing).

9-67

Why does MC decrease when MP increases? In our example each bag of fertilizer costs the farmer $30. When a bag of fertilizer has an MP of 5 bales of cotton, the MC of *each* of these 5 extra bales is equal to the
$6 extra $30 spent to produce them divided by 5, or $______.

9-68

But if a bag of fertilizer had an MP of 6 bales of cotton, the MC of each
6, $5 of the 6 bales is equal to $30 divided by ______, or $______.

9-69

From this we can see that the larger the MP of a bag of fertilizer, the
smaller (larger/smaller) is the MC of each additional bale of cotton; and the
larger smaller the MP of a bag of fertilizer, the (larger/smaller) is the MC of each extra bale of cotton.

9-70

And we can also see that if the MP of a bag of fertilizer *decreases*, the
increase — MC of each additional bale of cotton will (increase/decrease); and if the MP *increases*, the MC of each additional bale of cotton will (increase/
decrease — decrease).

9-71

Now we know *why* MC at first decreases and then increases. It is because
MP — ________ at first increases and then decreases.

9-72

Every firm is subject to the Law of Diminishing Returns in the short
fixed — run. In the short run, some resources or inputs are ________
variable (either order) — resources and some are ________ resources. As the firm uses more and more of the variable inputs and a constant amount of the fixed
increase — inputs, MP may at first ________ , but eventually MP will
decrease, decrease — ________ . The result is that MC will at first ________ , but
increase — sooner or later MC will ________ .

9-73

We have now discovered *why* the TVC and TC curves are not straight lines. Let's reconsider the cost schedules which we used in frame **9-9** and which are reprinted below.

Short-run costs of production schedule
Pounds of instant coffee per hour

Output of instant coffee (100 lbs.)	Total fixed cost	Total variable cost	Total cost
0	$200	$ 0	$200
1	200	40	240
2	200	60	260
3	200	90	290
4	200	130	330
5	200	180	380
6	200	240	140
7	200	310	510
8	200	390	590

9-74

MC in the short run is the change which occurs in either
TVC, TC (either order) — * ________ or * ________ when the firm increases its production by one unit—by 100 pounds of instant coffee.

9-75

In other words, the amount of *increase* in TC or in TVC when the firm

MC produces another unit of its product is the __________ of producing another unit.

9-76

And because MC at first decreases and then increases, TVC and TC will

smaller at first increase by amounts that become (larger/smaller), and thereafter

larger increase by amounts that become (larger/smaller).

9-77

Here is the graph of TVC and TC which appeared in frame **9-26**.

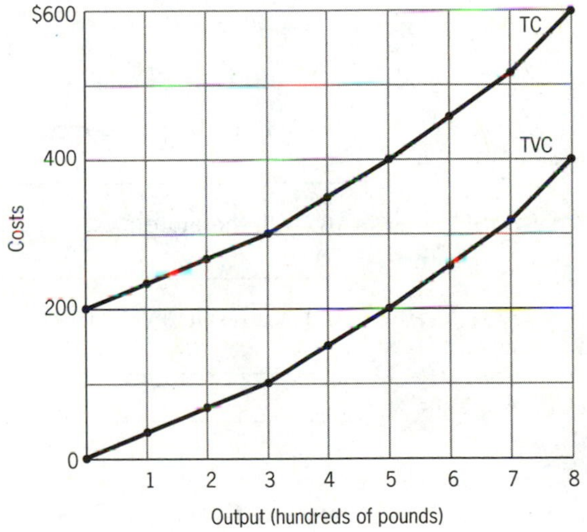

As the firm increases its production of instant coffee, the *slope* of each

less curve at first gets (more/less) steep, but beyond 200 pounds of instant

more coffee, each becomes (more/less) steep.

9-78

The initial decrease, followed by an increase in the steepness (or slope) of the TVC and TC curves, reflects the fact that MC initially

decreases, increases __________ and eventually __________ .

9-79

Because MC behaves in this way, as a firm increases its production the

will not TVC and TC curves (will/will not) be straight lines. Their slopes, as pro-

less duction increases, at first become (more/less) steep and then become

more (more/less) steep.

9-80 Review Frame

MC is defined as * ____.

the amount by which TVC or TC increases when the firm increases its output by one unit

MP is defined as * ____.

the amount by which total output increases when the firm increases the employment of a variable input by one unit

State the Law of Diminishing Returns: * ____.

As the firm increases its employment of a variable input, the MP of that input will at first increase and then decrease.

9-81 Review Frame

As the firm's output *increases*, MP will * ____.

at first increase and then decrease

MC will, therefore, * ____.

at first decrease and then increase

And as a result, TVC and TC will * ____.

at first increase by amounts that become smaller and then increase by amounts that become larger

Average Costs

9-82

Remember the total-cost schedule we examined in frame **9-43**? The costs are repeated in the table below.

Short-run costs of production schedule
Motorcycles per hour

Output of motorcycles	Total fixed cost	Total variable cost	Total cost
0	$400	$ 0	$ 400
1	400	500	900
2	400	900	1,300
3	400	1,500	1,900
4	400	2,400	2,800
5	400	3,500	3,900
6	400	4,800	5,200
7	400	6,300	6,700
8	400	8,000	8,400

If the firm were producing 5 motorcycles per hour, TFC is $400. If we divide the TFC of $400 by 5 motorcycles, we find that the ***average***

$80 ***fixed cost*** (AFC) is $_______ .

9-83

If the firm were to produce 8 motorcycles an hour, the AFC of a

$400, 8 motorcycle would equal $_______ divided by _______ motorcycles,

$50 or $_______ per motorcycle.

9-84

Complete the following AFC schedule using the TFC figures in the table in frame **9-82**.

(answer)	Output of motorcycles	AFC
$400	1	$_______
$200	2	_______
$133⅓	3	_______
$100	4	_______
$80	5	_______
$66⅔	6	_______
$57 1/7	7	_______
$50	8	_______

9-85

smaller
decreases

In the frame above you can see that the greater the firm's production, the (larger/smaller) is the AFC. In other words, as output increases, AFC (increases/decreases) and vice versa.

9-86

constant
larger

As production increases, AFC continually declines because a (constant/changing) number of dollars is being divided by a (larger/smaller) number of motorcycles.

9-87

The fact that AFC decreases in the short run when production is increased is known to many businesses. They call it "spreading the overhead." And to reduce the overhead cost on each unit of output or AFC,

increase they try to _______ their output.

9-88

variable

output (production)

Just as we can compute AFC, we can also compute ***average variable cost*** (AVC) and ***average total cost*** (ATC). To determine the AVC at any level of production, we must *divide* total __________ cost by __________ .

9-89

TC, production (output)

Likewise, to compute the ATC at any production level, we divide ____________________ by ____________________ .

9-90

Here are the cost figures for motorcycle production once again.

Short-run costs of production schedule
Motorcycles per hour

Output of motorcycles	Total fixed cost	Total variable cost	Total cost
0	$400	$ 0	$ 400
1	400	500	900
2	400	900	1,300
3	400	1,500	1,900
4	400	2,400	2,800
5	400	3,500	3,900
6	400	4,800	5,200
7	400	6,300	6,700
8	400	8,000	8,400

Complete the following table by computing the missing AVCs and ATCs. (The figures already in the table have been rounded off to the nearest dollar.)

	Output of motorcycles	AFC	AVC	ATC
$500, $900	1	$400	$_______	$_______
$450, $650	2	200	_______	_______
$500,	3	133	_______	633
$600, $700	4	100	_______	_______
$700, $780	5	80	_______	_______
$800,	6	67	_______	867
$900,	7	57	_______	957
$1,000, $1,050	8	50	_______	_______

9-91

If you look at the ATC at *any* level of output, you find that ATC is equal

AFC, AVC (either order) — to ________ plus ________ .

9-92

You will also see that as the output of motorcycles *increases*, AVC at first (increases/decreases) and thereafter (increases/decreases); and ATC at the start (rises/falls) and then (rises/falls).

decreases, increases
falls, rises

9-93

Because both AVC and ATC decline at first and then increase, we find that there is a *minimum* (or a lowest) AVC and ATC. The minimum AVC

$450, $633 — is $________ . The minimum ATC is $________ .

9-94

2 — AVC is the least—a minimum—when the firm produces ________

3 — bikes an hour. But ATC is a minimum if the firm produces ________ bikes per hour.

9-95

greater than — The output at which ATC is at a minimum is (greater than/equal to/less than) the output at which AVC is at a minimum.

9-96

Why do AVC and ATC decrease at first and then increase? To make the reason clear, let's start by recalling that TVC and TC at first increase by amounts that become (larger/smaller) and thereafter increase by amounts that become (larger/smaller). Or, in other words, recall that MC

smaller
larger

decreases, increases — at first ________ and then ________ .

9-97

Now, to take a simple noneconomic example, suppose your *average* on the first two examinations in a course is 80 percent. If on the *third* examination you obtain a mark of:

rise — 90 percent, your examination average will (rise/fall/not change);
fall — 70 percent, your examination average will (rise/fall/not change);
not change — 80 percent, your examination average will (rise/fall/not change).

9-98

Putting this in economic terms, if the AVC of 2 units of output is $80 and the MC of the *third* unit of output is:

increase — $90, the AVC of producing the product will (increase/decrease/not change);

decrease — $70, the AVC of producing the product will (increase/decrease/not change);

not change — $80, the AVC of producing the product will (increase/decrease/not change).

9-99

greater, less — In short, AVC increases as long as MC is (greater/less) than the AVC; but AVC will decrease when the MC is (greater/less) than the AVC.

9-100

So as output is expanded AVC declines for a while because MC is less than AVC, and AVC rises because MC is greater than AVC. But why does ATC decline at first and then rise? You remember that

AFC, AVC (either order), decreases — ATC equals __________ *plus* __________ and AFC always __________ when production increases.

9-101

When AVC is declining, AFC is also declining. The result is that ATC

decline (decrease) — will __________ .

9-102

ATC, however, continues to decrease after AVC has begun to increase. Why is this? Looking back at the schedules you completed in frame **9-90** and which are reprinted here, we see that AVC is at a minimum when the firm produces 2 bikes an hour. If it increases its production to

$50, $67 — 3 bikes an hour, AVC will *increase* by $________ , but AFC will *decrease* by $________ .

Output of motorcycles	AFC	AVC	ATC
1	$400	$ 500	$ 900
2	200	450	650
3	133	500	633
4	100	600	700
5	80	700	780
6	67	800	867
7	57	900	957
8	50	1,000	1,050

9-103

$17, less The amount by which AVC increases is $________ (more/less) than the
decrease amount by which AFC decreases. So ATC will (increase/decrease)
$17 by $________ .

9-104

But when the firm increases its production from 3 to 4 bikes an hour,
$67, more AVC increases by $________ (more/less) than the decrease in AFC. ATC
increase, $67 will, therefore, ________ by $ ________ .

9-105

All this means is that if a firm has any fixed costs:

ATC will decrease even though AVC is increasing, as long as the de-
greater crease in AFC is (greater/less) than the increase in AVC.

AVC The output at which ________ is a minimum will be *less than*
ATC the output at which ________ is at a minimum.

9-106

Now let's put AFC, AVC, and ATC all on the same graph. These three costs, using the figures you computed in frames **9-84** and **9-90**, are plotted below.

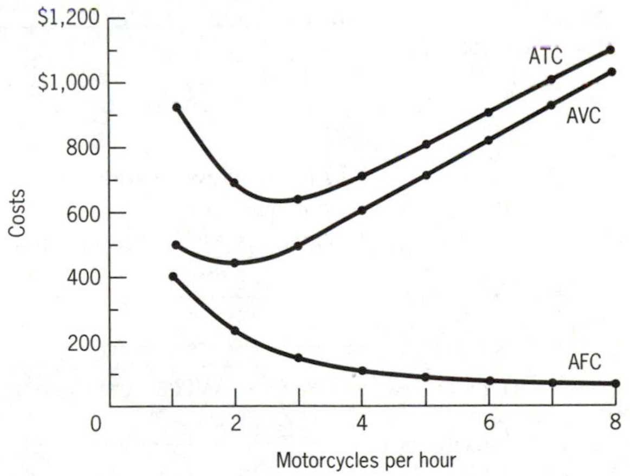

ATC Since ATC = AFC + AVC, AFC must be equal to ________
AVC *minus* ________ .

9-107

The *vertical distance* between the ATC and AVC curves is equal to
AFC ________ . And as we move from left to right on the graph we find
decreases that this distance (increases/decreases/stays the same).

9-108

On the graph we again see that as the firm increases its production, both AVC and ATC ________ in the beginning, but eventually both ________ . The output at which ATC is at a minimum is, however, ________ than the output at which AVC is at a minimum.

decrease
increase
greater

9-109 Review Frame

Now let's take four frames to review what we have learned about average costs.

In your own words, explain how you compute or determine:

AFC: * ________________________________ .

AVC: * ________________________________ .

ATC: * ________________________________ .

Divide TFC by output.
Divide TVC by output.
Divide TC by output (or add AFC and AVC).

9-110 Review Frame

As a firm increases its output in the short run, what happens to:

AFC? * ________________________________ .

AVC? * ________________________________ .

ATC? * ________________________________ .

Decreases
Decreases and then increases
Decreases and then increases

9-111 Review Frame

In your own words:

Why does AFC always decrease when the firm increases its output?

* ________________________________

________________________________ .

Why does AVC at first decrease and then increase? * ________

____

____

________________________________ .

TFC is being divided by larger and larger outputs.

MC at first is less than AVC, causing AVC to fall; as MC increases it becomes greater than AVC, causing AVC to rise.

9-112 Review Frame

In the short run some of a firm's costs are fixed, and AFC decreases as the firm expands its output. As a result, AVC will start to increase (before/after) ATC starts to increase, and the output at which ATC is a minimum is (greater/less) than the output at which AVC is a minimum.

before
greater

9-113

Now let's put the AVC, ATC, and MC curves on the same graph. The graph will look like this.

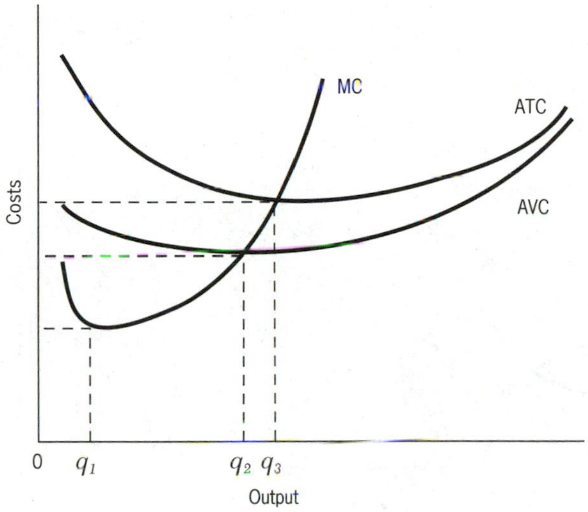

You see on the graph that ATC is a minimum when the firm produces
q_3 (q_1/q_2/q_3) units of output, and AVC is a minimum when the firm produces
q_2 (q_1/q_2/q_3).

9-114

less We can see that when ATC is decreasing, MC is (greater/less) than ATC.

greater And when ATC is increasing, MC is __________ than ATC.

9-115

falling Likewise, MC is less than AVC when AVC is (rising/falling), and MC is

rising (increasing) greater than AVC when AVC is __________ .

9-116

From the graph it is possible to draw two more conclusions.

First, when the AVC is a minimum (at output q_2), AVC and MC

equal (the same) are __________ .

Second, when the ATC is a minimum (at output q_3), ATC and MC

equal (the same) are __________ .

9-117

minimum In short, AVC and MC are equal when AVC is a __________ ; and

minimum ATC and MC are equal when ATC is a __________ .

9-118

To be sure you understand these relationships between MC on the one hand and AVC and ATC on the other hand, sketch in on the graph an AVC and an ATC curve. Then draw in an MC curve which cuts (or crosses) the two average-cost curves at the right spots.

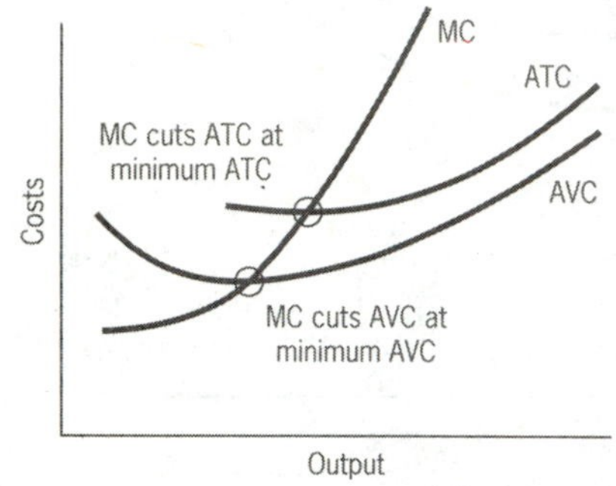

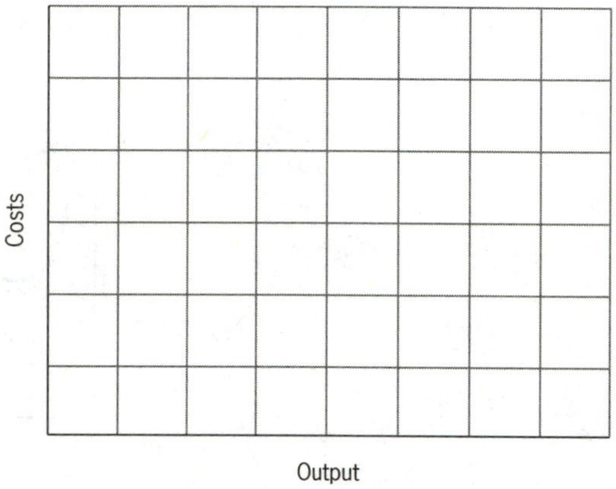

9-119

Look back at the curves you drew in the preceding frame. Does the vertical distance between the AVC and the ATC curves decrease as you move from left to right? (Yes/No)

If you said Yes, go on to frame 9-121. If you said No, go to frame 9-120.

9-120

Draw the AVC and ATC curves on the following graph. Draw the curve so that they show AFC falling as you move from left to right.

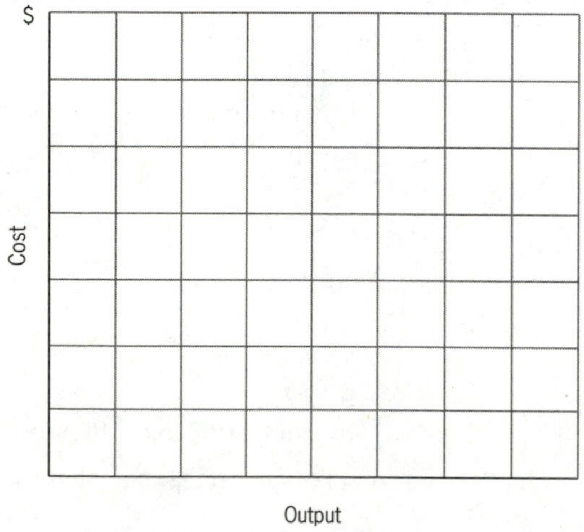

The vertical distance between ATC and AVC must decrease as output increases because this distance is AFC—which always decreases as output increases.

LONG-RUN COSTS

9-121

In the short run, as we know, some of the firm's costs are fixed and some are variable. But in the *long run*, all resources and all costs are variable.

fixed — Thus a firm, has *no* ________ costs or inputs in the long run.

9-122

When a firm has no fixed costs, the total costs of producing a product

variable — are all ________ costs.

9-123

We can then define the *long run* as a period of time long enough for a

resources (inputs) — firm to vary all the ________ the firm uses and during which time

costs — all the firm's ________ of production are variable.

9-124

Let's assume that in the short run the only fixed resource a firm has is

is not — its plant. In the long run the firm's plant (is/is not) fixed.

9-125

Let's also assume that in the long run a firm can choose to have any *one* of three different size plants in which to produce brooms. The *short-run* ATC schedule for each of the three broom plants is shown in the following table.

Short-run costs of production schedules
Hundreds of brooms per day

Plant number 1		Plant number 2		Plant number 3	
Output	ATC (per broom)	Output	ATC (per broom)	Output	ATC (per broom)
1	$3.00	1	$4.00	1	$7.00
2	2.00	2	3.00	2	6.00
3	1.50	3	2.00	3	5.00
4	2.00	4	1.00	4	4.00
5	3.00	5	.50	5	3.00
6	4.00	6	.75	6	2.00
7	5.00	7	2.00	7	1.00
8	6.00	8	3.00	8	2.00
9	7.00	9	4.00	9	3.00
10	8.00	10	5.00	10	4.00

If the firm were going to produce *just 100 brooms a day*, the use of

1 — plant number ________ would enable it to produce them at the lowest (least) ATC in the short run.

9-126

In the long run the firm would choose plant number 1 to produce 100 brooms. The short-run ATC of producing 100 brooms in plant number

$3 1 is $________ per broom.

9-127

If the firm produces 100 brooms in plant number 1, the ATC of each

less broom is $3. This figure is (greater/less) than the ATC of producing the same number of brooms in either plant number 2 or plant number 3.

9-128

Suppose the firm were planning to produce 400 brooms, and it could select any one of the three plants to produce this output. It would select

2 plant number ________, and the ATC of each broom in this plant

$1 would be $________ a broom.

9-129

If the firm were going to produce 800 brooms, it would choose plant

3 number ________, in which the ATC of each broom would be

$2 $________.

9-130

To produce any particular output, the firm selects the plant in which the

least ATC of producing that output will be (greatest/least).

9-131

The *long-run average cost* (LR ATC) of producing 800 brooms is $2, because this is the average cost of producing a broom when the firm produces this output in the plant in which the short-run ATC of 800 brooms is the least, or a minimum. The LR ATC of 400 brooms is

$1 $________ a broom.

9-132

The ATC is $3 per broom when 100 brooms are produced in plant num-

LR ATC ber 1. It is also the * ________ of producing 100 brooms.

9-133

Using the short-run cost schedules in the table in frame **9-125**, complete the following schedule.

	Output (hundreds of brooms)	LR ATC (per broom)
$3.00	1	$______
$2.00	2	______
$1.50	3	______
$1.00	4	______
$.50	5	______
$.75	6	______
$1.00	7	______
$2.00	8	______
$3.00	9	______
$4.00	10	______

9-134

long
average

The schedule you completed in frame **9-133** is known as a (short/long)-run (average/marginal) cost schedule.

9-135

quantities (amounts)
variable

The long-run average-cost schedule indicates the average cost of producing different ________ of a product when *all* of the firm's inputs are ________ .

9-136

short-run ATC

The LR ATC of producing a quantity of a product is equal to the lowest ° ____________ of producing that quantity of the product.

9-137

long-run average cost

The number of possible plant sizes does not have to be limited to 3 or to any other small number. The firm may find that *every* different output in the long run calls for and should be produced in a different size plant. Still, the least costly way of producing each output the firm might want to produce, when it can choose any plant size it might want, is called the °____________ schedule.

9-138

decreases, increases

If we look at the LR ATC schedule which we completed in frame **9-133**, we find that as the firm increases its production of brooms, LR ATC at first (increases/decreases) and then (increases/decreases).

9-139

Below is a graph of the LR ATC schedule. You can see how LR ATC decreases at first and then increases. But this behavior of LR ATC is *not* caused by the Law of Diminishing Returns, because in the long run there

fixed — are no __________ resources, or inputs.

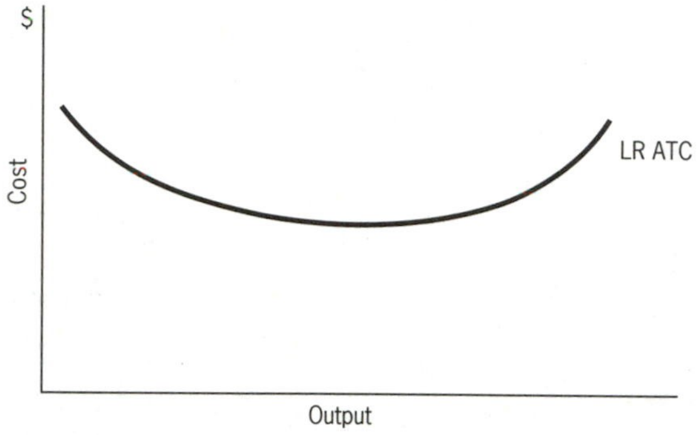

9-140

Because some resources are fixed in the short run, AVC and ATC will decrease at first and then increase. But in the long run, the behavior of LR ATC *cannot* be attributed to the fact that more and more

variable — __________ inputs are used along with a constant amount of the

fixed — __________ inputs to increase production, because there are no

fixed — __________ inputs in the long run.

9-141

LR ATC decreases at first because of the *economies of scale*. But as the firm continues to expand its production it eventually encounters *diseconomies of scale*. These *dis*economies will cause LR ATC to

increase — __________ .

9-142

Look again at the short-run ATC schedules in the table in frame **9-125**. The *minimum* short-run ATC of producing with plant number 1 is equal

$1.50, 300 — to $__________ and is achieved when the firm produces __________ brooms in a day.

9-143

If the firm has plant number 2, the minimum short-run ATC is

500 — reached when the firm produces __________ brooms a day and is equal

$0.50 — to __________ .

9-144

decreased

Increasing the plant size from number 1 to number 2 has (increased/decreased/left unchanged) the *minimum* short-run ATC of producing brooms.

9-145

increase, $0.50

$1

Were the firm to increase the plant size from number 2 to number 3, the minimum short-run ATC would (increase/decrease) from $______ to $______ .

9-146

economies

When the minimum short-run ATCs *decrease* as the firm increases the size of its plant, economists say there are (economies/diseconomies) in producing on a larger scale.

9-147

increase

But if the firm continues to expand the size of its plant, diseconomies will sooner or later appear; and the minimum short-run ATCs will ______ .

9-148

Here is another LR ATC schedule.

Output	LR ATC
10	$100
20	80
30	65
40	55
50	50
60	65
70	90
80	125

50, 80

10, 50

Between ______ and ______ units of output there are diseconomies of scale, but between ______ and ______ units of output there are economies of scale.

9-149

economies of scale

diseconomies of scale

Decreasing LR ATC is the result of * ______ while increasing LR ATC is brought about by the * ______ .

9-150 Review Frame

variable	In the long run, all costs are ________ because all resources are
variable	________. The long-run average cost of producing a certain amount
minimum (least, lowest)	of a product is equal to the ________ short-run cost of producing that quantity of the product. As the firm expands its production in
decrease	the long run, average cost will at first ________ because of the
economies, increase	________ of scale. Thereafter average cost will ________ due to
diseconomies	the ________ of scale.

Now take the Review Test for Section 9 at the back of the book.

Product Price and Output: Pure Competition

section **10**

The price and the total output, or production, of any product is determined by the cost of producing it and the demand for it. But the price and total production of a product also depend upon whether the product is produced by a competitive industry or by a monopolist, and whether we are talking about the short run or the long run.

In this section we will learn how demand and cost determine price and output in both the short run and the long run when the product is produced by a purely competitive industry. In the next section we will study price and output determination in the short and long runs when a monopolist produces the product.

The purely competitive industry which we study in this section has three important characteristics. *First*, the industry producing the product consists of a large number of firms; and each of these firms is so small that it cannot affect the price at which the product is sold. *Second*, each firm sells a product which is identical to the product produced by every other firm in the industry. *Third*, there are in the long run no barriers to prevent the entry of new firms into the industry or the exit of established firms from the industry.

Throughout this and the next section we make three additional assumptions:

1. The aim or goal of any business firm—pure competitor or monopolist—is the largest possible (maximum) profit or, if it cannot earn a profit, the smallest possible (minimum) loss.
2. The costs of producing a product do not depend upon whether the firm producing the product is a pure competitor or monopolist.
3. The number of buyers of the product is so large that no one buyer can in any way affect the product price or output.

We also assume that you are already familiar with the price elasticity of demand and marginal revenue concepts covered in Section 8.

THE SHORT RUN

10-1

Let's suppose that in the short run a purely competitive producer of snowblowers has the cost schedules shown in the following table.

Short-run costs of production schedule (Snowblowers per hour)

Output	TFC	TVC	TC	MC	AFC	AVC	ATC
0	$200	$ 0	$ 200				
1	200	175	375	$175	$200	$175	$375
2	200	300	500	125	100	150	250
3	200	500	700	200	66⅔	166⅔	233⅓
4	200	800	1,000	300	50	200	250
5	200	1,200	1,400	400	40	240	280
6	200	1,700	1,900	500	33⅓	283⅓	316⅔
7	200	2,300	2,500	600	28 4/7	328 4/7	357 1/7

do — The cost schedules shown above (do/do not) include a normal profit. Suppose that the price at which any producer of snowblowers can sell a snowblower is $250. If the firm produces and sells 1 snowblower,

$375 — its TC will be $__________ , and its total revenue (TR) will be

$250 — $__________ .

10-2

At this price, if the firm produces 1 snowblower, it will have a total

loss, $125 — economic (profit/loss) of __________ .

10-3

If the firm produces 3 snowblowers and sells them at this same price,

$700, $750 — $250, its TC will be $__________ , its TR will be $__________ , and

$+50 — its total economic profit (+) or loss (−) will be $__________ .

10-4

If the firm were to produce no snowblowers, it would have no revenue.

$200 — But it would have a TC of $__________ and as a result would have a

$−200 — total economic profit (+) or loss (−) of $__________ .

10-5

When a firm produces no output in the short run, it has a total economic

loss, fixed — (profit/loss) which is equal to its total __________ cost.

10-6

Assuming that the price of snowblowers is $250, here are schedules indicating a firm's TR, its TC, and its total economic profit or loss when it produces 0 through 7 snowblowers per hour.

Output of snowblowers	TR	TC	Total economic profit (+) or loss (−)
0	$ 0	$ 200	−$200
1	250	375	− 125
2	500	500	0
3	750	700	+ 50
4	1,000	1,000	0
5	1,250	1,400	− 150
6	1,500	1,900	− 400
7	1,750	2,500	− 750

If the firm wants the maximum total economic profit (or the minimum total loss), it should produce __________ snowblowers per hour. Its total profit would then be $__________ an hour.

3
$50

10-7

Because this producer is a purely competitive seller of snowblowers, the demand for its product is ***perfectly elastic***. This means that marginal revenue is (greater than/equal to/less than) the price of the product. (If you didn't know the answer, you should go back and review perfectly elastic demand and marginal revenue in frames **8-126** through **8-145**.)

equal to

10-8

The schedules in frame **10-6** assume that the price of snowblowers is $250, that this price does not change when the firm changes the amount it produces, and that the MR from the sale of each additional snowblower is $__________ .

$250

10-9

Now look at the MC schedule in the table in frame **10-1**. As we have seen, to have the maximum total economic profit, the firm must produce 3 snowblowers an hour when the price of snowblowers (and the __________ from the sale of each additional snowblower) is $250.

MR

10-10

This means that the firm must *not* produce any snowblowers when the MR is (greater/less) than the MC of producing the extra snowblower, and it should produce snowblowers so long as the MR is (greater/less) than the MC of the extra snowblower.

less
greater

10-11

The 4th snowblower has an MC of $300 and an MR of $250. If the firm produced this 4th snowblower, its TC would increase by

$300, $250 $_________, its TR would increase by $_________, and its total

decrease, $50 economic profit would (increase/decrease) by $_________.

10-12

The firm should produce the 3d snowblower because when it increases its production from 2 to 3 snowblowers, its TC increases by

$200, $250 $_________, its TR increases by $_________, and total

increases, $50 economic profit (increases/decreases) by $_________.

10-13

We have discovered a principle: to maximize profits, a firm must pro-

MR duce all units of a product so long as the (MC/MR) is greater than the

MC (MC/MR) of the last unit.

10-14

MC A profit-minded firm must *not* produce where (MC/MR) has become

MR greater than (MC/MR).

10-15

As output increases we reach a production level at which the MR is *equal* to the MC of producing the last unit of the product. For example, suppose the MR from the sale of the 101st bushel of corn is $4.20 and that the MC to the farmer of producing the 101st bushel is also $4.20. If the farmer produced the 101st bushel, the TC would increase by

$4.20, $4.20 $_________, the TR would increase by $_________, and the total

not change (neither increase nor decrease) profit would * ________________.

10-16

A firm *will* produce any unit of a product that has an MR equal to its MC. Our principle determining how much a firm should produce to maximize its profit thus becomes: Produce a product so long as MC has

greater, MR not become (greater/smaller) than _________.

10-17

Going back to snowblowers, suppose the price of snowblowers were $180. Under pure competition, the MR from the sale of each additional

$180 snowblower is $_________.

10-18

Refer to the production schedule in frame **10-1**. If the firm is going to maximize its profits or minimize its losses, when the price of snowblowers is $180, it should produce __________ snowblowers an hour. At this output it will have a TR of $__________ and a total economic (profit/loss) of $__________ .

2
$360
loss, $140

10-19

If the firm were to increase its production from 2 to 3 snowblowers an hour, its TR would increase by $__________ , its TC would increase by $__________ , and its total economic loss would (decrease/increase) by $__________ .

$180
$200, increase
$20

10-20

And if the firm cut its production from 2 to 1 snowblowers, its TR would decrease by $__________ , its TC would decrease by $__________ , and its total economic loss would (decrease/increase) by $__________ .

$180
$125, increase
$55

10-21

Even if the firm cut its production to 0, the firm would have a total economic loss of $__________ because at zero output this is the amount of the firm's total * __________ .

$200
fixed cost (cost)

10-22

Faced with the prospect of producing 2 snowblowers and having a loss of $140, or 0 snowblowers and suffering a loss of $200, the firm will choose to produce __________ snowblowers because * __________ .

2
$140 is a smaller loss than $200

10-23

Just to confirm these conclusions, look at the schedule that follows. It shows the firm's TR, TC, and total economic profit or loss when the price of snowblowers is $180.

Output of snowblowers	TR	TC	Total economic profit (+) or loss (−)
0	$ 0	$ 200	$ −200
1	180	375	−195
2	360	500	−140
3	540	700	−160
4	720	1,000	−280
5	900	1,400	−500
6	1,080	1,900	−820
7	1,260	2,500	−1,240

loss — No matter what output the firm produces, it has an economic (profit/loss).

10-24

2 — But the firm's total economic loss is a minimum when it produces ____ snowblowers an hour.

10-25

profit — When the price of snowblowers is $250, the firm has an economic (profit/loss); it produces the output that results in the maximum profit or minimum loss.

loss — When the price goes to $180, the firm has an economic (profit/loss) when it produces its "best" output.

10-26

Suppose the price of snowblowers were $233⅓. The firm:

will — (will/will not) produce the 1st snowblower,
will — (will/will not) produce the 2d snowblower,
will — (will/will not) produce the 3d snowblower,
will not — (will/will not) produce the 4th snowblower.

10-27

MC, MR — At a price of $233⅓, the firm will not produce the 4th snowblower because its ________ is greater than its ________ .

10-28

greater — The firm will produce the 1st, 2d, and 3d snowblowers because their MR is ________ than their MC.

10-29

$700, $700 / $0, will — So at a price of $233⅓, the firm will produce just 3 snowblowers. The firm's TC will be $________ , its TR will be $________ , and its total economic profit will be $________ . It (will/will not) be making a normal profit.

10-30

If the price of snowblowers is \$233⅓, the firm has neither an economic profit nor a loss at this output. If the price of snowblowers were greater

profit — than \$233⅓, the firm would have an economic ________ . If the price were anything less than \$233⅓, it would have an economic

loss — ________ .

10-31

Look at the *average*-cost schedules for snowblowers in frame **10-1**. You

ATC — will find that \$233⅓ is the *minimum* (AFC/AVC/ATC) shown there.

10-32

So we have this principle: A firm can earn an economic profit only if the

above — product price is (above/below) the minimum ATC. Economic losses re-

price, lowest — sult if the ________ is below the (highest/lowest) ATC.

10-33

But a firm will have neither an economic profit nor a loss if the price of

minimum ATC — the product is equal to * ________________ .

normal — Here it will be realizing a ________ profit.

10-34

Now let's assume that the price of snowblowers is only \$140. The firm's TR, TC, and total economic profit or loss at various outputs are shown in the following table.

Output of snowblowers	TR	TC	Total economic profit (+) or loss (−)
0	\$ 0	\$ 200	\$−200
1	140	375	−235
2	280	500	−220
3	420	700	−280
4	560	1,000	−440
5	700	1,400	−700
6	840	1,900	−1,160
7	980	2,500	−1,520

loss — At every output the firm has an economic (profit/loss).

10-35

The firm's total economic loss is at a minimum when it produces

0 — ________ snowblowers an hour. Thus, when the price of snowblowers is \$140, in the short run the firm will produce ________ snowblowers

0 — each hour.

10-36

When does a firm "close down" in the short run and produce none of its product? Look at the AVC schedule in frame **10-1**. The *minimum*

$150 AVC is $__________ .

10-37

less The price of $140 is (greater/less) than the minimum AVC.

10-38

Suppose the price of snowblowers were just equal to the minimum AVC of $150. The firm would produce no more than 2 snowblowers an hour.

$300, $500 At this output TR will be $__________ , TC will be $__________ ,

$ − 200 and total economic profit (+) or loss (−) will be $__________ .

10-39

What do *you* think a firm would do if, when the price of snowblowers is $150, it has a choice of producing *either* 0 or 2 snowblowers an hour?

We asked what you think. For what we think read on.

____

____ .

10-40

At a price of $150, if a firm produced 2 snowblowers it would have a total economic loss of $200. If it closed down, it would have a total

$200 economic loss of $__________ .

10-41

Regardless of whether the firm produces 0 or 2 snowblowers an hour, its economic loss is $200. So the firm could toss a coin to decide whether to produce or not, because it makes no difference whether it produces 0 to 2 snowblowers. But if the price of the product is *less than* $150, it does make a difference; if it then produces 2 snowblowers, its total loss

greater will be __________ than $200.

10-42

Thus, a firm will close down and produce nothing in the short run

AVC whenever the product price is less than the minimum (AVC/ATC).

10-43

Let's look at this another way. If a firm produces some output greater than zero, and the product price is less than the minimum AVC, the

less firm's TR will be (greater/less) than its TVC.

10-44

If TR is less than TVC, a firm suffers a total economic loss which is equal to the amount by which TVC exceeds TR *plus* the firm's total

fixed ________ cost.

10-45

So if the product price is less than minimum AVC, the firm's total economic *loss* is equal to (TVC − TR) + TFC. In other words, the firm's total economic loss is (greater/less) than its TFC.

greater

10-46

A firm's total economic loss when it produces *no* output is equal to its (TVC/TFC).

TFC

10-47

If a firm must choose between a total economic *loss* equal to its TFC or a total economic loss equal to its TFC *plus* the excess of TVC over TR, it will choose * ________________.

to lose its TFC

10-48

Thus, a firm will produce no output in the short run when the product price is ________ than the minimum AVC, because to produce any output would result in a total economic loss ________ than its TFC.

less

greater

10-49

But when the product price is greater than the minimum AVC and less than the minimum ATC, the firm will produce some output. It will suffer some economic loss, but the total will be less than its ________.

TFC

10-50

So we arrive at this overall conclusion about what output a firm will produce in the short run: It will produce so long as MR is ________ than or equal to the MC of the last unit, *provided* that the price of the product is ________ than or equal to ________ average ________ cost.

greater

greater,

minimum (lowest), variable

10-51

A firm will continue to increase its output up to the level at which the production of *one more* unit requires a marginal ________ greater than the marginal ________.

cost

revenue

10-52

equal to In other words, the business firm will produce that output at which the MC of the last unit produced is (greater than/equal to/less than) the MR of that last unit.

10-53

Understanding how much the firm will produce when we know its cost of production and the price of the product enables us to find out how much it will produce *at different product prices.*

Let's use the cost schedules in the table in frame **10-1**. Suppose the different prices that might be charged for snowblowers are those shown in the table below. How much would the firm produce at each price in the schedule?

	Price of snowblowers	Quantity the firm will produce
0	$140	______
3	200	______
4	300	______
5	400	______
6	500	______
7	600	______

10-54

smaller You will observe in the schedule which you completed in frame **10-53** that the lower the product price, the (greater/smaller) the quantity the firm will produce, and vice versa.

10-55

rise To induce the firm to produce more snowblowers, the price of snowblowers had to (rise/fall).

10-56

increases As a firm increases its output of a product, the MC of producing that product (increases/decreases). To get a firm to produce more of that product, the price and the MR from the sale of that product must

increase (increase/decrease).

10-57

supply The schedule which you completed in frame **10-53** shows the quantity of snowblowers the firm will produce each hour and offer to sell at various prices. Any schedule which contains this kind of information is a (demand/supply/cost/MR) schedule.

10-58

Looking at the firm's MC schedule, we can find what the price of a product must be to induce the firm to supply various quantities of its product. For example, to induce the firm to supply 6 snowblowers an hour, the price of snowblowers must be at least $__________.

$500

10-59

Before the firm will supply 7 snowblowers an hour, the price must be at least $__________. And a price of $300 will result in the firm supplying __________ snowblowers an hour.

$600
4

10-60

In short, we can find out what quantity the firm will supply at each price—which equals MR in a purely competitive industry—by looking at the firm's __________-cost schedule.

marginal

10-61

As a matter of fact, the firm's supply schedule *is* its __________ schedule, provided the price of the product is greater than the minimum __________ of producing the product.

MC
AVC

10-62

On the following graph are a firm's short-run average and marginal-cost curves. Indicate on this graph the firm's supply curve by drawing a heavy line with your pen or pencil.

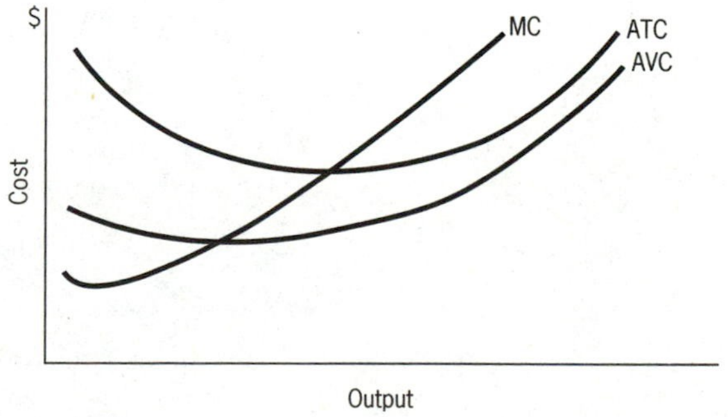

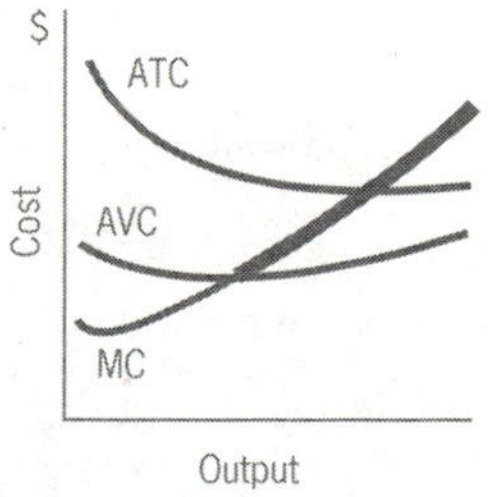

10-63

The part of the firm's MC curve which is above the AVC curve is the firm's __________ curve.

supply

10-64

The MC curve above minimum AVC tells us how much of its product a purely competitive firm will supply at various prices *because* the com-

MC — petitive firm will produce all units which have an ________ less than or equal to the product price provided this price is equal to or greater than minimum AVC.

10-65 Review Frame

In a purely competitive industry, the price of the product and the MR

equal (the same) — from the sale of each additional unit are * ________________ , and the demand for the product produced by each firm is

perfectly elastic (such that the product price is not affected by the output of any one firm) — * ________________________________ .

10-66 Review Frame

To maximize its total economic profits or minimize its total economic

MR (or price) — losses, a firm will produce all units of its product which have an ____

MC — greater than or equal to their ________ , provided the price of the

the minimum AVC — product is greater than or equal to * ________________ .

10-67 Review Frame

If the price of the product in the short run is:

profit — greater than minimum ATC, the firm will produce at a (profit/loss);

greater than minimum AVC and less than minimum ATC, the firm

loss — will produce at an economic (profit/loss);

close down (produce nothing) — less than minimum AVC, the firm will * ______________ and

TFC — its total loss will be equal to its ________ .

10-68 Review Frame

The purely competitive firm's short-run supply schedule is its

MC, AVC — ________ schedule above the minimum ________ . Product

increase — price must ________ to induce the firm to supply a greater quantity

increases — of its product, because the MC of producing the product ________ .

10-69

Having learned how much a single purely competitive firm will produce in the short run at various prices, let's find out what the price will be when a product is produced by group (or industry) of purely competitive firms. In any competitive market the price of the commodity depends

demand, supply — upon the ________ for and the ________ of the commodity.

10-70

Here is the supply schedule of a firm which sells snowblowers in a purely competitive market.

Price of snowblowers	Quantity supplied (per hour)
$600	7
500	6
400	5
300	4
200	3
140	0

If the price of snowblowers were $600, the quantity supplied by this
7 firm would be ________ snowblowers per hour.

10-71

Let's suppose that there are 1,000 producers of snowblowers and that each of them has the same cost schedule. If one firm were to supply 7 snowblowers an hour when their price is $600, then each of the 999
7 other firms in the industry would also supply ________ snowblowers an hour at this price.

10-72

When the price of snowblowers is $600, each firm will supply 7 snowblowers an hour; the 1,000 firms together will supply a total of
7,000 ________ snowblowers each hour.

10-73

Complete the supply schedule for the snowblower industry by indicating the total quantity the 1,000 firms will supply at each price. You will have to look back at frame **10-70** to find the quantities supplied by one firm.

	Price of snowblowers	Quantity supplied (per hour)
	$600	7,000
6,000	500	________
5,000	400	________
4,000	300	________
3,000	200	________
0	140	________

10-74

Look at the industry supply schedule in frame **10-73**. As the price of snowblowers increases, the total quantity supplied ________ , and as the price decreases, the total quantity supplied ________ .

increases
decreases

10-75

Why does the total quantity supplied diminish when the price of the product falls and increase when the product price rises? Because each firm will produce a (larger/smaller) quantity when the price of the product rises and vice versa.

larger

10-76

And each firm will increase its production only when the product price rises, because the marginal ________ of producing additional units of the product ________ as the firm increases its production.

cost
increases

10-77

If the product price falls and the firm continues to produce the same output, it will soon find that the ________ of the last units it produces is greater than their ________ .

MC
MR

10-78

So to maximize its total economic profits, the firm would have to give up the production of those units which have an MC greater than their MR. This it could only do by (increasing/decreasing) its total production.

decreasing

10-79

To find the *total* quantity supplied at any price by all the firms in an industry, we ________ the quantities supplied by each firm at that price.

add (total)

10-80

If we add the quantities supplied by each firm at some particular price, we find the total quantity supplied by the industry at that price. When we do this for several different prices, we have found the industry's ________ schedule.

supply

10-81

Given each firm's supply schedule, we can, by adding, find the ________ supply schedule. To know what the price of the product will be, we must also know the ________ schedule for the product.

industry's (total)
demand

10-82

Here is the demand schedule for snowblowers, together with the supply schedule which you worked out in frame **10-73**.

Quantity demanded (per hour)	Price of snowblowers	Quantity supplied (per hour)
3,000	$600	7,000
4,000	500	6,000
5,000	400	5,000
6,000	300	4,000
7,000	200	3,000
8,000	140	0

$400 The price of snowblowers will be $__________ . There will be

5,000 __________ snowblowers produced and sold each hour by the firms in this industry.

10-83

Look back at the cost schedules in the table in frame **10-1**. When the price of snowblowers is $400, the MR from the sale of each additional

$400, 5 snowblower is $__________ . Each firm will produce __________ snowblowers an hour. The 1,000 firms, each with the same cost schedule,

5,000 will produce a total of __________ snowblowers an hour.

10-84

Any single firm can sell each of the 5 snowblowers at a price of $400. Its

$2,000, $1,400 TR will be $__________ , its TC will be $__________ , and its total

profit, $600 economic (profit/loss) is __________ .

10-85

$280 The ATC of each of the 5 snowblowers is $__________ , the price of

$400 each snowblower is $__________ , and the economic profit on each

$120 snowblower is $__________ .

10-86

Suppose that the demand for snowblowers were not that shown in frame **10-82**. Suppose it is, instead, that given in the next table. The number of firms and their costs are the same, so the supply is the same.

Quantity demanded (per hour)	Price of snowblowers	Quantity supplied (per hour)
2,200	$600	7,000
2,400	500	6,000
2,600	400	5,000
2,800	300	4,000
3,000	200	3,000
3,200	140	0

$200 The equilibrium price of snowblowers would be __________ ,

3,000 and the equilibrium quantity would be __________ .

10-87

At this equilibrium price of $200, each firm would produce

3, $600 __________ snowblowers an hour. Its TR would be $__________

$700 and its TC would be $__________ . It would have a total economic

loss, $100 (profit/loss) of $__________ .

10-88

The firm produces at an economic loss because the equilibrium price is

ATC less than the __________ of producing the product.

10-89

How low would the price of the product have to drop before the quantity supplied by each firm and the total quantity supplied would be zero?

$150 Below $__________ .

10-90 Review Frame

Demand and supply determine the equilibrium price and equilibrium quantity in a purely competitive industry. In the short run the supply

adding (totaling), supply schedule for the industry is found by __________ the __________ schedules of all firms in industry.

The equilibrium price of the product is the price at which the total

equal quantity supplied by all firms is __________ to the total quantity

demanded __________ . The equilibrium quantity is the total quantity demanded

price and supplied at the equilibrium __________ .

10-91 Review Frame

MR The equilibrium price is also equal to the __________ the individual firm can obtain from the sale of one additional unit of its product. So

MC the firm will produce so long as __________ has not become greater than product price.

10-92 Review Frame

greater
less, minimum ATC
TFC

In the short run the firms in an industry will earn an economic profit if the product price is (greater/less) and they will suffer an economic loss if it is (greater/less) than ________________ . In no case, however, will a firm's loss exceed its __________ .

THE LONG RUN

10-93

variable, variable

In the long run, as we already know, all of a firm's costs are (fixed/variable) because all of the resources it employs are (fixed/variable).

10-94

cannot

The short run is *defined* as a period of time during which *the number of firms* in a purely competitive industry is fixed. This means that in the short run the number of firms producing a product such as snowblowers (can/cannot) either increase or decrease.

10-95

variable
can

But in the long run the number of firms in a purely competitive industry, like all the resources employed by a firm, is (fixed/variable). So the long run is *defined* as a period of time during which the number of firms in a purely competitive industry (can/cannot) increase or decrease.

10-96

increase (rise, etc.)
decrease (fall, etc.)

One of the characteristics of a purely competitive industry is the absence of any barriers preventing the entry of new firms or the exit of old firms in the long run. When new firms *enter*, the number of firms in the industry will __________ ; and when old firms *leave*, the number of firms will __________ .

10-97

earning an economic profit
suffering economic losses

New firms enter an industry in the long run when the firms already in the industry are (earning an economic profit/suffering an economic loss), but firms leave an industry when they are (earning economic profits/suffering economic losses).

10-98

enter
leave

In other words, when the product price is greater than the ATC of producing it, firms will (enter/leave) an industry. But when the price is less than ATC, they will (enter/leave) the industry.

10-99

If the price of the product produced by a purely competitive industry were equal to the ATC of producing it, the firms already in the industry would be:

(a) earning economic profits
(b) suffering economic losses
(c) neither (a) nor (b)

(c) Which one? ___________

10-100

neither enter nor leave — In this case, firms would (enter/leave/neither enter nor leave) the in-

normal — dustry, for they would all be earning ___________ profits.

10-101

So we know two things about the period of time which economists call the long run. It is a period in which firms can vary the amount

resources, enter — of all the ___________ they employ, and firms can ___________ or

leave — ___________ the industry.

10-102

And as we already know, when all resources are variable, the cost of producing various quantities of the firm's product is shown in its

long-run — (short-run/long-run) cost schedules.

10-103

Following are the long-run cost schedules of a firm producing snowblowers.

Long-run costs of production schedules (Snowblowers per hour)

Quantity of snowblowers	Total cost	Average total cost	Marginal cost
3	$2,100	$700	—
4	2,400	600	$300
5	2,500	500	100
6	2,700	450	200
7	3,000	428 4/7	300
8	3,400	425	400
9	3,900	433 1/3	500
10	4,500	450	600
11	5,200	472 8/11	700

There is only one total-cost and one average-total-cost schedule be-

fixed — cause, in the long run, there are *no* ___________ costs. All costs,

variable — therefore, are ___________ costs and equal to the firm's total costs.

10-104

total

Long-run marginal cost (LR MC) is the increase in long-run (total/average) cost which occurs when the firm increases its production by 1 snowblower.

10-105

decreases, increases

Because of the economies and diseconomies of scale, long-run average total cost at first (increases/decreases) and then (increases/decreases).

10-106

falls, rises

Since long-run average cost (LR ATC) behaves in this way, we find that LR MC (rises/falls) at first and thereafter (rises/falls).

10-107

marginal

To maximize its economic profits or minimize its losses in the long run, the purely competitive firm will produce snowblowers so long as MR, or price, is greater than or equal to LR ________ cost.

10-108

10

If, for example, the price of snowblowers were $600, the firm would produce ________ snowblowers an hour.

10-109

$6,000, $4,500

$+1,500

The firm's TR would be $________, its TC would be $________, and its total economic profit (+) or loss (−) would be $________.

10-110

enter

earning economic profits

At this price of $600 per snowblower, firms would (enter/leave) the industry because firms in the industry are * ________________.

10-111

increase

When new firms enter the industry because firms already in the industry are earning economic profits, the new firms (increase/decrease) the number of snowblowers supplied at the market price of $600.

10-112

increases

increases

Assuming that the demand for snowblowers does not change, the entry of new firms into the industry not only ________ the number of firms in the industry, but also (increases/decreases) the supply of snowblowers.

10-113

When we studied the fundamentals of demand and supply in Section 3 we learned how an increase in the supply of a good would affect the equilibrium price of the good. Applying what we learned there, this increase in the supply of snowblowers will result in a (rise/fall) in the price of snowblowers.

fall

10-114

When the price has been pushed down to $500 by the entry of new firms, each firm in the industry—assuming they all have the same cost schedules—will supply ________ snowblowers per hour and earn a total economic profit of $________ .

9
$600

10-115

This fall in the price causes the quantity of snowblowers supplied by each firm to (increase/decrease) and the economic profit earned by each firm in the industry to (rise/fall).

decrease
fall

10-116

As long as any economic profits are being earned by the firms in the industry, new firms will continue to enter the industry. Thus, the price of the product will continue to (rise/fall) and profits to (increase/decrease).

fall, decrease

10-117

Firms will stop coming into the industry and the price will stop falling only when economic profits earned by the firms in the industry are equal to $________ . This can only happen when the price of the product is equal to the ________ total cost of producing the product. The firms will now be earning a ________ profit.

0
average
normal

10-118

Look again at the LR cost schedules in frame **10-103**. Suppose the product price were $300. The MR from the sale of each additional snowblower would be $________ .

$300

10-119

At this price each firm in the industry would produce ________ snowblowers an hour, have a TR of $________ , have a TC of $________ , and have a total economic profit (+) or loss (−) of ________ .

7
$2,100
$3,000
$−900

10-120
Suffering economic losses at a price of $300, firms would start to ________ the industry.

leave

10-121
The exit of firms from the industry would cause the supply of snowblowers to (increase/decrease) and the price of snowblowers to (rise/fall).

decrease, rise

10-122
When the price has risen to $400, each firm remaining in the industry would be producing ________ snowblowers an hour and have a total economic profit (+) or loss (−) of $________ .

8
$−200

10-123
As long as any economic losses are suffered by firms in the industry, firms will continue to ________ the industry, the product price will continue to (rise/fall), and economic losses will continue to (increase/decrease).

leave
rise
decrease

10-124
Now suppose the product price were $425. The MR from each snowblower would be $________ , and each firm would produce ________ snowblowers an hour.

$425
8

10-125
At this price, the firm's TR is $________ , its TC is $________ , and its total economic profit (+) or loss (−) is $________ , and a ________ ________ will be gained.

$3,400, $3,400
$0, normal
profit

10-126
If the price of snowblowers is $425, firms will tend neither to enter nor to leave the industry, because * ____ .

the firms in the industry are neither earning economic profits nor suffering economic losses

10-127
$425 is a very particular price. If you will examine the cost schedules in frame **10-103**, you will find that it is a price which is exactly equal to the minimum LR ________ total cost of producing snowblowers.

average

10-128

If the price of the product is *at all above* the minimum LR ATC, the firms in the industry will (earn economic profits/suffer economic losses). This will cause firms to __________ the industry, the supply of the product to __________ , and the price of the product to __________ .

earn economic profits
enter
increase
fall

10-129

And if the product price is *at all below* the minimum LR ATC, firms in the industry will (earn economic profits/suffer economic losses). In turn, the result will be that firms __________ the industry, the supply of the product __________ , and the price of the product __________ .

suffer economic losses
leave
decreases, rises

10-130

Entry and exit continue in the long run as long as there is any motive for entering or leaving the industry. Entry and exit *stop* only when the firms in the industry have neither __________ nor __________ and are earning only __________ __________ .

economic profits, economic losses (either order)
normal profits

10-131

Economic profits and losses are absent in a purely competitive industry only when the price of the product is equal to the __________ LR ATC.

minimum (lowest, least)

10-132

In a purely competitive industry, *long-run equilibrium* exists when no firm wishes to enter or to leave the industry. This occurs when both the economic profits and the losses of firms in the industry are equal to $__________ , and the __________ of the product is equal to the *__________ of producing it.

$0, price
minimum LR ATC

10-133

We know from our study of short-run costs that where short-run average total cost (SR ATC) is a minimum, SR ATC and short-run __________ cost are equal.

marginal

10-134

Likewise with long-run costs: When LR ATC is at a minimum, it is equal to LR __________ cost.

marginal

10-135

So we know several things about a purely competitive firm when its industry is in long-run equilibrium. The LR ________ is at a minimum, and the price is * ________________ LR ATC.

ATC

equal to (the same as)

10-136

Since in long-run equilibrium it is true that:
price is equal to LR ATC,
LR ATC is at a minimum,
minimum LR ATC equals LR MC,

we can therefore conclude that the ________ of the product is also equal to the ________ . (Things equal to the same thing are equal to each other.)

price

LR MC

10-137 Review Frame

In the long run, all of the firm's ________ and ________ are variable; also, firms are able to ________ and to ________ a purely competitive industry.

resources, costs (either order)

enter, leave (either order)

10-138 Review Frame

Firms will enter an industry when * ________________________ and they will leave an industry when * ________________________ .

firms in the industry are earning economic profits

they are suffering economic losses

10-139 Review Frame

The entry of new firms into an industry causes the supply of the product to ________ , the price of the product to ________ , and economic profits in the industry to ________ .

On the other hand, the exit of old firms from an industry causes the supply of the product to ________ , the price of the product to ________ , and economic losses in the industry to ________ .

increase, decrease

decrease

decrease

increase, decrease

10-140 Review Frame

When a purely competitive industry is in long-run equilibrium, firms tend neither to * ________________ the industry because economic profits and losses in the industry are * ________ .

enter nor to leave

zero

10-141 Review Frame

In long-run equilibrium the product price is equal to both __________ and __________, and LR ATC is * __________.

LR ATC, LR MC (either order), at a minimum

Now take the Review Test for Section 10 at the back of the book.

Product Price and Output: Pure Monopoly

section 11

Having discovered in the last section what price a purely competitive firm will charge and how much it will produce in both the short run and the long run, let's find out in this section what price a pure monopolist will charge and how much it will produce in the short and long run.

To learn these things will not require so many frames as it took to understand the purely competitive firm and industry. But before we examine the pure monopolist, it will be worthwhile to recall the assumptions we made at the beginning of the last section. These assumptions are:

1. The goal of a firm is to maximize its profits or minimize its losses.
2. Whether or not a firm is a monopolist does not influence the costs of production.
3. There are a large number of buyers of the product produced by a firm.
4. You already know what is meant by price elasticity of demand and marginal revenue.

The pure monopoly studied in this section has three essential characteristics. *First*, only one firm—the pure monopolist—produces the product of this industry. *Second*, the product produced by this firm has no close or good substitutes. *Third*, entry into the industry is blocked and it is impossible for new firms to enter.

11-1

A pure monopolist, because it is an imperfect competitor, finds that the more it produces, the (higher/lower) is the price at which it can sell its product.

lower

11-2

It also knows that the higher the price it sets on the product it produces, the (more/less) of the product that can be sold.

less

11-3

inverse
inverse

In short, the relationship between the price the pure monopolist charges and the quantity of product demanded is (direct/inverse). Put another way, the relationship between the output of the monopolist and the price at which its output can be sold is (direct/inverse).

11-4

less than perfectly elastic (if you did not answer correctly, you should review frames 8-79 through 8-125.)

In more technical language, the demand for the product of a pure monopolist is (perfectly elastic/less than perfectly elastic).

11-5

Here is the demand schedule for electric golf carts, which, we assume, are manufactured and sold by a pure monopolist. Also shown in the table are the total revenues (TR) the monopolist would receive if it charged the various prices given in the demand schedule.

Demand and total-revenue schedule (Golf carts per hour)

Price	Quantity demanded	Total revenue
$1,200	0	$ 0
1,100	1	1,100
1,000	2	2,000
900	3	2,700
800	4	3,200
700	5	3,500
600	6	3,600
500	7	3,500
400	8	3,200
300	9	2,700
200	10	2,000

6, $600

The monopolist's TR is at a maximum when it produces and sells ______ golf carts an hour and charges a price of $______ for every cart.

11-6

No

Is the goal of the monopolist to have the maximum TR, that is, to maximize its TR? (Yes/No)

11-7

profit

The goal of the monopolist is to maximize, not its TR, but its total ______________. To know how many golf carts this monopolist will decide to produce and sell in order to accomplish this goal, we also have

cost to know the ______________ of producing golf carts at various levels of output.

11-8

Following is the monopolist's short-run total-cost schedule for golf carts along with its TR schedule. Indicate in the column at the right its total economic profit or loss when it produces 0 through 10 golf carts an hour.

	Quantity of golf carts (per hour)	Total revenue	Total costs	Total economic profit (+) or loss (−)
$−100	0	$ 0	$ 100	$______
$+600	1	1,100	500	______
$+1,300	2	2,000	700	______
$+1,700	3	2,700	1,000	______
$+1,800	4	3,200	1,400	______
$+1,600	5	3,500	1,900	______
$+1,100	6	3,600	2,500	______
$+300	7	3,500	3,200	______
$−800	8	3,200	4,000	______
$−2,200	9	2,700	4,900	______
$−3,900	10	2,000	5,900	______

11-9

The monopolist's total economic profit is at a maximum, or its economic

4 loss is a minimum, when it produces ________ golf carts an hour.

11-10

Now look back to the demand schedule in frame **11-5**. When it sells 4

$800 golf carts, each cart can be sold at a price of $________ .

11-11

Now, here are the MR and MC schedules that go along with the TR and short-run TC schedules in frame **11-8**. (If you have forgotten how to determine the MR for an imperfect competitor, review frames **8-79** through **8-96**.)

Quantity of golf carts (per hour)	TR	TC	MR	MC
0	$ 0	$ 100		
1	1,100	500	$1,100	$ 400
2	2,000	700	900	200
3	2,700	1,000	700	300
4	3,200	1,400	500	400
5	3,500	1,900	300	500
6	3,600	2,500	100	600
7	3,500	3,200	−100	700
8	3,200	4,000	−300	800
9	2,700	4,900	−500	900
10	2,000	5,900	−700	1,000

When the monopolist produces 4 golf carts an hour, it has produced
MR, MC all carts which have an (MC/MR) greater than or equal to their (MC/MR).

11-12

To maximize profits, or minimize losses, the monopolist must *not* pro-
MC, MR duce any golf carts whose (MC/MR) is greater than their (MC/MR).

11-13

In the table below is the complete set of short-run cost schedules as well as demand and revenue schedules.

Output of golf carts	TFC	TVC	TC	MC	AFC	AVC	ATC	Price	TR	MR
0	$100	$ 0	$ 100					$1,200	$ 0	
1	100	400	500	$ 400	$100	$400	$500	1,100	1,100	$1,100
2	100	600	700	200	50	300	350	1,000	2,000	900
3	100	900	1,000	300	33⅓	300	333⅓	900	2,700	700
4	100	1,300	1,400	400	25	325	350	800	3,200	500
5	100	1,800	1,900	500	20	360	380	700	3,500	300
6	100	2,400	2,500	600	16⅔	400	416⅔	600	3,600	100
7	100	3,100	3,200	700	$14\frac{2}{7}$	$442\frac{6}{7}$	457⅐	500	3,500	−100
8	100	3,900	4,000	800	12½	487½	500	400	3,200	−300
9	100	4,800	4,900	900	11⅑	533⅓	$544\frac{4}{9}$	300	2,700	−500
10	100	5,800	5,900	1,000	10	580	590	200	2,000	−700

When the monopolist produces 4 carts an hour and sells each for $800,
$350 total economic profit is $1,800. The ATC of each cart is $______ and
$450 the economic profit *on each cart* is $______.

11-14

If the monopolist produced just 1 golf cart an hour, it could sell this 1
$1,100, $500 cart at a price of $______. The ATC of this cart would be $______
$600 and the economic profit on each cart would be $______.

11-15

does not
does not

From this example we can learn two things. To maximize *total* profit, the pure monopolist: (does/does not) charge the highest possible price, and (does/does not) try to earn the largest possible profit on each cart.

11-16

In fact, some monopolists in the short run do not earn any economic profit at all. Following are the demand, TR, MR, TC, and MC schedules for another monopolist—the publisher of a textbook in advanced economic theory.

Number of books (per hour)	Price	TR	MR	TC	MC
0	$8	$ 0		$12	
1	7	7	$7	15	$3
2	6	12	5	17	2
3	5	15	3	20	3
4	4	16	1	24	4
5	3	15	−1	29	5

3
$5

To maximize total profit, or minimize total loss, this monopolist-publisher should print and sell ______ textbooks an hour, and should sell each book at a price of $______ .

11-17

$15
$20
$−5

Were the monopolist to do this, each hour TR would be $______ , TC would be $______ , and total economic profit (+) or loss (−) would be $______ .

11-18

$12
fixed

Even if the publisher stops printing the book, it has some costs in the short run. TC when it prints 0 books is $______ , and this, as we know, is called the total ______ cost.

11-19

$12

If the monopolist-publisher prints 3 books an hour, it loses $5 an hour. If it closes down and prints no books, it loses $______ an hour.

11-20

print 3 books

The monopolist would (close down/print 3 books) an hour to maximize its economic profits or minimize its economic losses.

11-21

Let's change the cost of producing the book just a little.

Number of books (per hour)	Price	TR	MR	TC	MC
0	$8	$ 0		$12	
1	7	7	$7	27	$15
2	6	12	5	33	6
3	5	15	3	40	7
4	4	16	1	48	8
5	3	15	−1	57	9

$27 — If the monopolist produced just 1 book, its TC would be $ ______ ,

$7 — TR would be $ ______ , and its total economic profit (+) or loss (−)

$−20 — would be $ ______ .

11-22

greater — This loss is (greater/less) than its TFC, and the monopolist would decide

close down (produce no output) — to * ______________ in the short run.

11-23

So, like the purely competitive firm, the monopolist in the short run may earn an economic profit or suffer a loss. At the output which maximizes profit or minimizes loss, it can earn an economic profit if the price at

total — which it sells the product is greater than the average ______ cost of producing the product.

11-24

But it will suffer an economic loss if the price at which it can sell the product is less than ATC. And it will close down, like the pure compet-

average variable — itor, whenever this price is less than the ______ ______ cost.

TFC — By so doing, it will restrict its loss to the amount of ______ .

11-25 Review Frame

To maximize total economic profit, or minimize total economic loss, a

MR — pure monopolist will produce so long as ______ is greater than or

MC — equal to ______ . The price it charges is the price its (cost/

demand — demand/supply) schedule tells it is the price at which its total output can be sold.

11-26 Review Frame

In the short run, a monopolist will:

greater — earn a profit if price is (greater/less) than ATC,

less — suffer a loss if price is (greater/less) than ATC,

AVC — close down if price is less than ________ ,

TFC — never have a total loss greater than ________ .

11-27 Review Frame

does not / does not / does not always earn

A monopolist (does/does not) charge the highest price it can get, it (does/does not) earn the largest possible profit on each unit produced, and (always earns/does not always earn) an economic profit in the short run.

11-28

variable / fixed

In the long run, the pure monopolist's costs are all ________ costs; similarly, none of its resources is ________ .

11-29

Here are the *long-run* cost, demand, and MR schedules of the monopolist that manufactures electric golf carts.

Output of golf carts (per hour)	Long-run TC	Long-run ATC	Long-run MC	Price	TR	MR	Total economic profit (+) or loss (−)
3	$1,200	$400		$1,100	$3,300		$2,100
4	1,500	375	$300	1,000	4,000	$700	2,500
5	1,700	340	200	900	4,500	500	2,800
6	1,800	300	100	800	4,800	300	3,000
7	2,000	285$\frac{5}{7}$	200	700	4,900	100	2,900
8	2,300	287½	300	600	4,800	−100	2,500
9	2,700	300	400	500	4,500	−300	1,800
10	3,200	320	500	400	4,000	−500	800
11	3,800	345$\frac{5}{11}$	600	300	3,300	−700	−500
12	4,500	375	700	200	2,400	−900	−2,100

6 / $800

To maximize total economic profit, or minimize total economic loss, in the long run the golf cart manufacturer should produce ________ carts an hour and charge a price of $________ per cart.

11-30

MR / MC

This means that it should produce carts so long as ________ is greater than or equal to long-run ________ .

11-31

Suppose a monopolist should find that no matter what output it produces in the long run, it suffers an economic loss. The best thing for it to do is:

(a) go on producing the output at which loss is a minimum;
(b) close down and produce no output.

(b) Which one? ________

11-32

If a monopolist closes down and produces no output, its loss will be zero

fixed — in the long run, because it has no ________ costs in the long run.

11-33

revenue / cost — We may conclude that, in the long run, a pure monopolist's total (revenue/cost) will be greater than or equal to its total (revenue/cost).

11-34

ATC / price — Put another way, in the long run its (price/ATC) must be less than or equal to its (price/ATC).

11-35

greater than — The pure monopolist that produces electric golf carts is typical of most monopolists in the long run. The price it charges is (greater than/less than/equal to) the long-run ATC of producing the product.

11-36

greater than — We also find that the actual long-run average cost of producing the product is (greater than/equal to) the *minimum* long-run average total cost.

11-37

greater than — And the price the monopolist charges is (greater than/equal to) the long-run marginal cost of the last unit of the product it produces.

11-38

entry / cannot — In a purely competitive industry during the long run, the (entry/exit) of firms would bring the price of the product *down* to the level of ATC. But when an industry is a pure monopoly, new firms (can/cannot) enter the industry in the long run.

11-39 Review Frame

In order to maximize total economic profit, the pure monopolist in the long run will produce how much of its product?

So long as MR is greater than or equal to long-run MC.

* ______________________________

____

11-40 Review Frame

In the long run the *typical* monopolist:

will

will not

does not sell

(will/will not) earn total profit,

(will/will not) produce the output at which the long-run average total cost is at a minimum,

(sells/does not sell) its product at a price which equals the long-run MC of the last unit produced.

Now take the Review Test for Section 11 at the back of the book.

The Prices and Employment of Resources

section **12**

Before a business firm can produce it must first employ such economic resources as labor, land, capital, and entrepreneurial ability.

Like the total output and market price of a product, the employment of a resource and the price paid for its use depend upon demand and supply. Just as every business firm has to decide how much of its product to produce, every firm must decide how much of each resource to employ. Some firms are monopolists and must determine what price to charge for the product they produce. Some firms that employ resources are monopsonists and these firms must decide what price they will pay for the use of resources.

In this section we will learn how demand and supply determine the price and total employment of a resource. We will discover that the price and employment of a resource depend not only upon demand and supply but also upon:

1. Whether the resource is used by a group of perfectly competitive employers or by one employer (a monopsonist), and
2. Whether only one or all of the resources employed by a firm are variable.

Throughout this section we assume that the aim of a firm is the maximum total profit (or minimum total loss); and that the number of suppliers of any resource is so large that no one supplier can affect the price of that resource.

The market for a resource is perfectly competitive if a large number of firms employ the resource and no one of these employers is able to affect the price of the resource. Monopsony exists when only one firm employs a resource.

ONE VARIABLE RESOURCE

Perfectly Competitive Employers, Perfectly Competitive Sellers

12-1

perfectly

A producer of plastic cups knows that it can sell as few or as many cups as it wishes to produce at the market price of $1.00 a cup. This producer sells cups in a (perfectly/imperfectly) competitive market.

12-2

In the *short run* the only way this producer can increase its production of cups is to employ more workers. If it employs fewer workers, production will decrease. As far as this manufacturer of cups is concerned,
variable labor—the number of workers—is a (fixed/variable) resource.

12-3

The manufacturer's fixed resources are the plant in which it produces cups and its stock of raw materials. The table below shows the total hourly production when it employs from 4 to 12 workers an hour.

Compute the marginal product of each worker. (If you have forgotten how to figure MP, review frames **9-53** through **9-58**.)

Production schedule (Plastic cups per hour)

	Number of workers employed (per hour)	Output of cups (per hour)	Marginal product of labor (cups)
	4	40	
8	5	48	______
7	6	55	______
6	7	61	______
5	8	66	______
4	9	70	______
3	10	73	______
2	11	75	______
1	12	76	______

12-4

As this manufacturer increases the number of workers it employs, total production of cups increases. Beyond 5 workers, the MP of each worker
decreases (increases/decreases).

12-5

If the firm employed 4 workers an hour, it would be able to produce
40 ________ cups each hour. Each of these cups would be sold for a price
$40 of $1.00 apiece. So the firm's total revenue (TR) would be $________ an hour when it employs 4 workers.

12-6

If the firm wished to manufacture 70 cups an hour, it would have to hire
9, $70 ________ workers. Its TR would then be $________ an hour.

12-7

Now complete the schedule below to show the firm's TR when it employs from 4 to 12 workers an hour. Remember that the firm can sell every cup it produces for $1.00 apiece.

Production and total-revenue schedule (Plastic cups per hour)

	Number of workers employed (per hour)	Output of cups (per hour)	MP of labor (cups)	Total revenue
$40	4	$40		$______
$48	5	48	8	______
$55	6	55	7	______
$61	7	61	6	______
$66	8	66	5	______
$70	9	70	4	______
$73	10	73	3	______
$75	11	75	2	______
$76	12	76	1	______

12-8

An examination of the TR schedule you completed in frame **12-7** reveals that as the firm increases the number of workers it employs, its TR
increases (increases/decreases). Were the firm to decrease the number of workers
fall it employs, its TR would (rise/fall).

12-9

Suppose the firm increases the number of workers it employed from 4
8 to 5. Its total output would increase by ________ cups, and its TR would
$8 increase by $________ .

12-10

The $8 *increase* in the firm's TR that occurs when it increases its employment of labor from 4 to 5 is called the ***marginal revenue product*** (MRP) of the 5th worker. Assume the firm increases the amount of labor
$7 it employs from 5 to 6. TR will increase by $________, and this increase
6 in TR is the MRP of the ________th worker.

12-11

We can define the MRP of labor—or of any other resource—as the amount by which ________ increases when the firm increases its employment of that resource by ________ additional unit.

TR

one (1)

12-12

The production and total-revenue schedule you completed in frame **12-7** is reprinted below. Compute the MRP of the 5th through the 12th worker and enter these amounts in the table.

Production and revenue schedules
(Plastic cups per hour)

	Number of workers employed	Output of cups	MP of labor	Total revenue	Marginal revenue product
	4	40		$40	
$8	5	48	8	48	$________
$7	6	55	7	55	________
$6	7	61	6	61	________
$5	8	66	5	66	________
$4	9	70	4	70	________
$3	10	73	3	73	________
$2	11	75	2	75	________
$1	12	76	1	76	________

12-13

Look at the MRP schedule you completed in the previous frame. As the firm increases the amount of labor it employs, the MRP of labor (increases/decreases/remains constant), and vice versa.

decreases

12-14

In short, the less labor the firm employs, the (greater/smaller) is the MRP of the last worker it employed; and the more labor it employs the (greater/smaller) is the MRP of the last worker.

greater

smaller

12-15

The MRP of the 7th worker is $6 and the MP is 6 cups. The MRP is equal to MP multiplied by $________ a cup.

$1

12-16

8 $5 is the MRP of the ________th worker employed by the firm;

MP it is equal to the ________ of this worker multiplied by $1.

12-17

In this example $1 is the *price* which the firm receives for *every* cup it sells. And, as you already know, when the firm sells its product in a perfectly competitive market, the price it receives is always equal to the

MR from (MC of/MR from) the last cup.

12-18

In short, when the firm sells cups in a purely competitive market, the

MP MRP from each is *equal to* the ________ of the last worker hired

MR *multiplied* by the ________ (or price) obtained from the sale of the last additional cup.

12-19

When the cup manufacturer increases its employment of labor beyond 5 workers, the MRP of labor decreases, because the MP (increases/

decreases, remains constant decreases/remains constant) while MR (increases/decreases/remains constant).

12-20 Review Frame

TR The MRP of a resource is the amount by which ________ increases

employs one more unit of the resource when the firm * ________________________________

____;

MP and is equal to the ________ of the last unit of the resource multi-

MR plied by the ________ from the sale of one more unit of its product.

12-21 Review Frame

When a firm sells its product in a perfectly competitive market and MP is decreasing, the firm finds that:

MR the price at which it sells its product and ________ are equal;

decrease MRP will also (increase/decrease).

12-22

Let's now see how many workers the cup producer will employ if it wishes to maximize total profit. Suppose it can hire as few or as many workers as it wishes by paying each worker $7.50 an hour. If it hired just

$7.50 one worker, the total cost (TC) of labor would be $________ .

12-23

$15 Were it to employ 2 workers, the TC of labor would be $________ .

12-24

Now complete the schedule below indicating the TC of labor to the cup manufacturer when it employs from 4 through 12 workers an hour, and when the price it must pay for each worker is $7.50 an hour.

	Number of workers employed (per hour)	Total cost of labor
$30.00	4	$________
$37.50	5	________
$45.00	6	________
$52.50	7	________
$60.00	8	________
$67.50	9	________
$75.00	10	________
$82.50	11	________
$90.00	12	________

12-25

Look at the table you completed in frame **12-24**. If the firm increases
increases the amount of labor it employs, the TC of its labor (increases/decreases) and vice versa.

12-26

The amount by which the TC of a resource increases when the firm employs one additional unit of the resource is called the ***marginal resource cost*** (MRC). Whenever this cup manufacturer increases the amount of labor it employs, it finds that the MRC of an additional worker
$7.50 is $________ .

12-27

The cup producer can hire as little or as much labor as it desires at a *constant* price of $7.50 an hour. It is also aware that the MRC of every extra worker is $7.50 an hour. From these facts we may conclude that: When the price an employer has to pay to hire a resource is *not* affected by the amount of the resource it employs, the MRC and the resource
equal (identical) price are ________ .

12-28

And when the price of the resource is constant, the MRC is also

constant ___________ .

12-29

The schedules you completed in frame **12-12** are reprinted below.

Number of workers employed	Output of cups	MP of labor	Total revenue	Marginal revenue product
4	40		$40	
5	48	8	48	$8
6	55	7	55	7
7	61	6	61	6
8	66	5	66	5
9	70	4	70	4
10	73	3	73	3
11	75	2	75	2
12	76	1	76	1

If the price and MRC of labor were $7.50 an hour and the employer increased the amount of labor employed from 4 to 5 workers, TR would

$8, $7.50 increase by $___________ , TC would increase by $___________ , and

increase, 50 total profit would (increase/decrease) by ___________ cents.

12-30

would The cup manufacturer (would/would not) employ the 5th worker be-

increase cause it would (increase/decrease) total profit.

12-31

If the manufacturer increases the employment of labor from 5 to 6

$7 workers, TR would increase by $___________ , TC would increase by

$7.50, decrease, 50 $___________ , and total profit would (increase/decrease) by ___________ cents.

12-32

would not The cup producer (would/would not) employ the 6th worker because

it would decrease total profit ____ .

12-33

Now we have a principle which tells us when a firm will hire a unit of
MRP resource. It will employ any resource unit which has an (MRP/MRC)
MRC greater than its (MRP/MRC). It will *not* employ any unit of a resource
MRC, MRP which has an (MRP/MRC) greater than its (MRP/MRC).

12-34

Suppose the price and the MRC of a worker were $7. Using the MRP
would *figures* in frame **12-29**, the cup manufacturer (would/would not) hire
would not the 5th worker, and (would/would not) hire the 7th worker.

12-35

But what about the 6th worker whose MRP is $7? Let's *assume* that a firm hires any resource unit whose MRP is equal to its MRC. Our principle is then: An employer will *not* employ any resource unit whose MRP
less is (greater/less) than its MRC, and *will* employ any unit whose MRP is
greater (greater/less) than or equal to its MRC.

12-36

We can now determine how much labor the cup producer will hire at the various market prices that might exist for this kind of labor. If the price of labor happened to be $8 an hour, the firm would hire

5 ________ workers, and if its price happened to be $7 an hour, it

6 would hire ________ workers.

12-37

Now complete the following schedule showing how much labor the cup manufacturer would hire at each of the prices shown for labor.

	Price of labor	Number of workers firm would hire (per hour)
	$8	5
	7	6
7	6	______
8	5	______
9	4	______
10	3	______
11	2	______
12	1	______

12-38

The schedule you completed in the preceding frame indicates the amount of labor the firm would want to hire at the different possible market prices for this kind of labor having regard to its MRP. Is this schedule a supply or a demand schedule? ____________

demand

12-39

We can conclude by examining the schedules in frames **12-29** and **12-37** that a firm's demand schedule for any variable resource is the ____________ schedule for the resource.

MRP

12-40 Review Frame

MRC is the amount by which the __________ of a resource increases when the firm employs * ______________________________ . When a firm can employ as little or as much of a resource as it desires without affecting its market price, the MRC is equal to * ____________ ______________________________ .

TC

one more unit of the resource

the market price of the resource

12-41 Review Frame

To maximize its total profit (or minimize its loss), a firm will hire all units of a resource which have an ____________ greater than or equal to their ____________ , and will not hire any units of a resource which have an ____________ greater than their ____________ .

MRP

MRC

MRC, MRP

12-42

The cup manufacturer we have been talking about was able to sell all the cups it decided to produce at a constant market price of $1.00 apiece because it sold its cups in a (perfectly/imperfectly) competitive market.

perfectly

Perfectly Competitive Employers, Imperfectly Competitive Sellers

12-43

Many firms, however, do not sell their products in perfectly competitive markets. They find that the *more* they produce and sell of their product, the (higher/lower) is the price they get for it. The *less* they produce and sell, the (higher/lower) is the price they can obtain.

lower

higher

12-44

Following are the daily production, price, and TR schedules for a firm which prints and sells copyrighted paperback books in an imperfectly competitive market. The price column indicates the price the producer must charge for the book if it wishes to sell all it prints. In the spaces provided, compute the MRP of the 4th through 12th worker.

Production, price, and revenue schedules (per day)

	Number of workers employed	Output of books	MP	Price per book	Total revenue	Marginal revenue product
	4	160		\$4.00	\$ 640.00	
\$272.00	5	240	80	3.80	912.00	\$______
\$204.00	6	310	70	3.60	1,116.00	______
\$142.00	7	370	60	3.40	1,258.00	______
\$86.00	8	420	50	3.20	1,344.00	______
\$36.00	9	460	40	3.00	1,380.00	______
\$31.20	10	490	30	2.88	1,411.20	______
\$16.80	11	510	20	2.80	1,428.00	______
\$7.20	12	520	10	2.76	1,435.20	______

12-45

decreases — Like the firm that sells its product in a perfectly competitive market, the imperfectly competitive seller finds that the MRP of labor (increases/decreases) when it increases its employment of labor.

12-46

lower — But *unlike* the perfectly competitive seller, the imperfectly competitive seller *cannot* sell all it wishes at a constant price. To increase sales it must (raise/lower) the price it charges for its books.

12-47

less than — And the imperfectly competitive seller, you recall, finds that the MR from the sale of an additional book is (greater than/less than/equal to) the price at which it sells the additional book.

12-48

For example, when the book publisher lowers its price from \$2.80 to

10 — \$2.76 a copy, its sales of books increase by ______________ copies and

\$7.20 — TR increases by \$__________ .

12-49

When it obtains an additional $7.20 in revenue from the sale of *10* more books, the MR from the sale of *each* additional book is ________ cents.

72

12-50

This MR of 72 cents is less than the $________ price at which the publisher sells each of the 10 additional copies of the book.

$2.76

12-51

But for both perfectly and imperfectly competitive sellers the MRP obtained by employing an extra unit of a resource is equal to the MP of the resource multiplied by the ________ from the sale of an additional unit of the product.

MR

12-52

The MP of the 12th worker is ________ copies of the book. The MR from the sale of each of these books is, as we found in frame **12-49**, 72 cents.

10

12-53

So the MRP of the 12th worker is equal to ________ copies *times* ________ cents, or is equal to $________ .

10

72, $7.20

12-54

This MRP of $7.20 (is/is not) the amount you found in frame **12-44** to be the MRP of the 12th worker.

is

12-55

The imperfectly competitive seller is just as anxious to maximize total profit (or minimize total loss) as the perfectly competitive seller. If this imperfectly competitive seller of books could employ as many or as few workers as it wished at a price of $160 a day, the MRC of each day of labor would be $________ .

$160

12-56

Using the schedules in frame **12-44** and at a price of $160 a day for labor, the publisher would employ ________ workers a day. At a price of $100 a day it would hire ________ .

6

7

12-57

Complete the following schedule showing how much labor the book publisher would hire at the various market prices for labor shown.

	Price of labor	Number of workers firm would hire (per day)
7	$142.00	_______
8	86.00	_______
9	36.00	_______
10	31.20	_______
11	16.80	_______
12	7.20	_______

12-58

demand
more

According to the ____________ schedule in frame **12-57**, the lower the price the firm has to pay for labor, the (more/less) labor it would employ, and vice versa.

12-59

lower
price

A firm will employ more labor only if the market price of labor decreases, because the more labor a firm employs, the (higher/lower) is the MRP of labor. And a firm hiring labor in a perfectly competitive market will employ only those workers whose MRP is greater than or equal to the __________ (and the MRC) of labor.

12-60

MP, MR

You already know that the MRP of any resource is equal to its __________ multiplied by the __________ from the sale of an extra unit of the firm's product.

12-61

decreases
remains constant

The MRP of any resource employed by a firm which *sells* its product in a *perfectly competitive* market decreases when the firm employs more of the resource, because the MP of the resource (increases/decreases/remains constant) while the MR from the sale of extra units of its production (increases/decreases/remains constant).

12-62

decrease

Simple logic tells us that if MRP equals MP $\times$ MR, and if MP decreases while MR is constant, MRP must __________ .

12-63

decrease
decrease

But the MRP of any resource employed by a firm selling its product in an *imperfectly* competitive market decreases because as the firm employs more of the resource, MP will (increase/decrease/remain constant) and MR will (increase/decrease/remain constant).

12-64

decrease

Again logic tells us that if MRP equals MP × MR, and if both MP and MR decrease, then MRP must ________ .

12-65 Review Frame

MP, MR (either order)
decreases

Regardless of whether a firm sells its product in a perfectly or imperfectly competitive market, MRP = ________ × ________ , and MRP ________ when the firm uses more of the resource.

12-66 Review Frame

MRP
MRC
MRC, MRP

Both perfectly and imperfectly competitive sellers of a product hire all units of a resource which have an ________ greater than or equal to their ________ , and they do not hire units of a resource which have an ________ greater than their ________ .

12-67 Review Frame

MP
MP, MR

Beyond some level of employment, MRP decreases as the firm increases its employment of a resource. The perfectly competitive seller of a product finds that MRP decreases because ________ decreases. The imperfectly competitive seller also finds that MRP decreases because both ________ and ________ decrease.

12-68 Review Frame

MRP

Any firm's demand schedule for a variable resource is its ________ schedule for that resource.

A Perfectly Competitive Resource Market

12-69

perfect

The firms we have been talking about *sold* their products in either perfectly or imperfectly competitive markets. But they could hire as little or as much of the variable resources as they wished without affecting the price they had to pay for the resource. This means that as employers of the resource they were (perfect/imperfect) competitors.

12-70

And in a perfectly competitive resource market the price of the resource

demand, supply

is determined by the __________ for and the __________ of the resource.

12-71

The suppliers of any resource—such as labor—are the households in the

business firms

economy. The demanders are * ______________________________ which produce products from these resources.

12-72

We already know that the demand schedule of any firm for a resource

MRP

is its __________ schedule for the resource, and that in a perfectly competitive resource market the number of firms demanding the re-

many

source is (one/few/many).

12-73

Let's suppose that in the market for the kind of labor employed by the maker of plastic cups there are 1,000 firms, and that each of these firms has the *same* demand schedule for this labor. The plastic cup producer had the following MRP and demand schedule for labor.

Price of labor	Number of workers demanded (per hour)
$8	5
7	6
6	7
5	8
4	9
3	10
2	11
1	12

If the market price of labor were $8, the total quantity of labor de-

5,000

manded by the 1,000 firms would be __________ workers.

12-74

Using the cup manufacturer's demand schedule in frame **12-73**, complete the market demand schedule on the following page.

	Number of workers demanded (per hour)	Price	Number of workers supplied (per hour)
	5,000	$8	9,000
6,000	______	7	8,000
7,000	______	6	7,000
8,000	______	5	6,000
9,000	______	4	5,000
10,000	______	3	4,000
11,000	______	2	3,000
12,000	______	1	2,000

12-75

Frame **12-74** also contains the market supply schedule for this kind of labor. Like other supply schedules, the higher the price paid for labor,
greater — the (greater/smaller) is the total quantity of labor supplied and vice versa.

12-76

Using the market demand and supply schedules in frame **12-74**: The
$6 — equilibrium price (or wage rate) for labor is $______ , and the equi-
7,000 — librium quantity of this labor is ______ workers.

12-77

$6 — In this labor market the MRC of labor for any firm is $______ . The manufacturer of plastic cups whose MRP schedule is given in frame
7, 61 — **12-29** would hire ______ workers each hour and produce ______ cups an hour.

12-78 Review Frame

large — In a perfectly competitive resource market there are a (large/small) number of employers or demanders of the resource. By itself, each employer
unable — is (able/unable) to affect the market price of the resource.

12-79 Review Frame

add (total, sum) — To find the market demand for a resource we ______ the demands of all firms using the resource.

12-80 Review Frame

The equilibrium price of any resource in a perfectly competitive market is the price at which the total quantity ____________-ed is equal to the total quantity ____________-ed. The total amount of the resource employed by all users is * ____

____.

demand

suppli- (either order)

the quantity demanded (or supplied) at the equilibrium price

Monopsonists

Many employers hire the resources they use in perfectly competitive markets: they can hire as much as they want of the resource without causing its price to rise or to fall.

But many other employers find that the less they hire of a resource, the lower is the price they have to pay for it. And the more they hire, the higher is the price they have to pay. These employers are *imperfectly competitive* resource employers: the amount of the resource they employ determines the price they have to pay for it.

One example of an imperfectly competitive resource employer is the *monopsonist*. It is the only employer of the resource; no other firms employ this resource. It may or may not sell the product in a perfectly competitive market. But the market in which it hires the resource is a monopsony—one buyer or demander.

The monopsonist, like the perfectly competitive employer, has to decide how much of the resource to employ to maximize total profit (or minimize total loss). Unlike the perfectly competitive employer, however, a monopsonist finds that it controls the resource price by controlling the amount of the resource it decides to employ.

Let's examine the monopsonist and find out how much of a variable resource it will employ and the price that it will pay for it.

12-81

Here is the supply schedule for the labor which is the variable resource employed by a monopsonist.

Price (per hour)	Number of workers supplied (per hour)
$ 4.00	0
5.60	1
7.20	2
8.80	3
10.40	4
12.00	5
13.60	6
15.20	7
16.80	8

Were the monopsonist to pay workers $7.20 an hour, it would be able
2 to obtain ____________ workers each hour. To employ 5 workers each
$12 hour it would have to pay each worker $____________ an hour.

12-82

Suppose the monopsonist employed 2 workers every hour. It would have to pay each worker $7.20 an hour, and the TC of its labor would be
$14.40 $____________ an hour.

12-83

Complete the following schedule to show the TC of labor to the monopsonist when it employs 0 through 8 workers an hour.

	Price (per hour)	Quantity of labor supplied (hours)	TC of labor (per hour)
0	$ 4.00	0	$____________
$5.60	5.60	1	____________
$14.40	7.20	2	____________
$26.40	8.80	3	____________
$41.60	10.40	4	____________
$60.00	12.00	5	____________
$81.60	13.60	6	____________
$106.40	15.20	7	____________
$134.40	16.80	8	____________

12-84

Suppose the firm were employing 4 workers. If it decided to hire a 5th
$18.40 worker, its TC of labor would *increase* by $____________ .

12-85

We already know that the $18.40 increase in the total cost of labor when the monopsonist increases the number of workers it employs each hour
marginal resource from 4 to 5 is called the ____________ ____________
5 cost of the ____________th worker.

12-86

$28 The MRC of the 8th worker is $____________ an hour, while the
$8.80 MRC of the 2d worker is ____________ an hour.

12-87

From the information given in the schedules below, compute the MRC of the 1st through the 8th worker per hour.

	Price (per hour)	Number of workers supplied (per hour)	TC of labor (per hour)	MRC of labor
	\$ 4.00	0	\$ .00	
\$5.60	5.60	1	5.60	\$________
\$8.80	7.20	2	14.40	________
\$12.00	8.80	3	26.40	________
\$15.20	10.40	4	41.60	________
\$18.40	12.00	5	60.00	________
\$21.60	13.60	6	81.60	________
\$24.80	15.20	7	106.40	________
\$28.00	16.80	8	134.40	________

12-88

Examination of the schedules in frame **12-87** reveals two things. First,
greater — with the exception of the 1st worker, the MRC of labor is (greater/less) than the *price* that must be paid by the monopsonist to obtain the workers.

12-89

Second, as the firm increases the number of workers it employs, the
increases — MRC of workers (increases/decreases/remains constant).

12-90

Why is the MRC of any worker greater than the price paid for that worker? Suppose the firm were employing 2 workers at a price of \$7.20 an hour. To obtain a 3d worker it would have to pay the 3d worker a
\$8.80 — price of \$________ .

12-91

In addition, the firm would have to increase the price it pays the first 2
\$1.60 — workers from \$7.20 to \$8.80 an hour. This is an increase of \$________ a worker for each of these 2 workers.

12-92

The $8.80 it pays for the third worker *plus* the $1.60 an hour increase it

$12 must give to *each* of the first 2 workers adds up to $__________

MRC and this is the __________ of the 3d worker.

12-93

Because the monopsonist must increase the price it pays *all* workers when it increases the number of workers it employs, the MRC of any

greater worker—except the very first—is __________ than the price it pays these workers.

12-94

If a monopsonist finds that in order to obtain more labor it must increase the price it pays for labor, and the MRC of any worker is greater than the price for that worker, it will also find that the *more* workers it hires

greater the (greater/smaller) is the MRC of a worker.

12-95

In other words, as a monopsonist increases the employment of a resource

higher it finds that it must pay a (higher/lower) price for that resource, that the MRC is greater than the price it pays, and that the MRC will

increase (rise) __________ .

12-96

Now how much labor will this monopsonist employ? When we asked this same question about the purely competitive employer of labor, we found that we needed to know not only the MRC (or price) of workers, but

MRP also the __________ of each worker.

12-97

So to find out how much labor a monopsonist will employ we have to

MRC, MRP (either order) know both the __________ and the __________ of each worker.

12-98

In the schedules on the top of the next page are both the MRC and the MRP of each worker, together with the price the monopsonist must pay to employ the various amounts of labor.

Number of workers (per hour)	Price of labor (per hour)	MRC of labor	MRP of labor
0	$ 4.00		
1	5.60	$ 5.60	$21.60
2	7.20	8.80	20.80
3	8.80	12.00	20.00
4	10.40	15.20	19.20
5	12.00	18.40	18.40
6	13.60	21.60	17.60
7	15.20	24.80	16.80
8	16.80	28.00	16.00

would — The monopsonist (would/would not) hire the 1st worker because its

MRP, MRC — ______ is greater than its ______ .

12-99

would not, MRC — It (would/would not) hire the 7th worker because its ______

MRP — is greater than its ______ .

12-100

5 — To maximize total profit it would hire ______ workers.

12-101

If it employed 5 workers, it would have to pay a *price* of

$12 — $______ an hour for each of these 5 workers.

12-102

So the monopsonist, to maximize total profit (or minimize total loss), follows the same rule as the purely competitive employer of a resource:

greater — Employ all units which have an MRP ______ than or equal to their MRC, and do *not* employ any units which have an MRC

greater — ______ than their MRP.

12-103

supply — The price which the monopsonist pays for a variable resource is the price which the (MRP/MRC/supply) schedule indicates it must pay to obtain the amount of the resource that will maximize profits.

12-104

cannot — If you will look back at the MRP schedule in frame **12-98**, you will find that you (can/cannot) tell whether this monopsonist *sells* its product in a perfectly or imperfectly competitive market.

12-105

A monopsonist may be a perfectly competitive seller or an imperfectly competitive seller. Regardless of which it is, as an employer of a variable resource it hires the resource up to the amount at which the MRP and the MRC are ____________ .

equal

12-106 Review Frame

A monopsonist finds that if it wishes to increase the amount of a variable resource it employs, it must ____________ the price it pays for each unit of the resource. As a result of this finding, the MRC is ____________ than the price paid for the resource and will ____________ when the monopsonist increases its employment of the resource.

increase

greater

increase

12-107 Review Frame

In your own words:

How much of a variable resource will the monopsonist employ?

* ____

All units which have an MRP greater than or equal to their MRC (or up to the amount at which MRP and MRC are equal).

What price will it pay for each unit of the resource? * ____________

The price which will enable it to employ that amount of the resource.

12-108 Review Frame

A perfectly competitive employer of a variable resource finds that it can hire as few or as many units of the resource as it wishes at a ____________ price. As a result, the MRC is ____________ the market price of the resource.

constant (fixed), equal to (the same as)

12-109 Review Frame

Because the perfectly competitive employer hires all units of the variable resource which have an ____________ greater than or equal to their market price, the firm's ____________ schedule *is* its ____________ schedule for that resource.

MRP

MRP, demand

12-110 Review Frame

The total or market demand schedule for a resource hired by perfectly competitive employers is found by * ______________________________ ______________________________ .

totaling the demand schedules of these employers

12-111 Review Frame

This market demand schedule, along with the supply schedule for the resource, determines the equilibrium ____________ of the resource. This equilibrium price, in turn, is the price at which each perfectly competitive employer can hire all it wishes of the resource and is equal to the ____________ of that resource.

price

MRC

ALL RESOURCES VARIABLE

Only in very short periods of time does a firm find that only one of the several resources it employs to produce its product is variable. In the time period which economists call the long run, all of a firm's resources are variable.

We have already learned what amount of a resource a firm will hire in order to maximize its total profit when only that resource is variable. Now let's find out what amount of each resource a firm will employ when *all* of its resources are variable.

12-112

There is a firm in almost every town and city in the country that collects wastepaper from homes and factories and sells it to wastepaper dealers. This firm really requires only two resources, trucks and common labor. Its product is ____________ .

wastepaper

12-113

Provided there is at least one worker for every truck, the more workers the firm employs, the (more/less) paper it can collect in a day. And the more trucks the firm utilizes, the (greater/smaller) is the quantity of paper it can gather in a day.

more
greater

12-114

But this firm knows that the greater the amount of either resource it employs, the (larger/smaller) is the MP of that resource.

smaller

12-115

Let's assume that the firm can *sell* all the paper it collects at a price of 4 cents a pound over and above what it pays to those from whom it collects paper. This means that the MR from the sale of each additional pound of paper is ____________ cents.

4

12-116

It also means that the MRP of each worker the firm employs is equal to

4 the MP of that worker multiplied by ____________ cents, and that

4 the MRP of each truck equals its MP times ____________ cents.

12-117

When the firm employs either more workers or more trucks, the MP of workers or trucks decreases, and this causes the MRP of trucks and

decrease workers to ____________ .

12-118

The wastepaper collector can rent each truck it wishes to employ for $24 a day and hire each worker it wants to utilize for $12 a day. The MRC

$24 of each truck is $____________ a day, and the MRC of each worker

$12 is $____________ a day.

12-119

It has been the practice of the firm to put 2 workers in each truck and to hire enough workers and trucks to collect 10,000 pounds of paper a day. At 4 cents a pound over and above the price paid for the paper, the

$400 firm's TR is $____________ a day.

12-120

To collect this 10,000 pounds of paper a day, the firm has had to hire 4 trucks at $24 a day and 8 workers at $12 a day. The firm, thus, has a TC

$192, $208 of $____________ a day and a daily economic profit of $__________ .

12-121

The paper collector wondered recently whether it couldn't collect more paper without spending any more on trucks and labor, or if it could collect the same amount of paper and spend less for trucks and labor.

increase Doing either of these things would (increase/decrease) total economic profits.

12-122

So the firm called in a consulting economist, who found that the MP of the 4th truck was 1,000 pounds of paper and that the MP of the 8th worker was 750 pounds of paper. The MRP of the 4th truck was,

$40 therefore, $____________ , and the MRP of the 8th worker was

$30 $____________ .

12-123

The consulting economist pointed out that the MRP of the 4th truck

$40, $24 divided by its MRC was equal to $________ ÷ $________ ,

1⅔ or ________ .

12-124

The MRP of the 8th worker divided by the worker's MRC was equal to

$30, $12, 2½ $________ ÷ $________ , or ________ .

12-125

was not And the ratio of the MRP to the MRC of trucks (was/was not) equal to the ratio of the MRP to the MRC of workers.

12-126

less In fact, the MRP/MRC ratio for trucks was (greater/less) than the MRP/MRC ratio for workers.

12-127

"You are *not*," the consulting economist told the paper collector, "using the two resources in the correct proportion, because the two MRP/MRC

are not ratios (are/are not) equal."

12-128

"If you will use the two resources in the best proportion, you can, without spending any more for trucks and men, increase your total economic

TR profit by increasing your ________ ."

12-129

"Of, if you like, you can increase your total profit without collecting any

TC more paper by decreasing your ________ ."

12-130

Let's see how the paper collector could collect more paper and obtain more revenue without spending any greater total amount on trucks and labor. Here are the MRP schedules for trucks and labor.

Number of trucks (per day)	Daily MRP of trucks	Number of workers (per day)	Daily MRP of workers
1	$64	7	$33
2	56	8	30
3	48	9	27
4	40	10	24
5	32	11	21
6	24	12	18
7	18	13	15
8	12	14	12
9	4	15	9

Suppose the paper collector laid off the 4th truck. Because this truck
$40 has an MRP of $______, laying it off would decrease TR by
$40 $______.

12-131

But if the firm laid off the 4th truck, TC would decrease by
$24 $______.

12-132

Let's take the $24 the firm saved by laying off the 4th truck and spend
2 it for more labor. For this $24 the firm can hire ______ additional workers.

12-133

According to the MRP schedule for workers in frame **12-130**, hiring the
$27 9th worker would increase TR by $______ and hiring the 10th
$24 worker would increase TR by $______.

12-134

$51 These 2 extra workers will increase TR by $______. The loss
$40 of the 4th truck decreased TR by $______. As a result of the substitution of the 2 workers for the 1 truck, the TR of the paper collector
increased, $11 has (increased/decreased) by $______.

12-135

Because the paper collector is still spending just $192 for trucks
increased and men, the replacement of the truck by 2 workers has (increased/
$11 decreased) daily total economic profit by $______.

12-136

higher
lower

Total revenue and total profit were increased without any increase in total cost by using *more* of the resource with the (higher/lower) MRP/MRC ratio and *less* of the resource with the (higher/lower) MRP/MRC ratio.

12-137

less
more

In other words, by spending the same total amount for resources a firm can increase its TR and total profit by employing (more/less) of the resource with the smaller and (more/less) of the resource with the larger MRP/MRC ratio.

12-138

decrease
increases

But, the consulting economist observed, every good thing must come to an end. As the paper collector uses more labor, the MRP of labor will (increase/decrease); and when the firm uses fewer trucks the MRP of trucks (increases/decreases).

12-139

$48
$24

Look back at the MRP schedules in frame **12-130**. The MRP of the 3d truck is $________ and the MRP of the 10th worker is $________ .

12-140

$24, 2

The ratio of MRP to MRC for the 3d truck is equal to $48 divided by $________ , or ________ .

12-141

$12, 2

And the MRP/MRC ratio for the 10th worker is $24 divided by $________ , or ________ .

12-142

are

So when the paper collector employs 3 trucks and 10 workers, the MRP/MRC ratios for trucks and workers (are/are not) equal.

12-143

rose

The two ratios did not start out equal: the ratio was originally $2\frac{1}{2}$ for workers and $1\frac{2}{3}$ for trucks. But when the firm cut back its use of trucks, the MRP of trucks increased and so the MRP/MRC ratio for trucks (rose/fell).

12-144

fall — And when the firm expanded its employment of labor, the MRP of labor decreased; this caused labor's MRP/MRC ratio to (rise/fall).

12-145

$48 — Not realizing that these changes in the two ratios have occurred, and having increased TR and total profit by substituting labor for trucks, the paper collector decides to replace the 3d truck with an 11th and 12th worker. Doing without the 3d truck decreases TR by $________ .

12-146

$21

$18

The firm takes the $24 saved on trucks and hires 2 more workers. The employment of the 11th worker adds $________ to TR and the employment of the 12th worker adds another $________ to TR.

12-147

$39

decrease, $9

Altogether, the 11th and 12th workers *added* $________ to TR, while the loss of the 3d truck *decreased* TR by $48. The replacement of 1 truck with 2 workers *did not* change the firm's TC, but it did (increase/decrease) its total economic profit by $________ .

12-148

more

less

What conclusions can be drawn from all this? First, that when the MRP/MRC ratios for two resources are *not* equal, a firm can increase its TR and total profits by spending (more/less) on the higher-ratio resource and (more/less) on the low-ratio resource.

12-149

decrease — Second, when two MRP/MRC ratios *are* equal, spending more on one and less on the other resource will ________ the firm's TR and total profits.

12-150

MRP, MRC

equal

In short, a firm is hiring two resources in the best, or ***least-cost***, proportion when the ________ / ________ ratios for the two resources are ________ .

12-151

revenue

economic profit

For any given total dollar and cents amount the firm spends on several resources, it can obtain the largest possible total ________ and total ________ ________ when it hires resources in the best proportion.

12-152

And resources are employed in the best proportion only when * ____________________.

their MRP/MRC ratios are equal

12-153

To summarize, if a firm desires to *minimize* the TC of obtaining its TR, it must employ resources in the best proportion: the ____________ of every resource divided by its ____________ must be ____________ for all resources.

MRP; MRC, equal (identical)

12-154

When the MRP/MRC ratio is not the same for all resources, the firm can decrease its TC without reducing its TR by employing (more/less) of the high and (more/less) of the low-ratio resource.

more; less

12-155 Review Frame

When resources are employed in the best proportion, * ____________ ____________ are equal.

the MRP/MRC ratios of all resources

12-156 Review Frame

If the MRP/MRC ratio is not the same for all resources, and the firm substitutes more of the high-ratio resources for less of the low-ratio resources, *either* the firm's TR will ____________ while TC remains constant, *or* its TC will ____________ while TR remains constant.

increase; decrease

12-157 Review Frame

In short, using resources in the best proportion means that a firm gets the most ____________ for the amount it spends on resources, or it is able to obtain its total revenue at the least ____________.

TR; TC

12-158 Review Frame

So if a firm is to maximize its profits, it must use resources in the ____________ ____________. This is the ***least-cost rule***.

best proportion

12-159

We now know in what proportion a firm must employ its several resources in order to maximize its profits. But this doesn't tell us the total amount of these resources to employ. However, *when only one resource is variable*, the firm can maximize its total profit by employing all units of the variable resource which have a ____________ greater than or equal to their ____________.

MRP; MRC

12-160

The principle is the same when *all* resources are variable. All units of each resource which have a MRP ______ than or equal to their MRC should be employed to maximize total profit.

greater

12-161

This means that the *last* unit of labor employed will have an MRP equal to its MRC. And the ______ of the last truck employed will be equal to the ______ of the last truck.

MRP
MRC (either order)

12-162

In short, to maximize total profit the MRP of the ______ unit of each resource employed must ______ the MRC of that unit of the resource.

last (final)
equal

12-163

So, to return to our paper collector and assuming the firm could collect as much paper as it wishes and sell it at the same price, is the firm maximizing profit? (Yes/No).

No

12-164

If you answered yes, you have forgotten the profit-maximizing rule set out in frames **12-35** and **12-105**—and repeated in frames **12-160** to **12-162** above—hire resources up to the amount where MRP and MRC are equal. Another way of expressing this is to say that profit-maximization is obtained when MRP/MRC of every resource equals 1. At present, the MRP/MRC ratio of the paper firm for both trucks and workers is ______. The firm should therefore hire (more/less) trucks and (more/less) workers.

2, more
more

12-165

Refer again to the table in frame **12-130**. If the firm hired 6 trucks, the MRP of the last truck would be $______. The MRC would be $ ______. The MRP/MRC ratio would then be $______/$______ = ______. And if the firm hired 14 workers, the MRP of the last worker would be $______. The MRC would be $______. The MRP/MRC ratio would then be $______/$______ = ______.

$24
$24
$24, $24, 1
$12, $12
$12, $12
1

12-166
Increasing the number of trucks from 3 to 6 has increased costs by

$24, $72 3 × $________ = $________ . Revenue has increased
MRP by the (MRP/MRC) of each of these three extra trucks, that is, by
$40, $32, $24 $(________ + ________ + ________) =
$96, increased $________ . Therefore, profit has (increased/decreased) by
$24 $________ .

12-167
Increasing the number of workers from 10 to 14 has increased costs by

$12, $48 4 × $________ = $________ . Revenue has increased
MRP by the (MRP/MRC) of each of these four extra workers, that is, by
$21, $18, $15 $(________ + ________ + ________ +
$12, $66 ________) = $ ________ . Therefore, profit has (in-
increased, $18 creased/decreased) by $ ________ .

12-168
Thus by following the profit-maximizing rule of increasing the hiring of

1 all resources until the MRP/MRC ratio of each is equal to ________
$24, $18 total profit of this firm has increased by $(________ + ________)
$42 = $________ .

12-169
Does following the ***profit-maximizing rule*** automatically ensure that the ***least-cost rule*** has also been followed? (Yes/No).

Yes: when MRP/MRC for each resource equals 1, then MRP/MRC for all resources are equal

12-170 Review Frame
Using A and B to stand for two different variable resources, A and B are employed in the *least-cost proportion* when

equal to
$$\frac{MRP_A}{MRC_A} \text{ is * \_\_\_\_\_\_\_\_ } \frac{MRP_B}{MRC_B}$$

12-171 Review Frame
When A and B are used in the *profit-maximizing amounts*,

equal to MRP_A is * ________ MRC_A

equal to MRP_B is * ________ MRC_B

12-172 Review Frame

For example, suppose the MRP_A and the MRC_A are equal when they are both \$3. This means that MRP_A/MRC_A will be equal to \$3 divided by \$3, or ______ .

1

12-173 Review Frame

So to use variable resources in *both* the best proportion *and* in the amounts that will maximize profits, the MRP/MRC ratio for all resources must be equal to ______ .

1

12-174 Review Frame

To maximize its total profit a firm must hire each variable resource up to the amount at which its ______ and ______ are ______ .

MRP, MRC (either order)
equal

12-175 Review Frame

To hire variable resources in the best proportion, the MRP/MRC ratio for all resources must be ______ .

equal

12-176 Review Frame

And when resources are hired in the best amounts and in the best proportion, the MRP/MRC ratio for each resource is * ______ ______ .

equal to 1

12-177

Suppose that the MRP and the MRC of a variable resource such as labor are both \$4; and that this labor is employed by a perfectly competitive employer. Now assume the market price of labor *increases*. This will cause the MRC of labor to (increase/decrease).

increase

12-178

With this increase in the MRC of labor, the MRP/MRC ratio for labor will be (greater/less) than 1.

less

12-179

To maximize total profit the MRP/MRC ratio for labor must be 1. If the firm is to bring the ratio back to 1, it must (increase/decrease) labor's MRP.

increase

12-180

less
decreasing

The only way to increase labor's MRP is for the firm to hire (more/less) labor. So when the price of labor increases, the firm will react by (increasing/decreasing) its employment of labor.

12-181

smaller

In other words, even when all resources are variable, a perfectly competitive employer will demand a (larger/smaller) quantity of a resource when its price increases and vice versa.

12-182

increased

An imperfectly competitive employer, however, does not employ variable resources at the market price. A monopsonist sets the price it pays when it decides how much of a resource to employ. But when the supply of a resource *decreases*, it finds that the MRC of any amount of that resource has (increased/decreased).

12-183

less

Because a decrease in the supply of a resource causes its MRC to increase, the monopsonist finds that its MRP/MRC ratio is __________ than 1.

12-184

increase
decrease

To bring the ratio back to 1, the monopsonist must either __________ MRP or __________ MRC or both.

12-185

less
less

The MRP of any resource increases when its employer hires (more/less) of it. MRC will decrease as the employer uses (more/less) of it.

12-186

decreasing
employ more of it

So even when all resources are variable, if the supply of one of them decreases the monopsonist will react by (increasing/decreasing) the quantity it employs of that resource. Were the supply of that resource to increase, the monopsonist would * __________________________ .

Now take the Review Test for Section 12 at the back of the book.

International Trade section 13

Monday through Friday the typical American worker gets up in the morning and gets ready to go to work. Before leaving the house he or she drinks a cup of coffee, probably with sugar in it, and reads the newspaper. The car is used to get to work. The wheels of the car have rubber tires on them, and the car's engine uses gasoline for fuel. There is nothing at all unusual about this.

But consider these facts. The coffee beans used to make the coffee, the sugar in the coffee, and the paper on which the newspaper is printed were not produced in the United States. They were imported from Brazil, the Philippines, and Canada. The car driven to work may be a Toyota imported from Japan. The gasoline that powers the car was produced from crude oil imported from Saudi Arabia. The natural rubber on the wheels of the car was imported from Malaysia. And so it goes all through the day: The worker consumes products imported from outside the United States.

Once the worker gets to work, no matter what the job is, the chances are that some of the products he or she helps to produce will be sold outside the United States. About $140 billion of the cars, chemicals, computers, consumer durables, and machinery manufactured in the United States is exported to foreign countries. From 50 to 60 percent of the crop harvested by the typical farmer will be sold abroad. Almost every American worker and every American industry exports some of its production to countries outside of the United States.

Today, American consumers and business firms import goods and services whose value is more than 12 percent of the GDP. American resource owners and business firms export goods and services with a value that is over 10 percent of the GDP. In short, the United States engages in international trade.

International trade is simply the sale of resources and products by people, business firms, and governments located in one nation to people, firms, and governments in other nations: the buyers and sellers are residents of different nations. International trade is much like the buying and selling that occurs within a nation. Buyers buy and sellers sell for the same basic reason.

The first thing we want to learn in this section is why trade takes place between buyers and sellers, whether these buyers and sellers are located in the same or different countries. The reason for trade—the reason why trade takes place—is explained by the theory of comparative advantage.

After we have learned what the theory of comparative advantage is, we will go on and explain:

1. What foreign exchange is and how it is used as a medium of exchange in international buying and selling.
2. How a nation summarizes its buying and selling activities with other nations in its international balance of payments.

THE THEORY OF COMPARATIVE ADVANTAGE

Trade takes place *across* national borders for the same fundamental reason that it takes place *within* a nation's borders: because individual persons and individual nations tend to specialize in the production of a few commodities. They produce much more than they consume of some things and much less than they consume of other things. As a result of this tendency to specialize, trade between individuals and between nations becomes necessary. Those who produce more of a commodity than they consume, trade their surplus for the commodities which they consume in amounts greater than their production. Surpluses of one thing are traded to make up for shortages of other things. In fact, if trade did not take place, it would be impossible for either nations or individuals to specialize: they would all have to try to be self-sufficient by producing some amount of every commodity they want to consume.

There are three questions we need to ask about specialization and the trade that it causes:

1. *What* will be the commodities on which a nation or an individual will specialize?
2. *Why* will nations and individuals specialize?
3. When nations or individuals specialize and trade one commodity for another, what will be the *terms of trade*?

Let's see if we can find the answers to these three questions by examining what economists call the theory, or principle, of comparative advantage. To illustrate and explain this theory we'll use a very simple example involving two countries. But the example will explain the principle, and it can be applied not only to two countries but also to two individuals or to two business firms.

13-1

The small country of Transalpine is capable of producing just two different commodities: corn and wheat. The production possibilities table below shows the various combinations of corn and wheat it is able to produce.

	A	B	C	D	E	F	G	H	I
Corn (bushels)	0	50	100	150	200	250	300	350	400
Wheat (bushels)	1,200	1,050	900	750	600	450	300	150	0

If it devoted *all* its resources to wheat, it would be able to produce no

A corn. In the table this is combination ______ .

13-2

So if Transalpine used all its resources to produce wheat, it would be

1,200 able to produce ______ bushels of wheat.

13-3

But if it decided to produce no wheat and use all its resources for corn,

I, 400 it would produce combination ______ and ______ bushels of corn.

13-4

Sylvania is another country capable of producing only corn and wheat. Here is its production possibilities table.

	A	B	C	D	E	F
Corn (bushels)	0	90	180	270	360	450
Wheat (bushels)	1,800	1,440	1,080	720	360	0

450 Using all its resources for corn, it can produce ______ bushels of corn. And if it uses all its resources for wheat, it can produce

1,800 ______ bushels of wheat.

13-5

Look back at the table in frame **13-1**. The table tells us that whenever Transalpine chooses to increase its production of corn by 50 bushels, it

decrease, 150 must (increase/decrease) its production of wheat by ______ bushels.

13-6

And to increase its production of wheat by 150 bushels, Transalpine must

50 sacrifice—go without or not produce—______ bushels of corn.

13-7

When Transalpine increases its production of corn by 50 bushels, the *opportunity cost* of this corn is the 150 bushels of wheat that it must go without or sacrifice. The opportunity cost when it increases its production of wheat by 150 bushels is the 50 bushels of corn that it must

sacrifice, go without (not produce)

________ or ________ ________.

13-8

Look now at Sylvania's production possibilities table in frame **13-4**. For Sylvania, the opportunity cost of 90 bushels of corn is

360 bushels of wheat

________________, and the opportunity cost

90 bushels of corn

of 360 bushels of wheat is ________________.

13-9

If it costs Transalpine 150 bushels of wheat to produce 50 bushels of corn, the opportunity cost of *1 bushel* of corn is 150 bushels of wheat

3

divided by 50, or ______ bushels of wheat.

13-10

Looking back at frame **13-4**, we can see that Sylvania can produce 360 bushels of wheat at a cost of 90 bushels of corn. For Sylvania, the op-

360

portunity cost of *1 bushel* of corn is ________ bushels of wheat

4

divided by 90, or ______ bushels of wheat.

13-11

We have discovered that the opportunity cost of 1 bushel of corn to Transalpine is 3 bushels of wheat and to Sylvania is 4 bushels of wheat.

This tells us that Transalpine has a ***comparative advantage*** in the production of corn because its opportunity cost of producing corn is

lower

(higher/lower) than Sylvania's.

13-12

We have also learned that Sylvania has a ***comparative disadvantage*** in corn production because its opportunity cost of producing corn is

higher

(higher/lower) than Transalpine's.

13-13

Who has the comparative advantage in the production of wheat?

50

It costs Transalpine ______ bushels of corn to produce 150 bushels of wheat.

50

Each bushel of wheat costs Transalpine ______ bushels of corn

150, ⅓

divided by ______, or ______ bushel of corn.

13-14

Try this one on your own. If Sylvania can produce 360 bushels of wheat at an opportunity cost of 90 bushels of corn, the opportunity cost of

¼ *1 bushel* of wheat is ________ bushel of corn.

13-15

Transalpine's opportunity cost of a bushel of wheat is ⅓ bushel of corn and Sylvania's is ¼ bushel of corn.

disadvantage
higher
Transalpine has a comparative (advantage/disadvantage) in producing wheat because its opportunity cost is (higher/lower).

13-16

advantage
lower
In frame **13-12** you saw that Sylvania has a comparative disadvantage in corn production. However, as you have just seen, Sylvania has a comparative (advantage/disadvantage) in producing wheat because its opportunity cost is (higher/lower).

13-17

We find that each country has a comparative advantage in the production of one of these commodities. Each country also has a comparative

disadvantage ____________ in the production of one of the commodities.

13-18

If these two countries were each to specialize, one in the production of corn and one in the production of wheat, which country ought to specialize in:

Transalpine
Sylvania
Corn? (Transalpine/Sylvania)
Wheat? (Transalpine/Sylvania)

13-19

Our general principle is that:

Countries should specialize and produce those commodities in which

comparative advantage they have a ____________ ____________ .

13-20

But why should specialization follow comparative advantage? Let's find out. The following table indicates how much corn and how much wheat Transalpine and Sylvania produced when they did *not* specialize. (Transalpine produced combination C in frame **13-1** and Sylvania combination D in frame **13-4**.) Complete the following table to show their combined production of corn and wheat.

Country	Corn	Wheat
Transalpine	100	900
Sylvania	270	720
Total	______	______

370, 1,620

13-21
In frame **13-1** we found that if Transalpine specializes entirely in corn, it can produce 400 bushels of corn. And in frame **13-4** we discovered that when Sylvania produces only wheat, it can produce 1,800 bushels of wheat. So if each produces *only* that commodity in which it has a comparative advantage, their *combined* production will be

400, 1,800 ______________ bushels of corn and ______________ bushels of wheat.

13-22
Compare the production in frames **13-20** (no specialization) and **13-21** (specialization according to comparative advantage). As you can see, specialization has led to an increase in the total corn production amounting

30 to ______________ bushels, and an increase in the combined wheat

180 production amounting to ______________ bushels.

13-23
In other words, by specializing in the commodity where each country has a comparative advantage, the two countries can obtain a greater

production (output) total ______________ with the same resources. This is, therefore, a

more (more/less) efficient use of resources.

13-24
In short, if producers will specialize in those commodities in which

comparative advantage they have a ______________ ______________, the results will be

greater total production * ________________________________ from the same resources and

more efficient the * ________________________________ use of resources.

13-25
Suppose Transalpine is going to grow only corn and Sylvania is going to grow nothing but wheat. If they both want to consume some corn and some wheat, Transalpine is going to have to trade some of its

corn, Sylvania, wheat ______________ for some of ______________'s ______________.

13-26

Imagine for just a minute that Transalpine trades 30 bushels of its corn for 150 bushels of Sylvania's wheat. This means that Transalpine is

5 getting ________ bushels of wheat for every *1* bushel of corn it gives up to Sylvania.

13-27

1/5 It also means that Sylvania is obtaining ________ bushel of corn for every *1 bushel* of wheat it turns over to Transalpine.

13-28

Put another way, the price Transalpine pays for a bushel of wheat is

1/5 ________ bushel of corn, and the price Sylvania pays for a bushel of

5 corn is ________ bushels of wheat.

13-29

Instead of talking about the price of a bushel of corn or of wheat, economists talk about the *terms of trade*. In our example, the terms of trade can be stated either as:

5 bushels of wheat for 1 bushel of corn; or

1/5 bushel of corn for 1 bushel of wheat.

are two ways This means that there (is just one way/are two ways) of expressing what the terms of trade are.

13-30

If 200 bushels of corn were to be exchanged for 600 bushels of wheat,

3 we could say that the terms of trade are ________ bushels of wheat for

corn, 1/3 1 bushel of ____________ or ________ bushel of corn for 1 bushel

wheat of ____________ .

13-31

What do *you* think is the best way to express the terms of trade:

(a) The number of bushels of corn that exchange for 1 bushel of wheat.

(b) The number of bushels of wheat that are traded for 1 bushel of corn.

(c) Either way—it doesn't really make any difference.

We hope you said (c). Does it really make any difference whether you say a dollar is worth ten dimes or a dime is one-tenth of a dollar?

Which one? ____________

13-32

But when two countries like Transalpine and Sylvania each specialize in one commodity and then trade, what will the terms of trade be? Since Transalpine found that its opportunity cost of *producing* a bushel of wheat was ⅓ bushel of corn, the *most* it would be willing to pay Sylvania

⅓ for a bushel of wheat would be ________ bushel of corn.

13-33

Let's express this another way. Transalpine would be willing to give up

3 *1* bushel of corn only if it obtained at least ______ bushels of wheat in return.

13-34

So if the terms of trade were *greater* than ⅓ corn for 1 wheat (which is the same as saying *less* than 3 wheat for 1 corn), Transalpine would be

unwilling (willing/unwilling) to trade.

13-35

Sylvania found that it would produce a bushel of corn at an opportunity cost of 4 bushels of wheat. In other words, 4 bushels of wheat is the

highest (lowest/highest) amount that Sylvania is willing to pay Transalpine for a bushel of corn.

13-36

This means the *least* Sylvania would take for 1 bushel of wheat is

¼ ______ bushel of corn.

13-37

If the terms of trade were *less* than ¼ bushel of corn for 1 bushel of

would not wheat, Sylvania (would/would not) be willing to trade.

13-38

Now let's summarize what we have just discovered about the willingness of Transalpine and Sylvania to trade.

Transalpine won't trade if the terms are *greater* than ⅓ corn for 1 wheat, and Sylvania won't trade if the terms are *less* than ¼ corn for 1 wheat.

It takes a willingness on the part of both countries before trade can

⅓ take place: the terms must be somewhere between ______ and

¼ ______ corn for 1 wheat.

13-39

We might also have put it this way:

Transalpine won't trade if the terms are *less* than 3 wheat for 1 corn.
Sylvania won't trade if the terms are *greater* than 4 wheat for 1 corn.

4 For trade to occur, the terms must be somewhere between ________

3 and ________ wheat for 1 corn.

13-40

It doesn't matter how we express the terms of trade. It does matter what the terms of trade are. But from our example we can see that we
do not (do/do not) know exactly what the terms will be.

13-41

We do know, however, in what *range* the terms of trade will have to be if trade is to take place at all. The terms must be in the range in which
both (one/both) parties are willing to trade.

13-42

If the terms were more than $\frac{1}{3}$ corn for 1 wheat (3 wheat for 1 corn),
opportunity Transalpine would not be willing to trade because its ________ cost of producing 1 wheat is only $\frac{1}{3}$ corn.

13-43

And if the terms were more than 4 wheat for 1 corn ($\frac{1}{4}$ corn for 1 wheat), Sylvania would not trade because its opportunity cost of producing 1
4 corn is only ________ wheat.

13-44

Let us assume that the terms of trade settle at $3\frac{1}{3}$ wheat for 1 corn. This
3/10 is the same as saying ________ corn for 1 wheat. Since Transalpine is specializing in corn, if it decides to keep 100 bushels of corn for itself,
300 it will have ________ bushels to trade.

13-45

Having regard to the terms of trade settled on in the previous frame, how many bushels of wheat will Transalpine expect in exchange for its
1000 300 bushels of corn? ________

13-46

Since Sylvania is specializing in wheat, after it has traded 1,000 bushels of wheat to Transalpine, it will have how many bushels of wheat left
800 for itself? ________

13-47

Look back at frame **13-20**. Before trade, Transalpine was able to consume ________ bushels of corn and ________ bushels of wheat. Through specialization and trade on the basis of comparative advantage, Transalpine now can consume ________ bushels of corn and ________ bushels of wheat. This is an/a (increase/decrease) of * ____________ .

100, 900

100, 1000

increase, 100 bushels of wheat

13-48

Before trade, Sylvania could consume ________ bushels of corn and ________ bushels of wheat. Now Sylvania can consume ________ bushels of corn and ________ bushels of wheat. This is an/a (increase/decrease) of * ______________________ .

270

720, 300

800, increase

30 bushels of corn and 80 bushels of wheat

13-49

So far we have talked only about trade between two countries. But individual persons and individual business firms tend to specialize in the production of one or a few commodities. And they specialize for the same reason that two countries like Transalpine and Sylvania specialize. If each individual or firm will specialize in those commodities in the production of which they have a ____________ advantage, together these individuals can obtain a greater total ____________ of these commodities with the same amounts of resources.

comparative

production (output)

13-50

But when countries specialize, trade between these countries is (necessary/desirable).

necessary

13-51

When trade between nations is possible, each nation will specialize in the commodities for whose production it has a comparative advantage and (export/import) these commodities to other nations.

export

13-52

They will (export/import) the commodities in which other nations specialize.

import

13-53 Review Frame

Here is a problem you can work to review your understanding of the principle of comparative advantage. The production possibilities tables for South Amasia and North Amasia follow.

South Amasia				
Steel (tons)	150	100	50	0
Oats (carloads)	0	20	40	60

North Amasia				
Steel (tons)	180	120	60	0
Oats (carloads)	0	30	60	90

South Amasia finds that the opportunity cost of 1 ton of steel is

⅖ carload of oats — * ________________ , and of 1 carload of

2½ tons of steel — oats is * ________________ .

13-54 Review Frame

½ carload of oats — North Amasia's opportunity cost of 1 ton of steel is * ________

2 tons of steel — ________ , and of 1 carload of oats is * ________________ .

13-55 Review Frame

South — ________ Amasia has a comparative advantage in steel, and

North — ________ Amasia has a comparative advantage in oats. North

oats — Amasia will specialize in the production of ________ and South

steel — Amasia in ________ .

13-56 Review Frame

oats
steel — North Amasia will exchange its (steel/oats) for South Amasia's (steel/oats).

The terms of trade will lie between:

⅖, ½ (either order) — ________ and ________ carload of oats for 1 ton of steel.

2½, 2 (either order) — ________ and ________ tons of steel for 1 carload of oats.

13-57 Review Frame

Specialization based on the principle of comparative advantage enables

increase — the two nations to ________ their combined production of steel and oats without an increase in the resources available to them.

FOREIGN EXCHANGE

Specialization is an economic fact of life in the modern world. Individuals and countries do not produce everything they consume. Nor do they consume all they produce. In short, specialization forces people and nations to trade.

Another economic fact is that there is very little barter: People and nations seldom trade one good or service directly for another good or service. Instead, they sell a commodity for money and use the money to buy other commodities. Money is used throughout the modern world as a medium of exchange to avoid all the inconveniences that accompany barter.

Nations like the United States use money to make specialization and trade within their borders more convenient. But here is a third economic fact: every nation uses a *different* money. The United States uses dollars, the English use pounds, the French use francs, and so on. This simple fact creates a basic problem that must be solved before international trade can take place. Let's see what this problem is and how it is solved.

13-58

import
export

I am an American citizen and wish to buy an automobile from a business firm in London, England. In technical terms, I wish to (import/export) the automobile and the English firm is anxious to (import/export) it.

13-59

dollars
pounds

The kind of money I have to spend is (dollars/pounds). But the kind of money the English firm will accept for the automobile is (dollars/pounds).

13-60

pounds, dollars

My problem is this: Before I can buy the car, I must first buy some (dollars/pounds) and pay for them with (dollars/pounds).

13-61

dollars, pounds

Let's say this another way. Before I can buy the car, I must first sell some (dollars/pounds) and be paid for them with (dollars/pounds).

13-62

demander
supplier

In economic language, I am at the same time both a (demander/supplier) of pounds and (demander/supplier) of dollars.

13-63

supplier
demander

The English firm willing to exchange its pounds for my dollars, in economic terms, is simultaneously a ______________ of pounds and a ______________ of dollars.

13-64

The markets in which one kind of money is exchanged for another kind of money are called ***foreign exchange markets***. In the foreign exchange market in which dollars are exchanged for pounds, Americans demand

pounds — and the English supply ______________ ; and the English demand and

dollars — Americans supply ______________ .

13-65

Because one kind of money is exchanged for another in these markets, ***foreign exchange*** is the name economists use for foreign money. From

is — the American point of view, the pound (is/is not) foreign exchange and

is not — the dollar (is/is not) foreign exchange.

13-66

But from the English viewpoint, it is the dollar and not the pound that

foreign exchange — is considered to be ______________ ______________ .

13-67

Looking at it from the point of view of Americans, if there were 100 different nations in the world and 100 different kinds of money, there

99 — would be (how many) ________ different kinds of foreign exchange.

13-68

Let's just suppose for a minute that an American can obtain *one* English pound by paying \$3. Economists would say that the *rate of exchange* for the pound (or the foreign exchange rate for the pound) is \$3. The rate

dollars — of exchange for the pound is the number of ________ an American must pay to acquire one English pound.

13-69

In other words, the American rate of exchange for the pound is the price

pound — in dollars of one ______________ .

13-70

If an English firm can sell 1 pound for \$3, it is *paying* ⅓ pound to buy

dollar — 1 dollar. From its viewpoint, the rate of exchange for the ____________

⅓ — is ________ pounds.

13-71

rate — In short, when 1 pound exchanges for \$3, the ______________ of

exchange, \$3, ⅓ pound — ______________ is ________ for the pound and ______________ for the dollar.

13-72

The rate of exchange for the dollar is the price in pounds of (how many)

one (1) ____________ dollar(s).

13-73

Suppose the rate of exchange for the pound were \$4. The rate of

¼ exchange for the dollar would be ________ pound. If the rate of exchange for the dollar were ⅕ pound, the rate of exchange for the

\$5 pound would be \$________ .

13-74

Now complete the following table to indicate the rates of exchange for the dollar at the various rates of exchange given for the pound.

	Rate of exchange for the pound	Rate of exchange for the dollar
⅕	\$5.00	____
¼	4.00	____
⅓	3.00	____
½	2.00	____
1	1.00	____

13-75

The table in frame **13-74** reveals a simple fact. When the rate of exchange for the pound *falls*, the rate of exchange for the dollar has to

rise (rise/fall). And when the rate of exchange for the dollar *rises*, the rate of

fall exchange for the pound must (rise/fall).

13-76

In short, the rates of exchange for the pound and the dollar are (directly/

inversely, rises (increases) inversely) related to each other; when one falls the other ____________ and vice versa.

13-77

But what determines the rate of exchange for the pound and for the dollar? Recall that the rate of exchange is nothing more than the

price ____________ paid for 1 unit of foreign exchange.

13-78

Foreign exchange is bought and sold in highly competitive markets. In *any* competitive market the price of the commodity bought and sold

demand, supply — there depends upon the ______ for and the ______ of that commodity.

13-79

rate of exchange — So the demand for and the supply of pounds determines the * ______ ______ for the pound.

13-80

Here are hypothetical demand and supply schedules for the English pound.

Quantity of pounds demanded	Foreign exchange rate	Quantity of pounds supplied
400	$5.00	800
500	4.50	700
600	4.00	600
700	3.50	500
800	3.00	400
900	2.50	300
1,000	2.00	200

One of the first things you see when you look at these schedules is that like the demand for and supply of most commodities, when the foreign exchange rate *increases*, the quantity of pounds *demanded*

decreases — (increases/decreases), and the quantity of pounds *supplied*

increases — (increases/decreases).

13-81

Later we'll explain why foreign exchange obeys the laws of demand and of supply. Right now we can see that with these demand and supply schedules, the equilibrium rate of exchange for the pound will

$4 — be $______ . This means that the equilibrium rate of exchange for

¼ — the dollar is ______ pound.

13-82

At this equilibrium rate of exchange, the quantity of pounds demanded

600 — and supplied—the equilibrium quantity—is ______ .

13-83

At the equilibrium, 600 pounds will be bought and sold at a price of $4 per pound. This means that 600 pounds will be exchanged for a *total* of

2,400 — ______ dollars.

13-84

quantity — In other words, $2,400 is the equilibrium (price/quantity) of dollars.

13-85

To summarize, the equilibrium rate of exchange for the dollar is

¼, $4 — ________ pound and for the pound is $________ .

600, $2,400 — And the equilibrium quantity is ________ pounds and $________ .

13-86 Review Frame

Now let's take four frames to review what we have learned so far about foreign exchange.

supplier, demander — A West German wishing to buy wine in France will be a (demander/supplier) of German deutschemarks and a (demander/supplier) of French francs.

deutschemarks, francs — A French firm that wants to buy coal in West Germany will demand (francs/deutschemarks) and supply (francs/deutschemarks).

13-87 Review Frame

foreign exchange — Another name for foreign money is ________ ________ .

price, one (1) — The rate of exchange is the ________ paid to obtain ________ unit(s) of foreign money.

13-88 Review Frame

If 5 French francs can be exchanged for $1, the rate of exchange for the

5 — dollar is ________ francs.

If the rate of exchange for the deutschemark is 40 cents, the rate of

2½ — exchange for the dollar is ________ deutschemarks.

13-89 Review Frame

The rate of exchange for any foreign money depends upon the

demand, supply — ________ for and the ________ of that money. The equilibrium exchange rate for the French franc will be the rate at which

demanded — the quantity of francs ________ equals the quantity of francs

supplied (either order) — ________ .

13-90

Now, just who are the people who *demand* English pounds in exchange for American dollars?

American — Well, one group that demands pounds are (American/English)

English — importers of (American / English) goods. And one group that

supplies — ________ pounds are English importers of American goods.

13-91

Many of the goods Americans import from England and the English import from the United States are consumer goods. Some of these goods, however, are not consumer goods. They are machinery, raw materials,

capital (producer) — and other forms of ______________ goods.

13-92

But American importers of consumer and capital goods are only one of the groups that demand English pounds. And English importers of American goods are just one group that supplies pounds.

American tourists travel in England and pay their bills in hotels, restaurants, and railway stations.

American business firms transport goods in English ships.

American consumers and business firms pay premiums on insurance policies issued by English companies.

Americans rent English motion pictures and pay royalties to English writers.

These are all examples of Americans purchasing (or importing) not

services — goods but ______________ from the English. And they all result in an

demand, supply — American ______________ for pounds and a ______________ of dollars.

13-93

One of the special services that Americans export to England is the *use of money*. For example, Americans who own stock in English business firms have invested their money in these firms, and for the use of this money they receive dividends. And Americans who have lent money to the English as an investment are paid interest for the use of this money.

Income from American investments in England, therefore, consists of

dividends, interest (either order) — ______________ and ______________ .

13-94

The income which American investments in England earn is payment

money — for the English use of ______________ owned by Americans.

13-95

These dividends and interest payments from the English are paid to Americans *in pounds*. The Americans who receive them, naturally, wish

dollars — to exchange them for ______________ .

13-96

The English, likewise, own stocks issued by American firms and have lent money to Americans. They have invested their money in the United States. Put another way, the English have (exported/imported) and Americans have (exported/imported) the use of money.

exported
imported

13-97

dollars

pounds, dollars

The dividends and interest paid to the English by Americans are paid in (dollars/pounds). After the English receive these dividends and interest payments, they will convert them. That is, they will demand ______ and supply ______ .

13-98

dollars
pounds

Like the English import of goods and services, the English import of the use of money creates a demand for (dollars/pounds) and a supply of (dollars/pounds) to pay the resulting interest and dividends.

13-99

supply of
demand for

And just like the American import of goods and services, the American import of the use of money results in a (demand for/supply of) dollars and a (demand for/supply of) pounds, to pay the resulting interest and dividends.

13-100

goods, services

stocks, loans

In summary, the demanders of pounds are:

Americans who import ______ and ______ from England, and

Englishmen who export the use of money to the United States for investment in ______ and ______ and wish to receive interest and dividends in their own currency.

13-101

Englishmen
the United States
Americans, England

And the suppliers of English pounds are:

(Englishmen/Americans) who import goods and services from (England/the United States), and

(Englishmen/Americans) who export the use of money to (England/the United States) and wish to receive interest and dividends in their own currency.

13-102

demand, supply

But there are two other groups who demand and supply pounds. Americans who wish to buy stocks in England and make loans to Englishmen will (demand/supply) pounds and (demand/supply) dollars.

13-103

supply
demand

And Englishmen who desire to buy stocks in the United States and make loans to Americans will ______ pounds and ______ dollars.

13-104

To make a financial investment in a foreign country means to buy

stocks, lend

________ in that country, or to ________ money in that country.

13-105

The final group of demanders and suppliers of foreign exchange is made up of those who want to *give* money away in foreign countries.

An Englishman wishing to give money to an American person or in-

supply, demand

stitution will ________ pounds and ________ dollars.

An American who wants to give money to an Englishman will demand

pounds, dollars

________ and supply ________ .

13-106 Review Frame

Now let's take two frames to review what we have learned about the groups that demand and supply foreign exchange. The four groups that *demand* pounds and *supply* dollars are:

import

Americans who wish to (export/import) goods and services,

exported

Englishmen who ________ the use of money and are being paid interest and dividends.

Americans who wish to make financial investments in England by

stocks, loans

buying ________ and making ________ in England,

give

Americans who want to ________ money to persons or institutions in England.

13-107 Review Frame

The *suppliers* of pounds and *demanders* of dollars are:

goods, services

Englishmen who import ________ and ________ ,

use

Americans who export the ________ of money and are being paid interest and dividends.

buy, make

Englishmen who wish to (buy/sell) stocks or (make/obtain) loans in the United States,

make

Englishmen who want to (make/receive) gifts of money.

13-108

The demand and supply schedules we looked at in frame **13-80** follow.

Quantity of pounds demanded	Foreign exchange rate	Quantity of pounds supplied
400	$5.00	800
500	4.50	700
600	4.00	600
700	3.50	500
800	3.00	400
900	2.50	300
1,000	2.00	200

decreases
increases

You will observe that when the rate of exchange for the pound *rises*, the quantity of pounds demanded (increases/decreases), and the quantity of pounds supplied (increases/decreases).

When the rate of exchange falls, the reverse is true.

13-109

In short, the Law of Demand applies to the demand for foreign exchange, and the Law of Supply applies to the supply of foreign exchange. But why do these laws apply not only to ordinary goods and services but also to foreign exchange?

Suppose the price of an automobile in England is 5,000 pounds. When the rate of exchange for the pound is $3, the *price* of the automobile in

15,000 dollars is $__________ .

13-110

But were the rate of exchange for the pound to fall to $2, the dollar price

10,000 of the automobile would be $__________ .

13-111

In other words, when the rate of exchange for the pound *falls*, the dollar

falls price of anything bought in England (rises/falls). And should the rate of exchange for the pound *rise*, the dollar price of anything purchased in

rise England would __________ .

13-112

Since a *decrease* in the rate of exchange for the pound causes the dollar price of anything bought in England to *decrease*, it will also result in

larger Americans demanding (larger/smaller) quantities of the things they buy in England.

13-113

When Americans demand larger quantities of the things they buy in

larger England, they will need a (larger/smaller) quantity of pounds to pay for them.

13-114

In short, a *decrease* in the rate of exchange for the pound:

decrease — causes the dollar price of things bought in England to ________ , which in turn causes the quantity of English commodities demanded

increase — to ________ ,

increase — which causes the quantity of pounds demanded to ________ .

13-115

The same kind of thing happens when the rate of exchange for the pound *increases*. The dollar price of things bought in England

increases — ________ , and the quantity of these things demanded

decreases — ________ . As a result the number of pounds demanded will

decrease — ________ .

13-116

inverse — In short, there will be a(n) (direct/inverse) relationship between the rate of exchange for the pound and the quantity of pounds demanded.

13-117 Review Frame

Now let's take two frames to review why the Laws of Demand and of Supply apply to foreign exchange.

Use a plus sign (+) to indicate an increase and a minus sign (−) to indicate a decrease.

− — An *increase* in the rate of exchange for the pound will ________

− — the rate of exchange for the dollar, ________ the pound price of American goods and services, and

+ — ________ the dollar price of English goods and services.

13-118 Review Frame

As a result of this increase in the rate of exchange for the pound:

The quantity of American commodities demanded by the English

+ — will ________ and the quantity of English commodities demanded by

− — Americans will ________ ;

The quantity of pounds supplied by Englishmen will ordinarily

+ — ________ and the quantity of pounds demanded by Americans will

− — ________ .

THE INTERNATIONAL BALANCE OF PAYMENTS

There are at present over 180 nations in the world. Each one of them keeps a record of its exports and imports of goods and services. Each country also records the gifts its residents make abroad and receive from abroad, the financial and real investments residents make in foreign countries, and the financial and real investments foreigners make in its country.

At the end of the year, a nation summarizes its total exports and imports and its other international financial transactions with *all* other nations. This annual summary is a nation's *international balance of payments*. Let's look at a country's international balance of payments to find out what kind of information it contains.

13-119

In the table at the bottom of this page is the simplified international balance of payments (IBP) for the United States in 1990. The top portion of the table summarizes the United States' trade in currently produced

current — goods and services and is therefore called the __________ account.

13-120

\+ — You will notice in the IBP table that economists put a (+/−) sign in front of the values of each of the exports. This indicates that the foreign

increased — exchange owned by Americans is (increased/decreased) by the amount shown.

13-121

You will also notice that there is a (−) sign in front of the value of each

imports, made outpayments — of the __________ . This indicates that Americans (made outpayments/received inpayments) for the amounts shown.

13-122

$390 — During the year the United States *exported* goods worth $__________

$498 — billion and *imported* goods worth $__________ . Thus the *Balance of*

$−108 — *trade* was $__________ . Insert this figure in the blank opposite *Balance of trade* in the table below.

Current account			
(1)	U. S. merchandise exports	$+390	
(2)	U. S. merchandise imports	−498	
(3)	Balance of trade		$__________
(4)	U. S. exports of services	+133	
(5)	U. S. imports of services	−107	
(6)	Balance on goods and services		__________
(7)	Net investment income	+12	
(8)	Net transfers	−22	
(9)	Balance on current account	...	__________
Capital account			
(10)	Capital inflows to the U.S.	+117*	
(11)	Capital outflows from the U.S.	−59	
(12)	Balance on capital account		__________
(13)	Current and capital account balance		__________
(14)	Official reserves		__________

*Includes a $64 billion statistical discrepancy which is believed to be comprised primarily of unaccounted capital inflows.

Source: *Survey of Current Business*, December 1991, p. 41.

13-123

negative — more — favorable

In 1990 the United States had (positive/negative) balance of trade. This is spoken of as an "unfavorable balance of trade." If the United States had had a trade surplus—(more/less) goods exported than imported—this would have been called a ______________ balance of trade.

13-124

services, in- — $+133

The United States not only exports cars and computers but also research, advertising, insurance, brokerage, franchises, and tourist services to residents of other countries. These are shown in line (4) of the table as exports of ______________ . In 1990 these resulted in (in-/out-) payments of $(+/−)______________ billion.

13-125

$−107

As well as exporting services, the United States also imports them. The result in 1990 was a figure of $________ billion in the balance of payments.

13-126

$+26 — $−82

Adding the exports and the imports figures resulted in a balance on services of $(+/−)______________ billion. Adding the balance on services to the *Balance of trade* gives us a *Balance on goods and services* of $(+/−)______________ billion. Enter this amount in the blank at the end of line (6) of the table.

13-127

more — in-, out- — $+12

In 1990 the United States still *appeared* to be a ***net international creditor***, that is to say, Americans appeared to own (more/less) bonds, shares, and equity abroad than foreigners owned in the United States. Thus there was a greater (in-/out-) flow than ________-flow of interest and dividends. This resulted in *Net investment income* of $(+/−)______________ billion. (Though the United States had become a net international debtor in 1986, this had not yet shown up in the net investment income flows by 1990.)

13-128

export

This inpayment of $12 billion is, in effect, for the (export/import) of the services of the real and financial investments that Americans had made abroad in excess of nonresident investments in the United States.

13-129

Transfers are in- and outpayments received and made by American institutions (including governments) and individuals. They include gifts, including foreign aid, pensions, and remittances to immigrants from their relatives abroad as well as remittances from immigrants to their relatives

$-22 "back home." In 1990 "net transfers" totaled $________ billion. This
more meant Americans sent (more/less) gifts, remittances, and pensions abroad than they received. In other words, Americans were (exporting/
importing importing) "thank you" notes.

13-130

Adding the *Balance on goods and services* to the balances on *Net investment income* and *Net transfers* gives us the *Balance on current ac-*

$-92 *count* of $(+/−)________ billion. Insert this figure in the table in the blank at the end of line (9).

13-131

deficit There was, therefore, a current account (deficit/surplus) in 1990. This
demand for meant that import transactions created a greater (supply of/demand for)

supplied foreign currencies than American export transactions ________.

13-132

The bottom portion of the table summarizes the net inflows and outflows of liquid capital for buying and selling real and financial assets. It is

capital therefore called the ________ account.

13-133

In 1990 nonresidents made net financial and real investments in the United States through buying bonds, shares, and property in the amount

$117, increase of $________ billion. Such transactions (increase/decrease) the supplies
in- of foreign currencies in the United States and thus are an (in-/out-) pay-
\+ ment to the United States, designated by a (+/−) sign.

13-134

During the year Americans also made net financial and real investments

$59 abroad to the extent of $________ billion. Such transactions led to an

out-, both, out- ________-flow of (foreign currency/dollars/both). As an ________-

— payment they are designated with a ________ sign.

13-135

Adding the capital inflows and outflows together, we find that the *Bal-*

$+58 *ance on capital account* was $(+/−)________ billion. Insert this figure in the table in the blank at the end of line (12).

13-136

surplus
more

This capital account (surplus/deficit) meant that nonresidents carried out (more/less) real and financial investments in the United States than Americans carried out abroad in 1990 with the result that the United

increased

States' position as a net international debtor ________________ .

13-137

Recall from frame **13-131** that in 1990 the United States had a current

deficit, $92

account (surplus/deficit) of $________ billion. We have now just found

surplus

that in the same year the United States had a capital account ________

$58, Yes

of $________ billion. Is there a connection? (Yes/No)

13-138

Americans cannot use foreign currency within the United States but only to buy foreign goods and services. Thus in 1990 of the $58 billion net

in-, capital
imports

(in-/out-) flow on the ______________ account, Americans used the whole $58 billion to partially *finance* the excess of (exports/imports) over

exports, current

______________ on the ______________ account.

13-139

surplus

So *what* brought about the capital account (surplus/deficit) that financed

deficit

the current account ______________ ? Was it:

(a) The United States' desire or need to import more than it exported that led foreigners to lend Americans foreign currency or to buy American shares and property

(b) The foreign desire to make real and financial investments being greater than the American desire to make similar investments abroad that led to the net inflow on capital account

We hope you said (b). Would a bank lend you money except to make a profit?

Which one? ________

13-140

When either Americans or nonresidents wish to buy United States'

dollars

bonds, shares, or property they need (dollars/foreign currency). Therefore when nonresidents wished to make more real and financial investments in the United States in 1990 than Americans wished to make

dollars

abroad, there was an increased demand for ______________ in the foreign exchange market. This caused the rate of exchange for the

dollar

______________ to increase. (Review frame **13-89** if you have forgotten this.) (Though the dollar has in fact fallen against other major currencies from the heights of the early 1980s, it has not yet fallen to the level needed to wipe out the trade deficit.)

13-141

The increased rate of exchange for the dollar resulted in United States' goods and services being (more/less) expensive to foreigners and thus led to (increased/decreased) foreign demand for United States' goods and services. Thus United States' exports ______ from what they would have been if the dollar had been lower.

more
decreased
decreased

13-142

When the rate of exchange for the dollar rose in the early 1980s, the rate of exchange for foreign currencies ______. This meant foreign goods and services became ______ to Americans. This led to ______ United States' demand for foreign goods and services and American imports ______.

fell
cheaper
increased
increased

13-143

When exports decrease and imports increase, net exports must ______. The result in 1990 was the *Balance on current account* of $______ billion.

decrease
$−92

13-144

The negative balance on the current account of $______ billion is not equal to the positive balance on the ______ account of $______ billion. The difference is the *Current and capital account balance* and equals $(+/−)______ billion. Insert this figure in the blank at the end of line (13).

$92
capital
$58
$−34

13-145

When the *Current and capital account balance* is positive, there is said to be a *Balance of payments surplus*. When the balance is negative, there is a *Balance of payments* ______. In 1990 there was a Balance of payments ______ of $______ billion.

deficit
deficit, $34

13-146

This $34 billion worth of foreign currencies below the amount needed to achieve a zero balance of the combined current and capital accounts was sold for ______ by the Federal Reserve Banks. Since this represents a(n) (increased/decreased) supply of dollars in the foreign exchange market, it constitutes an (in-/out-) payment. Therefore it is designated with a ______ sign.

dollars
decreased
in-
+

13-147

Therefore when the Federal Reserve Banks *sell* foreign currencies and thereby *decrease* their foreign exchange reserves, (upward/downward) pressure is exerted on the foreign exchange value of the dollar and this is designated with a ________ sign in the balance of payments. Since the Fed sold $________ billion worth of foreign currencies in 1990, the figure to be inserted is $(+/−)________ billion. Insert this figure in the blank at the end of line (14).

upward
+
$34
$+34

13-148

Adding the *Current and capital account balance* of $________ and the *Official reserves* figure of $________ finally gives us the balance of payments balance of $________ . Insert this figure in the blank on the last line of the table.

$−34
$+34
$0

13-149

That the balance of payments in 1990 should balance at $0 is not a fluke! If the Federal Reserve Banks in 1990 had not sold $________ billion worth of foreign currencies, so that the figure on line (14) of the table was $________ billion, then the figure on line (13) would have been $________ billion.

$34
$0
$0

13-150

Recall that the effect of the Federal Reserve Banks' selling $________ billion worth of foreign currencies for ____________ and thus ____________ the supply of ____________ on the foreign exchange markets was to put ________-ward pressure on the foreign exchange rate for the ____________ .

$34
dollars
decreasing, dollars
up
dollar

13-151

If this upward pressure had not occurred, the foreign exchange rate for the ____________ would have been ____________ and the *Balance on current account* would have been less (positive/negative) by $________ billion.

dollar, lower
negative
$34

13-152

With the *Balance on current account* less negative by $34 billion, its value

$−58 would have been $(+/−)________ billion. Adding this to the *Bal-*

$+58 *ance on capital account* of $(+/−)________ billion results in a *Cur-*

$0 *rent and capital account balance* of $________. With the change in

$0 *Official reserves* also $________, the sum of lines (13) and (14) of the

$0, as always table would have been $________ (as always/as a special case).

13-153

Recall from frame **13-127** and **13-128** that in 1990 the United States

creditor appeared to be a net international ________, as revealed in the

$+12 table by the *Net investment income* figure of $(+/−)________ billion.

13-154

The United States became a net international creditor through eco-

outflows from nomic policies that encouraged capital (inflows to/outflows from) the United States. While the United States was becoming a creditor

deficits nation it had capital account (surpluses/deficits) and current account

surpluses ________.

13-155

positive A net international creditor usually has (positive/negative) *Net investment income*, which can result in the *Balance on current account* being positive, or at least not negative, even when the *Balance on goods and*

negative *services* is ________.

13-156

For example, if in the United States' 1990 current account shown in frame **13-122** the *Balance on goods and services* had been $10 billion, with no change in *Net investment income* and in *Net transfers*, then the

$0 *Balance on current account* would have been $________ billion.

13-157

But if the Balance on goods and services had been $12 billion, the current account balance would have been $ + 2 billion, then (assuming no change in *Official reserves*) the *Balance on capital account* would have had to

$−2 be $________ billion.

13-158

out-, from
increasing
creditor

A *Balance on capital account* of $\$-2$ billion means that there would have been a net capital ________-flow (to/from) the United States and that the nation was thereby (increasing/decreasing) its position as a net international ____________ .

13-159

increased

If the United States had increased its position as a net international creditor in 1990 and in the following years, then *Net investment income* would have ____________ in subsequent years.

13-160

An increasing *Net investment income* permits:

(a) Negative net exports, without requiring that the deficit be financed by net capital inflows
(b) Increased capital outflows, creating an enhanced creditor position
(c) Both (a) and (b)

(c)

Which one? ________

13-161

deficit
unfavorable

Negative net exports or, in other words, a balance of trade ________ is spoken of as (favorable/unfavorable) because it is often associated with:

(a) Inability to compete internationally
(b) Unemployment
(c) Borrowing abroad; that is, "not paying one's way in the world"
(d) All of the above
(e) None of the above

(d)

Which one? ________

13-162

imports, exports

But from the point of view of consumers a balance of trade deficit is favorable because it means they are receiving more goods as (exports/imports) than they are forgoing as ____________ .

13-163

positive
in-

If the trade deficit is financed entirely by a (positive/negative) *Net investment income*, this implies that there are no net capital ________-flows.

13-164

With no net capital inflows, the United States' position as a net international ______________ would be maintained and the nation's positive *Net investment income* would not (increase/decrease).

creditor
decrease

13-165

However, if the *Balance on capital account* is positive, implying that there are net capital ________-flows simultaneously causing and financing the trade deficit, then the positive *Net investment income* will (increase/decrease) and eventually become ______________ .

in-
decrease, negative

13-166

When *Net investment income* has become negative, from then on a negative *Balance on goods and services* can only be financed by capital ________-flows and/or by decreasing the nation's *Official* ______________ : The nation becomes progressively more and more a net international ______________ .

in-
reserves
debtor

13-167

From 1984 to 1989 the Federal Reserve Board maintained real interest rates in the United States higher than in most of the world. The result was ________-flows of (dollars/foreign currencies) to buy (higher-/lower-) return United States bonds.

in-, foreign
currencies, higher-

13-168

These inflows of foreign currencies by 1986 had completely reversed the United States' status as the biggest net international (creditor/debtor), so that the United States is now the biggest net international ______________ .

creditor
debtor

13-169

To buy the higher-return United States' bonds the foreign currencies first had to be exchanged for ______________ . Thus the inflow of foreign currencies represents an increased (demand for/supply of) dollars causing the foreign exchange rate for dollars to ______________ .

dollars
demand for
rise

13-170

The higher exchange rate for the dollar leads to continuing current account ______________ because it simultaneously increases the price of American ______________ while decreasing the price of American ______________ .

deficits
exports
imports

13-171

Because the United States is now a net international debtor, *Net investment income* will eventually become ______________ . This means that the only way for consumers to enjoy more imports of goods and services than the nation exports is through yet more net capital _________-flows.

negative
in-

13-172

But increased net capital inflows mean increased net international ______________ and therefore increased _________-flows of *Net investment income*, creating a current account (surplus/deficit) *without* American consumers gaining more imports than the nation exports.

indebtedness, out-
deficit

13-173

It would be advantageous to American consumers to have again *on a sustainable basis* imports in excess of ______________ ; but for this to occur *Net investment income* must be ______________ . And this requires several years of massive net _________-flows of capital to match the massive _________-flows of recent years that led to the United States becoming a net international ______________ .

exports
positive
out-
in-
debtor

13-174

Massive net outflows of capital can be induced by the Federal Reserve Board bringing American real interest rates (below/above) the rate obtainable abroad.

below

13-175

Massive net outflows of capital mean that the *Balance on capital account* would be ______________ and that, therefore, the *Balance on current account* would be ______________ .

negative
positive

13-176

Net exports, therefore, would be (positive/negative) and this would be (favorable/unfavorable) to the American consumer. On the other hand, United States producers would find it ______________ and unemployment would ______________ .

positive
unfavorable
favorable
decrease

13-177

The return of the United States to a trade (surplus/deficit) or at least to a zero *Balance on goods and services* would (increase/decrease) the protectionist mood within the country and lead to (increased/decreased) barriers to trade.

surplus
decrease
decreased

13-178

favorable / more — This decrease in protectionism would be (favorable/unfavorable) to American consumers, for it would tend to permit the entry of (more/less) imports at ____________ prices.

lower

13-179 Review Frame

Look at this IBP of a Western European country.

Answer	Item		
	Merchandise exports	$17	
	Merchandise imports	16	
$+1	Balance of trade		$______
	Exports of services	3	
	Imports of services	1	
$+3	Balance on goods and services		______
	Net investment income	+3	
	Net transfers	−1	
$+5	Balance on current account		______
	Capital inflows	6	
	Capital outflows	8	
$−2	Balance on capital account		______
$+3	Current and capital account balance		______
$−3	Official reserves		______

Insert the correct figures in the six blanks on the right side of the table.

13-180 Review Frame

surplus — The country had a balance of payments ____________ .

13-181 Review Frame

From the figures in frame **13-179** it is apparent that the country is a net

exporter, creditor — (exporter/importer) of capital and is a net international ____________ .

13-182 Review Frame

increased — It is also apparent the country (increased/decreased) its *Official reserves*

$3, down- — by ________ billion and thereby acted to put (up-/down-)ward pressure on the foreign exchange rate for its currency.

13-183 Review Frame

If the country had not acted to absorb the $3 billion payments surplus in its *Official reserves* by buying them with its own currency, the excess

supply of, up- — (supply of/demand for) foreign currency would have put (up-/down-)ward pressure on the foreign exchange rate for its currency un-

decreased, $3 — til net exports of goods and services (increased/decreased) by $______ billion. The *Current and capital account balance* then would have be-

$0 — come ________ billion.

13-184 Review Frame

Exports and other transactions that increase the supply of foreign exchange demanding a country's own currency in foreign exchange mar-

up- kets put ________-ward pressure on the rate of exchange for its cur-

\+ rency and are shown as a (+/−) figure, while imports and other transactions that increase the supply of the country's own currency in foreign

downward exchange markets and put __________ pressure on its rate of

— exchange are shown as a ________ figure.

13-185 Review Frame

When a country increases its *Official reserves*, this is shown in the bal-

— ance of payments as a ________ figure because to increase these re-

its own currency serves the central bank has to buy them with ______________ .

increased Thus its supply in the foreign exchange markets is __________ and

down- this puts __________-ward pressure on its rate of exchange.

13-186 Review Frame

When imports are greater than exports, a nation has a balance of trade

deficit, − __________ . This is indicated by a (+/−) and means that the

less nation has earned (more/less) foreign exchange than it has spent.

13-187 Review Frame

surplus If a nation had a balance of trade of $ + 6, it had a trade __________

exports, imports and its __________ were greater than its ______________ .

13-188 Review Frame

If the figure given for *Official reserves* in the balance of payments is $ + 7

payments billion, this means the country had a balance of ______________

deficit, $7 (surplus/deficit) of $________ billion.

Now take the Review Test for Section 13 at the back of the book.

Review Tests

SECTION 1: GRAPHS AND THEIR MEANING

1. On the graph below:

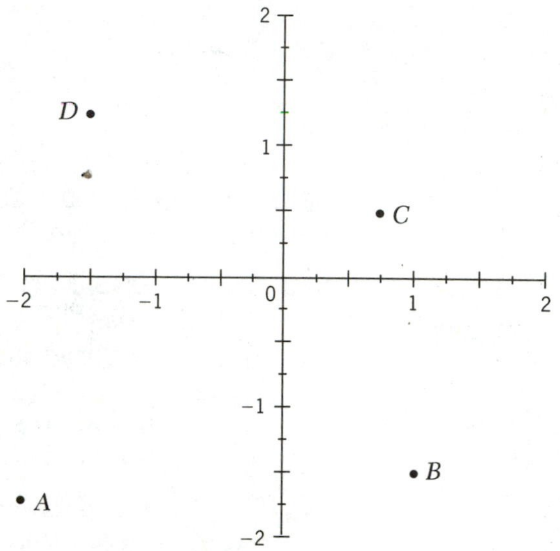

(a) Point A is located at ______________________

(b) Point B is located at ______________________

(c) Point C is located at ______________________

(d) Point D is located at ______________________

2. Locate each of the following points on the graph below.
   (a) $-2, +1$
   (b) $+1, -2$
   (c) $-1, -1$
   (d) $+1, +1$

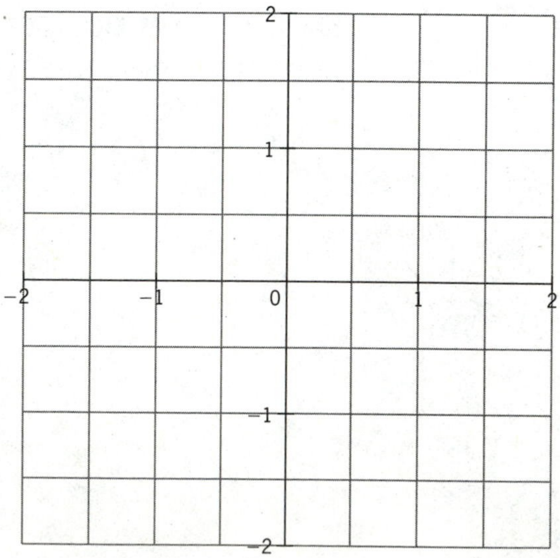

3. What does it mean to say that the relation between two variables is:

   (a) direct (or positive)? ____

   ____

   ____

   (b) inverse (or negative)? ____

   ____

   ____

4. What kind of a curve shows:

   (a) a direct relation between two variables? ________________________

   (b) an inverse relation between two variables? ________________________

5. Explain how you measure the slope of a straight line between two points. ____

   ____

   ____

6. When:

   (a) does a curve have a positive slope and what is the relation between the two variables? ________________________

   (b) does a curve have a negative slope and what is the relation between the two variables? ________________________

7. Explain how you measure the slope of a nonlinear line at a point on the curve.

   ____

   ____

   ____

   ____

8. On the graph below:

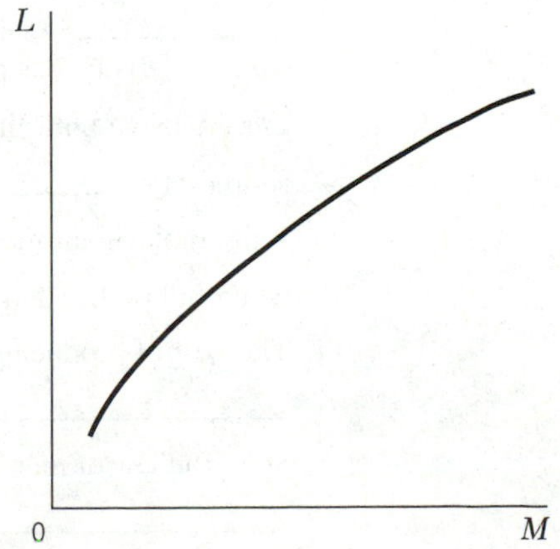

(a) the relation between L and M is ________________ .

(b) when M increases, L ____________ .

(c) the slope of the curve ____________ as M increases.

9. On the graph that follows:

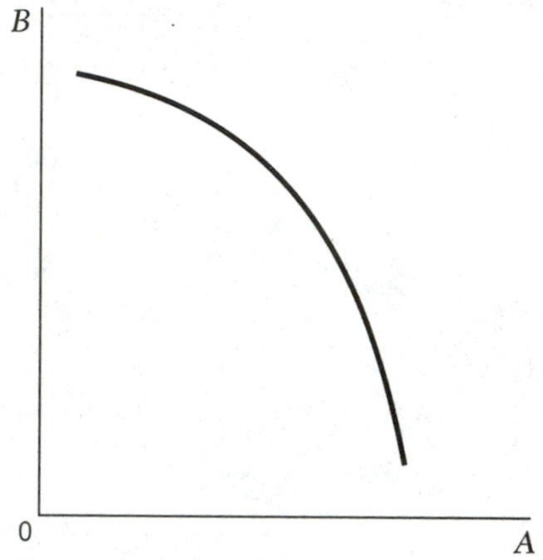

(a) the relation between A and B is ________________ .

(b) when A increases, B ____________ .

(c) the slope of the curve ____________ as A increases.

10. What does it mean when:

(a) the slope of the curve is zero at a point? ____________

____

____

(b) the slope of the curve is infinity at a point? ____________

____

SECTION 2: SCARCITY

1. Economics is the study of how societies use their ____________ ____________ to produce the ____________ and ____________ to satisfy ____________ human ____________ .

2. To be as efficient as possible at satisfying human wants an economy must achieve both the ____________ ____________ of its resources and ____________ ____________ .

3. Full employment means * ________________________ while full production means * ________________________ .

4. The cost of producing any good or service is * ____________ ____ .

5. State the law of increasing opportunity costs. * ____________ ____

Why do costs increase? * ______________________________

____

____

6. If an economy were producing less than it is capable of producing it could expand its production of goods and services by eliminating the ______________ and the ______________ of resources in the economy. The cost to the economy of this increased production would be ______________________________ .
7. To increase the amounts of goods and services it is capable of producing the economy must either * ______________________ or * ______________________________ . The cost to the economy of expanding its output in this way is ______________ .
8. What are the five Fundamental Economic Questions every society must answer?
   (a) ______________________________
   (b) ______________________________
   (c) ______________________________
   (d) ______________________________
   (e) ______________________________
9. Deciding:
   (a) what to produce means * ______________________
   ______________________________ .
   (b) how to produce means * ______________________
   ______________________________ .
   (c) for whom to produce means * ______________________
   ______________________________ .
10. When is an economy flexible? ______________________

    ____
11. In the circular flow diagram we see that:
    (a) resources flow from * ______________ to * ______________ .
    (b) goods and services flow from * ______________ to * ______________ .
    (c) there is also a flow of monies from firms to households to pay for * ______________ ; and that these monies are the ______________ of firms and the ______________ of households.
    (d) there is another flow of monies from households to firms to pay for ______________ ; and that these monies are the ______________ of firms and the ______________ of households.

(e) the flow of resources and goods and services is the ______________ flow and that the other flow is the ______________ flow.

(f) the dual role of

(1) business firms is to ______________ resources and ______________ goods and services.

(2) households is to ______________ resources and ______________ goods and services.

12. There are two major types of markets in the economy.

(a) There are ______________ markets and ______________ markets.

(b) In the resource markets business firms are ______________ and households are ______________.

(c) In the product markets business firms are ______________ and households are ______________.

SECTION 3: FUNDAMENTALS OF DEMAND AND SUPPLY

1. Define demand. ______________________________

____

2. What is the Law of Supply? ______________________________

____

3. When the price of any commodity increases, there will be a:
(a) decrease in the demand for the commodity
(b) decrease in the quantity demanded of the commodity

4. What is an increase in supply? ______________________________

____

5. How do you define a decrease in demand? ______________________________

____

6. Below are the demand and supply schedules for a commodity.

Quantity demanded (lbs.)	Price	Quantity supplied (lbs.)
2	$100	8
4	90	7
6	80	6
8	70	5
10	60	4
12	50	3
14	40	2
16	30	1

(a) The equilibrium price of this commodity is $__________.

(b) The equilibrium quantity of the commodity is __________ pounds.

7. Using the schedules in question 6:
   (a) When the price of the commodity is $100, there is a (shortage/surplus) of the commodity that amounts to 6 pounds.
   (b) If the price of the commodity were $40, there would be a 12-pound ________ of the commodity.
8. When the price of the commodity is:
   (a) $50, (buyers/sellers) will bid its price (up/down).
   (b) $90, (buyers/sellers) will bid the price (up/down).
9. What will be the effect of each of the following on the equilibrium price and the equilibrium quantity?

	Effect on	
	Price	Quantity
(a) An increase in demand	________	________
(b) An increase in supply	________	________
(c) A decrease in demand	________	________
(d) A decrease in supply	________	________

10. What will be the effect of each of the following on the equilibrium price and the equilibrium quantity?

	Effect on	
	Price	Quantity
(a) An increase in both demand and supply	________	________
(b) A decrease in demand and an increase in supply	________	________
(c) A decrease in both demand and supply	________	________
(d) An increase in demand and a decrease in supply	________	________

SECTION 4: NATIONAL INCOME ACCOUNTING

1. At the top of the next page are some national income accounting figures. Compute each of the following:
   (a) Net exports: $________
   (b) Net private domestic investment: $________
   (c) Gross national product: $________
   (d) Gross domestic product: $________
   (e) Net domestic product: $________
   (f) National income: $________
   (g) Personal income: $________

(h) Disposable income: $________

(i) Personal saving: $________

Consumption of fixed capital	$ 49
Imports	4
Rents	26
Personal taxes	98
Dividends	21
Gross private domestic investment	96
Proprietors' income	41
Indirect business taxes	26
Personal consumption expenditures	387
Exports	12
Compensation of employees	402
Corporate income taxes	22
Interest	27
Transfer payments	29
Government purchases	142
Net American income earned abroad	5
Undistributed corporate profits	24
Social security contributions	10

2. An economy's gross domestic product and the price index in three different years are as follows:

Year	GDP	Price index	Real (adjusted) GDP
1901	$180	120	$________
1902	200	100	________
1903	275	110	________

(a) In the spaces provided above, compute the real or adjusted GDP in each year.

(b) Which of the three years is the base year? ________

(c) $250 is the real GDP in the year ________ expressed in terms of the prices paid in the year ________.

(d) Between which pair of years was there inflation? ________ and ________ Deflation? ________ and ________

3. Define the gross domestic product. ____

____

4. The two approaches that are used to measure the GDP are called the ________ approach and the ________ approach.

5. The income *earned* by those who provide the economy with resources is called ________ income.

6. The two nonincome charges are ________________ and ________________.

7. Income received before personal taxes are paid is (personal/disposable) income. The income left after the payment of personal taxes is ______________ income.
8. Profits in the economy are the sum of four items. These four items are ______________, ______________, ______________, and ______________.
9. Including the values of intermediate goods in the gross domestic product is called ______________.
10. The compensation of employees is the sum of the following two items: ______________ ______________ and ______________.

SECTION 5: MACROECONOMIC ANALYSIS: AGGREGATE DEMAND AND AGGREGATE SUPPLY

1. Aggregate demand and aggregate supply determine the ______________ ______________ and the ______________ ______________ of the economy.
2. The aggregate-demand curve slopes ______________-ward because of the ______________-______________ effect, the ______________-______________ effect, and the ______________-______________ effect.
3. When the price level *falls*:
   (a) The demand for money ______________ and this ______________ the rate of interest and tends to ______________ the expenditures which are sensitive to the rate of interest.
   (b) Those holding assets the money value of which is fixed find that the purchasing power of these assets has ______________ and tend to ______________ their expenditures for final goods and services;
   (c) American goods become relatively ______________ to foreigners and imports become relatively ______________ to Americans. Therefore net exports ______________.
4. There are ______________ ranges along the aggregate-supply curve.
   (a) When the economy is in a severe recession or depression the economy is producing in the ______________ range and the aggregate-supply curve is ______________.
   (b) When the economy is producing its full-employment real GDP the economy is operating in the ______________ range and the aggregate-supply curve is ______________.

(c) Between these two ranges the economy is producing in the ________________ range and the aggregate-supply curve is ____________.

5. Were aggregate-demand to *increase* and the economy continued to operate:
   (a) in the Keynesian range, the increase in demand would ____________ the real GDP and * ________________ the price level;
   (b) in the intermediate range, the real GDP would ____________ and the price level would ____________;
   (c) in the classical range the real GDP would * ______________ and the price level would ____________.
6. A change in the price level causes (movement along/shift of) the AD curve.
7. AD can be affected in four ways as follows:
   (i) movement down AD curve
   (ii) movement up AD curve
   (iii) AD curve shifts to right
   (iv) AD curve shifts to left
   (v) Effect not certain

   State the effect of the following on AD by filling in each time one of the above:
   (a) A decrease in consumer real wealth (through, for example, stock market loss). ____________________
   (b) Expectation of increase in real income. ____________________
   (c) Consumers become heavily indebted. ____________________
   (d) A decrease in personal taxes. ____________________
   (e) An increase in interest rates. ____________________
   (f) A decreased expectation of profit. ____________________
   (g) An increase in business taxes. ____________________
   (h) Improved technology. ____________________
   (i) Excess factory capacity. ____________________
   (j) Government increases spending and taxes simultaneous with increase in interest rates. ____________________
   (k) Foreigners decrease buying of American exports because of increase in American price level.

   ____
   (l) Foreigners decrease buying of American exports because of increase in exchange rate for the dollar caused by higher American real interest rates.

   ____
8. AS can be affected in four ways as follows:
   (i) movement up AS curve
   (ii) movement down AS curve

(iii) AS curve shifts to right
(iv) AS curve shifts to left
State the effect of the following on AS by filling in each time one of the above:

(a) An increase in the price level. ______________

(b) An increase in AD. ______________

(c) A decrease in input prices. ______________

(d) An increase in productivity. ______________

(e) An increase in business taxes. ______________

(f) A decrease in subsidies to business. ______________

(g) A decrease in government regulation. ______________

9. Inflation is * ______________
and has two basic causes.

(a) It may result from a(n) __________ in aggregate demand or a(n) __________ in aggregate supply.

(b) The former kind of inflation is called __________-__________ inflation and the later type of inflation is called __________-__________ inflation.

10. Stagflation is* ______________,
the result of* ______________.

11. A *decrease* in aggregate supply will __________ real GDP, __________ unemployment, and __________ the price level.

SECTION 6: NATIONAL INCOME ANALYSIS

1. The four components of aggregate expenditures are __________, __________, __________, and __________.
2. Here is a consumption schedule.

Gross domestic product = disposable income	Consumption
$200	$200
250	240
300	280
350	320
400	360
450	400
500	440
550	480

(a) When the gross domestic product is $250, saving is equal to $__________ and the average propensity to consume is equal to $__________.

(b) Throughout the schedule the marginal propensity to consume is equal to ________ and the marginal propensity to save is equal to ________ .

(c) The multiplier has a value of ________ .

3. Assume the consumption schedule for an economy is the one given in question 2. Assume also that there is no government spending in the economy and that the governments collect no taxes.

(a) When net investment is $30, the equilibrium gross domestic product is equal to $________ .

(b) If net investment were to increase by $2, the equilibrium gross domestic product would (increase/decrease) by $________ .

4. Here is another consumption schedule.

GDP = DI	Consumption
$200	$180
250	225
300	270
350	315
400	360
450	405
500	450
550	495

(a) When no taxes are collected in this economy, when gross investment is $15, and when government purchases are $35, the equilibrium gross domestic product is equal to $________ .

(b) Suppose government purchases were to decrease from $35 to $25. The equilibrium gross domestic product would (rise/fall) by $________ .

(c) If governments decide to collect $30 in taxes at every level of gross domestic product, consumption at every gross domestic product will (increase/decrease) by $________ and saving at every gross domestic product will (increase/decrease) by $________ .

5. Assume that with no taxes the consumption schedule for the economy would be the one given in question 4. Gross investment is $24, government purchases are $38, and net taxes at every level of gross domestic product are $30.

(a) The equilibrium gross domestic product will be $________ .

(b) If net taxes should increase from $30 to $38, the equilibrium gross domestic product would ________________ by $________ .

(c) If both net taxes and government purchases decreased by $8, the equilibrium gross domestic product would (increase/decrease) by $________ .

(d) If net taxes were to increase by $5 and government purchases were to increase by $7, the equilibrium gross domestic product would (increase/decrease) by $________ .

6. Explain in your own words:
   (a) Why the gross domestic product actually produced in an economy tends to move toward the equilibrium gross domestic product. ____________________
   ____
   ____
   ____
   (b) Why a change in gross investment, or net exports, or government purchases has a multiplier effect upon the equilibrium gross domestic product. ____________________
   ____
   ____
   ____
   ____
7. Exports (add to/subtract from) aggregate expenditures and imports ____________ aggregate expenditures.
8. Exports are assumed to (increase/decrease/not change) as gross domestic product increases; imports are assumed to ____________ as gross domestic product increases; net exports are assumed to ____________ as gross domestic product increases.
9. The open-economy multiplier has a (higher/lower) value than the closed-economy multiplier because (exports/imports) are a (subtraction from/addition to) the spending stream.
10. The open economy multiplier = ____________ .
11. Assume the marginal propensity to consume is 0.8 and the equilibrium gross domestic product is $400.
    (a) To raise the equilibrium gross domestic product to $500 governments might either ____________ net taxes by $________ , or ____________ their purchases by $________ .
    (b) To lower the equilibrium gross domestic product to $350 governments may either ____________ net taxes by $________ , or ____________ their purchases by $________ .
    (c) To raise the equilibrium gross domestic product to $440 governments might ____________ both net taxes and government purchases by $________ .
12. A business firm will purchase capital goods when it (knows/expects) that this investment will ____________ its profits.
13. A decrease in the rate of interest in the economy will tend to (increase/decrease) the amount of gross investment in the economy.

14. When investment is autonomous, gross investment will ______________ when the gross domestic product increases. And when investment is induced, gross investment will ________ when the gross domestic product decreases.

SECTION 7: MONEY AND BANKING; FISCAL AND MONETARY POLICY

1. Define the money supply. ______________________________

____

____

2. The two demands for money are the __________ demand and the __________ demand.

   (a) The former demand is ______________ related to the ______________________________________.

   (b) The latter demand is ______________ related to the ______________________________________.

3. The equilibrium rate of interest in the economy is the rate at which ____

____

____

   (a) An increase in the money supply will __________ the rate of interest and __________ total spending in the economy.

   (b) An increase in the price level will __________ the rate of interest.

   (c) A decrease in the *real* GDP level will __________ the rate of interest.

4. In a commercial bank's balance sheet:

   (a) The bank's reserves are its ______________ and its ______________________________________.

   (b) The bank's other assets are chiefly its ______________ and ______________________________________.

   (c) The bank's net worth is equal to ______________________.

   (d) The bank's principal liability is its ______________________.

5. Here is the balance sheet of a commercial bank.

Assets		Liabilities and net worth	
Reserves	$300	Demand deposits	$900
Other assets	700	Net worth	100

Assume the reserve ratio is 25 percent.

(a) The bank's required reserves are $________ .

(b) The bank has excess reserves of $________ .

6. Commercial banks:

(a) create money when they ____

(b) destroy money when they ____

7. Assume that a commercial bank has the following balance sheet:

Assets		**Liabilities and net worth**	
Reserves	$225	Demand deposits	$1,000
Other assets	875	Net worth	100

(a) When the reserve ratio is 20 percent, it can safely increase the money supply by $________ .

(b) When the reserve ratio is 30 percent, it must reduce the money supply by $________ .

8. A commercial bank tends to limit the new loans it makes (or securities it buys) to an amount equal to its excess reserves because ____ .

9. Here is a consolidated balance sheet for the entire commercial banking system.

Assets		**Liabilities and net worth**	
Reserves	$ 6,500	Demand deposits	$30,000
Other assets	24,000	Net worth	500

(a) If the reserve ratio is 20 percent, the banking system is able to expand the money supply by $________ .

(b) When the reserve ratio is 25 percent, the banking system must contract the money supply by $________ .

(c) The size of the monetary multiplier can be found by ____

10. The three controls the Federal Reserve Banks can employ to change the money supply are ________________________, ________________________, and ________________________ .

11. To eliminate inflationary pressures the Federal Reserve Banks may ________ the reserve ratio, ________ the discount rate, or ________ government securities in the open market.

12. During periods of unemployment in the economy the Fed tends to __________ the reserve ratio, to __________ the discount rate, and to __________ government securities in the open market.
13. When the economy is operating along the intermediate range of the aggregate-supply curve and aggregate demand *decreases*:
    (a) If prices are flexible downward, both the real GDP and the price level will __________ ;
    (b) But if prices are inflexible downward, the real GDP will __________ and unemployment in the economy will __________ and the price level will ° __________ .
14. The Federal government is able to increase aggregate demand by ° __________

    ____
15. Were the economy operating in the intermediate range of the aggregate-supply curve:
    (a) Government could reduce unemployment by __________ aggregate demand, but this would __________ the price level.
    (b) Government could prevent further rises in the price level by __________ aggregate demand, but this would __________ unemployment.
16. Government may increase the real GDP and decrease unemployment without increasing the price level by increasing aggregate demand only when the economy is producing in the __________ range; and it may prevent rises in the price level without decreasing the real GDP and increasing unemployment only when the economy is producing in the __________ range.
17. To reduce or eliminate stagflation in the economy the Federal government must take the measures that will ° __________ . These measures are called __________-__________ policies.
18. The supply-side policies government might employ to increase the real GDP and to decrease unemployment are policies which ° __________ .

SECTION 8: PRICE ELASTICITY AND MARGINAL REVENUE

1. Following are a demand and a supply schedule.

Quantity demanded (tons)	Price	Quantity supplied (tons)
200	$1.80	2,200
600	1.40	1,800
1,000	1.00	1,400
1,400	.60	1,000
1,800	.20	600

(a) Between 20 cents and 60 cents, the coefficient of the elasticity of demand is equal to ______________ .

(b) Between \$1.40 and \$1.80, the coefficient of the elasticity of supply is equal to ______________ .

2. When demand is price elastic:

   (a) The elasticity coefficient is ______________ 1.

   (b) The percentage change in quantity demanded is ______________ the percentage change in price.

   (c) Total receipts of sellers will ______________ when the price of the commodity falls.

3. Suppose supply is price inelastic.

   (a) The elasticity coefficient will be ______________ 1.

   (b) The percentage change in quantity supplied will be ______________ the percentage change in price.

   (c) The total receipts of sellers will ______________ when the price of the commodity falls.

4. Define:

   (a) An imperfectly competitive seller: ______________________________

   ____

   (b) A perfectly competitive seller: ______________________________

   ____

5. What is marginal revenue? ______________________________

   ____

6. When demand is:

   (a) price elastic, marginal revenue is ______________ zero.

   (b) price inelastic, marginal revenue is ______________ zero.

   (c) unit elastic, marginal revenue is ______________ zero.

7. An imperfectly competitive seller finds that:

   (a) the demand for the product it produces is (<u>perfectly elastic/less than perfectly elastic</u>);

   (b) both the price it receives and marginal revenue ______________ when it sells more of its product;

   (c) marginal revenue is ______________ the price it receives for its product.

8. A perfectly competitive seller finds that:

   (a) the demand for the product it produces is ______________ price elastic;

   (b) both the price it receives and marginal revenue ______________ when it sells more of its product;

   (c) marginal revenue is ______________ the price it receives for its product.

SECTION 9: THE COSTS OF PRODUCTION

1. In the short run some of the resources a firm employs and some of its costs are ______________ and the rest are ______________. But in the long run all of the resources it employs and all of its costs are ______________.

2. What is a cost schedule? ____

____

3. As a firm increases its output in the short run its:

   (a) Total fixed cost will ______________.

   (b) Total variable cost will at first ______________ by amounts that become (larger/smaller) and then ______________ by amounts that become (larger/smaller).

   (c) Total costs will at first ______________________ and thereafter ______________________.

4. Define:

   (a) Marginal cost. ____

   ____

   (b) Marginal product. ____

   ____

5. State the Law of Diminishing Returns. ______________________________

____

____

6. Explain:

   (a) What happens to marginal cost in the short run as output increases? ____.

   (b) Why does marginal cost change in this way?

   ____.

7. How can you compute each of the following at any output?

   (a) Average fixed cost. ____

   (b) Average variable cost. ____

   (c) Average total cost: either divide ______________ by ______________; or add ______________ and ______________.

8. When the firm increases its output in the short run:

   (a) Average fixed cost ______________.

   (b) Average variable cost and average total cost ______________

   ____.

9. At the output at which average variable cost is a minimum, ______________ cost and ______________ cost are equal. And

at the output at which average total cost is at a minimum, ______________ cost and ______________ cost are equal.

10. As a firm increases its output in the long run, long-run average total cost at first ______________ because of the ______________ , and then ______________ because of the ______________ .
11. The long-run average total cost of producing any output is equal to the ______________ short-run average (fixed/variable/total)cost of producing that output.
12. In the long run a firm has no ______________ resources and no ______________ costs.

SECTION 10: PRODUCT PRICE AND OUTPUT: PURE COMPETITION

1. To maximize its total profit (or minimize its total loss) in the short run every firm will produce an output at which the ______________ and the ______________ of the last unit of the product produced are equal—provided that the price at which the firm can sell this output is greater than or equal to the ______________ cost of producing it.
2. The individual perfectly competitive firm finds that the marginal revenue from the sale of an additional unit of its product is always equal to ________________________ . As a result, the firm's supply schedule in the short run is its ________________ ________________________ .
3. The supply of the product produced by a perfectly competitive industry in the short run is found by ________________________ ____________ . The equilibrium market price of this product will be the price at which the ______________ and the ______________ are equal.
4. When the short-run equilibrium market price is greater than the minimum average total cost, the firm will have an economic (profit/loss); when it is less than the minimum average total cost, the firm will have an economic (profit/loss); and when it is less than the minimum average variable cost, the firm will produce ____________ output and suffer an economic loss equal to its ____________ .
5. During the short run firms (can/cannot) enter and leave the perfectly competitive industry. In the long run firms will enter the industry when firms already in the industry are * ________________________ and will leave the industry when they are * ________________________________ .
6. When the perfectly competitive industry is in long-run equilibrium, all firms in the industry are earning ______________ economic prof-

its and have ______________ economic losses. In addition, the price of the product will equal the ______________ of producing it; the long-run average cost of producing the product will equal the ______________ long-run average cost; and the price of the product will also equal the ______________ of the last unit of the product produced.

SECTION 11: PRODUCT PRICE AND OUTPUT: PURE MONOPOLY

1. Here are the short-run cost, demand, and marginal-revenue schedules facing a pure monopolist.

Output	Average total cost	Marginal cost	Price	Marginal revenue
0			$110	
1	$50	$ 50	100	$100
2	35	20	90	80
3	33⅓	30	80	60
4	35	40	70	40
5	40	60	60	20
6	50	100	50	0

The monopolist will produce ______________ units of its product and charge a price of $______________ for it. It will have a total revenue of $______________ and a total economic (profit/loss) of $__________ .

2. In the long run the typical monopolist charges a price which is ______________ the long-run average total cost of producing its product, produces an output at which the long-run average total cost is ______________ the minimum long-run average total cost, and charges a price which is ______________ the marginal cost of the last unit of the product produced.

SECTION 12: THE PRICES AND EMPLOYMENT OF RESOURCES

1. Define:

   (a) Marginal revenue product. ______________________________

   ____

   (b) Marginal resource cost. ______________________________

   ____

2. If any firm wishes to maximize its total profit (or minimize total loss), what amount of a variable resource will it employ? ______________

____

3. As a firm increases its employment of a variable resource, the marginal revenue product of the resource will eventually ______________ .

4. A firm that employs a variable resource in a perfectly competitive market finds that as it increases its employment of the resource, the marginal resource cost ______________ , the marginal resource cost is equal to ______________ , and its demand schedule for the resource is its ______________ schedule for the resource.

5. What is:
   (a) The total demand for a resource which is employed in a perfectly competitive market? ______________
   ____
   (b) The market price of that resource? ______________
   ____

6. A monopsonist finds that as it increases the amount of a variable resource it employs, the marginal resource cost of that resource ______________ .

7. Here are the marginal-revenue-product, supply, and marginal-resource-cost schedules facing a monopsonist.

Amount of variable resource	Marginal revenue product	Resource price	Marginal resource cost
0		$10	
1	$60	20	$ 20
2	70	30	40
3	60	40	60
4	50	50	80
5	40	60	100

   (a) What amount of this variable resource will the monopsonist employ? ______________
   (b) What price will it pay for each unit of the resource? $______________

8. When has a firm employed several variable resources in the least-cost combination? ______________

9. When has a firm employed variable resources in the profit-maximization combination? ______________
____

SECTION 13: INTERNATIONAL TRADE

1. Suppose two countries, Haven and Diablo, are both capable of producing only two commodities: pails and brooms. Their production possibilities follow.

Haven						
Pails	40	30	20	10	0	
Brooms	0	20	40	60	80	
Diablo						
Pails	100	80	60	40	20	0
Brooms	0	60	120	180	240	300

(a) Haven has a comparative advantage in the production of ______________ and Diablo in the production of ______________.

(b) ______________ will tend to specialize in the production of pails and ______________ in the production of brooms.

(c) The terms of trade will be ______________________________

____

2. How do nations benefit if they specialize in the production of those commodities in which they have a comparative advantage?:

____

____

3. Define:

(a) Foreign exchange. ______________________________

____

(b) The rate of exchange. ______________________________

____

4. An American importer of goods from Japan is a (demander/supplier) of dollars and a (demander/supplier) of yen. If the rate of exchange for the yen is ¾ cent ($0.0075), the rate of exchange for the dollar is ______________ yen.

5. The four principal groups of suppliers of American dollars and demanders of Mexican pesos are ______________________________

______________________________,

______________________________,

and ______________________________.

6. As the rate of exchange for the French franc increases, the quantity of francs demanded by Americans ______________________________ and the quantity of francs supplied by the French ______________. The actual rate of exchange for the franc will tend to be the rate at which ______________________________.

7. In the current account of a nation's international balance of payments the two kinds of exports and imports are ______________ and ______________.

8. A nation has a balance of trade surplus when its ______________________ and a balance of trade deficit when its ______________________.
9. To find a nation's balance of payments add the following three items to its balance on goods and services: ____________, ____________, and ____________.
10. A nation has a balance of payments:
    (a) surplus when ______________________.
    (b) deficit when ______________________.
11. A nation with a balance of payments surplus or deficit balances the surplus or deficit by ______________________.

ANSWERS TO REVIEW TESTS

Section 1

1. (a) −2, −1¾; (b) 1, −1½; (c) ¾, ½; (d) −1½, 1¼
2.

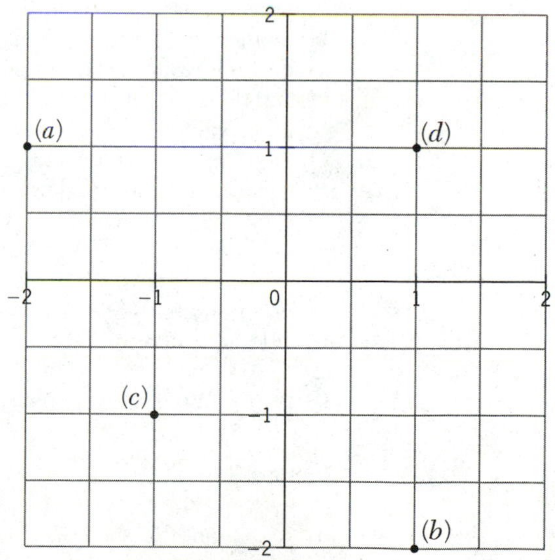

3. (a) they increase and decrease together (when one increases the other increases and vice versa); (b) when one increases the other decreases and vice versa.
4. (a) one that slopes upward; (b) one that slopes downward
5. Divide the vertical difference between the two points by the horizontal difference.
6. (a) when as one variable increases, the other variable increases, direct; (b) when as one variable increases, the other variable decreases, inverse

7. Draw a straight line tangent to the nonlinear line at the point and then measure the slope of the straight line.
8. (a) positive (direct); (b) increases; (c) decreases
9. (a) negative (inverse); (b) decreases; (c) increases
10. (a) the curve is horizontal at that point; (b) the curve is vertical at that point

Section 2

1. scarce resources, goods, services, unlimited, wants
2. full employment, full production
3. all the economy's available resources are employed, the most efficient methods of production are employed
4. the amount of other goods that must be sacrificed or done without
5. As the production of a good or service increases, the opportunity cost of producing it increases. Because as more resources are employed to produce a good or service the additional output that results from the employment of additional units of the resource will decrease. This occurs because the additional resources are employed along with *fixed* quantities of other resources.
6. unemployment, underemployment (either order), zero
7. obtain additional resources, improve its technology (either order), zero
8. (a) what to produce; (b) how to produce it; (c) for whom to produce; (d) what to do to ensure full employment of resources; (e) how to provide for flexibility in the economy (any order)
9. (a) deciding what combination of goods and services to produce; (b) deciding what resources are more efficient in producing a product and the right amount of resources needed to produce it; (c) deciding how to divide up or distribute the total output of the economy among the people of the economy
10. When it is able to adjust its output to take account of changes in wants, changes in the resources available, and in technology.
11. (a) households, business firms; (b) business firms, households; (c) resources, costs, incomes; (d) goods and services, receipts, expenditures; (e) real, money; (f) (1) employ, produce; (2) provide, use
12. (a) product, resource (either order); (b) demanders (buyers), suppliers (sellers); (c) suppliers (sellers), demanders (buyers)

Section 3

1. A schedule of the quantities demanded at various prices during a specific period of time.
2. As price increases, the quantity supplied increases and vice versa.
3. (b) decrease in the quantity demanded of the commodity
4. An increase in the quantities supplied at each price in the supply schedule.
5. A decrease in the quantities demanded at each price in the demand schedule.
6. (a) $80; (b) 6 pounds
7. (a) surplus; (b) shortage
8. (a) buyers, up; (b) sellers, down

9. (a) increase, increase; (b) decrease, increase; (c) decrease, decrease; (d) increase, decrease
10. (a) indeterminate, increase; (b) decrease, indeterminate; (c) indeterminate, decrease; (d) increase, indeterminate

Section 4

1. (a) $8; (b) $47; (c) $638; (d) $633; (e) $584; (f) $563; (g) $536; (h) $438; (i) $51
2. (a) $150, $200, $250; (b) 1902; (c) 1903, 1902; (d) 1902, 1903, 1901, 1902
3. The market value of all the final goods and services produced in the economy during a year.
4. expenditures, income (either order)
5. national
6. consumption of fixed capital (depreciation), indirect business taxes (either order)
7. personal, disposable
8. proprietors' income, dividends, corporate income taxes, undistributed corporate profits (any order)
9. double counting
10. wages and salaries, wage and salary supplements

Section 5

1. real GDP, price level (either order)
2. down, wealth, interest-rate, foreign-purchases (any order)
3. (a) decreases, decreases, increase; (b) increased, increase; (c) cheaper, more expensive, increase
4. 3; (a) Keynesian, horizontal; (b) classical, vertical; (c) intermediate, upsloping
5. (a) increase, not affect; (b) rise, rise; (c) not be affected, rise
6. movement along
7. (a) AD curve shifts to left; (b) AD curve shifts to right; (c) AD curve shifts to left; (d) AD curve shifts to right; (e) AD curve shifts to left; (f) AD curve shifts to left; (g) AD curve shifts to left; (h) AD curve shifts to right; (i) AD curve shifts to left; (j) effect not certain; (k) movement up AD curve; (l) AD curve shifts to left
8. (a) movement up AS curve; (b) movement up AS curve; (c) AS curve shifts to right; (d) AS curve shifts to right; (e) AS curve shifts to left; (f) AS curve shifts to left; (g) AS curve shifts to right
9. a rise in the price level; (a) increase, decrease; (b) demand-pull, cost-push
10. a rise in the price level accompanied by a fall in real GDP (a rise in unemployment), a decrease in aggregate supply
11. decrease, increase, increase

Section 6

1. consumption, gross investment, government purchases, net exports (any order)
2. (a) $10, 0.96 (96%); (b) 0.8 (80%), 0.2 (20%); (c) 5

3. (a) $350; (b) increase, $10
4. (a) $500; (b) fall, $100; (c) decrease, $27, decrease, $3
5. (a) $350; (b) decrease, $72; (c) decrease, $8; (d) increase, $25
6. (a) At GDPs above the equilibrium GDP, firms find that they can't sell all they produce and reduce the GDP; at GDPs below the equilibrium GDP, they find that they can sell more than they are producing and expand the GDP. (b) The change in gross investment or government purchases changes the GDP, which causes consumption to change, which in turn brings about still further changes in the GDP and consumption.
7. add to, subtract from
8. not change, increase, decrease
9. lower, imports, subtraction from
10. 1/MPS + MPM
11. (a) decrease, $25, increase, $20; (b) increase, $12.50, decrease, $10; (c) increase, $40
12. expects, increase
13. increase
14. not change, decrease

Section 7

1. The currency and checkable deposits not owned by depository institutions, the Federal government, or the Federal Reserve Banks.
2. transactions, asset; (a) directly, nominal GDP; (b) inversely, rate of interest
3. the money supply equals the total quantity of money demanded (for asset and transaction purposes); (a) lower, increase; (b) increase; (c) decrease
4. (a) vault cash (currency), deposits at the Federal Reserve Bank (either order); (b) loans, securities (either order); (c) its assets minus its liabilities; (d) demand deposits
5. (a) $225; (b) $75
6. (a) make new loans or buy securities from the public; (b) fail to make new loans as old loans are repaid or sell securities to the public
7. (a) $25; (b) $75
8. It fears the loss of reserves and the negative excess reserves that result when it lends more than this.
9. (a) $2,500; (b) $4,000; (c) finding the reciprocal of the reserve ratio (dividing 1 by the reserve ratio)
10. changing the reserve ratio, changing the discount rate, open-market operations (any order)
11. increase, increase, sell
12. decrease, decrease, buy
13. (fall); (b) fall, rise, remain constant
14. increasing its purchases, decreasing its net tax collections, or increasing the money supply
15. (a) increasing, raise; (b) decreasing; increase
16. Keynesian, classical
17. increase aggregate supply, supply-side
18. lower the costs of producing final goods and services

Section 8

1. (a) $\frac{1}{4}$; (b) $\frac{4}{5}$
2. (a) greater than; (b) greater than; (c) increase
3. (a) less than; (b) less than; (c) decrease
4. (a) A seller that must lower the price it charges in order to sell more of the commodity supplied; (b) A seller that can sell as much or as little as it wishes at a constant price.
5. The amount the total revenue of a seller changes when it sells one additional unit of the product produced.
6. (a) greater than; (b) less than; (c) equal to
7. (a) less than perfectly elastic; (b) decrease; (c) less than
8. (a) perfectly; (b) remain constant; (c) equal to

Section 9

1. fixed, variable (either order), variable
2. A schedule which indicates the cost of producing different quantities of a product.
3. (a) remain constant; (b) increase, smaller, increase, larger; (c) increase by amounts that become smaller, increase by amounts that become larger
4. (a) The amount by which total cost (and total variable cost) increases when the firm increases its production by one unit; (b) The amount by which the total output of the firm increases when it increases its employment of the variable resource by one unit.
5. As a firm employs more and more of a variable resource along with fixed amounts of other resources, the marginal product of the variable resource may at first increase but will eventually decrease.
6. (a) It decreases at first and then increases; (b) Because marginal product increases at first and then decreases.
7. (a) Divide total fixed cost by the output; (b) Divide total variable cost by the output; (c) total cost, the output, average fixed cost, average variable cost.
8. (a) decreases; (b) decrease at first and then increase
9. marginal, average variable (either order), marginal, average total (either order)
10. decreases, economies of scale, increases, diseconomies of scale
11. minimum (lowest), total
12. fixed, fixed

Section 10

1. marginal cost, marginal revenue (either order), minimum average variable
2. the market price of the product, marginal-cost schedule where marginal cost is greater than the minimum average variable cost
3. adding the supply schedules of all the firms in the industry, total quantity demanded, total quantity supplied (either order)
4. profit, loss, no, total fixed cost
5. cannot, earning an economic profit, suffering an economic loss
6. no, no, long-run average cost, minimum, marginal cost

Section 11

1. 4, $70, $280, profit, $140
2. greater than, greater than, greater than

Section 12

1. (a) The amount by which the firm's total revenue changes when it employs one additional unit of a variable resource; (b) The amount by which the firm's total cost changes when it employs one additional unit of a variable resource.
2. It will employ the resource up to the amount at which the marginal revenue product and the marginal resource cost are equal.
3. decrease
4. remains constant, the market price of the resource, marginal revenue product
5. (a) The sum of the demands of all firms that employ the resource; (b) The price at which the quantity demanded and quantity supplied are equal.
6. increases
7. (a) 3; (b) $40
8. When the ratio of the marginal revenue product to the marginal resource cost is the same for all resources.
9. When the ratio of the marginal revenue product to the marginal resource cost for all resources is equal to 1.

Section 13

1. (a) pails, brooms; (b) Haven, Diablo; (c) between 2 and 3 brooms for one pail (or between ⅓ and ½ pails for 1 broom)
2. They obtain a greater output of commodities with the same resources.
3. (a) foreign money; (b) The price paid in your own money to obtain one unit of foreign exchange.
4. supplier, demander, 133⅓
5. American importers of goods and services, Mexican exporters of the use of money, American givers, American investors (any order)
6. decreases, increases, the quantity demanded of francs equals the quantity supplied
7. goods, services
8. exports of goods exceed its imports of goods, imports of goods exceed its exports of goods
9. net investment income, net transfers, balance on capital account
10. (a) the current and capital account balance is a plus (+) amount (it ends the year with a balance due from the rest of the world); (b) the current and capital account balance is a minus (−) amount (it ends the year with a balance due to the rest of the world)
11. buying and selling foreign currency (exchange) and its own money